BASIC LITERATURE OF
AMERICAN PUBLIC ADMINISTRATION
1787–1950

Basic Literature of American
PUBLIC ADMINISTRATION
1787–1950

Selected and edited by

Frederick C. Mosher

HM

HOLMES & MEIER
PUBLISHERS, INC.
new york • london

/

First published in the United States of America 1981 by
Holmes & Meier Publishers, Inc.
30 Irving Place
New York, N.Y. 10003

Great Britain:
Holmes & Meier Publishers, Ltd.
131 Trafalgar Road
Greenwich, London SE10 9TX

Library of Congress Cataloging in Publication Data
Main entry under title:

Basic literature of American public administration,
    1787–1950.

    1. United States—Politics and government—
Addresses, essays, lectures.   2. Public administration—United States—History—Addresses, essays,
lectures.   I. Mosher, Frederick C.
JK 411.B34   1980   350'.000973   79-28553

ISBN 0-8419-0574-6
ISBN 0-8419-0575-4 pbk.

Manufactured in the United States of America

Contents

Preface

During the early 1970s the editor of this volume began to collect documents and articles relevant to the development of public administration for the use of graduate students in their exploration of the field and its background. The central aim of this undertaking was to provide them with a convenient set of references to the major landmarks in the growth of thought and of official action in this country. The selection of materials was progressively refined in consequence of student responses and discussions, which contributed greatly to the choices later made for publication. The first part of the collection, consisting of official documents—declarations, constitution, charters, laws, official reports—was published in 1976 as *Basic Documents of American Public Administration: 1776–1950*. This volume, though delayed somewhat by intervening commitments, is a companion rather than a sequel to the first one. It consists of articles, excerpts from books, speeches, and other pieces by individual authors which are thought to have contributed significantly to the evolution of public administration in the United States.

In many respects, the two volumes are parallel. Both are directed to the American scene. They are not global or international or comparative with other countries. Some of the pieces that follow were written by Europeans,[1] but they were chosen because of their relevance to and impact upon American public administration. The temporal boundaries of the two collections are roughly the same: from the founding of the republic to the middle of the twentieth century. The terminal date of both volumes, 1950, was selected partly because of the difficulty, at the time of this writing, to identify with confidence the truly seminal documents of the field which have appeared in the decades following 1950. Both works are divided into four parts, which are roughly consonant. The first part of each covers approximately the first century of the American republic when public administration was hardly recognized as a discipline or a science or even a legitimate field of study, although it was of course practiced as it has been since the beginnings of organized societies. The second part of each book deals with the developmental phase of public administration from the latter years of the nineteenth century to the 1920s. The third part concentrates on the period when a mature doctrine of public administration became generally, though not

---

1. Notably the excerpts or articles from de Tocqueville and Fayol of France, Weber of Germany, and Keynes and Finer of Britain.

1

universally, recognized and accepted. This period was approximately co-extensive with the late twenties, the Depression, and the New Deal. The fourth part of both volumes concerns the challenges of World War II and the immediate postwar period, both in terms of new and expanded responsibilities of government itself and the growing involvement of other disciplines and perspectives in the conduct of public affairs. A good many, but not all, of the developments of public administration since 1950 evolved from actions, observations, and insights enunciated during and immediately following World War II.

In this volume, as in the earlier one, the selections are arranged generally in chronological order. But in the interest of intellectual coherence, I have taken a few liberties with history. Some of the pieces that follow were written and published some years, even decades, before they were read or well known to American practitioners or scholars in public administration. Some, like the writings of Max Weber, were not translated into English for two or more decades after they were written. In the arrangement of essays which follow, I have made some attempt to relate the selections to the time of impact upon American public administration, rather than the time of first publication. In a number of instances, an article has been inserted in a part of this volume later than its publication date because the article was not known or had little influence when it was first published.[2] The article by Dwight Waldo was inserted in a part of the volume dealing with an earlier period than its date of publication because its contents primarily concerned that period.

The choice of inclusions in this volume has been more difficult than the selection of official documents for the first volume. The official documents at least expressed governmental intent to pursue certain objectives in public administration. Most of the literature about public administration was written with no certain expectation of changing the objectives or the manner of pursuing public purpose through new laws or actions. Some of it was directed to explaining, understanding, and theorizing about developments in the past and the situation at the time of writing. A good part of it was normative in the sense that it endeavored to develop principles and practices of good administration, applicable to the future. There were a few exceptions, but most of the literature was directed to other scholars in the field and their students, many of whom, it was hoped and expected, would be influential in the conduct of government. There is an academic flavor to much of the literature of public administration. It is a least once removed from the sphere of practice, a situation which continues in the present.

Since 1950, there have been growing complaints about the distance between the academic treatment of public administration and its practice in everyday life—complaints from both sides. The scholars complain of the practitioners' ignoring (or ignorance of) their products; the practitioners complain that the scholarly works are too theoretical to be relevant to their

2. Notably the pieces by Weber and Follett.

work. This was less true during the years with which this volume deals, before 1950. The majority of the scholars, including most of the authors quoted in this volume, had had direct experience in government or in other administration, or at least had done research in the going problems of public administration. There was, through the first half of the twentieth century, a fairly close relationship between academic study and administrative practice. This is attested by the fact that the two volumes, one dealing with official documents and one with scholarly literature, may each be logically organized in four parts roughly cognate both in temporal periods covered and in content.

It is interesting in this connection that until about 1950 the great bulk of students of public administration were trained as, or regarded themselves as, students of political science. Though they were increasingly joined or influenced by scholars in business administration and by nonscholar civic leaders, the overarching discipline was the study of government. Furthermore, until about the same time, public administration was generally regarded as a leading subfield of political science. No fewer than nine, nearly one third, of the authors quoted in this volume were at one time presidents of the American Political Science Association. Since 1950, the dominance of political science in the study of public administration has progressively declined with the growing interest and participation of other disciplines: economics, sociology, psychology, anthropology, mathematics, engineering, and others. Study and research in the field has been increasingly interdisciplinary. During the same period, the stature of public administration within the discipline of political science has also declined. For some years, it has not even been recognized by many political scientists as a separate subfield.

The growth in literature relevant to public administration since the turn of the twentieth century has been geometric. My choices have necessarily been limited, and they are admittedly somewhat arbitrary and subjective. My basic criterion has been that the pieces here reproduced or excerpted should be made familiar and conveniently available to teachers, scholars, and students of public administration. I have selected articles and chapters of books which seemed to me: landmarks in the development of the study and understanding of the field; precedents to governmental action in public administration; or seeds from other disciplines, like business administration, economics, sociology, and psychology, which grew or would grow after 1950 to have significant impact on public administration.

This work and its predecessor, *Basic Documents of American Public Administration,* are not intended to constitute a history of public administration. Their purpose is to provide the most relevant materials for scholars and students interested in the development of the field, materials that are hard or in some places impossible, to come by and are nowhere collected. Many of these are frequently quoted in a single sentence or alluded to in footnotes, and a few have been incorrectly interpreted. By far the best historical treatment of public administration is found in the four volumes by Leonard D. White, but his work ended with 1901. I hope that some competent scholar will take up where White left off and carry the history more nearly to date. These two volumes of mine may contribute to such a venture.

This volume is by no means definitive. Most of the authors represented in the collection have written other material relevant to public administration. In a number of cases, I have selected single chapters or excerpts from books and authors whose other chapters or different books and articles may be equally significant. The reader may find this a convenient jumping-off place for further readings by the same authors. And for purposes of literary parsimony, I have had to exclude a multitude of writings by other authors who might properly have been included.

A Reader's Guide

Each of the four parts that follow is introduced by a brief editorial comment about the period under consideration, its temporal boundaries, and its social and political context. Most of the individual selections are preceded by editorial notes of a few sentences about the author and the nature of and the rationale for the selection that follows. Only a few of the selections are quoted in full. They have been edited with some care, in the interest of brevity and relevance. I have sought to eliminate sections that are not directly concerned with public administration, are of only temporary or transitory significance, or are technical or legalistic. Where the deletions are substantial in length, they are indicated by a space break and ornament; where only a few words or sentences have been deleted, this is indicated by ellipses. Most of the significant deletions are explained in the notes introducing the selections. Footnotes from the originals have been largely eliminated; those essential to the meaning of the text have been retained. Virtually all the selections are verbatim copies from the originals as they first appeared in the English language. They therefore reflect the practices in grammar, spelling, punctuation, capitalization, and style of their authors and of the time period in which they were written.

Acknowledgments

This collection would hardly have been possible without the collaboration, conscious or unconscious, of quite a number of people. First are those many graduate students at the University of Virginia who were asked to labor through much of it as part of their course work and who offered comments and criticisms, sometimes caustic, of various inclusions and exclusions in earlier drafts. Second are a series of research assistants, likewise graduate students, who not only dug out and reproduced copies of the selections, as well as a great many other documents that were deleted, but also offered suggestions, advice, and editorial assistance. Among these was John M. Holmes, who made the original search and helped bring together the first draft. A number of others who succeeded him were of great assistance: Rita Epperson, George Gregory Raab, Laura Hudson, Mary Stevens, Gregg A. Cooke, James S. Tomashoff, and Max O. Stephenson, Jr. I can hardly name all those who have contributed to the clerical and typing tasks. Finally, I am most grateful to Professor Edith K. Mosher, to whom I am married, who helped, as she long has, with her advice, criticism, and suggestions.

I am of course responsible.

F.C.M.

PART I

THE HERITAGE

The literary and philosophic precedents for the study of public administration in the United States, as distinguished from its practice, seem to have been pretty thin. Many of the great documents about government which have survived from the colonial and post-Revolutionary periods treat the subject peripherally, not as a central focus for systematic examination and generalization. Administration, and more particularly centralized administration, was perceived more as an enemy than as a servant of the people, so that much of what was written was addressed to protection from the abuses of administration rather than to its effective conduct. Indeed, the American Revolution itself was at least in considerable part an outburst against administration, especially in the area of finances, as it had been exercised from London and by the colonial governors.

Actually, even before the adoption of the Constitution, Americans had had a great deal of experience in the administration of the colonial and later state governments, and of their subordinate counties, cities, and towns. The administrative failures of the Confederation following the Revolution probably played as significant a role as its political failures (if the two can be separated) in generating the Constitution itself. The first debates of the first Congress under the Constitution concerned administrative organization; they were lucid and knowledgeable, even if controversial. And George Washington, the only president of the United States enabled to build an administrative system from the ground up, was aware of the importance of his administrative responsibilities and gave much attention to them. From all accounts, he was a first-class administrator; he set precedents which last to this day. During those early years, other leaders—Hamilton, Jefferson, John Adams, Wolcott, Pickering, and Gallatin—built up a "philosophy of public management that is remarkably modern."[1] Many of those leaders and others wrote extensively about issues in public administration in official reports, memoranda, and private letters. Probably the most prolific and consistent in this field was Hamilton, but his views, like those of his contemporaries, were not then synthesized into a general statement about public administration.[2] However effective the administration of the republic may have been during the early years, it endowed subsequent scholars and students with little basis for the systematic study of public administration in this country. During

1. According to Leonard D. White, *The Federalists: A Study in Administrative History* (Macmillan, 1948), p. vii.

2. That he and at least some of the others did have consistent philosophies of public administration is attested by Lynton K. Caldwell, who contrasted *The Administrative Theories of Hamilton and Jefferson* (Russell and Russell, 1964). Caldwell wrote that Hamilton and Jefferson each "developed a coherent, well-considered plan of administration. . . ." (p. vii).

the middle decades of the nineteenth century, the perceived importance and prestige of public administration so declined that concerned citizens directed their efforts to civic reform, moral rather than administrative. And in the 1880s, American scholars interested in administrative matters turned to the monarchical regimes of Europe rather than the experience of their own country.[3]

It would be impossible to encompass within a few pages the writings about public administration in the first century of the American republic. Instead, I have drawn from two principal sources: parts of the essays of Alexander Hamilton and James Madison contained in *The Federalist Papers,* which contributed to an understanding of the field's subsequent development; and sections of Alexis De Tocqueville's *Democracy in America,* written forty years later and descriptive—perhaps more perceptively than anything written before or since—of American society, including the nature of politics and administration in this country. For purposes of this volume, the Tocqueville observations are particularly interesting because they were written at about the midway point between the original federalists and the public management movement.

The Federalist Papers

Clinton Rossiter opened his edited version of *The Federalist Papers* (New American Library, 1961) with the unequivocal declaration that: *"The Federalist* is the most important work in political science that has ever been written, or is likely ever to be written, in the United States. It is, indeed, the one product of the American mind that is rightly counted among the classics of political theory" (p. vii). The continuing and ever growing stature of the work after nearly two centuries is the more remarkable in view of the circumstances and purposes of its initial writing. The papers were a series of hastily written letters, published at brief intervals in New York newspapers, meant to explain and defend the draft Constitution of the United States and to persuade the legislators of New York State to ratify it. They were produced on a subject of intense controversy during the period between the Constitutional Convention of 1787 and its ratification in New York and other states during the following years. All of the eighty-five letters were signed with the pseudonym *Publius.* Their authors were Alexander Hamilton, who organized the venture and wrote the majority of the papers, James Madison, and

---

3. See the introduction and the passages concerning Woodrow Wilson in Part II of this book.

John Jay, who contributed only five, concerned principally with foreign affairs and defense.

The Federalist Papers dealt broadly—but sometimes quite specifically—with federalism and the powers and relationships of the national government and the states, the three branches of government, and the defects of the Articles of Confederation. Interspersed among the letters and underlying all of them were philosophical comments about the role of government in a free society, the importance of unity and energy in government, and the problem of reconciling an effective government with the liberty, protection, and representation of a free people. The subject of public administration was not a central theme. Nonetheless, of major importance for the future study of public administration as well as of government generally were two letters by Madison, numbers 10 and 51. The first of these, perhaps the most celebrated of all *The Federalist Papers*, remains to the present time the charter for students of pluralism and interest groups. The second extended the argument to the separation of powers among the three branches of government. Both are reproduced below.

Hamilton alluded to the importance of public administration in a number of places, and his letters on the presidency (numbers 67 to 77) treated important aspects of it though hardly providing a rounded theory of administration. Of these, excerpts from number 70, dealing with energy and unity in the executive, and number 76, concerning appointments of major offices of the government, are reprinted below.

F.C.M.

James Madison (1751–1836)

No. 10

Among the numerous advantages promised by a well-constructed Union, none deserves to be more accurately developed than its tendency to break and control the violence of faction. The friend of popular governments never finds himself so much alarmed for their character and fate, as when he contemplates their propensity to this dangerous vice. He will not fail, therefore, to set a due value on any plan which, without violating the principles to which he is attached, provides a proper cure for it. The instability, injustice, and confusion introduced into the public councils, have, in truth, been the mortal diseases under which popular governments have everywhere perished; as they continue to be the favorite and fruitful topics from which the

Edward G. Bourne, ed., *The Federalist*, Vol. I (Washington and London: M. Walter Dunne, Publisher, 1901), pp. 62–70.

adversaries to liberty derive their most specious declamations. The valuable improvements made by the American constitutions on the popular models, both ancient and modern, cannot certainly be too much admired; but it would be an unwarrantable partiality, to contend that they have as effectually obviated the danger on this side, as was wished and expected. Complaints are everywhere heard from our most considerate and virtuous citizens, equally the friends of public and private faith, and of public and personal liberty, that our governments are too unstable, that the public good is disregarded in the conflicts of rival parties, and that measures are too often decided, not according to the rules of justice and the rights of the minor party, but by the superior force of an interested and overbearing majority. However anxiously we may wish that these complaints had no foundation, the evidence of known facts will not permit us to deny that they are in some degree true. It will be found, indeed, on a candid review of our situation, that some of the distresses under which we labor have been erroneously charged on the operation of our governments; but it will be found, at the same time, that other causes will not alone account for many of our heaviest misfortunes; and, particularly, for that prevailing and increasing distrust of public engagements, and alarm for private rights, which are echoed from one end of the continent to the other. These must be chiefly, if not wholly, effects of the unsteadiness and injustice with which a factious spirit has tainted our public administrations.

By a faction, I understand a number of citizens, whether amounting to a majority or a minority of the whole, who are united and actuated by some common impulse of passion, or of interest, adversed to the rights of other citizens, or to the permanent and aggregate interests of the community.

There are two methods of curing the mischiefs of faction: the one, by removing its causes; the other, by controlling its effects.

There are again two methods of removing the causes of faction: the one, by destroying the liberty which is essential to its existence; the other, by giving to every citizen the same opinions, the same passions, and the same interests.

It could never be more truly said than of the first remedy, that it was worse than the disease. Liberty is to faction what air is to fire, an aliment without which it instantly expires. But it could not be less folly to abolish liberty, which is essential to political life, because it nourishes faction, than it would be to wish the annihilation of air, which is essential to animal life, because it imparts to fire its destructive agency.

The second expedient is as impracticable as the first would be unwise. As long as the reason of man continues fallible, and he is at liberty to exercise it, different opinions will be formed. As long as the connection subsists between his reason and his self-love, his opinions and his passions will have a reciprocal influence on each other; and the former will be objects to which the latter will attach themselves. The diversity in the faculties of men, from which the rights of property originate, is not less an insuperable obstacle to a uniformity of interests. The protection of these faculties is the first object of government. From the protection of different and unequal faculties of acquiring property, the possession of different degrees and kinds of property immediately results; and from the influence of these on the sentiments and views of the respective proprietors, ensues a division of the society into different interests and parties.

The latent causes of faction are thus sown in the nature of man; and we see them everywhere brought into different degrees of activity, according to the different circumstances of civil society. A zeal for different opinions concerning religion, concerning government, and many other points, as well of speculation as of practice; an attachment to different leaders ambitiously contending for pre-eminence and power; or to persons of other descriptions whose fortunes have been interesting to the human passions, have, in turn, divided mankind into parties, inflamed them with mutual animosity, and rendered them much more disposed to vex and oppress each other than to co-operate for their common good So strong is this propensity of mankind to fall into mutual animosities, that where no substantial occasion presents itself, the most frivolous and fanciful distinctions have been sufficient to kindle their unfriendly passions and excite their most violent conflicts. But the most common and durable source of factions has been the various and unequal distribution of property. Those who hold and those who are without property have ever formed distinct interests in society. Those who are creditors, and those who are debtors, fall under a like discrimination. A landed interest, a manufacturing interest, a mercantile interest, a moneyed interest, with many lesser interests, grow up of necessity in civilized nations, and divide them into different classes, actuated by different sentiments and views. The regulation of these various and interfering interests forms the principal task of modern legislation, and involves the spirit of party and faction in the necessary and ordinary operations of the government.

No man is allowed to be a judge in his own cause, because his interest would certainly bias his judgment, and, not improbably, corrupt his integrity. With equal, nay with greater reason, a body of men are unfit to be both judges and parties at the same time; yet what are many of the most important acts of legislation, but so many judicial determinations, not indeed concerning the rights of single persons, but concerning the rights of large bodies of citizens? And what are the different classes of legislators but advocates and parties to the causes which they determine? Is a law proposed concerning private debts? It is a question to which the creditors are parties on one side and the debtors on the other. Justice ought to hold the balance between them. Yet the parties are, and must be, themselves the judges; and the most numerous party, or, in other words, the most powerful faction must be expected to prevail. Shall domestic manufactures be encouraged, and in what degree, by restrictions on foreign manufactures? are questions which would be differently decided by the landed and the manufacturing classes, and probably by neither with a sole regard to justice and the public good. The apportionment of taxes on the various descriptions of property is an act which seems to require the most exact impartiality; yet there is, perhaps, no legislative act in which greater opportunity and temptation are given to a predominant party to trample on the rules of justice. Every shilling with which they overburden the inferior number, is a shilling saved to their own pockets.

It is in vain to say that enlightened statesmen will be able to adjust these clashing interests, and render them all subservient to the public good. Enlightened statesmen will not always be at the helm. Nor, in many cases, can such an adjustment be made at all without taking into view indirect and remote considerations, which will rarely prevail over the immediate interest which one party may find in disregarding the rights of another or the good of the whole.

The inference to which we are brought is, that the CAUSES of faction cannot be removed, and that relief is only to be sought in the means of controlling its EFFECTS.

If a faction consists of less than a majority, relief is supplied by the republican principle, which enables the majority to defeat its sinister views by regular vote. It may clog the administration, it may convulse the society; but it will be unable to execute and mask its violence under the forms of the Constitution. When a majority is included in a faction, the form of popular government, on the other hand, enables it to sacrifice to its ruling passion or interest both the public good and the rights of other citizens. To secure the public good and private rights against the danger of such a faction, and at the same time to preserve the spirit and the form of popular government, is then the great object to which our inquiries are directed. Let me add that it is the great desideratum by which this form of government can be rescued from the opprobrium under which it has so long labored, and be recommended to the esteem and adoption of mankind.

By what means is this object attainable? Evidently by one of two only. Either the existence of the same passion or interest in a majority at the same time must be prevented, or the majority, having such coexistent passion or interest, must be rendered, by their number and local situation, unable to concert and carry into effect schemes of oppression. If the impulse and the opportunity be suffered to coincide, we well know that neither moral nor religious motives can be relied on as an adequate control. They are not found to be such on the injustice and violence of individuals, and lose their efficacy in proportion to the number combined together, that is, in proportion as their efficacy becomes needful.

From this view of the subject it may be concluded that a pure democracy, by which I mean a society consisting of a small number of citizens, who assemble and administer the government in person, can admit of no cure for the mischiefs of faction. A common passion or interest will, in almost every case, be felt by a majority of the whole; a communication and concert result from the form of government itself; and there is nothing to check the inducements to sacrifice the weaker party or an obnoxious individual. Hence it is that such democracies have ever been spectacles of turbulence and contention; have ever been found incompatible with personal security or the rights of property; and have in general been as short in their lives as they have been violent in their deaths. The theoretic politicians, who have patronized this species of government, have erroneously supposed that by reducing mankind to a perfect equality in their political rights, they would, at the same time, be perfectly equalized and assimilated in their possessions, their opinions, and their passions.

A republic, by which I mean a government in which the scheme of representation takes place, opens a different prospect, and promises the cure for which we are seeking. Let us examine the points in which it varies from pure democracy, and we shall comprehend both the nature of the cure and the efficacy which it must derive from the Union.

The two great points of difference between a democracy and a republic are: first, the delegation of the government, in the latter, to a small number of citizens elected by the rest; secondly, the greater number of citizens, and greater sphere of country, over which the latter may be extended.

The effect of the first difference is, on the one hand, to refine and enlarge the public views, by passing them through the medium of a chosen body of citizens, whose wisdom may best discern the true interest of their country, and whose patriotism and love of justice will be least likely to sacrifice it to temporary or partial considerations. Under such a regulation, it may well happen that the public voice, pronounced by the representatives of the people, will be more consonant to the public good than if pronounced by the people themselves, convened for the purpose. On the other hand, the effect may be inverted. Men of factious tempers, of local prejudices, or of sinister designs, may, by intrigue, by corruption, or by other means, first obtain the suffrages, and then betray the interests, of the people. The question resulting is, whether small or extensive republics are more favorable to the election of proper guardians of the public weal; and it is clearly decided in favor of the latter by two obvious considerations:

In the first place, it is to be remarked that, however small the republic may be, the representatives must be raised to a certain number, in order to guard against the cabals of a few; and that, however large it may be, they must be limited to a certain number, in order to guard against the confusion of a multitude. Hence, the number of representatives in the two cases not being in proportion to that of the two constituents, and being proportionally greater in the small republic, it follows that, if the proportion of fit characters be not less in the large than in the small republic, the former will present a greater option, and consequently a greater probability of a fit choice.

In the next place, as each representative will be chosen by a greater number of citizens in the large than in the small republic, it will be more difficult for unworthy candidates to practice with success the vicious arts by which elections are too often carried; and the suffrages of the people being more free, will be more likely to centre in men who possess the most attractive merit and the most diffusive and established characters.

It must be confessed that in this, as in most other cases, there is a mean, on both sides of which inconveniences will be found to lie. By enlarging too much the number of electors, you render the representatives too little acquainted with all their local circumstances and lesser interests; as by reducing it too much, you render him unduly attached to these, and too little fit to comprehend and pursue great and national objects. The federal Constitution forms a happy combination in this respect; the great and aggregate interests being referred to the national, the local and particular to the State legislatures.

The other point of difference is, the greater number of citizens and extent of territory which may be brought within the compass of republican than of democratic government; and it is this circumstance principally which renders factious combinations less to be dreaded in the former than in the latter. The smaller the society, the fewer probably will be the distinct parties and interests composing it; the fewer the distinct parties and interests, the more frequently will a majority be found of the same party; and the smaller the number of individuals composing a majority, and the smaller the compass within which they are placed, the more easily will they concert and execute their plans of oppression. Extend the sphere, and you take in a greater variety of parties and interests; you make it less probable that a majority of the whole will have a common motive to invade the rights of other citizens; or if such a common motive exists, it will be more difficult for all who feel it to discover their own strength, and to act in unison with each other. Besides other impediments, it may be remarked that, where there is a consciousness of unjust or dishonorable purposes, communication is always checked by distrust in proportion to the number whose concurrence is necessary.

Hence, it clearly appears, that the same advantage which a republic has over a democracy, in controlling the effects of faction, is enjoyed by a large over a small republic,—is enjoyed by the Union over the States composing it. Does the advantage consist in the substitution of representatives whose enlightened views and virtuous sentiments render them superior to local prejudices and schemes of injustice? It will not be denied that the representation of the Union will be most likely to possess these requisite endowments. Does it consist in the greater security afforded by a greater variety of parties, against the event of any one party being able to outnumber and oppress the rest? In an equal degree does the increased variety of parties comprised within the Union, increase this security. Does it, in fine, consist in the greater obstacles opposed to the concert and accomplishment of the secret wishes of an unjust and interested majority? Here, again, the extent of the Union gives it the most palpable advantage.

The influence of factious leaders may kindle a flame within their particular States, but will be unable to spread a general conflagration through the other States. A religious sect may degenerate into a political faction in a part of the Confederacy; but the variety of sects dispersed over the entire face of it must secure the national councils against any danger from that source. A rage for paper money, for an abolition of debts, for an equal division of property, or for any other improper or wicked project, will be less apt to pervade the whole body of the Union than a particular member of it; in the same proportion as such a malady is more likely to taint a particular county or district, than an entire State.

In the extent and proper structure of the Union, therefore, we behold a republican remedy for the diseases most incident to republican government. And according to the degree of pleasure and pride we feel in being republicans, ought to be our zeal in cherishing the spirit and supporting the character of Federalists.

No. 51

To what expedient, then, shall we finally resort, for maintaining in practice the necessary partition of power among the several departments, as laid down in the Constitution? The only answer that can be given is, that as all these exterior provisions are found to be inadequate, the defect must be supplied, by so contriving the interior structure of the government as that its several constituent parts may, by their mutual relations, be the means of keeping each other in their proper places. Without presuming to undertake a full development of this important idea, I will hazard a few general observations, which may perhaps place it in a clearer light, and enable us to form a more correct judgment of the principles and structure of the government planned by the convention.

In order to lay a due foundation for that separate and distinct exercise of the different powers of government, which to a certain extent is admitted on all hands to be essential to the preservation of liberty, it is evident that each department should have a will of its own; and consequently should be so constituted that the members of each should have as little agency as possible in the appointment of the members of the others. Were this principle rigorously adhered to, it would require that all the appointments for the supreme executive, legislative, and judiciary magistracies should be drawn from the same fountain of authority, the people, through channels having no communication whatever with one another. Perhaps such a plan of constructing the several departments would be less difficult in practice than it may in contemplation appear. Some difficulties, however, and some additional expense would attend the execution of it. Some deviations, therefore, from the principle must be admitted. In the constitution of the judiciary department in particular, it might be inexpedient to insist rigorously on the principle: first, because peculiar qualifications being essential in the members, the primary consideration ought to be to select that mode of choice which best secures these qualifications; secondly, because the permanent tenure by which the appointments are held in that department, must soon destroy all sense of dependence on the authority conferring them.

It is equally evident, that the members of each department should be as little dependent as possible on those of the others, for the emoluments annexed to their offices. Were the executive magistrate, or the judges, not independent of the legislature in this particular, their independence in every other would be merely nominal.

But the great security against a gradual concentration of the several powers in the same department, consists in giving to those who administer each department the necessary constitutional means and personal motives to resist encroachments of the others. The provision for defense must in this, as in all other cases, be made commensurate to the danger of attack. Ambition must be made to counteract ambition. The interest of the man must be connected with the constitutional rights of the place. It may be a reflection on human nature, that such devices should be necessary to control the abuses of government. But what is government itself, but the greatest of all reflections on human nature? If men were angels, no government would be necessary. If angels were to govern men, neither external nor internal controls on government would be necessary. In framing a government which is to be administered by men over men, the great difficulty lies in this: you must first enable the government to control the governed; and in the next place oblige it to control itself. A dependence on the people is, no doubt, the primary control on the government; but experience has taught mankind the necessity of auxiliary precautions.

This policy of supplying, by opposite and rival interests, the defect of better motives, might be traced through the whole system of human affairs, private as well as public. We see it particularly displayed in all the subordinate distributions of power, where the constant aim is to divide and arrange the several offices in such a manner as that each may be a check on the other—that the private interest of every individual may be a sentinel over the public rights. These inventions of prudence cannot be less requisite in the distribution of the supreme powers of the State.

But it is not possible to give to each department an equal power of self-defense. In republican government, the legislative authority necessarily predominates. The remedy for this inconveniency is to divide the legislature into different branches; and to render them, by different modes of election and different principles of action, as little connected with each other as the nature of their common functions and their common dependence on the society will admit. It may even be necessary to guard against dangerous encroachments by still further precautions. As the weight of the legislative authority requires that it should be thus divided, the weakness of the executive may require, on the other hand, that it should be fortified. An absolute negative on the legislature appears, at first view, to be the natural defense with which the executive magistrate should be armed. But perhaps it would be neither altogether safe nor alone sufficient. On ordinary occasions it might not be exerted with the requisite firmness, and on extraordinary occasions it might be perfidiously abused. May not this defect of an absolute negative be supplied by some qualified connection between this weaker department and the weaker branch of the stronger department, by which the latter may be led to support the constitutional rights of the former, without being too much detached from the rights of its own department?

If the principles on which these observations are founded be just, as I persuade myself they are, and they be applied as a criterion to the several State constitutions, and to the federal Constitution, it will be found that if the latter does not perfectly correspond with them, the former are infinitely less able to bear such a test.

There are, moreover, two considerations particularly applicable to the federal system of America, which place that system in a very interesting point of view.

First. In a single republic, all the power surrendered by the people is submitted to the administration of a single government; and the usurpations are guarded against by a division of the government into distinct and separate departments. In the compound republic of America, the power surrendered by the people is first divided between two distinct governments, and then the portion allotted to each subdivided among distinct and separate departments. Hence a double security arises to the rights of the people. The different governments will control each other, at the same time that each will be controlled by itself.

Second. It is of great importance in a republic not only to guard the society against the oppression of its rulers, but to guard one part of the society against the injustice of the other part. Different interests necessarily exist in different classes of citizens. If a majority be united by a common interest, the rights of the minority will be insecure. There are but two methods of providing against this evil: the one by creating a will in the community independent of the majority—that is, of the society itself; the other, by comprehending in the society so many separate descriptions of citizens as will render an unjust combination of a majority of the whole very improbable, if not impracticable. The first method prevails in all governments possessing an hereditary or self-appointed authority. This, at best, is but a precarious security; because a power independent of the society may as well espouse the unjust views of the major, as the rightful interests of the minor party, and may possibly be turned against both parties. The second method will be exemplified in the federal republic of the United States. Whilst all authority in it will be derived from and dependent on the society, the society itself will be broken into so many parts, interests, and classes of citizens, that the rights of individuals, or of the minority, will be in little danger from interested combinations of the majority. In a free government the security for civil rights must be the same as that for religious rights. It consists in the one case in the multiplicity of interests, and in the other in the multiplicity of sects. The degree of security in both cases will depend on the number of interests and sects; and this may be presumed to depend on the extent of country and number of people comprehended under the same government. This view of the subject must particularly recommend a proper federal system to all the sincere and considerate friends of republican government, since it shows that in exact proportion as the territory of the Union may be formed into more circumscribed Confederacies, or States, oppressive combinations of a majority will be facilitated; the best security, under the republican forms, for the rights of every class of citizens, will be diminished; and consequently the stability and independence of some member of the government, the only other security, must be proportionally increased. Justice is the end of government. It is the end of civil society. It ever has been and ever will be pursued until it be obtained, or until liberty be lost in the pursuit. In a society under the forms of which the stronger faction can readily unite and oppress the weaker, anarchy may as truly be said to reign as in a state of nature, where the weaker individual is not secured against the violence of the stronger; and as, in the latter state, even the stronger individuals are prompted, by the uncertainty of their condition, to submit to a government which may protect the weak as well as themselves; so, in the former state, will the more powerful factions or parties be gradually induced, by a like motive, to wish for a government which will protect all parties, the weaker as well as the more powerful. It can be little doubted that if the State of Rhode Island was separated from the Confederacy and left to itself, the insecurity of rights under the popular form of government within such narrow limits would be displayed by such reiterated oppressions of factious majorities that some power altogether independent of the people would soon be called for by the voice of the very factions whose misrule had proved the necessity of it. In the extended republic of the United States, and among the great variety of interests, parties, and sects which it embraces, a coalition of a majority of the whole society could seldom take place on any other principles than those of justice and the general good; whilst there being thus less danger to a minor from the will of a major party, there must be less pretext, also, to provide for the security of the former, by introducing into the government a will not dependent on the latter, or, in other words, a will independent of the society itself. It is no less certain than it is important, notwithstanding the contrary opinions which have been entertained, that the larger the society, provided it lie within a practical sphere, the more duly capable it will be of self-government. And happily for the REPUBLICAN CAUSE, the practicable sphere may be carried to a very great extent, by a judicious modification and mixture of the FEDERAL PRINCIPLE.

Alexander Hamilton (1755–1804)

No. 70

There is an idea, which is not without its advocates, that a vigorous Executive is inconsistent with the genius of republican government. The enlightened well-wishers to this species of government must at least hope that the supposition is destitute of foundation; since they can never admit its truth, without at the same time admitting the condemnation of their own principles. Energy in the Executive is a leading character in the definition of good government. It is essential to the protection of the community against foreign attacks; it is not less essential to the steady administration of the laws; to the protection of property against those irregular and high-handed combinations which sometimes interrupt the ordinary course of justice; to the security of liberty against the enterprises and assaults of ambition, of faction, and of anarchy. Every man the least conversant in Roman story, knows how often that republic was obliged to take refuge in the absolute power of a single man, under the formidable title of Dictator, as well against the intrigues of ambitious individuals who aspired to the tyranny, and the seditions of whole classes of the community whose conduct threatened the existence of all government, as against the invasions of external enemies who menaced the conquest and destruction of Rome.

There can be no need, however, to multiply arguments or examples on this head. A feeble Executive implies a feeble execution of the government. A feeble execution is but another phrase for a bad execution; and a government ill executed, whatever it may be in theory, must be, in practice, a bad government.

Taking it for granted, therefore, that all men of sense will agree in the necessity of an energetic Executive, it will only remain to inquire, what are the ingredients which constitute this energy? How far can they be combined with those other ingredients which constitute safety in the republican sense? And how far does this combination characterize the plan which has been reported by the convention?

The ingredients which constitute energy in the Executive are, first, unity; secondly, duration; thirdly, an adequate provision for its support; fourthly, competent powers.

The ingredients which constitute safety in the republican sense are, first, a due dependence on the people, secondly, a due responsibility.

Those politicians and statesmen who have been the most celebrated for the soundness of their principles and for the justice of their views, have declared in favor of a single Executive and a numerous legislature. They have with great propriety, considered energy as the most necessary qualification of the former, and have regarded this as most applicable to power in a single hand, while they have, with equal propriety, considered the latter as best adapted to deliberation and wisdom, and best calculated to conciliate the confidence of the people and to secure their privileges and interests.

That unity is conducive to energy will not be disputed. Decision, activity, secrecy, and despatch will generally characterize the proceedings of one man in a much more eminent degree than the proceedings of any greater number; and in proportion as the number is increased, these qualities will be diminished.

This unity may be destroyed in two ways: either by vesting the power in two or more magistrates of equal dignity and authority; or by vesting it ostensibly in one man, subject, in whole or in part, to the control and co-operation of others, in the capacity of counsellors to him. Of the first, the two Consuls of Rome may serve as an example; of the last, we shall find examples in the constitutions of several of the States. New York and New Jersey, if I recollect right, are the only States which have intrusted the executive authority wholly to single men. Both these methods of destroying the unity of the Executive have their partisans; but the votaries of an executive council are the most numerous. They are both liable, if not to equal, to similar objections, and may in most lights be examined in conjunction.

❊   ❊   ❊

Wherever two or more persons are engaged in any common enterprise or pursuit, there is always danger of difference of opinion. If it be a public trust or office, in which they are clothed with equal dignity and authority, there is peculiar danger of personal emulation and even animosity. From either, and especially from all these causes, the most bitter dissensions are apt to spring. Whenever these happen, they lessen the respectability, weaken the authority, and distract the plans and operation of those whom they divide. If they should unfortunately assail the supreme executive magistracy of a country, consisting of a plurality of persons, they might impede or frustrate the most important measures of the government, in the most critical emergencies of the state. And what is still worse, they might split the community into the most violent and irreconcilable factions, adhering differently to the different individuals who composed the magistracy.

Men often oppose a thing, merely because they have had no agency in planning it, or because it may have been planned by those whom they dislike. But if they have been consulted, and have happened to disapprove, opposition then becomes, in their estimation, an indispensable duty of self-love. They seem to think themselves bound in honor, and by all the motives of personal infallibility, to defeat the success of what has been resolved upon contrary to their sentiments. Men of upright, benevolent tempers have too many opportunities of remarking, with horror, to what desperate lengths this disposition is sometimes carried, and how often the great interests of society are sacrificed to the vanity, to the conceit, and to the obstinacy of individuals, who have credit enough to make their passions and their caprices interesting to mankind. Perhaps the question now before the public may, in its consequences, afford melancholy proofs of the effects of this despicable frailty, or rather detestable vice, in the human character.

Upon the principles of a free government, inconveniences from the source just mentioned must necessarily be submitted to in the formation of the legislature; but it is unnecessary, and therefore unwise, to introduce them into the constitution of the Executive. It is here too that they may be most pernicious. In the legislature, promptitude of decision is oftener an evil than a benefit. The differences of opinion, and the jarrings of parties in that department of the government, though they may sometimes obstruct salutary plans, yet often promote deliberation and circumspection, and serve to check excesses in the majority. When a resolution too is once taken, the opposition must be at an end. That resolution is a law, and resistance to it punishable. But no favorable circumstances palliate or atone for the disadvantages of dissension in the executive department. Here, they are pure and unmixed. There is no point at which they cease to operate. They serve to embarrass and weaken the execution of the plan or measure to which they relate, from the first step to the final conclusion of it. They constantly counteract those qualities in the Executive which are the most necessary ingredients in its composition,—vigor and expedition, and this without any counterbalancing good. In the conduct of war, in which the energy of the Executive is the bulwark of the national security, every thing would be to be apprehended from its plurality.

It must be confessed that these observations apply with principal weight to the first case supposed—that is, to a plurality of magistrates of equal dignity and authority a scheme, the advocates for which are not likely to form a numerous sect; but they apply, though not with equal, yet with considerable weight to the project of a council, whose concurrence is made constitutionally necessary to the operations of the ostensible Executive. An artful cabal in that council would be able to distract and to enervate the whole system of administration. If no such cabal should exist, the mere diversity of views and opinions would alone be sufficient to tincture the exercise of the executive authority with a spirit of habitual feebleness and dilatoriness.

But one of the weightiest objections to a plurality in the Executive, and which lies as much against the last as the first plan, is, that it tends to conceal faults and destroy responsibility. Responsibility is of two kinds—to censure and to punishment. The first is the more important of the two, especially in an elective office. Man, in public trust, will much oftener act in such a manner as to render him unworthy of being any longer trusted, than in such a manner as to make him obnoxious to legal punishment. But the multiplication of the Executive adds to the difficulty of detection in either case. It often becomes impossible, amidst mutual accusations, to determine on whom the blame or the punishment of a pernicious measure, or series of pernicious measures, ought really to fall. It is shifted from one to another with so much dexterity, and under such plausible appearances, that the public opinion is left in suspense about the real author. The circumstances which may have led to any national miscarriage or misfortune are sometimes so complicated that, where there are a number of actors who may have had different degrees and kinds of agency, though we may clearly see upon the whole that there has been mismanagement, yet it may be impracticable to pronounce to whose account the evil which may have been incurred is truly chargeable.

It is evident from these considerations, that the plurality of the Executive tends to deprive the people of the two greatest securities they can have for the faithful exercise of any delegated power, *first,* the restraints of public opinion, which lose their efficacy, as well on account of the division of the censure attendant on bad measures among a number, as on account of the uncertainty on whom it ought to fall; and, *secondly,* the opportunity of discovering with facility and clearness the misconduct of the persons they trust, in order either to their removal from office or to their actual punishment in cases which admit of it.

The idea of a council to the Executive, which has so generally obtained in the State constitutions, has been derived from that maxim of republican jealousy which considers power as safer in the hands of a number of men than of a single man. If the maxim should be admitted to be applicable to the case, I should contend that the advantage on that side would not counterbalance the numerous disadvantages on the opposite side. But I do not think the rule at all applicable to the executive power. I clearly concur in opinion, in this particular, with a writer whom the celebrated Junius pronounces to be "deep, solid, and ingenious," that "the executive power is more easily confined when it is ONE"; that it is far more safe there should be a single object for the jealousy and watchfulness of the people; and, in a word, that all multiplication of the Executive is rather dangerous than friendly to liberty.

No. 76

The President is "to NOMINATE, and, by and with the advice and consent of the Senate, to appoint ambassadors, other public ministers and consuls, judges of the Supreme Court, and all other officers of the United States whose appointments are not otherwise provided for in the Constitution. But the Congress may by law vest the appointment of such inferior officers as they think proper, in the President alone, or in the courts of law, or in the heads of departments. The President shall have power to fill up ALL VACANCIES which may happen DURING THE RECESS OF THE SENATE, by granting commissions which shall EXPIRE at the end of their next session."

It has been observed in a former paper, that "the true test of a good government is its aptitude and tendency to produce a good administration." If the justness of this observation be admitted, the mode of appointing the officers of the United States contained in the foregoing clauses, must, when examined, be allowed to be entitled to particular commendation. It is not easy to conceive a plan better calculated than this to promote a judicious choice of men for filling the offices of the Union; and it will not need proof, that on this point must essentially depend the character of its administration.

It will be agreed on all hands, that the power of appointment, in ordinary cases, ought to be modified in one of three ways. It ought either to be vested in a single man, or in a SELECT assembly of a moderate number, or in a single man, with the concurrence of such an assembly. The exercise of it by the people at large will be readily admitted to be impracticable; as waiving every other consideration, it would leave them little time to do anything else. When, therefore, mention is made in the subsequent reasonings of an assembly or body of men, what is said must be understood to relate to a select body or assembly, of the description already given. The people collectively, from their number and from their dispersed situation, cannot be regulated in their movements by that systematic spirit of cabal and intrigue, which will be urged as the chief objections to reposing the power in question in a body of men.

Those who have themselves reflected upon the subject, or who have attended to the observations made in other parts of these papers, in relation to the appointment of the President, will, I presume, agree to the position, that there would always be great probability of having the place supplied by a man of abilities, at least respectable. Premising this, I proceed to lay it down as a rule, that one man of discernment is better fitted to analyze and estimate the peculiar qualities adapted to particular offices, than a body of men of equal or perhaps even of superior discernment.

The sole and undivided responsibility of one man will naturally beget a livelier sense of duty and a more exact regard to reputation. He will, on this account, feel himself under stronger obligations, and more interested to investigate with care the qualities requisite to the stations to be filled, and to prefer with impartiality the persons who may have the fairest pretensions to them. He will have FEWER personal attachments to gratify, than a body of men who may each be supposed to have an equal number; and will be so much the less liable to be misled by the sentiments of friendship and of affection. A single well-directed man, by a single understanding, cannot be distracted and warped by that diversity of views, feelings, and interests, which frequently distract and warp the resolutions of a collective body. There is nothing so apt to agitate the passions of mankind as personal considerations, whether they relate to ourselves or to others, who are to be the objects of our choice or preference. Hence, in every exercise of the power of appointing to offices, by an assembly of men, we must expect to see a full display of all the private and party likings and dislikes, partialities and antipathies, attachments and animosities, which are felt by those who compose the assembly. The choice which may at any time happen to be made under such circumstances, will of course be the result either of a victory gained by one party over the other, or of a compromise between the parties. In either case, the intrinsic merit of the candidate will be too often out of sight. In the first, the qualifications best adapted to uniting the suffrages of the party, will be more considered than those which fit the person for the station. In the last, the coalition will commonly turn upon some interested equivalent: "Give us the man we wish for this office, and you shall have the one you wish for that." This will be the usual condition of the bargain. And it will rarely happen that the advancement of the public service will be the primary object either of party victories or of party negotiations.

The truth of the principles here advanced seems to have been felt by the most intelligent of those who have found fault with the provision made, in this respect, by the convention. They contend that the President ought solely to have been authorized to make the appointments under the federal government. But it is easy to show, that every advantage to be expected from such an arrangement would, in substance, be derived from the power of NOMINATION, which is proposed to be conferred upon him; while several disadvantages which might attend the absolute power of appointment in the hands of that officer would be avoided. In the act of nomination, his judgment alone would be exercised; and as it would be his sole duty to point out the man who, with the approbation of the Senate, should fill an office, his responsibility would be as complete as if he were to make the final appointment. There can, in this view, be no difference between nominating and appointing. The same motives which would influence a proper discharge of his duty in one case, would exist in the other. And as no man could be appointed but on his previous nomination, every man who might be appointed would be, in fact, his choice.

But might not his nomination be overruled? I grant it might, yet this could only be to make place for another nomination by himself. The person ultimately appointed must be the object of his preference, though perhaps not in the first degree. It is also not very probable that his nomination would often be overruled. The Senate could not be tempted, by the preference they might feel to another, to reject the one proposed; because they could not assure themselves, that the person they might wish would be brought forward by a second or by any subsequent nomination. They could not even be certain, that a future nomination would present a candidate in any degree more acceptable to them; and as their dissent might cast a kind of stigma upon the indvidual rejected, and might have the appearance of a reflection upon the judgment of the chief magistrate, it is not likely that their sanction would often be refused, where there were not special and strong reasons for the refusal.

To what purpose then require the co-operation of the Senate? I answer, that the necessity of their concurrence would have a powerful, though, in general, a silent operation. It would be an excellent check upon a spirit of favoritism in the President, and would tend greatly to prevent the appointment of unfit characters from State prejudice, from family connection, from personal attachment, or from a view to popularity. In addition to this, it would be an efficacious source of stability in the administration.

It will readily be comprehended, that a man who had himself the sole disposition of offices, would be governed much more by his private inclinations and interests, than when he was bound to submit the propriety of his choice to the discussion and determination of a different and independent body, and that body an entire branch of the legislature. The possibility of rejection would be a strong motive to care in proposing. The danger to his own reputation, and, in the case of an elective magistrate, to his political existence, from betraying a spirit of favoritism, or an unbecoming pursuit of popularity, to the observation of a body whose opinion would have great weight in forming that of the public, could not fail to operate as a barrier to the one and to the other. He would be both ashamed and afraid to bring forward, for the most distinguished or lucrative stations, candidates who had no other merit than that of coming from the same State to which he particularly belonged, or of being in some way or other personally allied to him, or of possessing the necessary insignificance and pliancy to render them the obsequious instruments of his pleasure.

To this reasoning it has been objected that the President, by the influence of the power of nomination, may secure the complaisance of the Senate to his views. This supposition of universal venalty in human nature is little less an error in political reasoning, than the supposition of universal rectitude. The institution of delegated power implies, that there is a portion of virtue and honor among mankind, which may be a reasonable foundation of confidence; and experience justifies the theory. It has been found to exist in the most corrupt periods of the most corrupt governments. The venalty of the British House of Commons has been long a topic of accusation against that body, in the country to which they belong as well as in this; and it cannot be doubted that the charge is, to a considerable extent, well founded. But it is as little to be doubted, that there is always a large proportion of the body, which consists of independent and public-spirited men, who have an influential weight in the councils of the nation. Hence it is (the present reign not excepted) that the sense of that body is often seen to control the inclinations of the monarch, both with regard to men and to measures. Though it might therefore be allowable to suppose that the Executive might occasionally influence some individuals in the Senate, yet the supposition, that he could in general purchase the integrity of the whole body, would be forced and improbable. A man disposed to view human nature as it is, without either flattering its virtues or exaggerating its vices, will see sufficient ground of confidence in the probity of the Senate, to rest satisfied, not only that it will be impracticable to the Executive to corrupt or seduce a majority of its members, but that the necessity of its co-operation, in the business of appointments, will be a considerable and salutary restraint upon the conduct of that magistrate. Nor is the integrity of the Senate the only reliance. The Constitution has provided some important guards against the danger of executive influence upon the legislative body: it declares that "No senator or representative shall during the time FOR WHICH HE WAS ELECTED, be appointed to any civil office under the United States, which shall have been created, or the emoluments whereof shall have been increased, during such time; and no person, holding any office under the United States, shall be a member of either house during his continuance in office."

Alexis de Tocqueville (1805-1859)

In May of 1831, two young French noblemen, Alexis de Tocqueville and Gustave de Beaumont, landed in New York City to begin an extensive exploration of the United States, its society, its government, its economy, and its mores. Their initial mission, which they accomplished, was to survey prison reform in America on commission from the French government. Beyond that, they sought to study democracy as it operated in this country, its elements, its virtues and its defects and dangers, its probable future. They divided their work. Beaumont concentrated on races and racial relations, the blacks and the Indians; Tocqueville, on democratic institutions generally. The studies of Tocqueville carried him far beyond American political institutions into the whole fabric of American society. After his return to France, he wrote *Democracy in America* in two extensive volumes, which was soon extolled and criticized in France, Britain, and the United States and later, to this day, hailed as a classic, not alone in political science but in the social sciences generally. It is doubtful that any study of a whole complex society in all of history has been more far-ranging and more perceptive than this one.

As seems inevitable in studies of its kind, *Democracy in America* was parochial. Tocqueville was struck by the differences between the United States and his native France and to a somewhat lesser extent between the United States and Britain, which he had also visited and observed. This led him to some interpretations which may now seem exaggerated and overemphasized and to some omissions which now seem important. He could hardly predict the impact of the industrial revolution, technology, urbanization, and related developments which at the time of his writing were only beginning. Nonetheless, Tocqueville was extraordinarily percipient about both the political and social roots of American democracy: the stress on equality and liberty, sovereignty in the people, the tendency to establish and join associations, local self-government, emphasis on the practical and technological rather than philosophical and scientific, and many others. He provides a groundwork, a benchmark against which to judge the vast changes of succeeding decades and the influences of the mores and values at the time of his visit upon those changes, their nature and their speed.

In no field is this more true than in public administration, a topic to which he devoted a good deal of attention. It is significant that, unlike *The Federalist Papers* and many other political documents up to his time, he began his political analysis at the level of the townships, counties, and municipalities and moved upward to the states (to which he gave rather sparse attention) and the national government. He clearly distinguished centralized government (which he thought America had) from centralized administration (which it did not have). This may explain why, a half century later, American scholars in their quest for a science of administration turned to continental Europe, even as Tocqueville, in his quest for an understanding of democracy on behalf of Europe, had turned to America.

The excerpts that follow are intended to draw together Tocqueville's summary of popular sovereignty and public administration and their impact in America. Included is a brief excerpt from his discussion of the role of lawyers who were, even then, dominant in all branches of government.

F.C.M.

Democracy in America

IV. The Principle of the Sovereignty of the People in America

Whenever the political laws of the United States are to be discussed, it is with the doctrine of the sovereignty of the people that we must begin. The principle of the sovereignty of the people, which is to be found, more or less, at the bottom of almost all human institutions, generally remains concealed from view. It is obeyed without being recognized, or if for a moment it be brought to light, it is hastily cast back into the gloom of the sanctuary. "The will of the nation" is one of those expressions which have been most profusely abused by the wily and the despotic of every age. To the eyes of some it has been represented by the venal suffrages of a few of the satellites of power; to others by the votes of a timid or an interested minority; and some have even discovered it in the silence of a people, on the supposition that the fact of submission established the right of command.

In America the principle of the sovereignty of the people is not either barren or concealed, as it is with some other nations; it is recognized by the customs and proclaimed by the laws; it spreads freely, and arrives without impediment at its most remote consequences. If there be a country in the world where the doctrine of the sovereignty of the people can be fairly appreciated, where it can be studied in its application to the affairs of society, and where its dangers and its advantages may be foreseen, that country is assuredly America.

From Chapters 4, 5, 13, and 16, *Democracy in America* (New York: The Colonial Press, 1900), translated by Henry Reeve. Vol. I: pp. 55–57; 77–81, 83–90; 92–95; 213–214; 275–277; and 283–285.

I have already observed that, from their origin, the sovereignty of the people was the fundamental principle of the greater number of British colonies in America. It was far, however, from then exercising as much influence on the government of society as it now does. Two obstacles, the one external, the other internal, checked its invasive progress. It could not ostensibly disclose itself in the laws of colonies which were still constrained to obey the mother-country: it was therefore obliged to spread secretly, and to gain ground in the provincial assemblies, and especially in the townships.

American society was not yet prepared to adopt it with all its consequences. The intelligence of New England, and the wealth of the country to the south of the Hudson . . . long exercised a sort of aristocratic influence, which tended to retain the exercise of social authority in the hands of a few. The public functionaries were not universally elected, and the citizens were not all of them electors. The electoral franchise was everywhere placed within certain limits, and made dependent on a certain qualification, which was exceedingly low in the North and more considerable in the South.

The American revolution broke out, and the doctrine of the sovereignty of the people, which had been nurtured in the townships and municipalities, took possession of the State: every class was enlisted in its cause; battles were fought, and victories obtained for it, until it became the law of laws.

A no less rapid change was effected in the interior of society, where the law of descent completed the abolition of local influences.

At the very time when this consequence of the laws and of the revolution was apparent to every eye, victory was irrevocably pronounced in favor of the democratic cause. All power was, in fact, in its hands, and resistance was no longer possible. The higher orders submitted without a murmur and without a struggle to an evil which was thenceforth inevitable. The ordinary fate of falling powers awaited them; each of their several members followed his own interests; and as it was impossible to wring the power from the hands of a people which they did not detest sufficiently to brave, their only aim was to secure its good-will at any price. The most democratic laws were consequently voted by the very men whose interests they impaired; and thus, although the higher classes did not excite the passions of the people against their order, they accelerated the triumph of the new state of things; so that by a singular change the democratic impulse was found to be most irresistible in the very States where the aristocracy had the firmest hold. The State of Maryland, which had been founded by men of rank, was the first to proclaim universal suffrage, and to introduce the most democratic forms into the conduct of its government.

When a nation modifies the elective qualification, it may easily be foreseen that sooner or later that qualification will be entirely abolished. There is no more invariable rule in the history of society: the further electoral rights are extended, the greater is the need of extending them; for after each concession the strength of the democracy increases, and its demands increase with its strength. The ambition of those who are below the appointed rate is irritated in exact proportion to the great number of those who are above it. The exception at last becomes the rule, concession follows concession, and no stop can be made short of universal suffrage.

At the present day the principle of the sovereignty of the people has acquired, in the United States, all the practical development which the imagination can conceive. It is unencumbered by those fictions which have been thrown over it in other countries, and it appears in every possible form according to the exigency of the occasion. Sometimes the laws are made by the people in a body, as at Athens; and sometimes its representatives, chosen by universal suffrage, transact business in its name, and almost under its immediate control.

In some countries a power exists which, though it is in a degree foreign to the social body, directs it, and forces it to pursue a certain track. In others the ruling force is divided, being partly within and partly without the ranks of the people. But nothing of the kind is to be seen in the United States; there society governs itself for itself. All power centres in its bosom; and scarcely an individual is to be meet with who would venture to conceive, or, still less, to express, the idea of seeking it elsewhere. The nation participates in the making of its laws by the choice of its legislators, and in the execution of them by the choice of the agents of the executive government; it may almost be said to govern itself, so feeble and so restricted is the share left to the administration, so little do the authorities forget their popular origin and the power from which they emanate.

V. Necessity of Examining the Condition of the States Before That of the Union at Large

General Remarks on the Administration of the United States

I have already premised that, after having examined the constitution of the township and the county of New England in detail, I should take a general view of the remainder of the Union. Townships and a local activity exist in every State; but in no part of the confederation is a township to be met with precisely similar to those of New England. The more we descend towards the South, the less active does the business of the township or parish become; the number of magistrates, of functions, and of rights decreases; the population exercises a less immediate influence on affairs; town meetings are less frequent, and the subjects of debate less numerous. The power of the elected magistrate is augmented and that of the elector diminished, whilst the public spirit of the local communities is less awakened and less influential. These differences may be perceived to a certain extent in the State of New York; they are very sensible in Pennsylvania; but they become less striking as we advance to the northwest. The majority of the emigrants who settle in the northwestern States are natives of New England, and they carry the habits of their mother country with them into that which they adopt. A township in Ohio is by no means dissimilar from a township in Massachusetts.

We have seen that in Massachusetts the mainspring of public administration lies in the township. It forms the common centre of the interests and affections of the citizens. But this ceases to be the case as we descend to States in which knowledge is less generally diffused, and where the township consequently offers fewer guarantees of a wise and active administration. As we leave New England, therefore, we find that the importance of the town is gradually transferred to the county, which becomes the centre of administration, and the intermediate power between the Government and the citizen. In Massachusetts the business of the county is conducted by the Court of Sessions, which is composed of a *quorum* named by the Governor and his council; but the county has no representative assembly, and its expenditure is voted by the national* legislature. In the great State of New York, on the contrary, and in those of Ohio and Pennsylvania, the inhabitants of each county choose a certain number of representatives, who constitute the assembly of the county. The county assembly has the right of taxing the inhabitants to a certain extent; and in this respect it enjoys the privileges of a real legislative body: at the same time it exercises an executive power in the county, frequently directs the administration of the townships, and restricts their authority within much narrower bounds than in Massachusetts.

Such are the principal differences which the systems of county and town administration present in the Federal States. Were it my intention to examine the provisions of American law minutely, I should have to point out still further differences in the executive details of the several communities. But what I have already said may suffice to show the general principles on which the administration of the United States rests. These principles are differently applied; their consequences are more or less numerous in various localities; but they are always substantially the same. The laws differ, and their outward features change, but their character does not vary. If the township and the county are not everywhere constituted in the same manner, it is at least true that in the United States the county and the township are always based upon the same principle, namely, that everyone is the best judge of what concerns himself alone, and the most proper person to supply his private wants. The township and the county are therefore bound to take care of their special interests: the State governs, but it does not interfere with their administration. Exceptions to this rule may be met with, but not a contrary principle.

The first consequence of this doctrine has been to cause all the magistrates to be chosen either by or at least from amongst the citizens. As the officers are everywhere elected or appointed for a certain period, it has been impossible to establish the rules of a dependent series of authorities; there are almost as many independent functionaries as there are functions, and the executive power is disseminated in a multitude of hands. Hence arose the indispensable necessity of introducing the control of the courts of justice over the administration, and the system of pecuniary penalties, by which the secondary bodies and their

*Tocqueville undoubtedly meant state rather than national.

representatives are constrained to obey the laws. This system obtains from one end of the Union to the other. The power of punishing the misconduct of public officers, or of performing the part of the executive in urgent cases, has not, however, been bestowed on the same judges in all the States. The Anglo-Americans derived the institution of justices of the peace from a common source; but although it exists in all the States, it is not always turned to the same use. The justices of the peace everywhere participate in the administration of the townships and the counties, either as public officers or as the judges of public misdemeanors, but in most of the States the more important classes of public offences come under the cognizance of the ordinary tribunals.

The election of public officers, or the inalienability of their functions, the absence of a gradation of powers, and the introduction of a judicial control over the secondary branches of the administration, are the universal characteristics of the American system from Maine to the Floridas. In some States (and that of New York has advanced most in this direction) traces of a centralized administration begin to be discernible. In the State of New York the officers of the central government exercise, in certain cases, a sort of inspection or control over the secondary bodies.

At other times they constitute a court of appeal for the decision of affairs. In the State of New York judicial penalties are less used than in other parts as a means of administration, and the right of prosecuting the offences of public officers is vested in fewer hands. The same tendency is faintly observable in some other States; but in general the prominent feature of the administration in the United States is its excessive local independence.

The Executive Power of the State

The executive power of the State may with truth be said to be represented by the Governor, although he enjoys but a portion of its rights. The supreme magistrate, under the title of Governor, is the official moderator and counsellor of the legislature. He is armed with a veto or suspensive power, which allows him to stop, or at least to retard, its movements at pleasure. He lays the wants of the country before the legislative body, and points out the means which he thinks may be usefully employed in providing for them; he is the natural executor of its decrees in all the undertakings which interest the nation at large. In the absence of the legislature, the Governor is bound to take all necessary steps to guard the State against violent shocks and unforeseen dangers. The whole military power of the State is at the disposal of the Governor. He is the commander of the militia, and head of the armed force. When the authority which is by general consent awarded to the laws is disregarded, the Governor puts himself at the head of the armed force of the State, to quell resistance and to restore order. Lastly, the Governor takes no share in the administration of townships and counties, except it be indirectly in the nomination of Justices of the Peace, which nomination he has not the power to cancel. The Governor is an elected magistrate, and is generally chosen for one or two years only; so that he always continues to be strictly dependent upon the majority who returned him.

Political Effects of the System of Local Administration in the United States

Centralization is become a word of general and daily use, without any precise meaning being attached to it. Nevertheless, there exist two distinct kinds of centralization, which it is necessary to discriminate with accuracy. Certain interests are common to all parts of a nation, such as the enactment of its general laws and the maintenance of its foreign relations. Other interests are peculiar to certain parts of the nation; such, for instance, as the business of different townships. When the power which directs the general interests is centred in one place, or vested in the same persons, it constitutes a central government. In like manner the power of directing partial or local interests, when brought together into one place, constitutes what may be termed a central administration.

Upon some points these two kinds of centralization coalesce, but by classifying the objects which fall more particularly within the province of each of them, they may easily be distinguished. It is evident that a central government acquires immense power when united to administrative centralization. Thus combined, it accustoms men to set their own will habitually and completely aside; to submit, not only for once, or upon one point, but in every respect, and at all times. Not only, therefore, does this union of power subdue them compulsorily, but it affects them in the ordinary habits of life, and influences each individual, first separately and then collectively.

These two kinds of centralization mutually assist and attract each other; but they must not be supposed to be inseparable. It is impossible to imagine a more completely central government than that which existed in France under Louis XIV; when the same individual was the author and the interpreter of the laws, and the representative of France at home and abroad, he was justified in asserting that the State was identified with his person. Nevertheless, the administration was much less centralized under Louis XIV than it is at the present day.

❧ ❧ ❧

We have shown that in the United States no central administration and no dependent series of public functionaries exist. Local authority has been carried to lengths which no European nation could endure without great inconvenience, and which has even produced some disadvantageous consequences in America. But in the United States the centralization of the Government is complete; and it would be easy to prove that the national power is more compact than it has ever been in the old nations of Europe. Not only is there but one legislative body in each State; not only does there exist but one source of political authority; but district assemblies and county courts have not in general been multiplied, lest they should be tempted to exceed their administrative duties, and interfere with the Government. In America the legislature of each State is supreme; nothing can impede its authority; neither privileges, nor local immunities, nor personal influence, nor even the empire of reason, since it represents that majority which claims to be the sole organ of reason. Its own determination is, therefore, the only limit to this action. In juxtaposition to it, and under its immediate control, is the representative of the executive power, whose duty it is to constrain the refractory to submit by superior force. The only symptom of weakness lies in certain details of the action of the Government. The American republics have no standing armies to intimidate a discontented minority; but as no minority has as yet been reduced to declare open war, the necessity of an army has not been felt. The State usually employs the officers of the township or the county to deal with the citizens. Thus, for instance, in New England, the assessor fixes the rate of taxes; the collector receives them; the town-treasurer transmits the amount to the public treasury; and the disputes which may arise are brought before the ordinary courts of justice. This method of collecting taxes is slow as well as inconvenient, and it would prove a per-petual hindrance to a Government whose pecuniary demands were large. It is desirable that, in whatever materially affects its existence, the Government should be served by officers of its own, appointed by itself, removable at pleasure, and accustomed to rapid methods of proceeding. But it will always be easy for the central government, organized as it is in America, to intro-duce new and more efficacious modes of action, proportioned to its wants.

The absence of a central government will not, then, as has often been asserted, prove the destruction of the republics of the New World; far from supposing that the American governments are not sufficiently centralized, I shall prove hereafter that they are too much so. The legislative bodies daily encroach upon the authority of the Government, and their tendency, like that of the French Convention, is to appropriate it entirely to themselves. Under these circumstances the social power is constantly changing hands, because it is subordinate to the power of the people, which is too apt to forget the maxims of wisdom and of foresight in the consciousness of its strength: hence arises its danger; and thus its vigor, and not its impotence, will probably be the cause of its ultimate destruction.

The system of local administration produces several different effects in America. The Americans seem to me to have outstepped the limits of sound policy in isolating the administration of the Government; for order, even in second-rate affairs, is a matter of national importance. As the State has no administrative functionaries of its own, stationed on different points of its territory, to whom it can give a common impulse, the consequence is that it rarely attempts to issue any general police regulations. The want of these regulations is severely felt, and is frequently observed by Europeans. The appearance of disorder which prevails on the surface leads him at first to imagine that society is in a state of anarchy; nor does he perceive his mistake till he has gone deeper into the subject. Certain undertakings are of importance to the whole State; but they cannot be put in execution, because there is no national administration to direct them. Abandoned to the exertions of the towns or counties, under the care of elected or temporary agents, they lead to no result, or at least to no durable benefit.

The partisans of centralization in Europe are wont to maintain that the Government directs the affairs of each locality better than the citizens could do it for themselves; this may be true when the central power is enlightened, and when the local districts are ignorant; when it is as alert as they are slow; when it is accustomed to act, and they to obey. Indeed, it is evident that this double tendency must augment with the increase of centralization, and that the readiness of the one and the incapacity of the others must become more and more prominent. But I deny that such is the case when the people is as enlightened, as awake to its interests, and as accustomed to reflect on them, as the Americans are. I am persuaded, on the contrary, that in this case the collective strength of the citizens will always conduce more efficaciously to the public welfare than the authority of the Government. It is difficult to point out with certainty the means of arousing a sleeping population, and of giving it passions and knowledge which it does not possess; it is, I am well aware, an arduous task to persuade men to busy themselves about their own affairs; and it would frequently be easier to interest them in the punctilios of court etiquette than in the repairs of their common dwelling. But whenever a central administration affects to supersede the persons most interested, I am inclined to suppose that it is either misled or desirous to mislead. However enlightened and however skilful a central power may be, it cannot of itself embrace all the details of the existence of a great nation. Such vigilance exceeds the powers of man. And when it attempts to create and set in motion so many complicated springs, it must submit to a very imperfect result, or consume itself in bootless efforts.

Centralization succeeds more easily, indeed, in subjecting the external actions of men to a certain uniformity, which at least commands our regard, independently of the objects to which it is applied, like those devotees who worship the statue and forget the deity it represents. Centralization imparts without difficulty an admirable regularity to the routine of business; provides for the details of the social police with sagacity; represses the smallest disorder and the most petty misdemeanors; maintains society in a *status quo* alike secure from improvement and decline; and perpetuates a drowsy precision in the conduct of affairs, which is hailed by the heads of the administration as a sign of perfect order and public tranquillity: in short, it excels more in prevention than in action. Its force deserts it when society is to be disturbed or accelerated in its course; and if once the co-operation of private citizens is necessary to the furtherance of its measures, the secret of its impotence is disclosed. Even whilst it invokes their assistance, it is on the condition that they shall act exactly as much as the Government chooses, and exactly in the manner it appoints. They are to take charge of the details, without aspiring to guide the system; they are to work in a dark and subordinate sphere, and only to judge the acts in which they have themselves cooperated by their results. These, however, are not conditions on which the alliance of the human will is to be obtained; its carriage must be free and its actions responsible, or ... the citizen had rather remain a passive spectator than a dependent actor in schemes with which he is unacquainted.

It is undeniable that the want of those uniform regulations which control the conduct of every inhabitant of France is not unfrequently felt in the United States. Gross instances of social indifference and neglect are to be met with, and from time to time disgraceful blemishes are seen in complete contrast with the surrounding civilization. Useful undertakings which cannot succeed without perpetual attention and rigorous exactitude are very frequently abandoned in the end; for in America, as well as in other countries, the people are subject to sudden impulses and momentary exertions. The European who is accustomed to find a functionary always at hand to interfere with all he undertakes has some difficulty in accustoming himself to the complex mechanism of the administration of the townships. In general it may be affirmed that the lesser details of the police, which render life easy and comfortable, are neglected in America; but that the essential guarantees of man in society are as strong there as elsewhere. In America the power which conducts the Government is far less regular, less enlightened, and less learned, but an hundredfold more authoritative than in Europe. In no country in the world do the citizens make such exertions for the common weal; and I am acquainted with no people which has established schools as numerous and as efficacious, places of public worship better suited to the wants of the inhabitants, or roads kept in better repair. Uniformity or permanence of design, the minute arrangement of details, and the perfection of an ingenious administration, must not be sought for in the United States; but it will be easy to find, on the other hand, the symptoms of a power which, if it is somewhat barbarous, is at least robust; and of an existence which is checkered with accidents, indeed, but cheered at the same time by animation and effort.

Granting for an instant that the villages and counties of the United States would be more usefully governed by a remote authority which they had never seen than by functionaries taken from the midst of them—admitting, for the sake of argument, that the country would be more secure, and the resources of society better employed, if the whole administration centred in a single arm—still the political advantages which the Americans derive from their system would induce me to prefer it to the contrary plan. It profits me but little, after all, that a vigilant authority should protect the tranquillity of my pleasures and constantly avert all dangers from my path, without my care or my concern, if this same authority is the absolute mistress of my liberty and of my life, and if it so monopolizes all the energy of existence that when it languishes everything languishes around it, that when it sleeps everything must sleep, that when it dies the State itself must perish.

It is not the administrative but the political effects of the local system that I most admire in America. In the United States the interests of the country are everywhere kept in view; they are an object of solicitude to the people of the whole Union, and every citizen is as warmly attached to them as if they were his own. He takes pride in the glory of his nation; he boasts of its success, to which he conceives himself to have contributed, and he rejoices in the general prosperity by which he profits. The feeling he entertains towards the State is analogous to that which unites him to his family, and it is by a kind of egotism that he interests himself in the welfare of his country.

The European generally submits to a public officer because he represents a superior force; but to an American he represents a right. In America it may be said that no one renders obedience to man, but to justice and to law. If the opinion which the citizen entertains of himself is exaggerated, it is at least salutary; he unhesitatingly confides in his own powers, which appear to him to be all-sufficient. When a private individual meditates an undertaking, however directly connected it may be with the welfare of society, he never thinks of soliciting the co-operation of the Government, but he publishes his plan, offers to execute it himself, courts the assistance of other individuals, and struggles manfully against all obstacles. Undoubtedly he is often less successful than the State might have been in his position; but in the end the sum of these private undertakings far exceeds all that the Government could have done.

As the administrative authority is within the reach of the citizens, whom it in some degree represents, it excites neither their jealousy nor their hatred; as its resources are limited, every one feels that he must not rely solely on its assistance. Thus, when the administration thinks fit to interfere, it is not abandoned to itself as in Europe; the duties of the private citizens are not supposed to have lapsed because the State assists in their fulfilment, but every one is ready, on the contrary, to guide and to support it. This action of individual exertions, joined to that of the public authorities, frequently performs what the most energetic central administration would be unable to execute. It would be easy to adduce several facts in proof of what I advance, but I had rather give only one, with which I am more thoroughly acquainted. In America the means which the authorities have at their disposal for the discovery of crimes and the arrest of criminals are few. The State police does not exist, and passports are unknown. The criminal police of the United States cannot be compared to that of France; the magistrates and public prosecutors are not numerous, and the examinations of prisoners are rapid and oral. Nevertheless in no country does crime more rarely elude punishment. The reason is, that every one conceives himself to be interested in furnishing evidence of the act committed, and in stopping the delinquent. During my stay in the United States I witnessed the spontaneous formation of committees for the pursuit and prosecution of a man who had committed a great crime in a certain county. In Europe a criminal is an unhappy being who is struggling for his life against the ministers of justice, whilst the population is merely a spectator of the conflict; in America he is looked upon as an enemy of the human race, and the whole of mankind is against him.

I believe that provincial institutions are useful to all nations, but nowhere do they appear to me to be more indispensable than amongst a democratic people. In an aristocracy order can always be maintained in the midst of liberty, and as the rulers have a great deal to lose order is to them a first-rate consideration. In like manner an aristocracy protects the people from the excesses of despotism, because it always possesses an organized power ready to resist a despot. But a democracy without provincial institutions has no security against these evils. How can a populace, unaccustomed to freedom in small concerns, learn to use it temperately in great affairs? What resistance can be offered to tyranny in a country where every private individual is impotent, and where the citizens are united by no common tie? Those who dread the license of the mob, and those who fear the rule of absolute power, ought alike to desire the progressive growth of provincial liberties.

On the other hand, I am convinced that democratic nations are most exposed to fall beneath the yoke of a central administration, for several reasons, amongst which is the following. The constant tendency of these nations is to concentrate all the strength of the Government in the hands of the only power which directly represents the people, because beyond the people nothing is to be perceived but a mass of equal individuals confounded together. But when the same power is already in possession of all the attributes of the Government, it can scarcely refrain from penetrating into the details of the administration, and an opportunity of doing so is sure to present itself in the end, as was the case in France. In the French Revolution there were two impulses in opposite directions, which must never be confounded— the one was favorable to liberty, the other to despotism. Under the ancient monarchy the King was the sole author of the laws, and below the power of the sovereign certain vestiges of provincial institutions, half destroyed, were still distinguishable. These provincial institutions were incoherent, ill compacted, and frequently absurd; in the hands of the aristocracy they had sometimes been converted into instruments of oppression. The Revolution declared itself the enemy of royalty and of provincial institutions at the same time; it confounded all that had preceded it—despotic power and the checks to its abuses—in indiscriminate hatred, and its tendency was at once to overthrow and to centralize. This double character of the French Revolution is a fact which has been adroitly handled by the friends of absolute power. Can they be accused of laboring in the cause of despotism when they are defending that central administration which was one of the great innovations of the Revolution? In this manner popularity may be conciliated with hostility to the rights of the people, and the secret slave of tyranny may be the professed admirer of freedom.

I have visited the two nations in which the system of provincial liberty has been most perfectly established, and I have listened to the opinions of different parties in those countries. In America I met with men who secretly aspired to destroy the democratic institutions of the Union; in England I found others who attacked the aristocracy openly, but I know of no one who does not regard provincial independence as a great benefit. In both countries I have heard a thousand different causes assigned for the evils of the State, but the local system was never mentioned amongst them. I have heard citizens attribute the power and prosperity of their country to a multitude of reasons, but they all placed the advantages of local institutions in the foremost rank. Am I to suppose that when men who are naturally so divided on religious opinions and on political theories agree on one point (and that one of which they have daily experience), they are all in error? The only nations which deny the utility of provincial liberties are those which have fewest of them; in other words, those who are unacquainted with the institution are the only persons who pass a censure upon it.

Government of the Democracy in America

Instability of the Administration in the United States

The authority which public men possess in America is so brief, and they are so soon commingled with the ever-changing population of the country, that the acts of a community frequently leave fewer traces than the occurrences of a private family. The public administration is, so to speak, oral and traditionary. But little is committed to writing, and that little is wafted away forever, like the leaves of the Sibyl, by the smallest breeze.

The only historical remains in the United States are the newspapers; but if a number be wanting, the chain of time is broken, and the present is severed from the past. I am convinced that in fifty years it will be more difficult to collect authentic documents concerning the social condition of the Americans at the present day than it is to find remains of the administration of France during the Middle Ages; and if the United States were ever invaded by barbarians, it would be necessary to have recourse to the history of other nations in order to learn anything of the people which now inhabits them.

The instability of the administration has penetrated into the habits of the people: it even appears to suit the general taste, and no one cares for what occurred before his time. No methodical system is pursued; no archives are formed; and no documents are brought together when it would be very easy to do so. Where they exist, little store is set upon them; and I have amongst my papers several original public documents which were given to me in answer to some of my inquiries. In America society seems to live from hand to mouth, like an army in the field. Nevertheless, the art of administration may undoubtedly be ranked as a science, and no sciences can be improved if the discoveries and observations of successive generations are not connected together in the order in which they occur. One man, in the short space of his life remarks a fact; another conceives an idea; the former invents a means of execution, the latter reduces a truth to a fixed proposition; and mankind gathers the fruits of individual experience upon its way and gradually forms the sciences. But the persons who conduct the administration in America can seldom afford any instruction to each other; and when they assume the direction of society, they simply possess those attainments which are most widely disseminated in the community, and no experience peculiar to themselves. Democracy, carried to its furthest limits, is therefore prejudicial to the art of government; and for this reason it is better adapted to a people already versed in the conduct of an administration than to a nation which is uninitiated in public affairs.

This remark, indeed, is not exclusively applicable to the science of administration. Although a democratic government is founded upon a very simple and natural principle, it always presupposes the existence of a high degree of culture and enlightenment in society. At the first glance it may be imagined to belong to the earliest ages of the world; but maturer observation will convince us that it could only come last in the succession of human history.

Causes Which Mitigate the Tyranny of the Majority in the United States

Absence of Central Administration

I have already pointed out the distinction which is to be made between a centralized government and a centralized administration. The former exists in America, but the latter is nearly unknown there. If the directing power of the American communities had both these instruments of government at its disposal, and united the habit of executing its own commands to the right of commanding; if, after having established the general principles of government, it descended to the details of public business; and if, having regulated the great interests of the country, it could penetrate into the privacy of individual interests, freedom would soon be banished from the New World.

But in the United States the majority, which so frequently displays the tastes and the propensities of a despot, is still destitute of the more perfect instruments of tyranny. In the American republics the activity of the central Government has never as yet been extended beyond a limited number of objects sufficiently prominent to call forth its attention. The secondary affairs of society have never been regulated by its authority, and nothing has hitherto betrayed its desire of interfering in them. The majority is become more and more absolute, but it has not increased the prerogatives of the central Government; those great prerogatives have been confined to a certain sphere; and although the despotism of the majority may be galling upon one point, it cannot be said to extend to all. However the predominant party in the nation may be carried away by its passions, however ardent it may be in the pursuit of its projects, it cannot oblige all the citizens to comply with its desires in the same manner and at the same time throughout the country. When the central Government which represents that majority has issued a decree, it must entrust the execution of its will to agents, over whom it frequently has no control, and whom it cannot perpetually direct. The townships, municipal bodies, and counties may therefore be looked upon as concealed break-waters, which check or part the tide of popular excitement. If an oppressive law were passed, the liberties of the people would still be protected by the means by which that law would be put in execution: the majority cannot descend to the details and (as I will venture to style them) the puerilities of administrative tyranny. Nor does the people entertain that full conscious-ness of its authority which would prompt it to interfere in these matters; it knows the extent of its natural powers, but it is unacquainted with the increased resources which the art of government might furnish.

This point deserves attention, for if a democratic republic similar to that of the United States were ever founded in a country where the power of a single individual had previously subsisted, and the effects of a centralized adminis-tration had sunk deep into the habits and the laws of the people, I do not hesitate to assert, that in that country a more insufferable despotism would prevail than any which now exists in the monarchical States of Europe, or indeed than any which could be found on this side of the confines of Asia.

The Profession of the Law in the United States Serves to Counterpoise the Democracy

In visiting the Americans and in studying their laws we perceive that the authority they have entrusted to members of the legal profession, and the influence which these individuals exercise in the Government, is the most powerful existing security against the excesses of democracy. This effect seems to me to result from a general cause which it is useful to investigate, since it may produce analogous consequences elsewhere.

In America there are no nobles or men of letters, and the people is apt to mistrust the wealthy; lawyers consequently form the highest political class, and the most cultivated circle of society. They have therefore nothing to gain by innovation, which adds a conservative interest to their natural taste for public order. If I were asked where I place the American aristocracy, I should reply without hesitation that it is not composed of the rich, who are united together by no common tie, but that it occupies the judicial bench and the bar.

The more we reflect upon all that occurs in the United States the more shall we be persuaded that the lawyers as a body form the most powerful, if not the only, counterpoise to the democratic element. In that country we perceive how eminently the legal profession is qualified by its powers, and even by its defects, to neutralize the vices which are inherent in popular government. When the American people is intoxicated by passion, or carried away by the impetuosity of its ideas, it is checked and stopped by the almost invisible influence of its legal counsellors, who secretly oppose their aristocratic propensities to its democratic instincts, their superstitious attachment to what is antique to its love of novelty, their narrow views to its immense designs, and their habitual procrastination to its ardent impatience.

The courts of justice are the most visible organs by which the legal profession is enabled to control the democracy. The judge is a lawyer, who, independently of the taste for regularity and order which he has contracted in the study of legislation, derives an additional love of stability from his own inalienable functions. His legal attainments have already raised him to a distinguished rank amongst his fellow-citizens; his political power completes the distinction of his station, and gives him the inclinations natural to privileged classes.

Armed with the power of declaring the laws to be unconstitutional, the American magistrate perpetually interferes in political affairs. He cannot force the people to make laws, but at least he can oblige it not to disobey its own enactments; or to act inconsistently with its own principles. I am aware that a secret tendency to diminish the judicial power exists in the United States, and by most of the constitutions of the several States the Government can, upon the demand of the two houses of the legislature, remove the judges from their station. By some other constitutions the members of the tribunals are elected, and they are even subjected to frequent re-elections. I venture to predict that these innovations will sooner or later be attended with fatal consequences, and that it will be found out at some future period that the attack which is made upon the judicial power has affected the democratic republic itself.

It must not, however, be supposed that the legal spirit of which I have been speaking has been confined, in the United States, to the courts of justice; it extends far beyond them. As the lawyers constitute the only enlightened class which the people does not mistrust, they are naturally called upon to occupy most of the public stations. They fill the legislative assemblies, and they conduct the administration; they consequently exercise a powerful influence upon the formation of the law, and upon its execution. The lawyers are, however, obliged to yield to the current of public opinion, which is too strong for them to resist it, but it is easy to find indications of what their conduct would be if they were free to act as they chose. The Americans, who have made such copious innovations in their political legislation, have introduced very sparing alterations in their civil laws, and that with great difficulty, although those laws are frequently repugnant to their social condition. The reason of this is, that in matters of civil law the majority is obliged to defer to the authority of the legal profession, and that the American lawyers are disinclined to innovate when they are left to their own choice.

It is curious for a Frenchman, accustomed to a very different state of things, to hear the perpetual complaints which are made in the United States against the stationary propensities of legal men, and their prejudices in favor of existing institutions.

The influence of the legal habits which are common in America extends beyond the limits I have just pointed out. Scarcely any question arises in the United States which does not become, sooner or later, a subject of judicial debate; hence all parties are obliged to borrow the ideas, and even the language, usual in judicial proceedings in their daily controversies. As most public men are, or have been, legal practitioners, they introduce the customs and technicalities of their profession into the affairs of the country. The jury extends this habitude to all classes. The language of the law thus becomes, in some measure, a vulgar tongue; the spirit of the law, which is produced in the· schools and courts of justice, gradually penetrates beyond their walls into the bosom of society, where it descends to the lowest classes, so that the whole people contracts the habits and the tastes of the magistrate. The lawyers of the United States form a party which is but little feared and scarcely perceived, which has no badge peculiar to itself, which adapts itself with great flexibility to the exigencies of the time; and accommodates itself to all the movements of the social body, but this party extends over the whole community, and it penetrates into all classes of society; it acts upon the country imperceptibly, but it finally fashions it to suit its purposes.

PART II

BIRTH AND GROWTH OF THE PUBLIC MANAGEMENT MOVEMENT

The systematic study of public administration, indeed its recognition as a legitimate field of scholarly inquiry, did not begin until nearly a century after the Constitutional Convention of 1787. The search for an intellectual base for management improvement began with the efforts to reform the civil service, which was riddled by patronage and the spoils system during the middle decades of the nineteenth century. Those efforts culminated in the Pendleton Act of 1883 and comparable legislation in a number of states. The Pendleton Act itself was based partly upon a study of the British civil service reforms and was a considerably watered-down attempt to imitate the British.[1] At about the same time, academic interest in public administration more general than civil service reform was beginning at a very few American universities. Notable among these was Johns Hopkins, which upon its opening in 1876 launched an experimental program, modeled upon European rather than American universities and emphasizing graduate research rather than collegiate instruction. Almost from its beginning, Johns Hopkins offered studies in political economy and public administration. As early as 1887, a distinguished faculty member described it as the leading training school for administrators and public officials in the United States and proposed establishment there of a school of administration and public affairs.[2] A growing number of professors around the country during the late nineteenth and early twentieth centuries became interested in and taught the subject, and a few universities (Pennsylvania, Chicago, Wisconsin, and a little later, Harvard) considered full-fledged programs. The main emphases were upon public and constitutional law, the history of political institutions, political economy, and comparative administration, focused primarily upon continental Europe. None of these early efforts resulted in continuing academic programs in public administration, but they contributed to growing interest in the subject and a degree of respectability to its study.

While the initial sparks of the public management movement were the reform of civil service and the scholarly study of public administration in certain universities, there were at least three other influences, which had major impact soon after the turn of the twentieth century. First was the reorganization of the War Department and the formation of the General Staff

1. For further information about civil service reform and a copy of the Pendleton Act itself, see Frederick C. Mosher, ed., *Basic Documents of American Public Administration, 1776–1950* (Holmes and Meier, 1976), pp. 46–47 and 53–61.
2. Arthur S. Link, ed., *The Papers of Woodrow Wilson*, Vol. 5 (Princeton University Press, 1968), p. 436, fn. 2. The professor referred to was Herbert Baxter Adams. It was intended that the school be launched under two codirectors, one of whom was expected to be Woodrow Wilson.

in 1902 and 1903. These were in major part consequences of the managerial disasters of the Spanish-American War, and, like the developments described above, reflected studies of European practice. The emphasis, much of which would subsequently be transferred to civil agencies, was upon integrated command, the use of staff, systematized planning, and training.[3]

Another major contributor to the public management movement was private business: the efforts to rationalize and make a science of business management, to apply quantifiable measures to all the ingredients of performance, to relate costs to products, to make enterprises more efficient. These became generally known as scientific management, a term usually associated with its inventor, Frederick W. Taylor. In an era when the dominance and success of private business were central elements of American society and when a major theme of that society was the application of an advancing science and technology, the scientific management movement had a pervasive influence. Administrative developments in government paralleled to a substantial extent the ideology and the tools being increasingly applied in the business world.

The final impulse behind the public management movement, perhaps the most important, was the application of objective research to the problems of city government, largely in reaction against local political machines and corruption. Beginning during the first decade of the twentieth century, with the New York Bureau of Municipal Research and its associated training program for administrators, the municipal research movement spread rapidly to other cities, to states, and to the national government. It became the core of managerial reform in government over the ensuing decades, as well as the seed for university research and training programs in public administration, the first of which began during the 1920s.

The public management movement came to comprehend a relatively coherent and consistent set of values, doctrines, and techniques about which there was a widespread consensus among its adherents—researchers, teachers, students, and practitioners. It incorporated most of the elements mentioned above: civil service reform (which became personnel management); a political science base, grounded in public law, political institutions, and democratic principles; scientific management; rationalization of military organization with emphasis upon planning and training; and municipal research and reform.

3.   See Mosher, *Basic Documents,* pp. 48–49 and 67–75.

Dwight Waldo (1913–)

The first selection is out of chronological order in terms of date of publication. Dwight Waldo's celebrated study *The Administrative State* (Ronald Press, 1948) appeared three to six decades after the other selections in Part II were written. But Waldo's book provides a fitting preface to the study of the public management movement. Its first chapter and some of its later sections offer perhaps the most perceptive and concise overview of the forces and the philosophy contributing to that movement that has been written. He had advantages that the participants in the movement could not enjoy: the twenty-twenty-vision hindsight of one who could view it a generation or two later, and the dispassionate perspective of an observer not immediately involved, who could interpret the movement against broader trends of history and society.

My selection of only a few pages dealing with the background of the movement may be a disservice to Waldo. Other sections of *The Administrative State* dealt analytically with basic issues of public administration as he perceived them at the close of World War II. Since that time, he has produced an impressive array of monographs, articles, speeches, book reviews, and other pieces on administrative thought and practice, making him one of the most eminent philosophers of public administration in this country.

The text that follows consists of the first chapter of *The Administrative State*, from which have been excised a few paragraphs dealing with more recent developments, and the first few pages of the tenth chapter concerning the evolution of the concept of economy and efficiency.

F.C.M.

The Administrative State

The Material and Ideological Background

If they are to be understood, political theories must be construed in relation to their material environment and ideological framework. The political

Chapters 1 and 10, *The Administrative State* (New York: Ronald Press, 1948), pp. 3–21 and 192–196. Copyright 1948 by The Ronald Press Co.; © renewed 1976 by Dwight Waldo. Reprinted by permission of John Wiley & Sons, Inc.

theories of American public administration are not exceptions. For, despite occasional claims that public administration is a science with principles of universal validity, American public administration has evolved political theories unmistakably related to unique economic, social, governmental, and ideological facts.

The Material Background

Among the factors that clearly have affected the form and content of American literature on public administration are the advent of the Great Society, the closing of the frontier and the waste of our natural resources, our tremendous wealth and our Business Civilization, the "corporate revolution" and the evolution of new corporate forms, urbanization, our peculiar constitutional and political system, the "second phase of the industrial revolution," the increase in specialization and professionalism and the rise of American scholarship, and the Great Wars, the Great Prosperity, and the Great Depression.

The Great Society.   Whatever else it may be, "public administration" is a response on the part of its creators to the modern world that Graham Wallas has named the Great Society.

The text of Woodrow Wilson's early essay, "The Study of Administration," was that "it is getting to be harder to *run* a constitution than to frame one." This classic of administrative writing appeared contemporaneously with the Interstate Commerce Act, and the coincidence is significant. The establishment of the Interstate Commerce Commission signalized the passage of the United States from a simple, agricultural society into a highly complex and interrelated Great Society. This new society was based upon a highly advanced division of labor and specialization of skill, a highly developed system of transportation and communication, a vast, sprawling technology—all based upon a new method of controlling environment called "scientific method."

American writers on public administration have accepted the inevitability and the desirability of the Great Society—with minor differences and with reservations as to detail. The importance of this acceptance cannot be overestimated. The most significant facts about any era to subsequent generations are likely to be precisely the ones accepted as unquestioningly as the fish accepts water. The "acceptance" of the Great Society by writers on public administration is quite as important as their various assertions—more so, since their assertions flow from their acceptance. They have not only accepted the Great Society; they have accepted the obligation to remedy its deficiencies and to make it a Good Society. This need not have been the case. Jefferson or Thoreau, William Morris or Tolstoi, presumably would not find the arguments of the administrative writers compelling.

Closing of the Frontier. The economic and social readjustments attendant upon the closing of the frontier, and the prodigious waste of our natural resources that continued into the new period of consolidation, stimulated writing on public administration and determined its direction. The economic and political formulae of classical economics became, perhaps, a useful Myth for the period in which they were elaborated; many people found them helpful and they produced some manifest blessings. But the postulate that there is a harmony of nature, which if undisturbed would be productive of the greatest good of the greatest number, lost its appeal for many thoughtful and sensitive people with the passing of time and the altering of circumstances. The increasing ratio of population to resources, the vastness of waste and confusion, the failure of the traditional ways to produce a tolerable life for large numbers of our population even in the midst of plenty—these led an ever-increasing number of academic, literary, and civic-minded people to abandon the old faith in a natural harmony in favor of a new ideal: that of a man-made harmony. That eminent work of the Progressive period, Herbert Croly's *Promise of American Life,* may be taken as the symbol of the decision of a considerable number of citizens that we could no longer rely simply upon great natural wealth and complete individual freedom to fulfill the American dream of economic independence. The validity of the ideal of a man-made harmony, created for the most part through the instrumentality of governmental bureaucracies, has almost universally been assumed by writers on public administration—else why should they write of public administration except to damn it?

The importance of the conservation movement in hastening and confirming the adoption of this new viewpoint was apparently very great. The idea of saving natural resources soon developed into a social philosophy—saving human beings; and ultimately into the idea of a "planned" and "administered" human community. The ferment of the conservation idea is easily discernible in the early journals, and while "conservation" is no longer a popular word among writers on public administration, its meaning has been absorbed into new terminology.

Our Business Civilization. Despite increasing pressure of population on resources and continuing prodigality in the use of resources, America remained a uniquely wealthy country, and ours became characteristically a Business Civilization. This has influenced our methods of administration and our literature of public administration. It has been generally "business" that has given support to the study of public administration—in research bureaus, professional associations, the colleges and universities, and regular or *ad hoc* administrative agencies. Labor, agriculture, the older professions, and "consumers" have not been as much concerned about it. Naturally, therefore, the results reflect business beliefs and practices. ("Pressures" need not be presumed.) The paternalism, the "benevolent Feudalism" of business have been reproduced in public administration. . . .

It is important also that the rise of public administration occurred during the golden age of private charity. In the past fifty years billions of dollars have been contributed, chiefly by the business community, to found and support dozens of activities which in other civilized countries are undertaken by the State. But for this golden flood and the opposition of the business community to the extension of governmental functions, many domains of activity would have fallen under public control much sooner than they have, or promise to be, and the problems of their administration thus posed and considered earlier. So, while business has stimulated and supported administrative study, it must be presumed that it nevertheless has reduced the amount and scope of speculation on the subject.

The Modern Corporation. The dependence of public administration on its business background has been furthered by the influence of the "corporate revolution" and the resulting emphasis on forms of organization characteristic of business corporations. . . . Demonstrably, the corporation, both in its "private" and in its "public" varieties, has influenced our administrative thought, just as the institutions of the fief and the guild influenced medieval political thought.

❊   ❊   ❊

The most interesting aspect of the influence of the corporate form lies in the fact that it has produced a literature of both centralization and decentralization. The example of private corporate practice has been one of the favorite weapons in the dialectic armory of those who have been interested in deprecating legislative or judicial influence and in aggrandizing executive power. On the other hand a number of persons have found in the practices of corporate interrelationships a hope that society can be planned and managed in the requisite degree without the disadvantages and dangers of great concentration of authority; that widespread public control and central direction can be combined with devolution in management and a democratic, "grass-roots" administration.

Coming of Urbanization. The passing of the United States from a predominantly rural to a predominantly urban mode of life has recorded itself in the literature of public administration. This literature, in fact, is one of the forms in which the reconciliation of the old American ideal, Democracy, has been made with the new American condition, Urbanization. Democracy may not be as fervent an ideal today as it was in the Gilded Age, but the fear of great numbers of our citizens who surveyed the "City Wilderness" and were sick at heart at what was manifest from South End to Nob Hill, the fear that the destruction of democracy and its ideal was imminent, has been in considerable measure met and overcome by advances in administrative practice and by the assurances of administrative writers. The American ideal has, in fact, become predominantly an urban ideal, with its emphasis upon the material and spiritual satisfactions of a city civilization. . . .

Our Constitutional System. Public administration has of course been conditioned in diverse ways by the peculiarities of our constitutional and political systems. For example, our unique interpretation and strong institutionalization of the theory of the separation of powers, and our federal system, have created administrative problems that administrative students have sought to deal with by developing a philosophy of integration and simplification. The need for integration, in fact, has seemed so urgent that with many the "canons of integration" gained the status of universals.

It may be noted also that the separation and division of power and the lack of a strong tradition of administrative action have contributed to the proliferation of organizations of private citizens, and of public servants acting more or less in their private capacities, in order that certain functions may be performed that are carried out directly by the bureaucracies in some other highly developed nations. This "private" nature of American public administration has posed problems of the proper division of function between public and private administration and of the proper relation between autonomous or semi-autonomous organizations and the state structure.

It may also be noted that our institutional framework was partly responsible for the rise of the "spoils system," which has retarded the advance of effective administration and the rise of a tradition of government service by the "best." The fact that we have not developed a strong tradition of service by any particular intellectual, social, or educational type has invited speculative writing on the nature of administrative functions; on the problem of who should perform them, how they should be selected, and how trained—a field of much controversy.

Second Phase of the Industrial Revolution. What has been called "the second phase of the industrial revolution" has reflected itself in American writings on public administration. Toward the close of the nineteenth century, when productive capacity began to exceed the capacity of available markets to absorb goods at productive prices, emphasis shifted from securing capital and enlarging facilities to raising profits by more effective use of productive equipment—machines and men. The chief result of this change in emphasis was the "scientific management" movement. Beginning with Frederick W. Taylor's attempt to overcome "soldiering" among laborers and his study of the variables involved in steel-cutting operations, scientific management spread upward under the spur of profit and the aegis of science, and outward under the prestige of American mass-production methods until it became an international philosophy with a vision of a New Order—one of the most interesting and distinctive social philosophies developed in modern times.

About 1910 scientific management began to be introduced into some branches of public administration, and to percolate among the students in their bureaus and schools. Today, no realm of administration has been left untouched, however lightly, by the new spirit; and some bureaus give lessons in efficiency to business. Perhaps as much as any other one thing, the "management" movement has molded the outlook of those to whom public administration is an independent inquiry or definable discipline.

Advance of Specialization. The course which American study of public administration has taken is also a function of the very great increase in specialization which has featured our recent national life; particularly the rise of American scholarship and the growth of professional spirit and organizations. Few social and intellectual events in the history of the world have been more remarkable than the change, in the space of a generation, from the jack-of-all-trades pioneer-yeoman as a general type and ideal, to the specialist, the expert, the man who "knows his job." The typical, middle-class American in the twentieth century is not the yeoman but the professional or "skilled" man. This is the type we honor and aim to produce in our schools. Especially if a man's skill is in some way connected with "science," we accord him the deference that in some societies is accorded men of Church or State.

This change in national life has helped to force the issue of the "amateur" in government service and to blacken the reputation of the politician. The respect paid to the ideal of the expert—especially the scientist—has had as a by-product the fact that our public service is probably equal in quality to any other in these categories—and that these categories tend to dominate the service. The general movement toward specialization and professionalization has inspired much literature urging that public administration must be made a "profession"—or professions—to achieve high standards and gain prestige.

The fissiparous tendencies of specialization have made more difficult the integration of our national life and raised the question of the necessity for a new kind of "integrator"—an administrator who is a specialist in "things in general." On the other hand, some have found heterogeneity and indirection desirable, and we have had a pale image of British literature on Guild Socialism in the proposals of a few writers advocating that professional bodies be entrusted with the execution of a rather large number of "public" functions.

The rise of American scholarship, the spread of a guild spirit among scholars, and the rise of professional schools have been a part of the general movement toward specialization. The utilization of an increasing amount of our economic surplus for educational purposes; the late nineteenth-century hegira of our students to Europe, especially to German universities; the heritage of legal and philosophical interests in social studies; the founding of professional schools, particularly those in business administration; and the endowment or other provision for chairs, departments, and schools of public administration—these factors have left an indelible print in a variety of ways upon the literature of public administration since the publication of Wilson's essay.

The Ideological Framework

Up to this point we have been trying to discern the relationship between American study of public administration and its material environment—economic, institutional, "historical," and so forth. But the relationship of administrative study to the main currents of American thought during the past fifty years is equally important. In some measure the distinction between material and ideological environment is a false one. The relationship of ideas to the existential world is a matter of profound scientific and philosophical dispute; and in the above attempt to delineate the influence of "events" there has been occasional reference to ideology. However, it is assumed that ideas affect as well as reflect the course of events.

The choice of "dominant ideas" must be in some degree arbitrary, but both because of their widespread acceptance by the national community and their obvious influence upon writings on public administration the following are chosen for brief examination: the democratic ideal and related ideas such as the "mission of America," the belief in "fundamental law," the doctrine of progress and "progressivism," the gospel of efficiency, and faith in science.

Democracy and the Mission of America. Democracy has long been not only the form of government for the people of America, but a faith and an ideal, a romantic vision. This has been peculiarly our form of patriotism, our form of spiritual imperialism. The "mission of America," whether stated in religious terms or not, has been conceived as witnessing Democracy before mankind, bearing democracy's ideals of freedom and equality, and its material blessings, to the nations of the world. Belief in this mission perhaps has become less widely and intensively held during the past fifty years. Nevertheless, the romantic vision of democracy has been dimmed remarkably little by our continued experience with "realistic democracy" and *realpolitik.* Of the general influence of the democratic ideal there can be no doubt.

How have the students of public administration fared with respect to this national Ideal? Have they allowed their devotion to scientific objectivity to cut themselves off from the national community of sentiment? A few lines from one of the foremost of these students will suggest the answer: "One of the most inspiring movements in human history is now in progress. . . . A wave of organized democracy is sweeping around the world, based on a broader intelligence and a more enlightened view of civic responsibility than has ever before obtained. The theory that government exists for common welfare, that a public office is a public trust, is . . . old. . . . But responsibility for making this theory a vital principle in an empire whose sovereignty is abstractly conceived as residing in a hundred million souls and in which every officer of government is constitutionally a servant has not been considered with enough seriousness. . . ." [F. A. Cleveland] These lines do more than suggest, they epitomize the answer to the problem: our students of administration have accepted the American faith and have made an heroic effort to realize this faith by improving our institutions.

This interpretation doubtless would appear wholly in error to those who think democracy incompatible with the extension of government services and instrumentalities—to the James M. Becks, the Ludwig von Miseses, and the Lawrence Sullivans. Nevertheless, American students of administration have not loved democracy the less, but the more, because of their critical attention to its institutions and their desire to extend its services. They have not loved it the less dearly when they have insisted that it be worthy of its mission abroad by being noble at home, and when they have concluded from viewing the international scene that democracy cannot compete with ethically inferior ideals without efficiency. If "The Devil has all the best tunes," it becomes necessary to plagiarize. Early writings are full of assurances that we can adopt the administrative devices of autocracy without accepting its spirit and its end. Beginning with Wilson's famous essay it has often been confessed, to be sure, that the forms and ethos of democracy impose limitations upon the administrative process which test patience and ingenuity and make efficiency very difficult. But the obligation to reconcile democracy and efficiency has ever been accepted, never rejected.

More important than the fact that this obligation has always been accepted is the fact that in the Progressive era a political theory was evolved that made a virtue of the obligation. The dilemma of democracy versus efficiency was avoided by the formula that *true* democracy and *true* efficiency are not necessarily—perhaps not possibly—incompatible. The assumptions and syllogisms of this line of thought are familiar: Democracy means an intelligent and informed citizenry organized into groups, preferably as few as possible, on the basis of issues. To realize this condition the proper institutions, such as the short ballot, a merit system, a budget system and a reporting system must function.

The imperatives of specialization of function and adequate control must be observed in the modern world; it is the citizen's proper function to learn, to judge, and to vote, while others specialize in actually running the business of government. In order for citizens to perform their functions adequately, machinery and issues must be simplified. Citizens must realize that there are two essentials in government: politics and administration, deciding and executing. When these two functions are properly separated and institutionalized it will be found that the resulting system is both democratic and efficient.

The Fundamental Law. The relationship of administrative study to the notion of a "fundamental law" is as important as its relationship to democracy. It was widely and very firmly believed in the nineteenth century that there is a "higher law," a "fundamental moral order," upon which a firm and moral society must rest and in accordance with the rules of which it must be built. The nature and ultimate sanction of this fundamental order were differently conceived, according to the individual, but it was firm in our Christian heritage; and the "cosmic machine" of Newton and Descartes had become endowed with the moral sanctions and aura of this Christian tradition. As the century drew to a close, however, and especially as the present century has unfolded, the acids of modernity corrode this belief, and the "convention" view of law and justice has tended to come to the fore. The revival of humanism and neo-rationalism, the "socializing" of Protestant Christianity, the emergence of pragmatism, the rise of the so-called legal realists and the purging of natural law concepts from our jurisprudence, such events as these have marked our intellectual history since the Civil War.

From the beginning, students of public administration have been relatively sophisticated about higher law and the fundamentality of constitutional provisions and traditional institutions, about natural rights and the formulae of classical economics. These things they have generally rejected as the defense mechanisms of vested and antisocial interests, to be ignored or spurned. Yet it would be a serious mistake to suppose that American students have escaped the influence of the "higher law" notions widely accepted by the American community. Faith in democracy, already discussed, is just such an idea. To the extent that democracy has been thought superior and ultimate as a form of government and way of life, it has itself served as the higher law to which everything else must be referred; we have seldom permitted ourselves to doubt that democracy accords with the moral constitution of the universe. There is indeed a distinct aura of evangelical protestantism about the writings of the municipal and civil service reformers. They have always felt that moral issues are involved, and until recently they have not hesitated to speak out on what they felt.

In other respects those who have produced our literature on public administration have adopted absolutist positions and insisted upon the moral imperatives of "the facts"; proposals for administrative change have too often hardened into "dogmas of administrative reform," propounded with solemnity and earnestness in the name of Science. But most important of all has been the manner in which the sanction of "principles" has been made to do duty for higher law.

Progress and Progressivism. The past fifty years in America have been distinguished by a belief in the "doctrine of progress," so notably so that progress gave its name to an era. To be sure, the Great Wars dammed and diverted the rising stream, and most educated people now ease "progress" into their conversation in quotation marks. Still, in view of the fact that the "idea .of progress" is peculiar to the modern world, the prevalence and intensity of the conviction among us has been a remarkable event in intellectual history; and it is pertinent to inquire how it has influenced administrative writers.

If the question is only: What has been the influence of the idea of progress? the answer, if not simple, must be brief. Americans, administrative students included, simply "accepted" progress—its reality and its desirability. It was a matter for apostrophe, not for argument. When in 1913 Woodrow Wilson exclaimed: "Progress! Did you ever reflect that the word is almost a new one? The modern idea is to leave the past and to press on to something new," he spoke for all the students and reformers who were writing and preparing to write on administrative subjects. His belief that man "by using his intellect can remake society, that he can become the creator of a world organized for man's advantage," has been a major premise which, though generally inarticulate, has fevered many brows and filled many pages.

But if the query is the broader one: What has been the influence of "Progressivism"? the answer is neither simple nor brief. For Progressivism was not an idea but a sheaf of ideas, old and new, and at times incompatible, held together by a buoyant faith in Progress. Progressivism found its basis in the old democratic faith, it was stimulated by the Muckrakers and the earnest efforts of Reformers, it attempted to bring ethical absolutism into the world of science, it recruited armies of Reform sworn to march in different directions into the Future, it found its highest expression in such men as Woodrow Wilson, Walter Weyl and Herbert Croly: it was a welter of ideas given a momentary unity by a common basis of optimism.

At the very heart of Progressivism was a basic conflict in social outlook. This conflict was between those whose hope for the future was primarily that of a planned and administered society, and those who, on the other hand, remained firm in the old liberal faith in an underlying harmony, which by natural and inevitable processes produces the greatest possible good if the necessary institutional and social reforms are made.

This latter group felt a resurgence of primitive democratic feeling. They knew that man is pure at heart and was but thwarted and corrupted by bad institutions, that the realization of the ideal of the free individual depended upon restricting government and maintaining the open market. These persons believed that "the cure for democracy is *more* democracy," and to that end they proposed such reforms as the initiative, the referendum, the recall, the direct election of senators, home rule, and proportional representation. They knew that the Future must well up from *below*. In opposition were those whose patience was exhausted waiting for the Promise of American Life to realize itself by natural and inevitable means, whose view of human nature was not so charitable and who had no faith in the devices of primitive democracy, who had begun to think of planning and who realized that builders need tools. These persons believed that democracy must re-think its position and remold its institutions; particularly it must create a strong right arm for the State in the form of an efficient bureaucracy. They knew that "the way to realize a purpose is not to leave it to chance," and that the Future must be given shape from *above*.

This is oversimplification, but it is a valid and useful generalization in viewing the past half century in perspective. It is oversimplification because the two movements, the two views, have overlapped. Everyone but the rascals could agree to "turn the rascals out," and "good government" is a formula wide enough to cover a multitude of differences. It is oversimplification also because formulae were evolved to bridge the gap between the two general trends; notably formulae reconciling "true democracy" with "true efficiency" were evolved by administrative writers and were accorded wide credence. Certainly the two viewpoints can be reconciled in the realm of the ideal: an "ideal democracy" in which the citizens are all intelligent, educated, and of good will, so that very little authoritative direction is necessary, and when necessary is performed with economy and competence. Some of the Progressives caught just such a vision and hence their insistence upon "citizenship" and their espousal of the ideal of "Efficient Citizenship." The Wisconsin of the elder La Follette and Charles McCarthy was a crude, earthly approximation of this *Civitas Dei*.

But although administrative students helped construct the most useful dialectic bridge between the two viewpoints, although they profess and believe in democracy, liberty, and equality, they have generally accepted the alternative of a planned and managed society. This conclusion is obvious—axiomatic—but it is not so obvious as to preclude students of administration from often presuming that they labor in a sphere from which "values" have been excluded. American society is greatly in the debt of those who have given their time, energy and substance to improve administration. Still, it is in order to inquire whether, in narrowing their sphere of attention to administration only, students of administration did not also accept an unnecessary shrinking of their ideals. A society in which there are many "efficient citizens" must surely weigh heavier in the balance of American ideals than one in which there are only "trained administrators." Undue attention to the "management" aspects of group life in other eras has produced the not very lofty works of Machiavelli, Hobbes, and Mandeville.

The Gospel of Efficiency. Every era, as Carl Becker has reminded us in his *Heavenly City of the Eighteenth Century Philosophers*, has a few words that epitomize its world-view and that are fixed points by which all else can be measured. In the Middle Ages they were such words as faith, grace, and God; in the eighteenth century they were such words as reason, nature, and rights; during the past fifty years in America they have been such words as cause, reaction, scientific, expert, progress—and efficient. Efficiency is a natural ideal for a relatively immature and extrovert culture, but presumably its high development and wide acceptance are due to the fact that ours has been, *par excellence,* a machine civilization. At any event, efficiency grew to be a national catchword in the Progressive era as mechanization became the rule in American life, and it frequently appears in the literature of the period entangled in mechanical metaphor.

However natural, it is yet amazing what a position of dominance "efficiency" assumed, how it waxed until it had assimilated or overshadowed other values, how men and events came to be degraded or exalted according to what was assumed to be its dictate. It became a movement, a motif of Progressivism, a "Gospel." Some of the reasons for the acceptance of efficiency as a necessary objective and a sufficient criterion for governmental reform have already been suggested: fear of exhaustion of our natural resources; the urge to make America worthy of her Mission by those who, observing the frugality and dispatch of European autocracy, blushed for democracy's slattern ways; and simple fear for the future existence of American democracy when German efficiency moved Westward in 1914. More fundamental is the fact that America was attempting to adjust old conceptions and traditional institutions to the requirements of a machine technology, and efficiency came to symbolize the ideal of reconciliation. "A new era has come upon us like a sudden vision of things unprophesied, and for which no polity has been prepared," wrote Woodrow Wilson in 1901, reflecting on the confusion about him. Accepting efficiency as the essential ingredient, students of administration have tried to prepare a proper polity.

Faith in Science.   His powers and comforts daily increased by the agency of Science, the average American of the past generation has felt an almost limitless confidence in whatever bears the label of Science. The change in the externals of life was so amazing, the vistas of the future presented in the Sunday supplements so astounding that anything seemed possible; a Golden Age of peace and plenty for all seemed just a short distance across the years, an age in which the living might hope to end their days among its wonders—provided that death had not by then been rendered obsolete. It was the Great Engineer Hoover who visioned the "disappearance of poverty" in our lifetime. Naturally, the uninitiated—and often the initiated—looked with awe upon this Magic (even when, in War or Depression, they have thought it Black Magic), and "scientific" became an "honorific" word—even religion and ethics found it expedient to become scientific.

The contrast between the Brave New World that seemed so near, and the alarms and excursions, the pettiness and stupidities, the confusion and force of the world-at-hand stimulated many persons to ask, "Why?" Following the lead of many of the scientists and of most of the persons whose province of study was human affairs, they frequently concluded that the New Day would not dawn until science were applied to the realm of human affairs just as it had been to the physical world, until the "power-controlling sciences" were as well developed as the "power-producing sciences." An easy and unwarranted optimism abounded that at least a technique for solving these problems of group life, if not an actual answer to the problems themselves, lay hidden within the mystery of science.

So the humanties were re-named, new terminologies invented, new buildings raised, new endowments secured. Students and reformers of all kinds fell to making human relations and governmental practices scientific: the students by engaging in a new and recondite branch of inquiry called Scientific Methodology, and the reformers either by applying current conceptions of scientific method or by the simpler method of putting a scientific wrapper on old nostrums. This faith in science and the efficacy of scientific method thoroughly permeates our literature on public administration. Science has its experts: so we must have "experts in government." Science relies upon exact measurement: so let the data of administration be measured. Science is concerned only with facts: so let the "facts" be sovereign. Science makes use of experiment: so let the mode of administrative advance be experimental.

Far from removing themselves from the realm of political theory, as many appear to believe, this devotion to a concept of reality called Science makes students of administration part of a well-known company of political theorists. Any political theory rests upon a metaphysic, a concept of the ultimate nature of reality. Students of administration, following a line of precedent which begins in the modern period with Hobbes, have simply been willing to accept the verdict of science—or more accurately, popular conceptions of the verdict of science—as to the nature of reality. It is appropriate to inquire whether these concepts of reality are consistent among themselves, whether they are valid within their proper realm, and whether, if valid, they have been extended beyond the bounds of their validity.

Economy and Efficiency

" 'Efficiency with economy,' " remarks an English writer on administration, "is too hackneyed a phrase to have much meaning nowadays; it suffers from being a combination of two of the most abstract words in our language."

This indictment is a serious one. For "economy and efficiency" have inspired reformer and researcher, teacher and student. They have often been held to be the ultimate administrative values, serving to unify and direct all inquiry.

The Rise of Economy and Efficiency

"Economy and efficiency" are related historically to, and were engendered by, the transition in American life from nineteenth-century to twentieth-century conditions. They have been used as weapons of attack and defense in a political struggle. They have, indeed, been "key concepts" in a political philosophy; that is, concepts difficult to define precisely because they are themselves regarded as ultimates, in terms of which other concepts are defined. He whose purpose is historical understanding must approach them with imagination and sympathy as he would *imperium* and *sacerdotium* or "the laws of Nature and Nature's God."

"Economy and efficiency," together with other concepts, such as "scientific," replaced a "moralistic" approach to governmental improvement. Dorman B. Eaton's *Civil Service Reform in Great Britain* (1879) may be taken to illustrate the moralistic approach. In this classic work "efficiency" is seldom, if ever, mentioned; and "economy" occurs infrequently. Instead, such words as "fidelity" and "honesty" sprinkle its pages. Appeal is made to national pride; emphasis is placed upon "the disgrace to republican institutions."

By the turn of the century, however, it was generally agreed that morality, while perhaps desirable, is not enough. Democracy must be *able*. Its citizens must be alert and active. The machinery of government must not waste time, money, and energy. The prodigal utilization of our resources must be remedied. If our good purposes fail because of inefficiency—as it appears they may—then *inefficiency is the cardinal sin.*

The Baptism of Efficiency.   In short, a term generally regarded as descriptive, "mechanical," became in fact invested with moral significance. To a considerable extent the exaltation of efficiency must be regarded as the secularization, materialization, of the Protestant conscience. The tenet of efficiency is an article in the faith of "muscular Christianity."

A century's-end essay by C. R. Woodruff evidences the rising force of "efficiency." "The Complexity of American Government Methods" is, as the title suggests, a diatribe against the divisions and dispersions of the American system of government. According to Woodruff, this loosely knit system, established to prevent tyranny in a simple agricultural society, encourages boss-rule and fosters inefficiency and corruption. He urges that we equip ourselves with responsible and efficient governments, adapted to meet our new problems. "Efficiency is of the first consideration in business affairs; it must be first in political affairs."

W. H. Allen's *Efficient Democracy* demonstrates the "moralization" of efficiency. "To be efficient," proclaimed the Director of the New York Bureau of Municipal Research, "is more difficult than to be good. . . . *The goodness that has lasting value to one's fellow-man will be greatly increased and more widely distributed if efficiency tests are applied to all persons and all agencies that are trying to make tomorrow better than today.*" "Goodness" is a "false criterion," for there is no agreement on its meaning and content. Viewed realistically, "good service" means "efficient service."

The high point in the popularity of "efficiency" came in the years immediately preceding the First Great War. It was a rallying cry of Progressivism. Indeed, it was recognized as a "movement" within the larger movement, and became in certain circles a veritable fetish. While it is not literally true, as W. E. Mosher remarks, that the phrase "economy and efficiency" was "first coined by the bureau movement," students and reformers of many kinds became quickly and thoroughly enthusiastic about this new approach during the Progressive years. Woodruff felt moved to remark in 1913 that "efficiency is a word which has been introduced into our municipal vocabulary within a very few years." The bureau movement was certainly instrumental in its popularization.

It is instructive to review the treatment of efficiency by an interpreter of the Progressive era. Seeking to distill the essence of "the efficiency movement" B. P. DeWitt wrote:

> The movement is incapable of any concise definition, and in fact of any definition at all, because it is itself a protest against generalizations and definitions, standing for the specific study and solution of particular problems. The fundamental ideas underlying the efficiency movement are that there is no panacea for municipal ill; that municipal home rule, commission government, and city managers are merely means to an end; that municipal problems depend for their solution upon the same scientific study and analysis that banking and railroad problems require; that any attempt to remove inefficiency and waste must be continuous and not intermittent; that honesty and good intentions cannot take the place of intelligence and ability; and finally that city business is like any other business and needs precisely the same kind of organization, management, and control.

To this liturgical passage he added the following characterization: "The efficiency movement repairs and adapts the machinery of government which the home rule movement frees, the commission movement simplifies, and the social movement uses in the interest of the people." "There are everywhere," wrote another prophet of the era, "signs of an increasing recognition by our more democratic governments that to fulfill their functions they must be efficient."

Exegesis and Apostasy

"Economy and efficiency," as we believe and argue below, are intimately bound up with "values" or "valuations." For this reason there can be great differences in the meaning ascribed to them. Thus, because they have the appearance of being "impartial" or "scientific" terms, they have occasionally served the ends of those whose purposes might be regarded as more or less reprehensible if stated in another idiom. There have always been reformers and students, chiefly associated with some bureaus of municipal research and taxpayers organizations, whose *primary* purpose is the lowering of taxes, no matter what the cost in human values. "Efficiency" means for them, economy, and "economy" means less money spent by government, more retained by taxpayers—simply that.

Efficiency versus Economy

On the other hand, many writers soon felt obliged to indicate that they meant by "economy and efficiency" something other and greater than penny-pinching. In the down-to-earth language of Walter Weyl in 1912, "it is important that efficiency be not identified with lessened governmental expenditures, with a cheeseparing and a special care for the preservation of government lead pencils and the soap and towels in the public offices. In these days of rapidly expanding governmental functions the bark of the 'watchdog of the treasury' is not the epitome of political wisdom."

This attempt to make clear that by "economy and efficiency" is not meant, or should not be meant, anything narrow, niggardly, or mechanical has continued down to the present day. Thus L. D. White speaks out on the subject of "the administrative gods, efficiency and economy," in his dialogue with T. V. Smith on the state of the civic arts: "Don't misunderstand what we administrators mean when we use the shorthand of efficiency and economy. . . . When we say efficiency we think of homes saved from disease, of boys and girls in school prepared for life, of ships and mines protected against disaster. . . . We do not think in terms of gadgets and paper clips alone. And when we talk of economy, we fight waste of all human resources, still much too scanty to meet human needs."

Similarly, J. M. Pfiffner, noting the fact that the research movement in local government has been based generally upon the assumption that the spending of less money by local government is in itself a desirable end, remarks:

> the inherent desirability of lower governmental expenditures is by no means a scientific conclusion, and it may not even be amenable to scientific proof. There are many other value criteria affecting expenditure. There are those who could present rather convincing data in favor of much greater expenditure than has ever been undertaken in public health, education, and recreation.

❊   ❊   ❊

Woodrow Wilson (1856–1924)

Woodrow Wilson is frequently hailed as the founder of "The Study of Administration," principally because of his article of that title written in 1886 when he was thirty years old. Actually, a very few other American scholars were already delving into the subject. Wilson's own interest in it was apparently whetted by his studies under Professor Richard T. Ely at Johns Hopkins in 1884–85 when Wilson was working toward his Ph.D. degree. After he had completed his classic work *Congressional Government* (Houghton Mifflin, 1885), he turned to comparative administration as a major field of inquiry. He emphasized "comparative" (meaning essentially European continental) because he did not think that there was much to learn from

American experience or even Great Britain's. In late 1885, in a preliminary paper entitled "Notes on Administration," he wrote:

> Neither the practice nor the theory of administration has ever been reduced to a science either in this country or in England. . . .
> The Germans and the French have done most in developing a *science* of administration. May this not be because administration has been made for them by a supreme central authority, so that they have been able to stand aside and speculate about it?[1]

The basic problem for Wilson was whether and how efficient administrative organization and methods, as developed in centralized, authoritarian nations like France and Germany, could be transferred or developed in the United States, whose primary dedication was to free democratic institutions. His resolution of the problem, enunciated in the paper below, was a clear-cut distinction between politics and administration—an idea which he apparently borrowed from German scholars.[2] In his essay Wilson was not altogether consistent with regard to this dichotomy, and it has been a subject of controversy ever since, particularly following the New Deal and World War II.

In the fall of 1886, Wilson was invited by the president of Cornell University to deliver a lecture on public administration. He accepted and presented his lecture on "The Study of Administration" in November of that year. Shortly thereafter, the editor of the newly established *Political Science Quarterly* asked permission to publish it. Wilson agreed but subsequently requested that two paragraphs which he thought "might convey a false impression when read" be changed or deleted. The two paragraphs were at the close of the second part of his speech. He revised the first of the two paragraphs but did not significantly change its content. The second, which dealt in part with centralization and decentralization, he deleted. In light of subsequent interpretations (and misinterpretations) of Wilson's thought, that omitted paragraph is reproduced below:

> Those who fear the growth of an undemocratic professional officialism in this country are frightening themselves with bugbears which no one who does not live under a highly centralized government ought to allow to haunt him. In urging a perfected organization of public administration I have said not a word in favour of making all administration centre in Washington. I have spoken of giving new life to local organisms, of reorganizing decentralization. The end which I have proposed for administrative study in America is the discovery of the best means of constituting a civil service cultured and self-sufficient enough to act with sense and vigour and yet so connected with popular thought by means of elections and constant public counsel as to find arbitrariness out of the question.[3]

F.C.M.

1. Quoted in *The Papers of Woodrow Wilson,* V, p. 49.
2. Notably Johann Kaspar Bluntschli. *Ibid.*
3. *Ibid.,* p. 359.

The Study of Administration

I suppose that no practical science is ever studied where there is no need to know it. The very fact, therefore, that the eminently practical science of administration is finding its way into college courses in this country would prove that this country needs to know more about administration, were such proof of the fact required to make out a case. It need not be said, however, that we do not look into college programmes for proof of this fact. It is a thing almost taken for granted among us, that the present movement called civil service reform must, after the accomplishment of its first purpose, expand into efforts to improve, not the *personnel* only, but also the organization and methods of our government offices: because it is plain that their organization and methods need improvement only less than their *personnel.* It is the object of administrative study to discover, first, what government can properly and successfully do, and, secondly, how it can do these proper things with the utmost possible efficiency and at the least possible cost either of money or of energy. On both these points there is obviously much need of light among us; and only careful study can supply that light.

Before entering on that study, however, it is needful:

I. To take some account of what others have done in the same line; that is to say, of the history of the study.

II. To ascertain just what is its subject-matter.

III. To determine just what are the best methods by which to develop it, and the most clarifying political conceptions to carry with us into it.

Unless we know and settle these things, we shall set out without chart or compass.

I.

The science of administration is the latest fruit of that study of the science of politics which was begun some twenty-two hundred years ago. It is a birth of our own century, almost of our own generation.

Why was it so late in coming? Why did it wait till this too busy century of ours to demand attention for itself? Administration is the most obvious part of government; it is government in action; it is the executive, the operative, the most visible side of government, and is of course as old as government itself. It is government in action, and one might very naturally expect to find that government in action had arrested the attention and provoked the scrutiny of writers of politics very early in the history of systematic thought.

Political Science Quarterly, Vol. 2 (June 1887), pp. 197–222.

But such was not the case. No one wrote systematically of administration as a branch of the science of government until the present century had passed its first youth and had begun to put forth its characteristic flower of systematic knowledge. Up to our own day all the political writers whom we now read had thought, argued, dogmatized only about the *constitution* of government; about the nature of the state, the essence and seat of sovereignty, popular power and kingly prerogative; about the greatest meanings lying at the heart of government, and the high ends set before the purpose of government by man's nature and man's aims. The central field of controversy was that great field of theory in which monarchy rode tilt against democracy, in which oligarchy would have built for itself strongholds of privilege, and in which tyranny sought opportunity to make good its claim to receive submission from all competitors. Amidst this high warfare of principles, administration could command no pause for its own consideration. The question was always: Who shall make law, and what shall that law be? The other question, how law should be administered with enlightenment, with equity, with speed, and without friction, was put aside as "practical detail" which clerks could arrange after doctors had agreed upon principles.

That political philosophy took this direction was of course no accident, no chance preference or perverse whim of political philosophers. The philosophy of any time is, as Hegel says, "nothing but the spirit of that time expressed in abstract thought"; and political philosophy, like philosophy of every other kind, has only held up the mirror to contemporary affairs. The trouble in early times was almost altogether about the constitution of government; and consequently that was what engrossed men's thoughts. There was little or no trouble about administration,—at least little that was heeded by administrators. The functions of government were simple, because life itself was simple. Government went about imperatively and compelled men, without thought of consulting their wishes. There was no complex system of public revenues and public debts to puzzle financiers; there were, consequently, no financiers to be puzzled. No one who possessed power was long at a loss how to use it. The great and only question was: Who shall possess it? Populations were of manageable numbers; property was of simple sorts. There were plenty of farms, but no stocks and bonds; more cattle than vested interests.

There is scarcely a single duty of government which was once simple which is not now complex; government once had but a few masters; it now has scores of masters. Majorities formerly only underwent government; they now conduct government. Where government once might follow the whims of a court, it must now follow the views of a nation.

And those views are steadily widening to new conceptions of state duty; so that, at the same time that the functions of government are every day becoming more complex and difficult, they are also vastly multiplying in number. Administration is everywhere putting its hands to new undertakings. The utility, cheapness, and success of the government's postal service, for instance, point towards the early establishment of governmental control of the telegraph system. Or, even if our government is not to follow the lead of the governments of Europe in buying or building both telegraph and railroad lines, no one can doubt that in some way it must make itself master of masterful corporations. The creation of national commissioners of railroads, in addition to the older state commissions, involves a very important and delicate extension of administrative functions. Whatever hold of authority state or federal governments are to take upon corporations, there must follow cares and responsibilities which will require not a little wisdom, knowledge, and experience. Such things must be studied in order to be well done. And these, as I have said, are only a few of the doors which are being opened to offices of government. The idea of the state and the consequent ideal of its duty are undergoing noteworthy change; and "the idea of the state is the conscience of administration." Seeing every day new things which the state ought to do, the next thing is to see clearly how it ought to do them.

This is why there should be a science of administration which shall seek to straighten the paths of government, to make its business less unbusinesslike; to strengthen and purify its organization, and to crown its duties with dutifulness. This is one reason why there is such a science.

But where has this science grown up? Surely not on this side of the sea. Not much impartial scientific method is to be discerned in our administrative practices. The poisonous atmosphere of city government, the crooked secrets of state administration, the confusion, sinecurism, and corruption ever and again discovered in the bureaus at Washington forbid us to believe that any clear conceptions of what constitutes good administration are as yet very widely current in the United States. No; American writers have hitherto taken no very important part in the advancement of this science. It has found its doctors in Europe. It is not of our making; it is a foreign science, speaking very little of the language of English or American principle. It employs only foreign tongues; it utters none but what are to our minds alien ideas. Its aims, its examples, its conditions, are almost exclusively grounded in the histories of foreign races, in the precedents of foreign systems, in the lessons of foreign revolutions. It has been developed by French and German professors, and is consequently in all parts adapted to the needs of a compact state, and made to fit highly centralized forms of government; whereas, to answer our purposes, it must be adapted, not to a simple and compact, but to a complex and multiform state, and made to fit highly decentralized forms of government. If we would employ it, we must Americanize it, and that not formally, in language merely, but radically, in thought, principle, and aim as well. It must learn our constitutions by heart; must get the bureaucratic fever out of its veins; must inhale much free American air.

If an explanation be sought why a science manifestly so susceptible of being made useful to all governments alike should have received attention first in Europe, where government has long been a monopoly, rather than in England or the United States, where government has long been a common franchise, the reason will doubtless be found to be twofold: first, that in Europe, just because government was independent of popular assent, there was more governing to be done; and, second, that the desire to keep government a monopoly made the monopolists interested in discovering the least irritating means of governing. They were, besides, few enough to adopt means promptly.

The English race ... has long and successfully studied the art of curbing executive power to the constant neglect of the art of perfecting executive methods. It has exercised itself much more in controlling than in energizing government. It has been more concerned to render government just and moderate than to make it facile, well-ordered, and effective. English and American political history has been a history, not of administrative development, but of legislative oversight,—not of progress in governmental organization, but of advance in law-making and political criticism. Consequently, we have reached a time when administrative study and creation are imperatively necessary to the well-being of our governments saddled with the habits of a long period of constitution-making. That period has practically closed, so far as the establishment of essential principles is concerned, but we cannot shake off its atmosphere. We go on criticizing when we ought to be creating. We have reached the third of the periods I have mentioned,—the period, namely, when the people have to develop administration in accordance with the constitutions they won for themselves in a previous period of struggle with absolute power; but we are not prepared for the tasks of the new period.

Such an explanation seems to afford the only escape from blank astonishment at the fact that, in spite of our vast advantages in point of political liberty, and above all in point of practical political skill and sagacity, so many nations are ahead of us in administrative organization and administrative skill. Why, for instance, have we but just begun purifying a civil service which was rotten full fifty years ago? To say that slavery diverted us is but to repeat what I have said—that flaws in our Constitution delayed us.

Of course all reasonable preference would declare for this English and American course of politics rather than for that of any European country. We should not like to have had Prussia's history for the sake of having Prussia's administrative skill; and Prussia's particular system of administration would quite suffocate us. It is better to be untrained and free than to be servile and systematic. Still there is no denying that it would be better yet to be both free in spirit and proficient in practice. It is this even more reasonable preference which impels us to discover what there may be to hinder or delay us in naturalizing this much-to-be-desired science of administration.

What, then, is there to prevent?
Well, principally, popular sovereignty. It is harder for democracy to organize administration than for monarchy. The very completeness of our most cherished political successes in the past embarrasses us. We have enthroned public opinion; and it is forbidden us to hope during its reign for any quick schooling of the sovereign in executive expertness or in the conditions of perfect functional balance in government. The very fact that we have realized popular rule in its fullness has made the task of *organizing* that rule just so much the more difficult. In order to make any advance at all we must instruct and persuade a multitudinous monarch called public opinion,—a much less feasible undertaking than to influence a single monarch called a king. An individual sovereign will adopt a simple plan and carry it out directly; he will have but one opinion, and he will embody that one opinion in one command. But this other sovereign, the people, will have a score of differing opinions. They can agree upon nothing simple: advance must be made through compromise, by a compounding of differences, by a trimming of plans and a suppression of too straightforward principles. There will be a succession of resolves running through a course of years, a dropping fire of commands running through a whole gamut of modifications.

In government, as in virtue, the hardest of hard things is to make progress. Formerly the reason for this was that the single person who was sovereign was generally either selfish, ignorant, timid, or a fool,—albeit there was now and again one who was wise. Nowadays the reason is that the many, the people, who are sovereign have no single ear which one can approach, and are selfish, ignorant, timid, stubborn, or foolish with the selfishnesses, the ignorances, the stubbornnesses, the timidities, or the follies of several thousand persons,—albeit there are hundreds who are wise. Once the advantage of the reformer was that the sovereign's mind had a definite locality, that it was contained in one man's head, and that consequently it could be gotten at; though it was his disadvantage that that mind learned only reluctantly or only in small quantities, or was under the influence of some one who let it learn only the wrong things. Now, on the contrary, the reformer is bewildered by the fact that the sovereign's mind has no definite locality, but is contained in a voting majority of several million heads; and embarrassed by the fact that the mind of this sovereign also is under the influence of favorites, who are none the less favorites in a good old-fashioned sense of the word because they are not persons but preconceived opinions; *i.e.,* prejudices which are not to be reasoned with because they are not the children of reason. Wherever regard for public opinion is a first principle of government, practical reform must be slow and all reform must be full of compromises. For wherever public opinion exists it must rule. This is now an axiom half the world over, and will presently come to be believed even in Russia. Whoever would effect a change in a modern constitutional government must first educate his fellow-citizens to want *some* change. That done, he must persuade them to want the particular change he wants. He must first make public opinion willing to listen and then see to it that it listen to the right things. He must stir it up to search for an opinion, and then manage to put the right opinion in its way.

The first step is not less difficult than the second. With opinions, possession is more than nine points of the law. It is next to impossible to dislodge them. Institutions which one generation regards as only a makeshift approximation to the realization of a principle, the next generation honors as the nearest possible approximation to that principle, and the next worships as the principle itself. It takes scarcely three generations for the apotheosis. The grandson accepts his grandfather's hesitating experiment as an integral part of the fixed constitution of nature.

Even if we had clear insight into all the political past, and could form out of perfectly instructed heads a few steady, infallible, placidly wise maxims of government into which all sound political doctrine would be ultimately resolvable, *would the country act on them?* That is the question. The bulk of mankind is rigidly unphilosphical, and nowadays the bulk of mankind votes. A truth must become not only plain but also commonplace before it will be seen by the people who go to their work very early in the morning; and not to act upon it must involve great and pinching inconveniences before these same people will make up their minds to act upon it.

And where is this unphilosophical bulk of mankind more multifarious in its composition than in the United States? To know the public mind of this country, one must know the mind, not of Americans of the older stocks only, but also of Irishmen, of Germans, of Negroes. In order to get a footing for new doctrine, one must influence minds cast in every mould of race, minds inheriting every bias of environment, warped by the histories of a score of different nations, warmed or chilled, closed or expanded by almost every climate of the globe.

II.

The field of administration is a field of business. It is removed from the hurry and strife of politics; it at most points stands apart even from the debatable ground of constitutional study. It is a part of political life only as the methods of the counting-house are a part of the life of society; only as machinery is part of the manufactured product. But it is, at the same time, raised very far above the dull level of mere technical detail by the fact that through its greater principles it is directly connected with the lasting maxims of political wisdom, the permanent truths of political progress.

The object of administrative study is to rescue executive methods from the confusion and costliness of empirical experiment and set them upon foundations laid deep in stable principle.

It is for this reason that we must regard civil service reform in its present stages as but a prelude to a fuller administrative reform. We are now rectifying methods of appointment; we must go on to adjust executive functions more fitly and to prescribe better methods of executive organization and action. Civil service reform is thus but a moral preparation for what is to follow. It is clearing the moral atmosphere of official life by establishing the sanctity of public office as a public trust, and, by making the service unpartisan, it is opening the way for making it businesslike. By sweetening its motives it is rendering it capable of improving its methods of work.

Let me expand a little what I have said of the province of administration. Most important to be observed is the truth already so much and so fortunately insisted upon by our civil service reformers; namely, that administration lies outside the proper sphere of *politics*. Administrative questions are not political questions. Although politics sets the tasks for administration, it should not be suffered to manipulate its offices.

This is distinction of high authority; eminent German writers insist upon it as of course. Bluntschli, for instance, bids us separate administration alike from politics and from law. Politics, he says, is state activity "in things great and universal," while "administration, on the other hand," is "the activity of the state in individual and small things. Politics is thus the special province of the statesman, administration of the technical official." "Policy does nothing without the aid of administration"; but administration is not therefore politics. But we do not require German authority for this position; this discrimination between administration and politics is now, happily, too obvious to need further discussion.

There is another distinction which must be worked into all our conclusions, which, though but another side of that between administration and politics, is not quite so easy to keep sight of; I mean the distinction between *constitutional and administrative* questions, between those governmental adjustments which are essential to constitutional principle and those which are merely instrumental to the possibly changing purposes of a wisely adapting convenience.

One cannot easily make clear to every one just where administration resides in the various departments of any practicable government without entering upon particulars so numerous as to confuse and distinctions so minute as to distract. No lines of demarcation, setting apart administrative from non-administrative functions, can be run between this and that department of government without being run up hill and down dale, over dizzy heights of distinction and through dense jungles of statutory enactment, hither and thither around "ifs" and "buts," "whens" and "howevers," until they become altogether lost to the common eye not accustomed to this sort of surveying, and consequently not acquainted with the use of the theodolite of logical discernment. A great deal of administration goes about *incognito* to most of the world, being confounded now with political "management," and again with constitutional principle.

Perhaps this ease of confusion may explain such utterances as that of

Niebuhr's: "Liberty," he says, "depends incomparably more upon administration than upon constitution." At first sight this appears to be largely true. Apparently facility in the actual exercise of liberty does depend more upon administrative arrangements than upon constitutional guarantees; although constitutional guarantees alone secure the existence of liberty. But—upon second thought—is even so much as this true? Liberty no more consists in easy functional movement than intelligence consists in the ease and vigor with which the limbs of a strong man move. The principles that rule within the man, or the constitution, are the vital springs of liberty or servitude. Because dependence and subjection are without chains, are lightened by every easy-working device of considerate, paternal government, they are not thereby transformed into liberty. Liberty cannot live apart from constitutional principle; and no administration, however perfect and liberal its methods, can give men more than a poor counterfeit of liberty if it rest upon illiberal principles of government.

A clear view of the difference between the province of constitutional law and the province of administrative function ought to leave no room for misconception; and it is possible to name some roughly definite criteria upon which such a view can be built. Public administration is detailed and systematic execution of public law. Every particular application of general law is an act of administration. The assessment and raising of taxes, for instance, the hanging of a criminal, the transportation and delivery of the mails, the equipment and recruiting of the army and navy, etc., are all obviously acts of administration; but the general laws which direct these things to be done are as obviously outside of and above administration. The broad plans of governmental action are not administrative; the detailed execution of such plans is administrative. Constitutions, therefore, properly concern themselves only with those instrumentalities of government which are to control general law. Our federal Constitution observes this principle in saying nothing of even the greatest of the purely executive offices, and speaking only of that President of the Union who was to share the legislative and policy-making functions of government, only of those judges of highest jurisdiction who were to interpret and guard its principles, and not of those who were merely to give utterance to them.

This is not quite the distinction between Will and answering Deed, because the administrator should have and does have a will of his own in the choice of means for accomplishing his work. He is not and ought not to be a mere passive instrument. The distinction is between general plans and special means.

There is, indeed, one point at which administrative studies trench on constitutional ground—or at least upon what seems constitutional ground. The study of administration, philosophically viewed, is closely connected with the study of the proper distribution of constitutional authority. To be efficient it must discover the simplest arrangements by which responsibility can be unmistakably fixed upon officials; the best way of dividing authority without hampering it, and responsibility without obscuring it. And this question of the distribution of authority, when taken into the sphere of the higher, the originating functions of government, is obviously a central constitutional question. If administrative study can discover the best principles upon which to base such distribution, it will have done constitutional study an invaluable service. Montesquieu did not, I am convinced, say the last word on this head.

To discover the best principle for the distribution of authority is of greater importance, possibly, under a democratic system, where officials serve many masters, than under others where they serve but a few. All sovereigns are suspicious of their servants, and the sovereign people is no exception to the rule; but how is its suspicion to be allayed by *knowledge?* If that suspicion could but be clarified into wise vigilance, it would be altogether salutary; if that vigilance could be aided by the unmistakable placing of responsibility, it would be altogether beneficent. Suspicion in itself is never healthful either in the private or in the public mind. *Trust is strength* in all relations of life; and, as it is the office of the constitutional reformer to create conditions of trustfulness, so it is the office of the administrative organizer to fit administration with conditions of clear-cut responsibility which shall insure trustworthiness. And let me say that large powers and unhampered discretion seem to me the indispensable conditions of responsibility. Public attention must be easily directed, in each case of good or bad administration, to just the man deserving of praise or blame. There is no danger in power, if only it be not irresponsible. If it be divided, dealt only in shares to many, it is obscured; and if it be obscured, it is made irresponsible. But if it be centred in heads of the service and in heads of branches of the service, it is easily watched and brought to book. If to keep his office a man must achieve open and honest success, and if at the same time he feels himself entrusted with large freedom of discretion, the greater his power the less likely is he to abuse it, the more is he nerved and sobered and elevated by it. The less his power, the more safely obscure and unnoticed does he feel his position to be, and the more readily does he relapse into remissness.

Just here we manifestly emerge upon the field of that still larger question,—the proper relations between public opinion and administration.

To whom is official trustworthiness to be disclosed, and by whom is it to be rewarded? Is the official to look to the public for his meed of praise and his push of promotion, or only to his superior in office? Are the people to be called in to settle administrative discipline as they are called in to settle constitutional principles? These questions evidently find their root in what is undoubtedly the fundamental problem of this whole study. That problem is: What part shall public opinion take in the conduct of administration?

The right answer seems to be, that public opinion shall play the part of authoritative critic.

But the *method* by which its authority shall be made to tell? Our peculiar American difficulty in organizing administration is not the danger of losing liberty, but the danger of not being able or willing to separate its essentials from its accidents. Our success is made doubtful by that besetting error of ours, the error of trying to do too much by vote. Self-government does not consist in having a hand in everything, any more than housekeeping consists necessarily in cooking dinner with one's own hands. The cook must be trusted with a large discretion as to the management of the fires and the ovens.

In those countries in which public opinion has yet to be instructed in its privileges, yet to be accustomed to having its own way, this question as to the province of public opinion is much more readily soluble than in this country, where public opinion is wide awake and quite intent upon having its own way anyhow. It is pathetic to see a whole book written by a German professor of political science for the purpose of saying to his countrymen, "Please try to have an opinion about national affairs"; but a public which is so modest may at least be expected to be very docile and acquiescent in learning what things it has *not* a right to think and speak about imperatively. It may be sluggish, but it will not be meddlesome. It will submit to be instructed before it tries to instruct. Its political education will come before its political activity. In trying to instruct our own public opinion, we are dealing with a pupil apt to think itself quite sufficiently instructed beforehand.

The problem is to make public opinion efficient without suffering it to be meddlesome. Directly exercised, in the oversight of the daily details and in the choice of the daily means of government, public criticism is of course a clumsy nuisance, a rustic handling delicate machinery. But as superintending the greater forces of formative policy alike in politics and administration, public criticism is altogether safe and beneficent, altogether indispensable. Let administrative study find the best means for giving public criticism this control and for shutting it out from all other interference.

But is the whole duty of administrative study done when it has taught the people what sort of administration to desire and demand, and how to get what they demand? Ought it not to go on to drill candidates for the public service?

There is an admirable movement towards universal political education now afoot in this country. The time will soon come when no college of respectability can afford to do without a well-filled chair of political science. But the education thus imparted will go but a certain length. It will multiply the number of intelligent critics of government, but it will create no competent body of administrators. It will prepare the way for the development of a sure-footed understanding of the general principles of government, but it will not necessarily foster skill in conducting government. It is an education which will equip legislators, perhaps, but not executive officials. If we are to improve public opinion, which is the motive power of government, we must prepare better officials as the *apparatus* of government. If we are to put in new boilers and to mend the fires which drive our governmental machinery, we must not leave the old wheels and joints and valves and bands to creak and buzz and clatter on as the best they may at bidding of the new force. We must put in new running parts wherever there is the least lack of strength or adjustment. It will be necessary to organize democracy by sending up to the competitive examinations for the civil service men definitely prepared for standing liberal tests as to technical knowledge. A technically schooled civil service will presently have become indispensable.

I know that a corps of civil servants prepared by a special schooling and drilled, after appointment, into a perfected organization, with appropriate hierarchy and characteristic discipline, seems to a great many very thoughtful persons to contain elements which might combine to make an offensive official class,—a distinct, semi-corporate body with sympathies divorced from those of a progressive, free-spirited people, and with hearts narrowed to the meanness of a bigoted officialism. Certainly such a class would be altogether hateful and harmful in the United States. Any measures calculated to produce it would for us be measures of reaction and of folly.

But to fear the creation of a domineering, illiberal officialism as a result of the studies I am here proposing is to miss altogether the principle upon which I wish most to insist. That principle is, that administration in the United States must be at all points sensitive to public opinion. A body of thoroughly trained officials serving during good behavior we must have in any case: that is a plain business necessity. But the apprehension that such a body will be anything un-American clears away the moment it is asked, What is to constitute good behavior? For that question obviously carries its own answer on its face. Steady, hearty allegiance to the policy of the government they serve will constitute good behavior. That *policy* will have no taint of officialism about it. It will not be the creation of permanent officials, but of statesmen whose responsibility to public opinion will be direct and inevitable. Bureaucracy can exist only where the whole service of the state is removed from the common political life of the people, its chiefs as well as its rank and file. Its motives, its objects, its policy, its standards, must be bureaucratic. It would be difficult to point out any examples of impudent exclusiveness and arbitrariness on the part of officials doing service under a chief of department who really served the people, as all our chiefs of departments must be made to do.

The ideal for us is a civil service cultured and self-sufficient enough to act with sense and vigor, and yet so intimately connected with the popular thought, by means of elections and constant public counsel, as to find arbitrariness or class spirit quite out of the question.

III.

Having thus viewed in some sort the subject-matter and the objects of this study of administration, what are we to conclude as to the methods best suited to it—the points of view most advantageous for it?

Government is so near us, as much a thing of our daily familiar handling, that we can with difficulty see the need of any philosophical study of it, or the exact point of such study, should it be undertaken. We have been on our feet too long to study now the art of walking. We are a practical people, made so apt, so adept in self-government by centuries of experimental drill that we are scarcely any longer capable of perceiving the awkwardness of the particular system we may be using, just because it is so easy for us to use any system. We do not study the art of governing: we govern. But mere unschooled genius for affairs will not save us from sad blunders in administration. Though democrats by long inheritance and repeated choice, we are still rather crude democrats. Old as democracy is, its organization on a basis of modern ideas and conditions is still an unaccomplished work. The democratic state has yet to be equipped for carrying those enormous burdens of administration which the needs of this industrial and trading age are so fast accumulating. Without comparative studies in government we cannot rid ourselves of the misconception that administration stands upon an essentially different basis in a democratic state from that on which it stands in a non-democratic state.

After such study we could grant democracy the sufficient honor of ultimately determining by debate all essential questions affecting the public weal, of basing all structures of policy upon the major will; but we would have found but one rule of good administration for all governments alike. So far as administrative functions are concerned, all governments have a strong structural likeness; more than that, if they are to be uniformly useful and efficient, they *must* have a strong structural likeness. A free man has the same bodily organs, the same executive parts, as the slave, however different may be his motives, his services, his energies. Monarchies and democracies, radically different as they are in other respects, have in reality much the same business to look to.

It is abundantly safe nowadays to insist upon this actual likeness of all governments, because these are days when abuses of power are easily exposed and arrested, in countries like our own, by a bold, alert, inquisitive, detective public thought and a sturdy popular self-dependence such as never existed before. We are slow to appreciate this; but it is easy to appreciate it. Try to imagine personal government in the United States. It is like trying to imagine a national worship of Zeus. Our imaginations are too modern for the feat.

But, besides being safe, it is necessary to see that for all governments alike the legitimate ends of administration are the same, in order not to be frightened at the idea of looking into foreign systems of administration for instruction and suggestion; in order to get rid of the apprehension that we might perchance blindly borrow something incompatible with our principles. That man is blindly astray who denounces attempts to transplant foreign systems into this country. It is impossible: they simply would not grow here. But why should we not use such parts of foreign contrivances as we want, if they be in any way serviceable? We are in no danger of using them in a foreign way. We borrowed rice, but we do not eat it with chopsticks. We borrowed our whole political language from England, but we leave the words "king" and "lords" out of it. What did we ever originate, except the action of the federal government upon individuals and some of the functions of the federal supreme court?

We can borrow the science of administration with safety and profit if only we read all fundamental differences of condition into its essential tenets. We have only to filter it through our constitutions, only to put it over a slow fire of criticism and distill away its foreign gases.

Let it be noted that it is the distinction, already drawn, between administration and politics which makes the comparative method so safe in the field of administration. When we study the administrative systems of France and Germany, knowing that we are not in search of *political* principles, we need not care a peppercorn for the constitutional or political reasons which Frenchmen or Germans give for their practices when explaining them to us. If I see a murderous fellow sharpening a knife cleverly, I can borrow his way of sharpening the knife without borrowing his probable intention to commit murder with it; and so, if I see a monarchist dyed in the wool managing a public bureau well, I can learn his business methods without changing one of my republican spots. He may serve his king; I will continue to serve the people; but I should like to serve my sovereign as well as he serves his. By keeping this distinction in view,—that is, by studying administration as a means of putting our own politics into convenient practice, as a means of making what is democratically politic towards all administratively possible towards each,—we are on perfectly safe ground, and can learn without error what foreign systems have to teach us. We thus devise an adjusted weight for our comparative method of study. We can thus scrutinize the anatomy of foreign governments without fear of getting any of their diseases into our veins; dissect alien systems without apprehension of blood-poisoning.

Our own politics must be the touchstone for all theories. The principles on which to base a science of administration for America must be principles which have democratic policy very much at heart. And, to suit American habit, all general theories must, as theories, keep modestly in the background, not in open argument only, but even in our own minds,—lest opinions satisfactory only to the standards of the library should be dogmatically used, as if they must be quite as satisfactory to the standards of practical politics as well. Doctrinaire devices must be postponed to tested practices. Arrangements not only sanctioned by conclusive experience elsewhere but also congenial to American habit must be preferred without hesitation to theoretical perfection. In a word, steady, practical statesmanship must come first, closet doctrine second. The cosmopolitan what-to-do must always be commanded by the American how-to-do-it.

Our duty is, to supply the best possible life to a *federal* organization, to systems within systems; to make town, city, county, state, and federal governments live with a like strength and an equally assured healthfulness, keeping each unquestionably its own master and yet making all interdependent and coöperative, combining independence with mutual helpfulness. The task is great and important enough to attract the best minds.

This interlacing of local self-government with federal self-government is quite a modern conception. It is not like the arrangements of imperial federation in Germany. There local government is not yet, fully, local *self*-government. The bureaucrat is everywhere busy. His efficiency springs out of *esprit de corps*, out of care to make ingratiating obeisance to the authority of a superior, or, at best, out of the soil of a sensitive conscience. He serves, not the public, but an irresponsible minister. The question for us is, how shall our series of governments within governments be so administered that it shall always be to the interest of the public officer to serve, not his superior alone but the community also, with the best efforts of his talents and the soberest service of his conscience? How shall such service be made to his commonest interest by contributing abundantly to his sustenance, to his dearest interest by furthering his ambition, and to his highest interest by advancing his honor and establishing his character? And how shall this be done alike for the local part and for the national whole?

If we solve this problem we shall again pilot the world. There is a tendency—is there not?—a tendency as yet dim, but already steadily impulsive and clearly destined to prevail, towards, first the confederation of parts of empires like the British, and finally of great states themselves. Instead of centralization of power, there is to be wide union with tolerated divisions of prerogative. This is a tendency towards the American type—of governments joined with governments for the pursuit of common purposes, in honorary equality and honorable subordination. Like principles of civil liberty are everywhere fostering like methods of government; and if comparative studies of the ways and means of government should enable us to offer suggestions which will practicably combine openness and vigor in the administration of such governments with ready docility to all serious, well-sustained public criticism, they will have approved themselves worthy to be ranked among the highest and most fruitful of the great departments of political study. That they will issue in such suggestions I confidently hope.

Frank J. Goodnow (1859–1939)

Woodrow Wilson and Frank J. Goodnow paralleled one another in age and, up to a point, in interests. Both earned law degrees and both became eminent scholars in administrative law, history, and political science. Wilson became president of Princeton University, and two years after he was elected to the presidency of the United States, Goodnow was named president of Johns Hopkins, where Wilson had earned his Ph.D. degree and had lectured. Around the turn of the century, both became interested and involved in local, particularly municipal, government, and shortly after writing his classic work, *Politics and Administration* (Macmillan, 1900), Goodnow became a professor in administrative law and municipal science at Columbia.

Goodnow's book was in some ways an extension and elaboration, in some ways a modification, of Wilson's main thesis in "The Study of Administration." Goodnow began by emphasizing the difference between and the proper separation of politics and administration, but in later chapters differentiated the functions of administration, some of which should be subject to political control, others free from politics. From these distinctions he deduced that certain kinds of offices should be politically appointed and removable while others should be protected by civil-service tenure. Goodnow's work was one of the most carefully reasoned analyses of the relations between politics and administration and a defense of the separation of the two in most circumstances.

F.C.M.

Politics and Administration

The Primary Functions of the State

Enough has been said, it is believed, to show that there are two distinct functions of government, and that their differentiation results in a differentiation, though less complete, of the organs of government provided by the

Chapters 1 and 4, *Politics and Administration* (New York: Macmillan, 1900), pp. 18–22 and 72–93.

formal governmental system. These two functions of government may for purposes of convenience be designated respectively as Politics and Administration. Politics has to do with policies or expressions of the state will. Administration has to do with the execution of these policies.

It is of course true that the meaning which is here given to the word "politics" is not the meaning which has been attributed to that word by most political writers. At the same time it is submitted that the sense in which politics is here used is the sense in which it is used by most people in ordinary affairs. Thus the Century Dictionary defines "politics": "In the narrower and more usual sense, the act or vocation of guiding or influencing the policy of a government through the organization of a party among its citizens—including, therefore, not only the ethics of government, but more especially, and often to the exclusion of ethical principles, the art of influencing public opinion, attracting and marshalling voters, and obtaining and distributing public patronage, so far as the possession of offices may depend upon the political opinions or political services of individuals."

An explanation of the word "administration" is not perhaps so necessary, since in scientific parlance it has not as yet acquired so fixed a meaning as has "politics." Block, in his *Dictionnaire de l'administration française,* defines "administration" as: "L'ensemble des services publiques destinés à concourir à l'exécution de la pensée du gouvernement et à l'application des lois d'intérêt général." The Century Dictionary speaks of it as: "The duty or duties of the administrator; specifically, the executive functions of government, consisting in the exercise of all the powers and duties of government, both general and local, which are neither legislative nor judicial."

These definitions, it will be noticed, both lay stress upon the fact that politics has to do with the guiding or influencing of governmental policy, while administration has to do with the execution of that policy. It is these two functions which it is here desired to differentiate, and for which the words "politics" and "administration" have been chosen.

The use of the word "administration" in this connection is unfortunately somewhat misleading, for the word when accompanied by the definite article is also used to indicate a series of governmental authorities. "The administration" means popularly the most important executive or administrative authorities. "Administration," therefore, when used as indicative of function, is apt to promote the idea that this function of government is to be found exclusively in the work of what are commonly referred to as executive or administrative authorities. These in their turn are apt to be regarded as confined to the discharge of the function of administration. Such, however, is rarely the case in any political system, and is particularly not the case in the American governmental system. The American legislature discharges very frequently the function of administration through its power of passing special acts. The American executive has an important influence on the discharge of the function of politics through the exercise of its veto power.

Further, in the United States, the words "administration" and "administrative," as indicative of governmental function, are commonly used by the courts in a very loose way. The attempt was made at the time of the formation of our governmental system, as has been pointed out, to incorporate into it the principle of the separation of powers. What had been a somewhat nebulous theory of political science thus became a rigid legal doctrine. What had been a somewhat attractive political theory in its nebulous form became at once an unworkable and unapplicable rule of law.

To avoid the inconvenience resulting from the attempt made to apply it logically to our governmental system, the judges of the United States have been accustomed to call "administrative" any power which was not in their eyes exclusively and unqualifiedly legislative, executive, or judicial, and to permit such a power to be exercised by any authority.

While this habit on the part of the judges makes the selection of the word "administration" somewhat unfortunate; at the same time it is indicative of the fact to which attention has been more than once directed, that although the differentiation of two functions of government is clear, the assignment of such functions to separate authorities is impossible.

Finally, the different position assigned in different states to the organ to which most of the work of executing the will of the state has been intrusted, has resulted in quite different conceptions in different states of what has been usually called administration. For administration has been conceived of as the function of the executing, that is, the executive authority. Recently, however, writers on administration have seen that, from the point of view both of theoretical speculation and of practical expediency, administration should not be regarded as merely a function of the executive authority, that is, the authority in the government which by the positive law is the executing authority. It has been seen that administration is, on the contrary, the function of executing the will of the state. It may be in some respects greater, and in others less in extent than the function of the executing authority as determined by the positive law.

There are, then, in all governmental systems two primary or ultimate functions of government, viz. the expression of the will of the state and the execution of that will. There are also in all states separate organs, each of which is mainly busied with the discharge of one of these functions. These functions are, respectively, Politics and Administration.

The Function of Administration

The function of executing the will of the state has been called administration. This function, it has been shown, must be subjected to the control of politics, if it is to be hoped that the expressed will of the state shall be executed, and thus become an actual rule of conduct. This control should not, however, extend further than is necessary to insure the execution of the state will. If it does, the spontaneous expression of the real state will tends to become difficult and the execution of that will becomes inefficient. In order to determine the exact limits to which this most necessary control should extend, it becomes necessary to analyze this function of administration.

On analysis we find that administration may be either of justice or of government. No legislature or legislative body can express the will of the state as to all matters of human conduct so clearly that no dispute as to its meaning may arise. The disputes which must necessarily arise must be set at rest before the will of the state in the concrete instances may be executed. For reasons both of convenience and of propriety, it is believed that the interpretation of the will of the state shall be made by some authority more or less independent of the legislature. The action of such non-legislative authority is usually spoken of as the administration of justice, and the authority to which this branch of the function of administration is intrusted is usually called the judicial authority.

The function of administration apart from its judicial side may be called the administration of government. The administration of government is also susceptible of differentiation. If it is analyzed it will be seen that it consists of several elements. On the border line of the administration of justice and the administration of government is a minor function of administration whose discharge is, by some governmental systems, intrusted to officers mainly busied with the administration of justice. In other systems this function is attended to by officers regarded as mainly administrative in character. To this branch of governmental activity no generic name can well be given. Its character can be made plain by concrete examples, as well as by a few words of general description.

Many laws passed by the lawgiving authority of the state are of such a character that they merely express the will of the state as a general rule of conduct. They do not, and, in the nature of things, cannot, express it in such detail that it can be executed without further governmental action, tending to bring a concrete individual or a concrete case within the class which the general rule of law purports to affect. Until the concrete case is thus brought within the general class affected by the law, the will of the state cannot be executed.

For example, the law may say that certain classes of individuals shall pay taxes on certain classes of property, and that these taxes shall vary in amount in accordance with the amount of such property. In order that the will of the state as to what tax a given individual shall pay on a given piece of property may be expressed, three things must be ascertained: viz. whether the given individual comes within the class, whether he has property of the kind specified, and what is its amount.

Again, the law may provide that certain kinds of buildings shall be built in a specified way. In order to insure that its provisions shall be complied with, the law may provide that the plans of all buildings shall be approved by some governmental authority before their erection may be begun.

In both of these cases some action must be taken by a governmental authority, in order to bring concrete cases under the operation of general rules. So far as this is the case, the discharge of this function of government bears a close resemblance to that of the administration of justice. In some cases the matter may be attended to by authorities recognized as distinctly judicial in character, in others the fitness of distinctly judicial authorities is not so marked. Indeed, in most cases judicial authorities engaged in the decision of suits relative to merely private rights are unfitted to attend to these matters.

Judicial authorities are unfitted for the performance of these duties because such performance requires the possession of considerable technical knowledge. The proper determination of the value of property for the purpose of taxation thus requires of those who assess it considerable knowledge of property values. The approval of plans of buildings should be made by those acquainted with building processes. Therefore these matters are, as a general thing, not classed as a part of the administration of justice, but rather as a part of the administration of government.

The election of any of the officers of the government cannot, further, be had without most important action on the part of governmental authorities. This must be as impartial and free from prejudice as possible, if it is to be hoped that the officers elected will represent the people—in other words, if it is to be hoped that the government will be popular. The action of election officers is thus also *quasi*-judicial in character.

In order, finally, that the general work of government may go on, the governmental organization must have at its disposal wide information and varied knowledge. This information, which is used not merely by the government, but as well by private students, must in many instances be acquired by some governmental authority which is reasonably permanent in character. For much of this information can be obtained only as the result of a series of observations, lasting through a long period of time. The authorities of the government which acquire this information must be absolutely impartial and as free from prejudice as possible, if it is to be hoped to get at the truth. Their work is, therefore, quite similar to the *quasi*-judicial work already described.

A second part of the administration of government is to be found in the mere execution of the expressed will of the state—the law. No one will deny that, if the expressed will of the state is to amount to anything as an actual rule of conduct, it must be executed. Before it can be executed it may be necessary that there shall be action taken by the judicial and *quasi*-judicial authorities to which allusion has been made. But after all this necessary action has been taken, the will of the state has to be executed. If the will of the state has been violated, the violator must be punished, and the conditions existing prior to such violation must, as far as may be, be restored.

Finally, in order that the will of the state may be either expressed or executed, a very complex governmental organization must be established, preserved, and developed. Legislators must be elected, judges must be chosen, and a whole series of officers must be provided for the discharge of the *quasi*-judicial duties already mentioned, the statistical and other similar work undertaken by the government, and for the direct execution of the will of the state. The establishment, preservation, and development of this vast force of officers and authorities should, in a popular government, be undertaken with the end in view of securing the freest possible expression by the people of the popular will, and of insuring the most efficient execution of that will after it has been expressed.

After this analysis of the function of administration we are in a position to answer the question put at the beginning of this chapter: What parts of this function of administration should be subjected to the control of the function of politics to the end that the expressed will of the state may be executed? It has already been shown that the administration of justice should be and is removed from this control. There remain to be considered the function of executing the law, which may be called the executive function, the *quasi*-judicial function, the statistical and semi-scientific functions, if we may so call them, and the function of establishing, preserving, and developing the governmental organization.

As regards the executive function, as it has been called, there can be no question of the necessity of subjecting it to the control of the body intrusted ultimately with the expression of the state will. If there is no relation of subordination between the body which makes law and the body which exe- cutes it, or if, where the legislature and the executive bodies are independent of each other so far as their governmental relations are concerned, no pro- vision is made outside of the governmental system for bringing about harmony between the making and the execution of the law, it is easy to conceive of a condition, in which the authorities provided for the execution of the law may refuse, for one reason or another, to execute it. This executive function must therefore of necessity be subordinated to the function of politics.

No such close connection, however, exists between the function of poli- tics and the other branches of the administration of government. No control of a political character can bring it about that administrative officers will discharge better their *quasi*-judicial duties, for example, any more than such a control can bring it about that judges will make better decisions.

No control which a political body can have over a body intrusted with the acquisition of facts and the gathering of information can result in the gathering of more facts or the acquisition of more exact information. The same is true, although not perhaps to the same degree, in the case of the necessary actions preliminary to the choice of officers by the electors. In these cases much must be left to official discretion, since what is demanded of the officers is not the doing of a concrete thing, but the exercise of judgment.

The courts, in the exercise of the control which the American system of government gives them over the acts of officers, have been obliged by the very force of things to recognize this distinction. Although it is possible for them to exercise a much more effective control than the legislature ever could exercise, they have voluntarily confined their jurisdiction to ministerial acts, and have refused to exercise a control over discretionary acts. The only possible exception to this statement is to be found in the fact that the courts will see to it that discretion is not grossly abused. This is the only point over which the legislature, or similar political body, can exercise a control over the discharge of this branch of administration. All that the legislature, or any political body, can do is to see to it, through the exercise of its control, that persons discharging these administrative functions are efficient and impartial. Their general conduct, but not their concrete actions, should be subject to control.

It is not only true that the control which the political body should and may have over the executive authority cannot, in the nature of things, be exercised over an administrative authority, i.e. an authority discharging that part of the function of administration not distinctly of an executive character; but any attempt to exercise such a control beyond the attempt to insure administrative integrity is likely to produce evil rather than good. For a close connection between politics and work of an administrative character is liable, in the case of the work done by the administration in the investigation of facts and the gathering of information, to pollute the sources of truth, in that it may give a bias to the investigator. It is liable in the case of an officer intrusted with the discharge of the quasi-judicial duties to produce corruption, in that it may take from him that impartiality which is so necessary. The same reasons which demand an impartial and upright administration of justice call for an impartial and upright administration of these matters of government. Private right may be as easily violated by a corrupt and partial administration of a tax law as by a corrupt and partial judicial decision. Political rights are easily violated by corrupt and partial election officers. Political control over administrative functions is liable finally to produce inefficient administration in that it makes administrative officers feel that what is demanded of them is not so much work that will improve their own department, as compliance with the behests of the political party.

Up to within comparatively few years, the existence of this branch of the administration of government has been practically ignored. Officers whose main duty was the execution of the law in the sense in which these words have been used in these pages have attended to these administrative matters. The distinctly administrative functions naturally were confused with the executive function. It was regarded as proper to attempt to exercise the same control over administrative matters as was exercised, and properly exercised, over the executive function. When, however, administrative matters began to assume greater prominence with the extension of the field of government,—an extension which was largely made in regard to subjects of an administrative rather than of an executive character,—the evil effects of such a treatment of matters of administration could not fail to appear. It is only in those countries which have recognized most fully that administration apart from its executive side is not from the point of view of theory, and should not be from the point of view of fact, connected with politics, that the greatest progess has been made in the improvement of the details of government, which, as in every other field of life, count for so much—much more, in fact, than the general principles.

The necessity for this separation of politics from administration is very marked in the case of municipal government. For municipal government is very largely a matter of administration in the narrow sense of the word. This is the truth at the bottom of the claim which is so often made, that municipal government is a matter of business. Of course the statement of the truth in this form is not correct. For municipal government is not business, but government. It is, however, almost exclusively a matter of administration, and a matter of local administration.

While it is true that politics should have no more to do with state than with municipal administration, using the word in the narrow sense, it is also true that the influence of politics on municipal government is worse than on state administration. This is so, because municipal government is in character more administrative than state government, and because, when politics affect municipal government it is liable to be not only local, but also state and national, politics. The result is, not only that municipal government is rendered partial, unjust, and inefficient, but that municipal interests are sacrificed to national and state interests . . .

The fact is, then, that there is a large part of administration which is unconnected with politics, which should therefore be relieved very largely, if not altogether, from the control of political bodies. It is unconnected with politics because it embraces fields of semi-scientific, *quasi*-judicial and *quasi*-business or commercial activity—work which has little if any influence on the expression of the true state will. For the most advantageous discharge of this branch of the function of administration there should be organized a force of governmental agents absolutely free from the influence of politics. Such a force should be free from the influence of politics because of the fact that their mission is the exercise of foresight and discretion, the pursuit of truth, the gathering of information, the maintenance of a strictly impartial attitude towards the individuals with whom they have dealings, and the provision of the most efficient possible administrative organization. The position assigned to such officers should be much the same as is that which has been by universal consent assigned to judges. Their work is no more political in character than is that of judges; and while it may be that their organization should differ somewhat from the judicial organization, still, the most advantageous discharge of the work devolved upon them makes it necessary that their position should be much the same as that which we assign to judicial officers.

It took the world a long time to recognize that judicial officers should occupy the position they now hold. In England, this position was not assigned to them by law until the passage of the Act of Settlement in 1701. In some of the Continental European countries such a position cannot even now be regarded as theirs. Before this position could be thus assigned to judges, the existence of the judicial function as a function not connected with politics had to be recognized. So, before we can hope that administrative officers can occupy a position reasonably permanent in character and reasonably free from political influence, we must recognize the existence of an administrative function whose discharge must be uninfluenced by political considerations. This England and Germany, and France though to a much less degree, have done. To this fact in large part is due the excellence of their administrative systems. Under such conditions the government may safely be intrusted with much work which, until the people of the United States attain to the same conception, cannot be intrusted to their governmental organs. For when so undertaken by governmental organs, it is inefficiently done, and inefficiently done because of our failure to recognize the existence of an administrative function which should be discharged by authorities not subject to the influence of politics.

The governmental authorities intrusted with the discharge of the administrative function should not only, like judges, be free from the influence of politics; they should also, again like judges, have considerable permanence of tenure. They should have permanence of tenure because the excellence of their work is often conditioned by the fact that they are expert, and expertness comes largely from long practice. Reasonable permanence of tenure is absolutely necessary for the semi-scientific, *quasi-* judicial, and technical branches of the administrative service. It is also extremely desirable for a much larger part of the administrative service, whose duties are not so important to the welfare of the state as those of the semi-scientific, *quasi-*judicial, and technical branches just mentioned. This is that vast class of clerical and ministerial officers who simply carry out orders of superiors in whose hands is the determination of general questions of administrative policy. Reasonable permanence of tenure is desirable for this class of officers because without it the maximum of administrative efficiency is impossible of attainment. Without it, it is true, the work of government can go on, but without it the cost of government is vastly increased, while the work is poorly done. Such permanence of tenure can be secured by provision of law, as in the case of Germany, or it may be secured by the demands of an enlightened public opinion, as is the case in England.

Care should be taken, however, that permanence of tenure be not given to those distinctly executive officers to whom is entrusted the general execution of the law. If permanence of tenure is provided for such officers, the government, as a whole, will tend to lose its popular character, since the execution of law has an important influence on the expression of the will of the state. An unenforced law is not really a rule of conduct, and the enforcement of law is in the hands of such officers. If, therefore, officers intrusted with the execution of the law are not subjected to some control of a political character provided in the governmental organization, as, for example, the control of the legislature, they should be subject to the control of the party which, in such case, is called upon to exercise that political control over the general function of administration so indispensable to a harmonious and efficient government.

Permanence of tenure in the case of the highest executive officers entrusted with large discretionary powers is incompatible with popular government, since it tends to further the formation of an immense governmental machine whose very efficiency may make it dangerous to the existence of popular government. It is to be remembered that too great strength in the administrative organization tends to make popular government impossible. Thus a strong administration, where the party organization is weak, may nullify the popular will through the control which the administration has, and in the nature of things must have, over the elections. This is largely true at the present time of Germany, and has been true in the past in France. On the other hand, it is to be remembered that an administrative system, where permanence of tenure in the lower grades of the service does not exist at all, can also be made use of, where there is a strong party organization, to nullify the popular will. This may be done through the wrongful exercise of the power of appointment, under a party system so formed as to make the popular will in the party difficult of expression.

In the semi-scientific, *quasi*-judicial, clerical, and ministerial divisions of the administrative system provision should be made for permanence of tenure, if efficient and impartial administration is to be expected, and if questions of policy are to be determined in accordance with the popular will. In its highest divisions, that is, those where the incumbents of offices have a determining influence on questions of policy, and particularly in case of the executive head, permanence of tenure should be avoided. Provision should in these cases be made for political control if it is hoped to secure the decision of questions of policy by bodies representative of the people.

Enough has been said, it is hoped, to show that while two primary functions of government may be differentiated, the questions arising out of the discharge of the one cannot, in a popular government, be considered apart from the questions arising out of the discharge of the other. In order that the execution of the will of the state shall conform to its expression, that is, in order that the functions of politics and administration may be coordinated, the political body in the governmental system must have control over the administrative body. There are limits, however, beyond which such a control should not be exercised. If it is extended to all officers in the administrative service, the government becomes inefficient and incapable of attending to many matters which for their advantageous attention must be attended to by the government. The too great extension of the political control, where the party organization has great strength and the administrative system is weak, tends further to defeat the very purpose for which it is formed. For the administrative organization may be made use of to further the ends of the party and to prevent the free expression of the state will.

On the other hand, if the attempt is made to strengthen the administrative system unduly in the hope of securing efficient administration, there is danger that, if the party organization is weak, the administrative organization may be made use of to influence the expression of the will of the state through its power over elections. Safety lies alone in frankly recognizing both that there should be a control over the general execution of the law and that there is a part of the work of administration into which politics should not enter. Only in this way may really popular government and efficient administration be obtained.

Henry Bruere (1882–1958)

In the late nineteenth and early twentieth centuries, most governmental activity in the United States was in the cities. And it was in urban areas where most political machines were based and where waste and corruption were most conspicuous. It is not surprising therefore that the leadership in governmental reform was assumed by groups dedicated to city improvement. They formed organizations known as bureaus of municipal research, a new kind of institution, indigenous to the United States. The bureaus were usually set up outside of the political mainstream and outside of governmental operations, were initially financed by philanthropists, and were led by persons of civic consciousness untainted by active affiliation with any political party. Their arms were to develop and apply specialized knowledge to municipal administration, a science of public management, and to encourage citizen enlightenment and participation in the problems and decisions of city governments. Such aims rested on a faith that efficiency in administration could and should be joined with the principles of democracy.

First and foremost of these new institutions was the New York Bureau of Municipal Research, founded in 1906, which was supplemented a few years later by its Training School for Public Service. The three principal figures in founding the bureau in New York and leading in its undertakings were William H. Allen, Henry Bruere, and Frederick A. Cleveland, sometimes dubbed the ABC of municipal research. The article by Henry Bruere that is excerpted below summarizes and synthesizes the nature and the goals of the New York Bureau and of the several hundred comparable bureaus which followed it.

                                                                    F.C.M.

Efficiency in City Government
Origin of the Movement

Through a catastrophe Galveston learned what many cities do not yet appreciate, that city government is the indispensable instrument of effective community co-operation. To equip its government to take leadership in rebuilding the wrecked city and to safeguard it from a recurrence of the disaster, the citizens of Galveston resorted to the commission plan whose growth and achievements were recently vividly described in *The Annals.* Similarly, the efficiency movement in cities grew out of recognition of the dependence of community welfare upon government activity. It began in 1906 in an effort to capture the great forces of city government for harnessing to the work of social betterment. It was not a tax-saving incentive nor desire for economy that inspired this first effort to apply modern efficiency tests to municipal government, but the conviction that only through efficient government could progressive social welfare be achieved, and that, so long as government remained inefficient, volunteer and detached effort to remove social handicaps would continue a hopeless task.

The efficiency movement is not trying to convert city government into a master philanthropist. On the contrary it aims to remove city government from its isolation, and to make it the customary and accepted common agency for "getting things done" by all groups of citizens in the execution of public purposes upon which they divide either because of racial, sectarian, social, economic or political differences.

It is an attempt to substitute for fractional, isolated, incomplete, ill-equipped and cross-purpose social welfare work a city-wide, community planned and community executed program of citizen well-being. It recognizes in health work, public education, public charities, police work, corrections, the administration of law and justice, housing control and public recreation, opportunity to deal directly with conditions engendering personal incapacity and community distress.

It is too much to say that effort to obtain efficiency in government originated with any single organization or was unknown before bureaus of municipal research began their work of co-operation with public officials. But it is probably true that not until 1906, when an experimental bureau of research was established, had any official or citizen agency directed its effort exclusively to learning the facts regarding city government and to constructive effort to promote efficient municipal administration.

Since 1906 citizens and officials of New York City have given persistent attention to the work of converting "ramshackle" into efficient government. Philadelphia, Cincinnati, Hoboken, Chicago, St. Louis and numerous smaller towns have organized and are financing agencies to bring about better city government through learning the facts regarding present government service, organization, methods and community needs.

Supplementing local work, the Metz Fund of $30,000, established by ex-Comptroller H. A. Metz, has as its purpose, placing country-wide in the hands of municipal officials, officers of boards of trade, civic associations and

Annals of the American Academy of Political and Social Science, Vol. 42 (May, 1912), pp. 3–5.

chambers of commerce, precise information regarding the best administrative and accounting practices worked out in any American city. The Training School for Public Service with $200,000 has begun an experiment in equipping men for public employment and civic work as distinct professional pursuits.

The President of the United States has organized a commission to apply the principles of efficiency to the federal government.

Each of these steps is directly traceable to the experimental test begun in New York in 1906 of basing citizen protest, citizen request, governmental plans, and administrative methods upon a scientific study of community conditions and the facts of governmental action, neglect, results and failures.

First Steps

So great has been the task, necessarily first undertaken, of instituting efficient business practices in city departments, that for these first years the major part of the work of citizen efficiency agencies has been devoted to co-operation with public officials in reorganizing budget making, accounting, purchasing, timekeeping, storekeeping, and to providing a fact basis for administration. For this reason, despite already extensive emphasis upon health, education, housing and dependency, the idea is very general that those interested in promoting efficiency in government are concerned only with business methods, efficient accounting and the technical aspects of budget making, etc.—in short the means and methods of government rather than its aim and policies.

Systematizing public business has been necessary to equip city government to do the work already committed to it and to prepare it for the assumption of increased responsibilities. However well-conceived and well-intentioned the program of city government may be, its value to the community will depend upon the frequency with which accomplishment is checked against purposes and intentions, results achieved measured against standards of possible results, misdirection of effort and other waste detected and diverted into channels of needed activity.

While the efficiency movement aims, it is true, at efficient business administration in cities, the scope of its purpose is as wide as the five standards by which it holds municipal efficiency must be tested. These standards are:

1. Efficiency of service program or objectives towards which government activities are directed.
2. Efficiency of organization, with reference to facilitating the economical execution of the service program.
3. Efficiency of method which will provide the best means for performing each separate function and task of city government.
4. Efficiency of personnel—conceived of as a specially trained, socially minded, skilfully directed and permanently employed corps of municipal workers to man

the organization, to devise, supervise and employ efficient methods and to execute an efficient program of service.

5. Efficient citizenship, equipped through intelligence regarding citizen needs, and armed with facts regarding government conditions and results, to co-operate with public officials in enlarging the usefulness of government and insuring its adherence to establish (sic) standards of efficiency.

❋ ❋ ❋

Richard S. Childs (1882–1979)

The origin of the city-manager plan is generally credited to the small city of Woodrow Wilson's birth, Staunton, Virginia, which in 1908 established by ordinance the post of "general manager," to be appointed by the city council, who would have complete charge of all the administrative work of the city's departments.[1] The manager plan soon succeeded the commission plan[2] as the model for municipal reformers and became incorporated as an integral part of the public management movement. It seemed to embody many of the aims of that movement: the separation of politics from administration; the professionalization of management; clear lines of authority and responsibility within the administrative organization; and others. Through adoption by a growing number of cities, the plan acquired momentum during the second and third decades of the century, momentum renewed after World War II and that continues to this day.

If not exactly the father of the city manager plan, Richard S. Childs was certainly its stepfather, its principal promoter and publicizer. A successful businessman, Childs early became interested in governmental reform, principally at the municipal level. In 1909, he organized and became secretary of the National Short Ballot Organization, and he found the city-manager plan a natural ally of the short ballot. For nearly seventy years, Childs promoted the city manager plan through helping and pushing state legislation and city charters; advising national, state, and local civic groups; lectures and articles; and personal contacts with legions of individuals. The article that follows, written by Childs in 1914, sets forth in plain and lucid terms the rationale and arguments for the city-manager plan in its early years.

1. However, the city of Ukiah, California, had established a comparable post of "chief executive officer" four years earlier. See Richard J. Stillman II, *The Rise of the City Manager* (Albuquerque: University of New Mexico Press, 1974), pp. 13–15.

2. The commission plan was inaugurated by the city of Galveston, Texas, in 1901, following a disastrous hurricane. It provided a relatively small commission of elected members, each of whom would be the administrative head of a city department and who, together, would act as the legislative body.

The Principles Underlying the City-Manager Plan

The city-manager plan . . . provides for a single elective board of directors, which may be called a commission or council. This commission receives nominal salaries or none (except, probably, in very large cities) and the members give only part of their time to municipal work, and thus are left free to continue their private careers without interruption. Their functions are to hire and supervise an appointive chief executive called the city manager, who holds office at their pleasure; also to pass ordinances and to contribute to the city government the amateur and representative element. If, for example, the city manager proposes the municipal operation of a street car line, the commission will have the duty of examining the proposition, first as to its wisdom, and second as to whether such a move accords with public sentiment with which they, as representative native citizens having wide personal acquaintance throughout the city, are supposed to be familiar. If the decision is favorable to municipal operation, they have the further responsibility of seeing that the city manager is competent to handle the job and that he does handle it properly in the years that follow.

The city manager, as chief executive, holds universal appointive power over the administrative establishment. He is not necessarily a local resident. Supposedly he is an expert in matters of municipal administration. In small cities he should be a practical civil engineer, thereby making a separate city engineer unnecessary. In larger cities broad executive experience would of course be a major requirement. The city manager's salary should be the largest in the city's service.

The logical exceptions to the appointive power of the city manager would be a civil service commission and an auditor. These would be appointive directly by the commission. In large cities, the auditor might well be given such powers as are possessed by the commissioners of accounts of New York City, who have power to compel witnesses under oath whether those witnesses are city employees or not, and to make free-lance investigations of city expenditures and work.

The city-manager plan differs from the commission plan in the fact that the commissioners do not assume the actual executive management of each of the city departments, but delegate the administrative work to the manager.

The plan preserves the basic merits of the commission plan, which are: (1) The short ballot, and (2) the unification of powers.

"Commission Government and the City-Manager Plan" (revised), *Annals of the American Academy of Political and Social Science,* Vol. 38 (1914), pp. 841–849.

By the "short ballot" is meant the limiting of the number of elective officers which are to be chosen by the voters. For example, it would be a violation of principle if the commission were made so large that the typical voter was called upon to vote for more than five offices simultaneously. When more than five officers are voted for at any one time, the voter ceases to make an individual choice for each office and begins to use ready-made tickets prepared for him by interested parties. This will hold true even if the ballot is non-partisan or in such form as to compel a separate mark for every candidate. The ticket, if it does not take the form of a column on the ballot, will nevertheless persist in the form of memoranda circulated through the press by organized civic and political bodies in such form that the voter can copy the list when marking his ballot. Obviously, when the ballot requires more choices than his majesty, the voter, cares to remember, power gravitates away from the voters into the hands of the ticket-makers, who thus acquire opportunities which are open to great abuse.

In Dayton and Springfield, Ohio, the only two good-sized cities which have thus far adopted the plan, the number of commissioners is five. In larger cities the number could be more than five, providing, however, that terms expire in rotation so that not more than five would be chosen at any one election, or provided that the ballot, as the voter sees it, is shortened in some other way, as by dividing the city into wards, each of them electing five or less. Proportional representation also provides a way of keeping the ballot short without necessarily making the commission a very small one.

"Unification of powers," the other basic merit which the city-manager plan takes over from the Galveston-Des Moines commission plan, means the reposing of all power in a single board. This gives to the whole mechanism the single controlling composite mind which is essential to the success of any organism. The mayor-and-council plan, for example, lacks unification of powers, since the mayor and the council are prevented by the charter from getting together and composing their differences by so simple an expedient as the taking of a joint vote. It would be a violation of the principles of the city-manager plan, therefore, to give to a separate mayor the power to veto the acts of the commission. It would then be a two-headed city instead of a one-headed one.

The advantages of having a city manager are obvious to any business man. For counsel, many minds are needed; for execution, a single head is required. Universal business practice demonstrates this as does also the superior luck which we have had with our typical public school systems where a school board does all its work through a hired superintendent. It is important to the plan that the city manager shall be appointive. Any scheme which would make him elective is fatal to the principle. Even the Dayton arrangement which subjects him to direct recall by the people is damaging to the principle involved, since it diverts responsibility from the commission. He must be the loyal servant of the commissioners, else they cannot be made to take responsibility for his acts. He must in no way be independent of them, although there is no objection to allowing the commission to contract with a city manager and promise to keep him in office for a certain number of years, not exceeding their own tenure, subject to mutual penalties. In large private businesses important managers frequently hold their positions under such contracts and a certain degree of security of office when arranged in this way is no more objectionable in city government than in business. It must, however, not be a charter matter, but something which the commissioners in their own judgment decide to risk.

To make it possible to hire the city manager from out of town not only is helpful in getting expert service, but is highly important to the coming profession of city management. If a city manager cannot look forward to similar positions elsewhere in case he is displaced or outgrows his town, a powerful incentive toward the development of personal efficiency is lost. The fact that the city manager, unlike a mayor, is not necessarily involved in local politics, permits comparative permanence in office of the chief executive of the city, a most important thing to the development of a smoothly running mechanism. In all plans involving elective executives, long tenures are rare. To rid us of the amateur and transient executives which our present mayors are, and to substitute, or at least permit the substitution of, experienced experts in municipal administration, is enough in itself to justify the coming of the city-manager plan.

How superior, too, is the method thus provided for the interchange of experience among our cities. At present we have various bureaus and publications attempting to do this work in an artificial way—on paper. The city manager of the future will bring to his task the experience of perhaps several cities in which he has himself served. To convey experience spelled out on paper is not to be compared to conveying it thus in a man's head.

Frederick W. Taylor (1856–1915)

The backdrop for much of the work toward management improvement of American cities was the contemporaneous development of more systematic management in industrial enterprises. The principal leader of the movement in the private sphere and the author of the term "scientific management" was Frederick W. Taylor. The son of a lawyer, Taylor was prevented from pursuing a legal career himself because of eye trouble. Instead, he started as an apprentice machinist and rose rapidly, first in the Midvale Steel Works, later in other companies, including particularly Bethlehem Steel, to posts of general manager and consulting engineer. Along this route, Taylor became increasingly concerned with inefficiency in the work place, lack of incentives and consequent "soldiering" of workers, and the inadequacies of managers in providing knowledge, leadership, and direction. He began in the late nineteenth century, through a series of experiments and innovations, to develop methods and principles for analyzing tasks and the best means of organizing and carrying them out. After the turn of the century, he became perhaps this nation's first management consultant and, through papers principally addressed to the American Society of Mechanical Engineers, the acknowledged leader in pushing management as a science and managing as a legitimate and learnable profession.

Among Taylor's major contributions were the development of incentive systems of pay; the importance of planning; standardization of materials, machines, methods, and products; cost analysis and cost accounting; time and motion studies; the importance of measurement and of inspection; management by exception; and functional foremanship. Taylor acquired a great many disciples in business management and a few in the public sphere. His followers formed the Society to Promote the Science of Management in 1912. Upon his death in 1915, it was renamed the Taylor Society, and it ultimately became the Society for the Advancement of Management.

The passage that follows is drawn from Taylor's principal work, *The Principles of Scientific Management,* published in 1911 and soon republished around the world in ten different languages. Most of what has been excised consists of examples and experiences in various specific fields. The core of Taylor's concepts of scientific management is retained.

F.C.M.

The Principles of Scientific Management

❋ ❋ ❋

... throughout all of these illustrations, it will be seen that the useful results have hinged mainly upon (1) the substitution of a science for the individual judgment of the workman; (2) the scientific selection and development of the workman, after each man has been studied, taught, and trained, and one may say experimented with, instead of allowing the workmen to select themselves and develop in a haphazard way; and (3) the intimate cooperation of the management with the workmen, so that they together do the work in accordance with the scientific laws which have been developed, instead of leaving the solution of each problem in the hands of the individual workman.

Abridged from Chapter 2, "The Principles of Scientific Management" in *Scientific Management* by Frederick Winslow Taylor (New York: Harper & Brothers, 1911), pp. 114–141. Copyright 1911 by Frederick W. Taylor; renewed 1939 by Louise M. S. Taylor; renewed 1947 by Harper & Row, Publishers, Inc.

In applying these new principles, in place of the old individual effort of each workman, both sides share almost equally in the daily performance of each task, the management doing that part of the work for which they are best fitted, and the workmen the balance.

It is for the illustration of this philosophy that this paper has been written, but some of the elements involved in its general principles should be further discussed.

The development of a science sounds like a formidable undertaking, and in fact anything like a thorough study of a science such as that of cutting metals necessarily involves many years of work. The science of cutting metals, however, represents in its complication, and in the time required to develop it, almost an extreme case in the mechanic arts. Yet even in this very intricate science, within a few months after starting, enough knowledge had been obtained to much more than pay for the work of experimenting. This holds true in the case of practically all scientific development in the mechanic arts. The first laws developed for cutting metals were crude, and contained only a partial knowledge of the truth, yet this imperfect knowledge was vastly better than the utter lack of exact information or the very imperfect rule of thumb which existed before, and it enabled the workmen, with the help of the management, to do far quicker and better work.

For example, a very short time was needed to discover one or two types of tools which, though imperfect as compared with the shapes developed years afterward, were superior to all other shapes and kinds in common use. These tools were adopted as standard and made possible an immediate increase in the speed of every machinist who used them. These types were superseded in a comparatively short time by still other tools which remained standard until they in their turn made way for later improvements.

The science which exists in most of the mechanic arts is, however, far simpler than the science of cutting metals. In almost all cases, in fact, the laws or rules which are developed are so simple that the average man would hardly dignify them with the name of a science. In most trades, the science is developed through a comparatively simple analysis and time study of the movements required by the workmen to do some small part of his work, and this study is usually made by a man equipped merely with a stop-watch and a properly ruled notebook. Hundreds of these "time-study men" are now engaged in developing elementary scientific knowledge where before existed only rule of thumb. Even the motion study of Mr. Gilbreth in bricklaying . . . involves a much more elaborate investigation than that which occurs in most cases. The general steps to be taken in developing a simple law of this class are as follows:

First. Find, say, 10 or 15 different men (preferably in as many separate establishments and different parts of the country) who are especially skilful in doing the particular work to be analyzed.

Second. Study the exact series of elementary operations or motions which each of these men uses in doing the work which is being investigated, as well as the implements each man uses.

Third. Study with a stop-watch the time required to make each of these elementary movements and then select the quickest way of doing each element of the work.

Fourth. Eliminate all false movements, slow movements, and useless movements.

Fifth. After doing away with all unnecessary movements, collect into one series the quickest and best movements as well as the best implements.

This one new method, involving that series of motions which can be made quickest and best, is then substituted in place of the ten or fifteen inferior series which were formerly in use. This best method becomes standard, and remains standard, to be taught first to the teachers (or functional foremen) and by them to every workman in the establishment until it is superseded by a quicker and better series of movements. In this simple way one element after another of the science is developed.

In the same way each type of implement used in a trade is studied. Under the philosophy of the management of "initiative and incentive" each work-man is called upon to use his own best judgment, so as to do the work in the quickest time, and from this results in all cases a large variety in the shapes and types of implements which are used for any specific purpose. Scientific management requires, first, a careful investigation of each of the many modifications of the same implement, developed under rule of thumb; and second, after a time study has been made of the speed attainable with each of these implements, that the good points of several of them shall be united in a single standard implement, which will enable the workman to work faster and with greater ease than he could before. This one implement, then, is adopted as standard in place of the many different kinds before in use, and it remains standard for all workmen to use until superseded by an implement which has been shown, through motion and time study, to be still better.

With this explanation it will be seen that the development of a science to replace rule of thumb is in most cases by no means a formidable under-taking, and that it can be accomplished by ordinary, every-day men without any elaborate scientific training; but that, on the other hand, the successful use of even the simplest improvement of this kind calls for records, system, and cooperation where in the past existed only individual effort.

There is another type of scientific investigation which has been referred to several times in this paper, and which should receive special attention, namely, the accurate study of the motives which influence men. At first it may appear that this is a matter for individual observation and judgment, and is not a proper subject for exact scientific experiments. It is true that the laws which result from experiments of this class, owing to the fact that the very complex organism—the human being—is being experimented with, are sub-ject to a larger number of exceptions than is the case with laws relating to material things. And yet laws of this kind, which apply to a large majority of men, unquestionably exist, and when clearly defined are of great value as a guide in dealing with men. In developing these laws, accurate, carefully planned and executed experiments, extending through a term of years, have been made, similar in a general way to the experiments upon various other elements which have been referred to in this paper.

Perhaps the most important law belonging to this class, in its relation to scientific management, is the effect which the task idea has upon the efficiency of the workman. This, in fact, has become such an important element of the mechanism of scientific management, that by a great number of people scientific management has come to be known as "task management."

The writer has described in other papers a series of experiments made upon workmen, which have resulted in demonstrating the fact that it is impossible, through any long period of time, to get workmen to work much harder than the average men around them, unless they are assured a large and a permanent increase in their pay. This series of experiments, however, also proved that plenty of workmen can be found who are willing to work at their best speed, provided they are given this liberal increase in wages. The workman must, however, be fully assured that this increase beyond the average is to be permanent. Our experiments have shown that the exact percentage of increase required to make a workman work at his highest speed depends upon the kind of work which the man is doing.

It is absolutely necessary, then, when workmen are daily given a task which calls for a high rate of speed on their part, that they should also be insured the necessary high rate of pay whenever they are successful. This involves not only fixing for each man his daily task, but also paying him a large bonus, or premium, each time that he succeeds in doing his task in the given time. It is difficult to appreciate in full measure the help which the proper use of these two elements is to the workman in elevating him to the highest standard of efficiency and speed in his trade, and then keeping him there, unless one has seen first the old plan and afterward the new tried upon the same man. And in fact until one has seen similar accurate experiments made upon various grades of workmen engaged in doing widely different types of work. The remarkable and almost uniformly good results from the *correct* application of the task and the bonus must be seen to be appreciated.

These two elements, the task and the bonus (which, as has been pointed out in previous papers, can be applied in several ways), constitute two of the most important elements of the mechanism of scientific management. They are especially important from the fact that they are, as it were, a climax, demanding before they can be used almost all of the other elements of the mechanism; such as a planning department, accurate time study, standardization of methods and implements, a routing system, the training of functional foremen or teachers, and in many cases instruction cards, slide-rules, etc. . . .

The necessity for systematically teaching workmen how to work to the best advantage has been several times referred to. It seems desirable, therefore, to explain in rather more detail how this teaching is done. In the case of a machine-shop which is managed under the modern system, detailed written instructions as to the best way of doing each piece of work are prepared in advance, by men in the planning department. These instructions represent the combined work of several men in the planning room, each of whom has his own specialty, or function. One of them, for instance, is a specialist on the proper speeds and cutting tools to be used. He uses the slide-rules which have been above described as an aid, to guide him in obtaining proper speeds, etc. Another man analyzes the best and quickest motions to be made by the workman in setting the work up in the machine and removing it, etc. Still a third, through the time-study records which have been accumulated, makes out a time-table giving the proper speed for doing each element of the work. The directions of all of these men, however, are written on a single instruction card, or sheet.

These men of necessity spend most of their time in the planning department, because they must be close to the records and data which they continually use in their work, and because this work requires the use of a desk and freedom from interruption. Human nature is such, however, that many of the workmen, if left to themselves, would pay but little attention to their written instructions. It is necessary, therefore, to provide teachers (called functional foremen) to see that the workmen both understand and carry out these written instructions.

Under functional management, the old-fashioned single foreman is superseded by eight different men, each one of whom has his own special duties, and these men, acting as the agents for the planning department . . . are the expert teachers, who are at all times in the shop, helping and directing the workmen. Being each one chosen for his knowledge and personal skill in his specialty, they are able not only to tell the workman what he should do, but in case of necessity they do the work themselves in the presence of the workman, so as to show him not only the best but also the quickest methods.

One of these teachers (called the inspector) sees to it that he understands the drawings and instructions for doing the work. He teaches him how to do work of the right quality; how to make it fine and exact where it should be fine, and rough and quick where accuracy is not required,—the one being just as important for success as the other. The second teacher (the gang boss) shows him how to set up the job in his machine, and teaches him to make all of his personal motions in the quickest and best way. The third (the speed boss) sees the the machine is run at the best speed and that the proper tool is used in the particular way which will enable the machine to finish its product in the shortest possible time. In addition to the assistance given by these teachers, the workman receives orders and help from four other men; from the "repair boss" as to the adjustment, cleanliness, and general care of his machine, belting, etc.; from the "time clerk," as to everything relating to his pay and to proper written reports and returns; from the "route clerk," as to the order in which he does his work and as to the movement of the work from one part of the shop to another; and, in case a workman gets into any trouble with any of his various bosses, the "disciplinarian" interviews him.

It must be understood, of course, that all workmen engaged on the same kind of work do not require the same amount of individual teaching and attention from the functional foremen. The men who are new at a given operation naturally require far more teaching and watching than those who have been a long time at the same kind of jobs.

The history of the development of scientific management up to date, however, calls for a word of warning. The mechanism of management must not be mistaken for its essence, or underlying philosophy. Precisely the same mechanism will in one case produce disastrous results and in another the most beneficent. The same mechanism which will produce the finest results when made to serve the underlying principles of scientific management, will lead to failure and disaster if accompanied by the wrong spirit in those who are using it. Hundreds of people have already mistaken the mechanism of this system for its essence. Messrs. Gantt, Barth, and the writer have presented papers to the American Society of Mechanical Engineers on the subject of scientific management. In these papers the mechanism which is used has been described at some length. As elements of this mechanism may be cited:

Time study, with the implements and methods for properly making it.

Functional or divided foremanship and its superiority to the old-fashioned single foreman.

The standardization of all tools and implements used in the trades, and also of the acts or movements of workmen for each class of work.

The desirability of a planning room or department.

The "exception principle" in management.

The use of slide-rules and similar time-saving implements.

Instruction cards for the workman.

The task idea in management, accompanied by a large bonus for the successful performance of the task.

The "differential rate."

Mnemonic systems for classifying manufactured products as well as implements used in manufacturing.

A routing system.

Modern cost system, etc., etc.

These are, however, merely the elements or details of the mechanism of management. Scientific management, in its essence, consists of a certain philosophy, which results, as before stated, in a combination of the four great underlying principles of management.*

When, however, the elements of this mechanism, such as time study, functional foremanship, etc., are used without being accompanied by the true philosophy of management, the results are in many cases disastrous. And, unfortunately, even when men who are thoroughly in sympathy with the principles of scientific management undertake to change too rapidly from the old type to the new, without heeding the warnings of those who have had years of experience in making this change, they frequently meet with serious troubles, and sometimes with strikes, followed by failure.

The writer, in his paper on "Shop Management," has called especial attention to the risks which managers run in attempting to change rapidly from the old to the new management. In many cases, however, this warning has not been heeded. The physical changes which are needed, the actual time study which has to be made, the standardization of all implements connected with the work, the necessity for individually studying each machine and placing it in perfect order, all take time, but the faster these elements of the work are studied and improved, the better for the undertaking. On the other hand, the really great problem involved in a change from the management of "initiative and incentive" to scientific management consists in a complete revolution in the mental attitude and the habits of all of those engaged in the management, as well of the workmen. And this change can be brought about only gradually and through the presentation of many object-lessons to the workman, which, together with the teaching which he receives, thoroughly convince him of the superiority of the new over the old way of doing the work. This change in the mental attitude of the workman imperatively demands time. It is impossible to hurry it beyond a certain speed. The writer has over and over again warned those who contemplated making this change that it was a matter, even in a simple establishment, of from two to three years, and that in some cases it requires from four to five years.

The first few changes which affect the workmen should be made exceedingly slowly, and only one workman at a time should be dealt with at the start. Until this single man has been thoroughly convinced that a great gain has come to him from the new method, no further change should be made. Then one man after another should be tactfully changed over. After passing the point at which from one-fourth to one-third of the men in the employ of the company have been changed from the old to the new, very rapid progress can be made, because at about this time there is, generally, a complete revolution in the public opinion of the whole establishment and practically all of the workmen who are working under the old system become desirous to share

---

First. The development of a true science. *Second.* The scientific selection of the workman. *Third.* His scientific education and development. *Fourth.* Intimate friendly cooperation between the management and the men.

in the benefits which they see have been received by those working under the new plan.

The writer would again insist that in no case should the managers of an establishment, the work of which is elaborate, undertake to change from the old to the new type unless the directors of the company fully understand and believe in the fundamental principles of scientific management and unless they appreciate all that is involved in making this change, particularly the time required, and unless they want scientific management greatly.

It will doubtless be claimed that in all that has been said no new fact has been brought to light that was not known to some one in the past. Very likely this is true. Scientific management does not necessarily involve any great invention, nor the discovery of new or startling facts. It does, however, involve a certain *combination* of elements which have not existed in the past, namely, old knowledge so collected, analyzed, grouped, and classified into laws and rules that it constitutes a science; accompanied by a complete change in the mental attitude of the working men as well as of those on the side of the management, toward each other, and toward their respective duties and responsibilities. Also, a new division of the duties between the two sides and intimate, friendly cooperation to an extent that is impossible under the philosophy of the old management. And even all of this in many cases could not exist without the help of mechanisms which have been gradually developed.

It is no single element, but rather this whole combination, that constitutes scientific management, which may be summarized as:

Science, not rule of thumb.

Harmony, not discord.

Cooperation, not individualism.

Maximum output, in place of restricted output.

The development of each man to his greatest efficiency and prosperity.

The writer wishes to again state that: "The time is fast going by for the great personal or individual achievement of any one man standing alone and without the help of those around him. And the time is coming when all great things will be done by that type of cooperation in which each man performs the function for which he is best suited, each man preserves his own individuality and is supreme in his particular function, and each man at the same time loses none of his originality and proper personal initiative, and yet is controlled by and must work harmoniously with many other men."

Henri Fayol (1841–1925)

In many ways, the career and the contributions of Henri Fayol in France parallel those of Frederick W. Taylor in the United States. Both men enjoyed a long experience in business enterprise first as specialized technicians, then as managers; both became keenly interested in the development of a science of management, basing their laws and principles on their own practical experience; and both in their later years sought to generalize their observations to other types of organized enterprise besides private business, notably to government. In one important respect, their approaches to management were distinctly different. Taylor, as noted earlier, started from the bottom of the organization—the workers and their machines, the foremen and their responsibilities, the day-to-day management of the shop. Fayol started from the top and dealt primarily with the overall governance and administration of a large-scale business. Taylor's perspective was from the bottom up; Fayol's, from the top down.

Henri Fayol retired in 1918 from the top management position of a large French coal and metallurgical concern by which he had been employed for most of his working life. Thereafter, he drafted and published his basic work, *Administration Industrielle et Generale,* which was translated into English and German in 1925, the year of his death. He also prepared a number of monographs and speeches, including some directed to public administration.[1] There can be no doubt that his work had much influence beyond the borders of France and specifically in the United States. Significant parts of Luther Gulick's "Notes on the Theory of Organization" (in Part III of this volume) were adapted and extended from Fayol's basic work, and almost every American student of public administration in the late twenties and the thirties will recognize most of his principles and elements of management, which are excerpted from his basic work in the passage that follows.

F.C.M.

1. For example, see his address on "The Administrative Theory in the State," delivered before the Second International Congress of Administrative Science at Brussels in 1923 and later reprinted in English as one of the *Papers on the Science of Administration,* edited by Luther Gulick and L. Urwick (New York: Institute of Public Administration, 1937).

General and Industrial Management

Definition of Management

All activities to which industrial undertakings give rise can be divided into the following six groups—

1. Technical activities (production, manufacture, adaptation).
2. Commercial activities (buying, selling, exchange).
3. Financial activities (search for and optimum use of capital).
4. Security activities (protection of property and persons).
5. Accounting activites (stocktaking, balance sheet, costs, statistics).
6. Managerial activities (planning, organization, command, co-ordination, control).

Be the undertaking simple or complex, big or small, these six groups of activities or essential functions are always present. The first five are well known—a few words will be enough to demarcate their respective spheres— but the managerial group calls for further explanation.

Managerial Activities

No one of the preceding groups is concerned with drawing up the broad plan of operations of the business, with assembling personnel, co-ordinating and harmonizing effort and activity. These functions do not come within the province of technical activity nor within the commercial, financial, security, or accounting group. They make up another group usually indicated by the term Management with somewhat ill-defined attributes and frontiers. Foresight, organization, co-ordination and control undoubtedly form part of management as it is commonly understood. Should command necessarily be included? It is not obligatory: command may be treated separately. Nevertheless I have decided to include it under management for the following reasons—

1. Selection and training of personnel and the setting up of the organization which are managerial responsibilities are very much concerned with command.
2. Most principles of command are principles of management—management and command are very closely linked. From the mere standpoint of facilitating study there would be reason to set these two groups together.
3. Furthermore, the grouping has the advantage that it makes management a very important function at least as worthy as the technical one of attracting and holding public attention.

Chapters 1, 4, and 5, *General and Industrial Management* (London: Pitman & Sons, 1949, reprint of 1925 edition), pp. 3, 4–5, 19–20, 22, 24, 25, 26, 33, 34, 36, 38–39, 43, 53, 97, 103, 107.

Therefore I have adopted the following definition: To manage is to forecast and plan, to organize, to command, to co-ordinate and to control. To foresee and provide means examining the future and drawing up the plan of action. To organize means building up the dual structure, material and human, of the undertaking. To command means maintaining activity among the personnel. To co-ordinate means binding together, unifying and harmonizing all activity and effort. To control means seeing that everything occurs in conformity with established rule and expressed command.

Management, thus understood, is neither an exclusive privilege nor a particular responsibility of the head or senior members of the business; it is an activity spread, like all other activities, between head and members of the body corporate. The managerial function is quite distinct from the other five essential functions. It should not be confused with government. To govern is to conduct the undertaking towards its objective by seeking to derive optimum advantage from all available resources and to assure the smooth working of the six essential functions. Management is merely one of the six functions whose smooth working government has to ensure, but it has such a large place in the part played by higher managers that sometimes this part seems exclusively managerial.

General Principles of Management

The managerial function finds its only outlet through the members of the organization (body corporate). Whilst the other functions bring into play material and machines the managerial function operates only on the personnel. The soundness and good working order of the body corporate depend on a certain number of conditions termed indiscriminately principles, laws, rules. For preference I shall adopt the term principles whilst dissociating it from any suggestion of rigidity, for there is nothing rigid or absolute in management affairs, it is all a question of proportion. Seldom do we have to apply the same principle twice in identical conditions; allowance must be made for different changing circumstances, for men just as different and changing and for many other variable elements.

Therefore principles are flexible and capable of adaptation to every need; it is a matter of knowing how to make use of them, which is a difficult art requiring intelligence, experience, decision and proportion. Compounded of tact and experience, proportion is one of the foremost attributes of the manager. There is no limit to the number of principles of management, every rule or managerial procedure which strengthens the body corporate or facilitates its functioning has a place among the principles so long, at least, as experience confirms its worthiness. A change in the state of affairs can be responsible for change of rules which had been engendered by that state.

I am going to review some of the principles of management which I have most frequently had to apply; viz.—

1. Division of work.

2. Authority.
3. Discipline.
4. Unity of command.
5. Unity of direction.
6. Subordination of individual interests to the general interest.
7. Remuneration.
8. Centralization.
9. Scalar chain (line of authority).
10. Order.
11. Equity.
12. Stability of tenure of personnel.
13. Initiative.
14. Esprit de corps.

1. Division of Work

Specialization belongs to the natural order; it is observable in the animal world, where the more highly developed the creature the more highly differentiated its organs; it is observable in human societies where the more important the body corporate the closer is the relationship between structure and function. As society grows, so new organs develop destined to replace the single one performing all functions in the primitive state.

The object of division of work is to produce more and better work with the same effort.

2. Authority and Responsibility

Authority is the right to give orders and the power to exact obedience. Distinction must be made between a manager's official authority deriving from office and personal authority, compounded of intelligence, experience, moral worth, ability to lead, past services, etc. In the make up of a good head personal authority is the indispensable complement of official authority. Authority is not to be conceived of apart from responsibility, that is apart from sanction—reward or penalty—which goes with the exercise of power. Responsibility is a corollary of authority, it is its natural consequence and essential counterpart, and wheresoever authority is exercised responsibility arises.

3. Discipline

Discipline is in essence obedience, application, energy, behaviour, and outward marks of respect observed in accordance with the standing agreements between the firm and its employees, whether these agreements have been freely debated or accepted without prior discussion, whether they be written or implicit, whether they derive from the wish of the parties to them or from rules and customs, it is these agreements which determine the formalities of discipline.

4. Unity of Command

For any action whatsoever, an employee should receive orders from one superior only.

5. Unity of Direction

This principle is expressed as: one head and one plan for a group of activities having the same objective. It is the condition essential to unity of action, coordination of strength and focusing of effort.

6. Subordination of Individual Interest to General Interest

This principle calls to mind the fact that in a business the interest of one employee or group of employees should not prevail over that of the concern, that the interest of the home should come before that of its members and that the interest of the State should have pride of place over that of one citizen or group of citizens.

7. Remuneration of Personnel

Remuneration of personnel is the price of services rendered. It should be fair and, as far as is possible, afford satisfaction both to personnel and firm (employee and employer).

8. Centralization

Like division of work, centralization belongs to the natural order; this turns on the fact that in every organization, animal or social, sensations converge towards the brain or directive part, and from the brain or directive part orders are sent out which set all parts of the organism in movement. Centralization is not a system of management good or bad of itself, capable of being adopted or discarded at the whim of managers or of circumstances; it is always present to a greater or less extent. The question of centralization or decentralization, is a simple question of proportion, it is a matter of finding the optimum degree for the particular concern.

9. Scalar Chain

The scalar chain is the chain of superiors ranging from the ultimate authority to the lowest ranks. The line of authority is the route followed—via every link in the chain—by all communications which start from or go to the ultimate authority.

10. Order

The formula is known in the case of material things "A place for everything and everything in its place." The formula is the same for human order "A place for everyone and everyone in his place."

11. Equity

Why equity and not justice? Justice is putting into execution established conventions, but conventions cannot foresee everything, they need to be interpreted or their inadequacy supplemented. For the personnel to be encouraged to carry out its duties with all the devotion and loyalty of which it is capable it must be treated with kindness, and equity results from the combination of kindliness and justice.

12. Stability of Tenure of Personnel

Time is required for an employee to get used to new work and succeed in doing it well, always assuming that he possesses the requisite abilities. If when he has got used to it, or before then, he is removed, he will not have had time to render worthwhile service.

13. Initiative

Thinking out a plan and ensuring its success is one of the keenest satisfactions for an intelligent man to experience. It is also one of the most powerful stimulants of human endeavour. This power of thinking out and executing is what is called initiative, and freedom to propose and to execute belongs too, each in its way, to initiative. At all levels of the organizational ladder zeal and energy on the part of employees are augmented by initiative. The initiative of all, added to that of the manager, and supplementing it if need be, represents a great source of strength for businesses.

14. Esprit de Corps

"Union is strength." Business heads would do well to ponder on this proverb. Harmony, union among the personnel of a concern, is great strength in that concern. Effort, then, should be made to establish it. Among the countless methods in use I will single out specially one principle to be observed and two pitfalls to be avoided. The principle to be observed is unity of command; the dangers to be avoided are (A) a misguided interpretation of the motto "divide and rule," (b) the abuse of written communications.

Elements of Management

1. Planning

The maxim, "managing means looking ahead," gives some idea of the importance attached to planning in the business world, and it is true that if foresight is not the whole of management at least it is an essential part of it. To foresee, in this context, means both to assess the future and make provision for it; that is, foreseeing is itself action already.

2. Organizing

To organize a business is to provide it with everything useful to its functioning: raw materials, tools, capital, personnel. All this may be divided into two main sections, the material organization and the human organization.

3. Command

The organization, having been formed, must be set going and this is the mission of command. This mission is spread over the different heads of the concern, each in charge of and responsible for his particular unit. For every manager the object of command is to get the optimum return from all employees of his unit in the interest of the whole concern. The art of command rests on certain personal qualities and a knowledge of general principles of management.

4. Co-ordination

To co-ordinate is to harmonize all the activities of a concern so as to facilitate its working, and its success. It is giving to the material and social, functional, organic whole such proportions as are suitable to enable it to play its part assuredly and economically.

5. Control

In an undertaking, control consists in verifying whether everything occurs in conformity with the plan adopted, the instructions issued and principles established. It has for object to point out weaknesses and errors in order to rectify them and prevent recurrence.

PART III

MATURATION OF AN ORTHODOX PUBLIC ADMINISTRATION

For purposes of historical convenience, the year 1937 may be considered the high-point of the public management movement. During that year, two related documents, one official and one unofficial, were published. In many ways, they represented the culmination of a half century of development and synthesis in the field of management generally and of public management specifically; and many of the subsequent writings and developments in the field stemmed from them. The official document was the *Report* of the President's Committee on Administrative Management (the Brownlow Committee)[1]; the unofficial one was a collection of eleven *Papers on the Science of Administration,* edited by Luther Gulick and L. Urwick and published by the Institute of Public Administration (which was an outgrowth of the New York Bureau of Municipal Research). The connection between the two was that the *Papers* were written or drawn together for the use of the members and staff of the Brownlow Committee, principally by Gulick, who was a member of that committee.

Gulick introduced his foreword to the *Papers* with the statement that: "The papers brought together in this collection are essays by men scientifically interested in the phenomena of administration. Most of these writers did their thinking independently, in some cases without any acquaintance with the others, or with their writings. The striking similarity of the analysis, nomenclature, and hypotheses, frequently set forth as principles, is thus doubly significant."[2]

In fact, two of the articles in the collection, which dealt primarily with human beings and their relationships in the management process,[3] seemed quite different in their approaches. But Gulick's observation was generally true.

The development of thinking in the field had been quite consistent and systematic for nearly thirty years. Leonard D. White had produced the first general text in the field in 1926, and it was followed the next year by a text by W. F. Willoughby. A growing number and variety of books and reports had been produced in more specialized fields, such as budgeting, personnel, public works, and planning. For the most part, they were all *simpatico* in their

1. Basic exerpts from the *Report* are reproduced in Mosher, *Basic Documents of American Public Administration,* pp. 110–138.

2. The majority of the papers dealt primarily with management of private business; almost half of them were by British and French authors, the remainder by Americans.

3. Mary Parker Follett, "The Process of Control"; and L. J. Henderson, T. N. Whitehead, and Elton Mayo, "The Effects of Social Environment," which was a summary of lessons from the Hawthorne studies. Both Follett and the Hawthorne studies are discussed in Part IV.

premises and approaches. In the fifty years after Woodrow Wilson had published his famous essay (see Part II) public administration had come of age. A number of professional associations of public officials in various fields—city management, state administration, social welfare, public works, city planning, police, municipal finance, and others—had been formed and their various headquarters moved under one roof at 1313 East Sixtieth Street in Chicago. In 1939, an integrating organization of officials and students in the field, the American Society for Public Administration, was established.

It should not be construed, however, that all was peace and unity during the 1930s or before or after that era. The Brownlow *Report* itself and the Roosevelt proposals that grew out of it became a bitter battleground between president and Congress, within Congress, among the general public, and even within the public administration fraternity itself. The depression and the New Deal brought an explosion of governmental responsibilities in the economy and the society, and a virtual revolution in the relationship of the federal government with the states and local units, all accompanied by vigorous disdisagreement and debate. Further, public administration was little geared to problems of national security and the preparation for and later the conduct of war, which would soon override virtually all other concerns.

The New Deal sharpened some of the issues in the administrative realm which had never been really settled: the role of the administration in relation to the chief executive and the legislature; its responsibilities in connection with policy making and with politics; specialism vs. generalism; the neutrality of the civil service; the nature of administrative responsibility; the degree to which there is or can be a science of administration, applicable to both public and private sectors.

The articles that follow, published between 1919 and 1941, represent both sides: the orthodox public administration (as expounded by White, the Commission of Inquiry on Public Service Personnel, Mosher and Kingsley, Gulick, and Beard); and some of the dissenters and questioners (Willoughby, Keynes, Barnard, and Key).

W. F. Willoughby (1867–1960)

A major issue among students of American government during the 1920s and 1930s concerned the relationship of administration with the executive and legislative powers respectively. One school of thought identified executive and administrative as virtually synonymous terms embodying the execution of the laws. It held that the chief executive should direct and be responsible for the carrying out of the will of the government as determined through the legislative process. An opposing school held that administration was essentially a fourth branch of government and that power over it rested in the legislative body. This opinion distinguished between the presidential power to "take care that the laws be faithfully executed" (Article II, Section 4, of the U.S. Constitution) and the actual execution of them, which, it held, is legally under the direction of the Congress. Protagonists of the second view did not preclude Congressional delegation of some or even most of those directive powers to the president so that, in practice, the two opposing positions might constitute a distinction without much operational difference.

In historical perspective, it appears that the executive-administrative proponents prevailed, especially following the heated arguments attending President Roosevelt's reorganization proposals in the late 1930s. But the issue is not dead and over the years has cropped up on a number of fronts: for example, the executive powers of the Comptroller General; presidential impoundments; the Congressional budget; legislative vetoes, to name a few. It is probably still true that a good many federal administrators wonder whether they are really working for the president and his executive office or for Congress and its various committees.

The principal professional advocate of the legislative-administrative connection was undoubtedly W. F. Willoughby, one of the outstanding scholars of public administration and government generally during approximately the first forty years of this century. Willoughby served on President Taft's Commission on Economy and Efficiency. In 1916, he became the first director of the Institute for Government Research which later, in 1927, became a core of the Brookings Institution. He was a principal author of the Budget and Accounting Act of 1921. He wrote a number of authoritative books, including the second general text on public administration, *Principles of Public Administration* (Brookings Institution, 1927), and wrote and edited countless monographs on various aspects of American government. The excerpt that follows is drawn from one of his earlier works, in which he sets forth his concept of the role and responsibility of public administration in relation to the executive and legislature, a theme he repeated and expanded upon in a number of his later works.

F.C.M.

The Government of Modern States

The Distribution of Governmental Powers Functionally

The splitting up of the territory of a State into political divisions and the distribution of governmental powers among such divisions constitutes but one method by which provision may be made for the effective exercise of these powers. The work that has to be done by a government is so complex that it is imperative that special organs shall be established for the performance of the several kinds of work to be done. This is necessary, not only that the benefits of specialization may be secured, but that responsibility may be more definitely located. It follows, therefore, that all governments must seek to determine the classes into which governmental powers fall, viewed from the standpoint of their character, and the provision that shall be made for the exercise of each. . . .

The Classification of Governmental Powers. In seeking to classify any body of data the first essential is the adoption of the principle or basis upon which such classification shall be made. In making a selection of a principle it is furthermore desirable that the choice should fall upon some characteristic which is at once fundamental rather than incidental, and will serve to bring out distinctions which will best serve the objects in view. In the present case no doubt exists regarding the principle that should be employed. A distinguishing feature of the modern government in its practical operations is that it is one of law. Every feature of its organization is a matter of legal determination, and every one of its acts, in order to possess validity, must rest upon a legal sanction. The practical problem of organizing and conducting a government is thus one of legal action. It resolves itself into the problem of determining how the law of the land, and particularly that part having to do with the operations of government, shall be declared, how differences of opinion regarding its meaning or applicability to particular cases shall be decided, and how the law as thus declared and interpreted shall be put into effect. The principle upon which governmental powers shall be classified functionally is thus universally recognized as that of the nature of the power exercised as determined by its relation to law.

The Traditional Threefold Classification of Governmental Powers into Legislative, Judicial, and Executive. Based upon this principle of classification, all the powers of government have long been conceived as falling within one or the other of three great classes, according as they have to do with: (1) the determination or enactment of law; (2) the interpretation of this law; and (3) its

Chapters 11 and 16, *The Government of Modern States* (New York: Century, 1919), pp. 227–233 and 385–390.

enforcement. To these three classes have been given the names, legislative, judicial, and executive. Structurally considered, government has thus been deemed to be made up of three great branches having for their functions the enactment, the adjudication and the enforcement of law.

A More Satisfactory Classification: That of a Fivefold Division of Powers into: Electoral, Legislative, Judicial, Executive, and Administrative. Notwithstanding the fact that this threefold division of governmental powers has received such general recognition as to give it the designation of the classical division of governmental powers, examination will show that it cannot stand the test of scientific analysis, and, furthermore, that attempts to act upon it not only lead to confusion of thought, but to serious difficulties in working out the practical problems of the distribution of governmental powers functionally. The defect in this system of classification lies in the fact that it fails to distinguish and make separate provision for the functions of electoral action and administration.

Administration as a Distinct Branch of Government. In the threefold classification of governmental powers no recognition is given to Administration as a separate function or branch of government. In so far as any account at all is taken of this function in that classification, it is confused with, and treated as a part of, the executive function. To so great an extent is this true that the two terms "executive" and "administrative" are used almost interchangeably. This is exceedingly unfortunate since, as we shall see, the two terms should be employed as connoting operations which are distinct in character.

To understand the difference between the two, when properly employed, it is necessary to distinguish between two things. The first of these is the difference between the function of seeing that laws are enforced and that of actually doing the things which the laws call for. This distinction is specially apparent where the actual exercise of authority is distributed among a number of organs or parts. Where this is the case it is evident that there must be some authority whose special function it is to see that the laws governing this distribution, determining the special duties of the several parts, and regulating the relations of the latter with each other are in fact complied with. Without some such authority the several parts cannot be correlated into a single harmonious system and made to work in proper cooperation with each other for the attainment of a common end.

The second distinction is that between the act of an organization as a whole, and that of one of its parts. There are many cases where governmental action should represent the action of the government as a unit. This applies especially to the whole field of international relations in which is involved the intercourse of sovereign States with each other. This makes it imperative that there shall be some organ or authority whose special function it is to represent the government in this capacity.

With these distinctions and requirements in mind, the essential difference that exists between the executive and the administrative function, using these terms in their proper technical sense, can be seen. The executive function is the function of representing the government as a whole, and of seeing that all of its laws are complied with by its several parts. The administrative function is the function of actually administering the law as declared by the legislative and interpreted by the judicial branches of the government. This distinction is usually made by declaring the executive function to be essentially political in character; that is, one having to do with the determination of general policies, and involving the exercise of judgment in its use; and the administrative function to be one concerned with the putting into effect of policies as determined by other organs.

The Administrative Branch

The last of the grand divisions into which government may be divided is that known as the administrative. This is the branch which has as its function the actual putting into execution of the policies adopted by the government. In studying this branch it is desirable again to describe its precise position in the general scheme of government and certain characteristics of its work, even though this may involve a measure of repetition of what has already been given.

Non-Political Character of the Administrative Branch. In our consideration of the distribution of governmental powers functionally, we have pointed out the essential difference between the executive and the administrative functions. The former is distinctly of a political character. It involves the making of far-reaching decisions in respect to governmental policies. In respect to the actual conduct of governmental affairs it has to do with seeing that policies that are adopted, or lines of action that are decided upon, are properly carried into effect rather than in undertaking the work proper of putting these policies and programs into execution. Or, to use the expression employed in our constitution, it consists in seeing that the laws are duly enforced, not in doing the work involved in enforcing such laws. The latter function, the administrative, on the other hand, strictly speaking involves the making of no decisions of a political character. Its participation in the making of such decisions is, or should be, merely that of furnishing to the policy-determining organs of government, the legislative and the executive, the facts which should be taken into account by those organs in reaching their decisions. Apart from this the duties of the administrative branch should consist solely in the execution of orders. In doing so political considerations should have no weight other than that the work ordered should be done in such a manner as to put into execution the policies decided upon.

The distinction here made is important in any form of government. It is especially so in a Popular Government where the people are divided into political parties. No greater abuse in government can take place than that of the administrative branch of government using its powers to promote the interests of any particular political party. Unfortunately, this is a principle which is only too often violated. . . .

Distinction Between the Function of Direction, Supervision, and Control and That of Execution. If the work involved in the administration of any service or enterprise is subjected to analysis certain important distinctions appear. The first of these is that between the function of direction, supervision, and control, on the one hand, and execution on the other. In small undertakings, and especially in ones managed directly by the owner of the enterprise, this distinction may not be of significance. In those cases it is feasible for the same person to exercise both functions, and the fact that the second must be performed in subordination to the first is lost sight of. In all large undertakings, and especially in those such as modern governments, comprehending the prosecution of varied lines of activities, the distinction is one of prime importance. Not only are the two functions to be clearly distinguished but, for the most part, their performance must be vested in separate hands. One organ should have responsibility for directing what work shall be undertaken, for determining the general conditions under which the work shall be done, for providing the funds required for its execution, and for currently exercising that general supervision and control that is required in order that assurance may be had that orders given are properly and efficiently carried out. Other organs should have the responsibility for the actual performance of the work so determined upon.

This distinction is one which, as we have pointed out in our consideration of the legislative branch of government, is clearly made in the goverment of the United States. As is there shown, the whole power of direction, supervision, and control of administrative affairs legally is vested in Congress. The executive departments and other administrative services are mere agencies of that body for the carrying out of its orders. A thorough comprehension of this fact is the first essential in understanding the true character of the administrative branch of our government. This is all the more necessary since in popular estimation, and, to a considerable extent, in appearance, the President seems to occupy this position. There can be no question regarding the great powers of direction, supervision, and control of the President over the administrative work of the government. These powers, however, are primarily exercised by him but as an agent of Congress, which as a matter of expediency has conferred them upon him. They are, moreover, greatly strengthened by three facts: (1) that the President, as chief executive, has the duty of seeing that all laws are duly enforced; (2) that to a large extent the power of appointing and removing administrative officers is vested in his hands; and, (3) that the position is now generally held by all parties, administrative officers, the public, and Congress itself, that the President should in a way be looked upon as the head of the administration. In taking this position, however, sight should never be lost of the fact that the real seat of administrative authority is in Congress and not in the President. The distinction is that between the position and powers of a board of directors and a president in an ordinary corporation.

Congress as a Board of Directors. Having drawn this distinction between the function of direction, supervision, and control and that of execution, it is evident that the problem is presented in the case of each of devising the means through which it may be effectively performed. In respect to the first but a few words will be required to make known the character of this problem.

The work of direction is performed by the process of legislation. The problem of organization and procedure in its performance is thus practically the same as that for the performance of the function of legislation properly speaking, and need not therefore be specially considered here. Mention, however, should be made of the fact that Congress, in common with most legislative bodies, has devised a system of committee organization and procedure with a view almost solely to the exercise of its law-making function. Only to a comparatively slight extent has it organized and formulated rules of procedure with special reference to the performance of its function as a board of directors. The result is that its organization and methods of procedure are not well adapted for the performance of this function. Especially is its whole committee system and procedure governing the consideration of appropriation bills which constitute the main means of giving administrative directions defective. Involved in this question is the great problem of budgetary procedure. This, however, is so technical a problem that it is impossible for us to undertake its consideration.

When a board of directors has given orders as to what shall be done it has discharged but one phase of its responsibilities. It is incumbent upon it to provide means by which it may insure that its orders are in fact carried out; in other words, means by which it may effectively exercise its function of supervision and control. The means available for this purpose consist in the requirement that its executing agents, the administrative services, shall keep accurate records of all their acts and financial operations; that at stated intervals, or whenever called upon, they shall submit to it detailed reports setting forth their transactions in such form that their character and purport may be readily understood; that it shall provide itself with an agency by which these accounts and reports may be critically examined; and, finally, that it shall make provision for itself considering the facts so brought to its attention, to the end that it may take such corrective action as the facts shown may warrant. All modern governments meet these requirements to a greater or less extent. Administrative departments are required to keep records and accounts and to submit reports. These accounts are subject to a critical examination made by an officer known as Auditor or Comptroller. And the facts thus rendered available are given consideration by the legislature. In few cases, however, have the technical problems involved in establishing a proper system of accounts and reports, and in providing for their audit, been satisfactorily worked out. Especially is this true of the United States Government, and most of our state and municipal governments. Nor have governments very generally evolved satisfactory means for considering such facts as are brought out by these documents. The result is that legislative bodies very generally fail to exercise that supervision and control over the conduct of administrative affairs that is essential if efficient and economical administration is to be had. It is desired to emphasize this point, since responsibility for bad administration is too often placed upon the executing agencies. That a large measure of responsibility falls upon them is undoubted. On the other hand, it is of great importance to recognize that primarily the responsibility rests upon the directing authority which has failed to perform properly its function of giving the direction in the proper form, of seeing that records and reports are kept and made in proper form, and of exercising in a proper way its function of supervision and control.

Leonard D. White (1891–1958)

In the years immediately following World War I, there was a flurry of articles, monographs, and a few books dealing with public administration. But the first full-fledged textbook was Leonard D. White's *Introduction to the Study of Public Administration*, published in 1926. White was then, and for many years after, a professor of political science at the University of Chicago. In the 1930s White, as a member of the United States Civil Service Commission, was a major innovator of federal personnel developments. But he is probably best remembered for his research and writing in public administration. His scholarly work spanned more than three decades and included, in addition to a number of revisions of his original text, by far the most thorough history of public administration, beginning with George Washington and carrying through to 1901.[1]

The passages that follow are drawn from the introductory chapter of the first edition of White's text, in which he defines and describes the field of public administration as he perceived it in 1926. Readers more than a half century later will probably be surprised at the similarities between White's observations and those of writers in the 1970s: for example, the emphasis upon science and technology, the management of resources, the comparisons and contrasts with business. They may also be surprised at his mention

---

1. The history appeared in four volumes, *The Federalists, The Jeffersonians, The Jacksonians,* and *The Republicans.*

of "muddling through," an expression which would many years later be made famous (or notorious) through the writings of another scholar.[2]

F.C.M.

Introduction to the Study of Public Administration

Administration and the Modern State

1. The Scope and Nature of Public Administration

There is an essential unity in the process of administration, whether it be observed in city, state, or federal governments, that precludes a "stratified" classification of the subject. To treat it in terms of municipal administration, state administration, or national administration, is to imply a distinction that in reality does not exist. The fundamental problems such as the development of personal initiative, the assurance of individual competence and integrity, responsibility, coordination, fiscal supervision, leadership, morale are in fact the same; and most of the subjects of administration defy the political boundaries of local and state government. Health administration, the licensing of medical practitioners, the control of trade, the reclamation of waste lands, have little fact relation to cities or counties or states as such. Nor do the respective phases of city, state, or federal government present any significant variation in the technique of their administration. At the outset, therefore, it seems important to insist that the administrative process is a unit, and to conceive it not as municipal administration, or state administration, or federal administration, but as a process common to all levels of government.

• Public administration is the management of men and materials in the accomplishment of the purposes of the state. This definition emphasizes the managerial phase of administration and minimizes its legalistic and formal aspect. It relates the conduct of government business to the conduct of the affairs of any other social organization, commercial, philanthropic, religious, or educational, in all of which good management is recognized as an element essential to success. It leaves open the question to what extent the administration itself participates in formulating the purposes of the state, and avoids any controversy as to the precise nature of administrative action.

• The objective of public administration is the most efficient utilization of

2.   Charles E. Lindblom, "The Science of 'Muddling Through' " (*Public Administration Review*, Spring 1959), pp. 79–88.

the resources at the disposal of officials and employees. These resources include not only current appropriations and material equipment in the form of public buildings, machinery, highways and canals, but also the human resources bound up in the hundreds of thousands of men and women who work for the state. In every direction good administration seeks for elimination of waste, the conservation of material and energy, and the most rapid and complete achievement of public purposes consistent with economy and the welfare of the workers.

• Public administration is, then, the execution of the public business; the goal of administrative activity the most expeditious, economical, and complete achievement of public programs. This obviously is not the sole objective of the state as an organized unit; the protection of private rights, the development of civic capacity and sense of civic responsibility, the due recognition of the manifold phases of public opinion, the maintenance of order, the provision of a national minimum of welfare, all bespeak the constant solicitude of the state. Administration must be correlated with other branches of government, as well as adjusted to the immense amount of private effort which in America far more than elsewhere supplements public enterprise. The following chapter deals with these adjustments, but here it is desirable to differentiate the adjacent fields of administration and administrative law.

It is said that "administrative law is that part of the public law which fixes the organization and determines the competence of the administrative authorities, and indicates to the individual remedies for the violation of his rights." This definition rightly indicates that the subject matter belongs to the field of law, and points to its major objective, the protection of private rights. The objective of public administration is the efficient conduct of public business.

These two goals are not only different, but may at times conflict. Administration is of course bound by the rules of administrative law, as well as by the prescriptions of constitutional law; but within the boundaries thus set, it seeks the most effective accomplishment of public purposes. . . .

Students of government are familiar with the traditional division of governmental activities into the legislative, executive, and judicial. It is important to understand that the work of the administration involves all three types of activity, although a strict application of the theory of separation of power would seem to confine it to "executive" business. After pointing out that the administrative commission exercises an authority which is in part executive, in part legislative, and in part judicial. Croly asserts "it is simply a means of consolidating the divided activities of government for certain practical social purposes," and proceeds to give a reasoned defense of this fusion of powers. Administration more and more tends, in fact, to reach into the established fields of legislation and adjudication, raising important problems which will be the subject of study in later chapters.

Students of public affairs are gradually discerning, in fact, that administration has become the heart of the modern problem of government. In an earlier and simpler age, legislative bodies had the time to deal with the major issues, the character of which was suited to the deliberations of the lay mind; they were primarily problems involving judgments on important questions of political ethics, such as the enfranchisement of citizens by abolishing property qualifications, the disposition of the public land, the disestablishment of the Anglican Church, or the liberalization of a monarchist state. The problems which crowd upon legislative bodies today are often entangled with, or become exclusively technical questions which the layman can handle only by utilizing the services of the expert. The control of local government, the regulation of utilities, the enforcement of the prohibition amendment, the appropriation for a navy, the organization of a health department, the maintenance of a national service of agricultural research, are all matters which can be put upon the statute book only with the assistance of men who know the operating details in each case. So we discover in the administrative service one official who knows all that can be known about the control of water-borne diseases, another who has at his finger-tips the substance of all available information on wheat rust, and another who cannot be "stumped" on appropriations for the national park service. These men are not merely useful to legislators overwhelmed by the increasing flood of bills; they are simply indispensable. They are the government. One may indeed suggest that the traditional assignment of the legislature as the pivotal agency in the governmental triumvirate is destined at no distant date to be replaced by a more realistic analysis which will establish government as the task of administration, operating within such areas as may be circumscribed by legislatures and courts.

2. The Emergence of Administration

It is from Great Britain of course that the United States derived its administrative institutions. Our local governments were patterned after the English model in the seventeenth century. Decentralized, self-governmental, dominated by the "squirearchy," they proved to be readily adaptable to the economic and social conditions of the New World. Even today the main lines of our administrative structure are profoundly influenced by their English origin; nowhere in the American commonwealths can be found the prototype of the continental intendant or his successor, the prefect.

But the modern social and economic environment in which administration operates, and the insistent demand for a greater and greater degree of state intervention are destined to force the issue whether a modern industrial, interventionist state can possibly operate on the restricted base of voluntary and substantially amateur effort which characterizes our administrative inheritance. The problems with which officials must grapple are now so varied in scope, so technical in character, so insistent for solution that it hardly seems possible that the state can hold its own except by adopting at least some of the essentials of bureaucratic administration. Is it not now imperative for democratic states to derive the advantage of a civil service characterized by permanence of tenure, special training for official position, professional interest on the part of the public official, undivided loyalty to the interests of the state? No one will understand that this suggestion is in favor of autocratic as contrasted with democratic institutions. But democracies can fruitfully borrow from more highly organized administrative systems those elements which can be properly adapted to their fundamental political institutions in order to make more effective the achievement of their own purposes and programs.

The fact is that the role of administration in the modern state is profoundly affected by the general political and cultural environment of the age. The *laissez faire* school of social philosophy, demanding the restriction of state activities to the bare minimum of external protection and police, created a situation in which administration was restricted in scope and feeble in operation. Officialdom was thought a necessary evil, bureaucracy an ever-present danger. On the continent irresponsible governments, able within large limits to defy the wishes of the people, and themselves often without programs of social betterment, contributed powerfully to the philosophic argument in favor of non-intervention by the state.

The industrial revolution and its many social, economic, and political implications are fundamentally responsible for the new social philosophy and the new concept of public administration. *Laissez faire* has been abandoned by philosophers and statesmen alike, and a new era of collective activity has been ushered in by the twentieth century. The expansion of industry on a national and international scale, the growth of transportation by railroad, motor truck, and airplane, the transformation of communication by modern postal systems, the press, the telegraph, telephone, wireless, and radio, the enormously increasing mobility of persons and ideas, the urbanization of industrial states and the crystallization of powerful social classes and economic interests have not only increased the area and intensity of administrative activity, but also have added new types of problems and magnified the importance and difficulty of the old.

The industrial revolution has necessitated, in short, a degree of social cooperation in which *laissez faire* has become impossible; and gradually the new environment is building up in men's minds a conception of the role of the state which approximates the function assigned it by the conditions of modern life. These new ideas involve the acceptance of the state as a great agency of social cooperation, as well as an agency of social regulation. The state becomes therefore an important means by which the program of social amelioration is effected. "The power of the civil service is increasing," writes an English scholar, "for the state has given up its old role of acting, in

Lassalle's phrase, as nightwatchman, as a mere dispenser of justice in the strictest sense of the word. Today it acts on the theory that the good of the individual and of society may be discovered by the processes of social reason and action, and be implemented through statutes."

The enlarging positive program of the state does not imply by any means a corresponding diminution of its repressive and regulative activities. The struggle of classes over the distribution of the social surplus has led to the intervention of the state on behalf of the economically weak (children, women, laboring classes) by insistence on minimum wage, limited hours of labor, and healthful working conditions; the persistence of various groups of "reformers" has brought about prohibitions and regulations of diverse kinds (sale of cigarettes, narcotics, alcohol, censorship of motion pictures); the need for guaranteeing so far as possible the integrity of the processes of self-government has led to the regulation of elections and political parties, and the elaboration of such repressive legislation as corrupt practice acts.

In every direction, therefore, the task of the modern state is enlarging. In every direction likewise the range of public administration is being extended, for every phase of the new program of the state is reflected in additional administrative activity.

For these reasons it is not surprising that in the last two decades increasing attention has been given to the business side of government. The remarkable thing is that for over a hundred years of our national existence, the only phase of administration to emerge in the arena of national issues was the spoils system.

The World War brought into vivid contrast the administrative methods of democratic and autocratic governments, and gave rise to sharp criticisms of the time-honored plan of "muddling through." At an early date the war was declared to be one between democracy and autocracy, but at a later date there was general agreement that democracy had been forced to adopt the administrative methods of autocracy to gain its end. . . .

On a less dramatic scale, international competition in trade and industry continues to sharpen the demand for efficiency in government. The United States Chamber of Commerce has taken an active interest in greater efficiency "because as business men they already believed in efficiency and economy and wanted to see it applied to the municipal, state, and national governments; because they realized that efficient and economical government was a prime requisite for prosperity and business success; and because as good citizens, they desired to see an honest, sound, and intelligent administration."

The scientific management movement has had a very important share in stimulating improvement in the methods of carrying on public business.

Commencing with the pioneer work of Frederick W. Taylor, the movement has developed constantly widening interests, and has eventually built up the outlines of a whole philosophy of social betterment on the basis of scientific control of the productive process.

The enormous improvements which have been made by scientific management in some industries have raised the question whether or not equally striking improvements are feasible in government. Whatever answer be given to this question, there can be no doubt that the achievements of scientific management have aroused a vast amount of dissatisfaction with antiquated methods which have characterized many public offices. More and more clearly it is being understood that the promise of American life will never be realized until American administration has been lifted out of the ruts in which it has been left by a century of neglect.

3. Science and Administration

In an earlier paragraph it was suggested that what differentiates the civil servant of antiquity from his twentieth century successor is the remarkable improvement of the equipment with which he works. The unexampled development of science and technology in the last half century has transformed not only the equipment but the tasks of administration as well. Science has revealed the objects to be achieved and also furnished the tools with which the state operates. Could one make a careful comparison of the actual work performed and methods used by an American commonwealth or municipality in 1825 with its work and methods in 1925, the contrast would be startling.

To what extent the modern state now depends upon science is not easily described, for the whole technical equipment of present-day administration rests upon scientific achievement. More than that, the modern administrator has in many cases become not only a scientist, but a research scientist. Few of the major tasks of modern administration can be carried on without the constant support of the technician; education, sanitation, construction (highways, reclamation, public buildings), regulation, conservation, public welfare administration, criminology, the management of funds, the management of personnel, control of the administrative process, all these and many more demand the services of the specialist and of his unique body of knowledge.

Science is making a vast contribution to the daily administrative task of the government, a fact of fundamental import to modern society. Before developing its significance, however, attention should be turned to a new contribution of science which has already been hailed by some as "the science of administration." That is, science is not only furnishing the tools with which administration works, it is transforming the methods of administration (in the sense of management) from rule of thumb empiricism to ascertained principle. Here it is that scientific management has been the leader. The search for the "one best way" of doing things has led to a constantly developing technique of research and a constantly greater refinement of method.

Although we are entitled to certain reserve in the use of the phrase "the science of management," we are wholly justified in asserting that a science of management appears to be immediately before us. In some respects indeed it is now fairly well established. By way of illustration the "standardized test" procedure may serve. Questions are developed to test the specific qualities established as essential for a given position. These questions are then given to persons whose competence is known, and a correlation established between the ranking obtained by the test and by the independent rating. In another direction the measurement of efficiency has produced certain interesting and significant procedures which have some claim to the term scientific. Mechanical problems connected with routing, equipment, ventilation, lighting, and the like have been dealt with on a strictly scientific basis. We may suppose that eventually more subtle and complicated problems will be attacked with the aid of scientific methods.

The growth of science and technology and their application to the business side of government has already created a new environment in which old theories need to be readjusted. It is manifestly impossible in an age when public administration depends upon the slide-rule, the clinical thermometer, the test tube, and higher mathematics, to continue on the Jacksonian notion that "the duties of all public officers are, or at least admit of being made, so plain and simple that men of intelligence may readily qualify themselves for their performance." The duties of public office are complicated, highly specialized, professional, and immensely important. They can be adequately performed only by permanent officials, with suitable professional and technical training, acting upon the direction of department heads of the broadest vision who are able by their personal leadership to mediate between the technician, the politician, and the public.

The impact of science upon administration raises many important questions. Among these is the most effective organization of the scientific personnel. Obviously something may be gained and something may be lost by attempting to segregate the function of research and scientific endeavor in the realm of administration.

Of equal importance is the provision of a working environment and an employment situation which will enable the government to secure and retain competent professional employees. Shall a scientist be entitled to patent a discovery made directly or indirectly in connection with his employment by the government? Shall the scientist be free to publish his results under his own name, or must he remain anonymous? Should the scientist receive the equivalent of the academic sabbatical leave in order to freshen his own interests? To what extent should his work and expenditures be under supervision of non-scientific fiscal agents? These questions and many others can be asked more easily than they can be answered.

4. Public and Non-Official Administration

The antecedents of American public administration are profoundly different from those of American business. For over a half century the spoils system held undisputed sway in government affairs, and for a century its influence has been great. The gigantic struggle to loosen the grip of the politician has inevitably left its marks upon the body of the civil service. Many of the conditions which seem to lessen the efficiency of government offices are the product of the legal protection evolved to guarantee even a moderate level of efficiency and integrity. These cannot be relaxed to any considerable degree without encouraging an immediate return to the evils of an age now happily waning. But in the city-manager cities can be observed the relaxation of legal safeguards as they are replaced by a new ideal of the public service.

Business has not been scarred by a similar struggle to free itself from incompetence, although it has had other almost equally difficult conditions to meet. Business, too, has been more strongly armed, for the incentive of profit and the spur of competition have compelled constant improvement. Profits also furnished business an intelligible test of success, but they are of no help whatever in assessing the achievements of government. Government has not the profit incentive, either as a collectivity or viewed from the standpoint of the individual employee, nor is it deeply affected in America by any sort of competition, whereas in Europe international rivalry has done much to strengthen both the civil and military establishments. The sustaining incentives for high productivity in government must in fact be sought elsewhere, and the search constitutes at once the most delicate and the most important task of the student of administration.

Government is constrained to a rigid observance of the principle of consistency, which may be ignored by business. "Consistency means reasoned relation between decisions for one class of case and decisions for another class, wherever it is a question of degree."

The principle of consistency must be applied as between successive cases, over the whole of the area concerned, for the complete period of time involved.

But business (excluding public utilities), philanthropy, religion, endowed education, are under no such compulsion. A state university must throw open its resources to all qualified applicants alike, but a privately endowed institution may impose an arbitrary limit on the gross numbers, or draw racial lines, or vary its entrance requirements at will, so far as its governing authorities deem wise. The Federal Trade Commission is gradually building up certain standards of consistency in the conduct of business as it defines unfair practices, but business is still free to vary its service and prices in ways forbidden to government. A significant study could be made of the development of the principle of consistency in the business world.

Government affairs differ in another respect from private affairs; their conduct is subject to a degree of accountability which is far more minute and pervasive than business. Appropriation acts are much more specific and rigid than allotments of commercial funds; auditors are insistent upon exact compliance with the terms of the law; Congressmen are always alert to discover any violation of the statute book.

Public administration has also its vantage points. There is even in America a glamor surrounding some branches of the public service which attracts young men toward such work as the consular service, the railway mail service, the secret service force of the federal government, the public health service, the reclamation service. The complex urge toward a government job has never been analyzed and we can only surmise its elements. The opportunity to travel (played up by the marine corps and the navy in their campaign for recruits), the lure of a "government" job, the dignity and honor of the occupation, all probably play a part.

Public administration offers an opportunity for constructive leadership in America which is hardly paralleled in unofficial circles. The large scale of the operations, the variety of the tasks, their immediate relation to the commonweal, all strike the imagination through a combination of appeals which industry and commerce do not ordinarily achieve. The city manager is more than an engineer, and his profession as manager is likely to strike deeper than his profession as engineer.

The state need not attempt to compete with business on a financial basis for its administrative leadership. It needs as fine administrative capacity as business, but must attract it by means of other considerations. It must of course provide an adequate scale of salaries and proper provision for retirement, but it will hold its own in the competition with industry by capitalizing the prestige value which attaches to a "big" organization, to a "big" opportunity, and to the honor of public position. The state can and presumably will provide in constantly more generous measure a career which will call for and receive, so far as needed, the best brains of each decade.

John Maynard Keynes (1883-1946)

Among the most significant elements of the New Deal were certainly the direct and purposive involvement of the federal government in the society and its assumption of vastly increased responsibility for the health of the economy. These developments had and would later have growing impact upon the policies and the content of public administration.

Probably the principal intellectual contributor to this change was John Maynard Keynes, a British economist. Keynes turned the study of economics around and indirectly veered public administration in the direction of economic considerations. His influence on American government was neither direct nor immediate. It now seems doubtful that Keynesian theory and proposals much influenced Franklin D. Roosevelt's policies during the first phase of the New Deal. Roosevelt's ventures were pragmatic and experimental; they were not grounded in economic theory. Roosevelt never went nearly as far as Keynes recommended. But Keynes's ideas gave rise and support to American political leaders and economists who would later push for increasing governmental intervention in economic matters and would rationalize many of the programs that were begun during the New Deal and others that would follow in succeeding decades.

On December 30, 1933, less than nine months after Roosevelt's first inauguration, Keynes wrote an open letter to the president that was published in its entirety in the *New York Times*. It urged, among other things, an aggressive program of public works and deficit financing. The following year, Keynes visited Roosevelt and, it is assumed, further pressed his views on the president. In 1936 his major book, *The General Theory of Employment, Interest, and Money* was published. And in 1938, he wrote another open letter to the president with specific reference to the slump that the United States was enduring that year.

Excerpted below are the major paragraphs of Keynes's first letter to Roosevelt in 1933 that symbolized and probably stimulated the enormous growth of influence of economic considerations upon public policy and administration, which would follow in succeeding years and decades.

F.C.M.

From Keynes to Roosevelt: Our Recovery Plan Assayed

The British Economist Writes an Open Letter to the President Finding Reasons, in Our Policies, for Both Hopes and Fears

London, Dec. 30, 1933

Dear Mr. President:

You have made yourself the trustee for those in every country who seek to mend the evils of our condition by reasoned experiment within the framework of the existing social system.

If you fail, rational change will be gravely prejudiced throughout the world, leaving orthodoxy and revolution to fight it out.

But if you succeed, new and bolder methods will be tried everywhere, and we may date the first chapter of the new economic era from your accession to office.

This is a sufficient reason why I should venture to lay my reflections before you, though under the disadvantages of distance and partial knowledge.

The Present Task

You are engaged on a double task, recovery and reform—recovery from the slump, and the passage of those business and social reforms which are long overdue. For the first, speed and quick results are essential. The second may be urgent, too: but haste will be injurious, and wisdom of long-range purpose is more necessary than immediate achievement. It will be through raising high the prestige of your administration by success in short-range recovery that you will have the driving force to accomplish long-range reform.

On the other hand, even wise and necessary reform may, in some respects, impede and complicate recovery. For it will upset the confidence of the business world and weaken its existing motives to action before you have had time to put other motives in their place. It may overtask your bureaucratic machine, which the traditional individualism of the United States and the old "spoils system" have left none too strong. And it will confuse the thought and aim of yourself and your administration by giving you too much to think about all at once.

NRA Aims and Results

Now I am not clear, looking back over the last nine months, that the order of urgency between measures of recovery and measures of reform has been

New York Times, December 31, 1933. Reprinted by permission of North American Newspaper Alliance.

duly observed, or that the latter has not sometimes been mistaken for the former. In particular, though its social gains are considerable, I cannot detect any material aid to recovery in the NRA. The driving force which has been put behind the vast administrative task set by this act has seemed to represent a wrong choice in the order of urgencies. The act is on the statute book; a considerable amount has been done toward implementing it; but it might be better for the present to allow experience to accumulate before trying to force through all its details.

That is my first reflection—that NRA, which is essentially reform and probably impedes recovery, has been put across too hastily, in the false guise of being part of the technique of recovery.

My second reflection relates to the technique of recovery itself. The object of recovery is to increase the national output and put more men to work. In the economic system of the modern world, output is primarily produced for sale; and the volume of output depends on the amount of purchasing power, compared with the prime cost of production, which is expected to come on the market.

Broadly speaking, therefore, an increase of output cannot occur unless by the operation of one or other of three factors. Individuals must be induced to spend more out of their existing incomes, or the business world must be induced, either by increased confidence in the prospects or by a lower rate of interest, to create additional current incomes in the hands of their employees, which is what happens when either the working or the fixed capital of the country is being increased; or public authority must be called in aid to create additional current incomes through the expenditure of borrowed or printed money.

In bad times the first factor cannot be expected to work on a sufficient scale. The second factor will only come in as the second wave of attack on the slump, after the tide has been turned by the expenditures of public authority. It is therefore, only from the third factor that we can expect the initial major impulse.

Now there are indications that two technical fallacies may have affected the policy of your administration. The first relates to the part played in recovery by rising prices. Rising prices are to be welcomed because they are usually a symptom of rising output and employment. When more purchasing power is spent, one expects rising output at rising prices. Since there cannot be rising output without rising prices, it is essential to insure that the recovery shall not be held back by the insufficiency of the supply of money to support the increased monetary turnover.

The Problem of Rising Prices

But there is much less to be said in favor of rising prices if they are brought about at the expense of rising output. Some debtors may be helped, but the national recovery as a whole will be retarded. Thus rising prices caused by deliberately increasing prime costs or by restricting output have a vastly inferior value to rising prices which are the natural result of an increase in the nation's purchasing power.

I do not mean to impugn the social justice and social expedience of the redistribution of incomes aimed at by the NRA and by the various schemes for agricultural restriction. The latter, in particular, I should strongly support in principle. But too much emphasis on the remedial value of a higher price-level as an object in itself may lead to serious misapprehension of the part prices can play in the technique of recovery. The stimulation of output by increasing aggregate purchasing power is the right way to get prices up; and not the other way around.

Thus, as the prime mover in the first stage of the technique of recovery, I lay overwhelming emphasis on the increase of national purchasing power resulting from governmental expenditure which is financed by loans and is not merely a transfer through taxation, from existing incomes. Nothing else counts in comparison with this.

Boom, Slump and War

In a boom, inflation can be caused by allowing unlimited credit to support the excited enthusiasm of business speculators. But in a slump governmental loan expenditure is the only sure means of obtaining quickly a rising output at rising prices. That is why a war has always caused intense industrial activity. In the past, orthodox finance has required a war as the only legitimate excuse for creating employment by government expenditure. You, Mr. President, having cast off such fetters, are free to engage in the interests of peace and prosperity the technique which hitherto has only been allowed to serve the purposes of war and destruction.

The set-back American recovery experienced this past Autumn was the predictable consequence of the failure of your administration to organize any material increase in new loan expenditure during your first six months of office. The position six months hence will depend entirely on whether you have been laying the foundation for larger expenditures in the near future.

The Favored Policy

In the field of domestic policy, I put in the forefront, for the reasons given above, a large volume of loan expenditure under government auspices. It is beyond my province to choose particular objects of expenditure. But preference should be given to those which can be made to mature quickly on a large scale, as, for example, the rehabilitation of the physical condition of the railroads. The object is to start the ball rolling.

The United States is ready to roll toward prosperity, if a good hard shove can be given in the next six months. Could not the energy and enthusiasm which launched the NRA in its early days be put behind a campaign for accelerating capital expenditures, as wisely chosen as the pressure of circumstances permits? You can at least feel sure that the country will be better enriched by such projects than by the involuntary idleness of millions. With great respect,

❧ ❧ ❧

Your obedient servant,
J. M. KEYNES

Commission of Inquiry on Public Service Personnel (1935)

At the close of 1933, the Social Science Research Council designated a five-member Commission of Inquiry on Public Service Personnel to study, report on, and make recommendations about personnel at all levels of government. The Commission conducted one of the most extensive surveys in history of public personnel practices here and abroad. It included a variety of hearings in various American cities, research conducted by its own staff, and a series of studies prepared by recognized experts in the field. The products of its research were published as monographs in five separate volumes. The summary report of the Commission, including its recommendations, was issued in 1935 under the title *Better Government Personnel*.

Two members of the Commission were Louis Brownlow, then director of the Public Administration Clearing House, and Charles E. Merriam, then chairman of political science at the University of Chicago. The staff was headed by Luther Gulick, then director of the Institute of Public Administration. These three were appointed by President Roosevelt in 1936 as the President's Committee on Administrative Management. It is therefore not surprising that many of the recommendations of the commission's study were reflected in the Brownlow Committee's later report.

The passage that follows is the opening section of *Better Government Personnel*, which summarizes the recommendations of the Commission.

F. C. M.

Better Government Personnel

*Summary of Recommendations of the Commission of Inquiry
on Public Service Personnel*

We find that our governmental units, federal, state, and local, do not generally offer the more capable men and women a fair chance, in any way comparable with that offered by private business, industry, or the professions, for a lifetime of honorable work affording opportunity for advancement based on merit and accomplishment. The spoils system, the use of the public payroll for charity, undiscriminating criticism of public employees, and the failure to adjust our ideas, our governmental institutions, and our public personnel policies to the social and economic changes since the Civil War, are primarily responsible for this condition. The cure is not to be found in negative prohibitive legislation, but in positive constructive action.

We therefore recommend that the day-to-day administrative work of government be definitely made a career service. By this we mean that steps shall be taken to make public employment a worthwhile life work, with entrance to the service open and attractive to young men and women of capacity and character, and with opportunity of advancement through service and growth to posts of distinction and honor.

To this end we present two groups of recommendations which deal, first, with the broad aspects of the program, and second, with a number of specific measures for immediate action.

Outlines for a New American Public Personnel Program

General Recommendations

1. A Career Service System should be established in the various governmental units, federal, state, and local, through the enactment and execution of appropriate laws, or through the development of existing personnel or civil service administration.

2. There should be developed in each of the larger governmental units an agency for personnel administration, to render constructive personnel service instead of devoting its entire attention to the policing of appointments, as has been all too common under civil service. The personnel agency must have adequate powers, staff, and appropriations to maintain and develop the career service system and render personnel service to the operating departments and their responsible officers.

3. All positions involving any compensation or fees from the public

Better Government Personnel, Report of the Commission of Inquiry on Public Service Personnel (New York: McGraw-Hill, 1935), pp. 3–9.

treasury under any unit of government should be designated as falling in one or another of the following categories: (a) the political or major-policy determining group, which would include legislators, elected chief executives, appointed executives of the cabinet or subcabinet grade who are expected to share political responsibility with their chiefs, and in some cases the members of boards and commissions; and immediate private secretaries of such officials; (b) the judges, but not the court employees; (c) the military service; and (d) the general service.

4. The general service should be placed on a career basis through subdivision, first of all, into career services, not into many classes as has been the past American practice. We do not believe that the public service should first be minutely classified into pigeonholes, for which the civil service commission tries to find men who exactly fit each compartment, but rather that the service should be divided into ladders, for which young men are normally selected to start on the bottom rung. These ladders must rise from different points depending upon the kinds of service, and an opportunity must be provided for advance at different rates of speed and for transfer from one ladder to another.

5. The career service should extend to all the nonpolitical top positions, including many posts not now covered by civil service in most jurisdictions. The tops of the ladders would thus reach posts of real eminence and honor.

6. The major classification of the general public service should be along the following lines: first, the administrative service; second, the professional and technical service; third, the clerical service; fourth, the skilled and trades service; and fifth, the unskilled service.

7. With the establishment of these career services on the basis of competitive entrance, and advancement on merit, the salaries of the top positions should be materially advanced, and adequate retirement provisions should be made for each group.

8. Recruitment to each one of the career services should be articulated with the American educational system and with the average age levels of young men and women who have reached the stage of education and development fitting them for the lower grades of the various services.

9. Certification by accredited professional associations and by legally established professional bodies should be made a prerequisite for all professional and technical positions to which this procedure is applicable.

10. Probation must be developed and utilized as a most important part of the selection process, and not neglected as at present in practically all jurisdictions. A probationary period of service of not less than six months should elapse before an appointment becomes in any way permanent.

11. The vicious practice of evading the merit system through temporary appointments which are continued indefinitely must be prevented by stricter legislation and control.

12. The system of promotion is fundamental for the maintenance of a career service; it should therefore be a first duty of personnel officers, and of

general administrators as well, to develop contacts between superior officers and subordinates, to encourage training in the service, to maintain service records, and to facilitate transfers, particularly during the early stages of a man's career, so that every employee may have a chance to advance, so that men of special capacity may be discovered promptly, and so that the petrification of personnel in stagnant and forgotten places may be prevented.

13. Public employees should be given security against dismissal or demotion for trivial, personal, religious, racial, political, or other arbitrary or extraneous reasons. Legislation thus guaranteeing tenure should not be enacted except in conjunction with (a) a system of recruitment, appointment, and probation which will insure the appointment of thoroughly capable persons only; (b) periodic service records with a procedure for transfer, adjustment, and reduction in pay with reduction of service; (c) the pensioning of superannuated employees; and (d) an adequate administrative procedure for discipline or discharge from the service.

14. Those who devote their lives to the public service deserve an honorable pension when the time comes for them to step aside from the arduous duties of government work, and relinquish their posts to the oncoming group. A financially sound pension system, based on contributions by the public and the employee, should be established to cover every permanent position, with provision for the transfer of credits with the transfer of the employee from jurisdiction to jurisdiction.

15. Cooperation should be established between the federal personnel administration and the state and local administrations through such measures as the joint use of eligible lists, the joint preparation and conduct of examinations, and the development of technical studies.

16. In the states similar cooperation should be established as between the state and the local personnel agencies, and there should be developed, either by the state or by the leagues of local governments, central technical services available to the units of government which cannot maintain complete personnel agencies of their own. The larger local government agencies should also be empowered to render personnel service at cost on a contractual basis to nearby smaller units of government.

17. The short ballot which we have always had in the federal government should be adopted also in states and local units.

18. Uneconomic and unworkable small units of local government must be modernized through consolidation of boundaries and positions, the establishment of joint services, and the use of central technical assistance particularly in maintaining personnel. In order that there may be careers in local government service, with promotion from city to city or county to county, local residence requirements should be abolished.

19. Public personnel officers throughout the United States should through their national association undertake far more extensive research in the technical problems of personnel administration, wherever possible in cooperation with qualified specialists in private business and in the universities.

Specific Recommendations

1. The immediate repeal of all national, state, or local laws or ordinances, such as the federal "Four Year Law" adopted in 1820, setting a definite term of office for appointive administrative officials.

2. The inclusion of all postmasterships in the civil service system and their recruitment primarily by promotion.

3. The inclusion of federal deputy collectors of internal revenue and marshals in the classified service.

4. The extension of the federal civil service classification to include under the merit system such professional and skilled services of the regular departments as are now excepted.

5. The immediate extension of the federal civil service system to include as far as may be practicable the personnel of the existing federal emergency administrations, boards, and agencies.

6. The extension of the merit system under the supervision of the United States Civil Service Commission, wherever practicable, to the personnel of state and local government agencies receiving or expending federal funds, as a condition of the grant, with the power to utilize existing local civil service agencies which are able and willing to meet standards set by the United States Civil Service Commission.

7. The extension of classification and salary standardization to the federal services outside the District of Columbia.

8. The amendment of veteran preference laws so that they will adequately recognize the war service experience of veterans without conflicting with merit principles or the efficiency of the public service.

9. The immediate repeal of section 213 of the Economy Act of 1932, which requires the discharge of one member of a married couple when both are employed in the federal service.

10. The repeal or amendment of all general provisions prescribing residence requirements or geographic apportionment of appointments.

11. The immediate establishment or designation in every governmental department or agency of adequate size, whether federal, state, or local, of a personnel officer, who should in the larger departments be freed of all other responsibilities.

12. The increase of the appropriations for personnel administration and the Civil Service Commission in the federal government and in state and local governments where this is necessary for the adequate maintenance of the merit system, as a step toward the ultimate development of a career service.

William E. Mosher (1877–1945) and J. Donald Kingsley (1908–1972)

The first text in *Public Personnel Administration* was the book of that title by William E. Mosher and J. Donald Kingsley, published in 1936.[1] Mosher, who had begun his career as a scholar and professor of German literature, conducted a study of classification and pay in the federal service for the New York Bureau of Municipal Research, which contributed to the passage of the first federal classification act in 1923. He later became director of the New York Bureau's training school. When that school moved to Syracuse University in 1924, Mosher became the first director and later first dean of the Maxwell School of Citizenship and Public Affairs at Syracuse, a post he held until his death. Among other achievements, he was a cofounder and the first president of the American Society of Public Administration. Kingsley, an instructor at Antioch College when this book was written, later wrote a most provocative work on the British civil service, *Representative Bureaucracy* (Antioch Press, 1944). His career included a wide variety of academic, governmental, and foundation positions.

The concluding chapter of *Public Personnel Administration,* most of which is reproduced below, was chiefly a critique of the traditional amateur civil service commissions with suggestions as to how they should be changed or replaced. This topic was not directly addressed in the recommendations of the Commission of Inquiry on Public Service Personnel. But it became a major theme of the Brownlow Committee on Administrative Management, of personnel reorganizations of some states and cities in later years, and most recently of President Carter's civil service reforms of 1978.

F.C.M.

---

1. The book, frequently revised, remains standard fare in the study of public administration. After Mosher's death near the close of World War II, authorship was transferred to O. Glenn Stahl. The seventh edition was published in 1976.

Public Personnel Administration

General Conclusions

Although the most important functions of the supervisory, executive, and administrative staffs are personnel functions, it must be apparent that the various phases of personnel administration, if for no other reason than their technical character, call for a staff agency which will be devoted exclusively to handling either in an administrative or in an advisory capacity the various techniques involved. These range from examinations and training programs to suggestion systems and the leadership necessary for successful employee organizations.

Like other important staff agencies, the personnel agency must be closely associated with the administrative head and must continuously enjoy the prestige, the understanding, and support of his office. This is the justification for the establishment of the office of vice-president in charge of personnel in some of the largest organizations in the field of private enterprise. Like other vice-presidents, such an official has his seat at the council table and his appropriate vote when policies and changes in policies are under consideration because nearly all administrative policies impinge upon personnel in one way or another.

If this conception of the importance of personnel in administration is approved, there can be no doubt but that the typical civil service commission as the standard personnel agency in government has not proved adequate to the execution of those several functions which are appropriate to a personnel agency. The appointment of three or five commissioners whose primary qualification is that they shall represent the two major parties is not conducive to the upbuilding of the merit system and even less conducive to the introduction of progressive employment policies. Available records go to show that most commissioners are lacking in personnel experience which is a *sine qua non* for fruitful cooperation with operating heads. This partially explains the lack of sympathy and misunderstanding, if not real estrangement, between the commission and those responsible for getting out the work of government. It also explains the neglect of many of the duties that normally fall to the lot of the division of personnel.

This indictment must be qualified by a recognition of the ability and devotion of many commissioners who have served at one time or another and are now serving in various jurisdictions of the country. They have contributed materially to the advancement of the merit principle and in scattering instances have overcome the prejudices of operating officials toward the

From Chapter 28, *Public Personnel Administration,* revised edition by William E. Mosher and J. Donald Kingsley (New York: Harper and Brothers, 1936), pp. 549–553. Copyright 1936, 1941 by Harper & Row, Publishers, Inc.

division of authority inherent in the typical civil service law. But even such commissioners have been seriously handicapped by a chronic lack of funds necessary for the proper conduct of their office.

It has been consistently maintained throughout this work that the official personnel agency must become a "part of the works," must have an acknowledged place in the official family. As a staff agency it should become a part of the staff. This can be accomplished under the standard law by insisting that those appointed to the commission both believe in the merit principle and have some understanding and experience in the problems of management. A second and equally important requirement is that a representative of the commission should have his regularly assigned seat in the cabinet of the chief executive. If properly qualified he would soon win the respect and cooperation of his associates by virtue of his substantive contributions to the formation of policy, particularly as new policies affect the personnel.

Any such innovation will depend on the development of an enlightened public opinion. Up to the present the chief executive has been under little constraint in making appointments to the civil service commission. The public's attitude has been one of indifference. How otherwise can nominations of men and women totally inexperienced in personnel and management and even of political henchmen be explained? The character of the commissioners themselves goes far toward explaining both the general lack of confidence in civil service laws and the prevailing attitude of administrative heads that may be summed up in the phrase that the commission is a necessary evil.

The above suggestions are made in the thought that whether well- or ill-founded the public in many localities retains its confidence in the commission in its present form as a desirable protective device.

But if further amendments are in order it is proposed that the functions of the commission be redistributed in the following manner: (1) assign all administrative duties including that of rule-making to a single executive head employed on a full-time basis; and (2) constitute the commission as such as a judicial body for the handling of appeals and endow it with only advisory responsibility on other matters. As has already been pointed out there is sufficient precedent for this policy to warrant its adoption.

In the opinion of the authors, however, the above are but half-way measures. It is held first of all that the handling of personnel is so largely an administrative matter and so interwoven with every phase of operation that it should be assigned to a single competent individual who has his accepted place as a peer of other administrative heads. Like theirs his responsibility should be directly to the chief executive. The proposed personnel director should be a man of the highest standing and of proved competency, selected through an open competitive examination and appointed for a long term or for an indefinite period and removable only for cause and after an appropriate public hearing. Such an official should have an adequate staff which would undoubtedly result in much larger appropriations than are now available for the conduct of the civil service commission. In the larger jurisdictions, provision would be made for the more or less permanent assignment of members of the staff to the several departments. By this means administration of personnel would be dealt with on a uniform basis and in close cooperation with those in direct charge of the working force. Transfers, promotions, and demotions would be handled without regard to departmental lines so far as this might be dictated by the interests of those concerned.

In view of the conviction that employees' rights should be safeguarded, it is further proposed that the personnel office be supplemented by a judicial body for the handling of appeals. Such a body should preferably consist of representatives of the administrative staff, the rank and file of employees, and the personnel office. But, as was just suggested, the civil service commission might serve in this capacity until such time as it is replaced by a properly constituted administrative court.

The final proposal envisages the elimination of the commission. This recommendation has been carefully argued in the preceding pages. It was specially stressed that the bipartisan commission has been no guarantee of non-partisanship, that the commissions have been and can be packed, and above all else, that under ordinary circumstances the commission is more or less "on the outside looking in." Finally, it was emphasized that the chief contribution of the civil service reform movement was not the agency of administration so much as the recognition of the principle of merit in the form of competitive examinations given by a competent staff. This principle would be conserved in the proposed reorganization.

Hand in hand with the increased concentration and centralization of responsibility for personnel should go the elimination of the spoils policy as it affects the upper tier of executives and sub-executives, that is, below the level of strictly policy-determining officials. The incumbents of such positions in any large-scale organization determine its tone, its pace, and its progress. That they have been filled in so many jurisdictions by birds of passage unfamiliar with the characteristics of public administration constitutes one of the severest handicaps under which government has labored. Furthermore, unless such positions are open on a competitive basis to those already in the service, it means that the top rungs of the promotional ladder are cut off.

Without the above thoroughgoing and fundamental reorganization of personnel management, it is difficult to see how a public-career service can be developed and made attractive to the abler young people who must be recruited into the service of government if government is not to collapse of its own weight.

Finally, it may be pointed out that there is no single economy which will net such savings or promote such efficiency as may be realized through the feasible improvement of the quality of the public personnel. Government today has ceased being an incidental or second-rate business of the people of the United States. From the point of view of the essential character of the services performed, from the point of view of the percentage of the national income spent, the public business has become the foremost business enterprise of the country. . . . And so we would close with the conviction that the most important and fruitful reform challenging the American public is placing public personnel on a new level and securing for the public service men and women of capacities commensurate with the vast responsibilities now vested in modern government.

Luther Gulick (1892–   )

As noted earlier, President Franklin D. Roosevelt appointed Luther Gulick one of the three members of the Brownlow Committee on Administrative Management. Gulick already had a distinguished and varied experience in public administration at all levels of government. Prior to World War I, he had served on the staff of the New York Bureau of Municipal Research. Following that war, in which he served as an officer, he became director of the bureau and later president of the Institute of Public Administration. During the course of the work of the Brownlow Committee, and primarily for the use of the committee's staff, Gulick and L. Urwick, a distinguished British student of administration, brought together a number of articles, speeches, and monographs, some of which had not been published and almost none of which was readily available. These *Papers on the Science of Administration* were published by the Institute of Public Administration in 1937. Gulick himself prepared two of the eleven papers in the collection. The most significant of them was his "Notes on the Theory of Organization," which had initially been written as a memorandum for the Brownlow Committee. That memorandum, a substantial part of which is reprinted below, became near gospel for students of public administration. After World War II, it came under severe criticism by some of the younger scholars in the field, initially and notably Herbert A. Simon, who alleged that Gulick's principles of administration were mere proverbs (see Part IV). But most of Gulick's paper did not enunciate principles. It was directed primarily to describing and classifying different aspects of organization and administration and the advantages and disadvantages of various alternatives.

Gulick subsequently served as administrator (city administrator of New York from 1954 to 1956, for example), consultant, researcher, author, and professor (at Columbia). His thinking, his analyses, his ideas have consistently been incisive and forward-looking. If such a title is appropriate for anyone, Luther Gulick is the dean of public administration.

Notes on the Theory of Organization

Every large-scale or complicated enterprise requires many men to carry it forward. Wherever many men are thus working together the best results are secured when there is a division of work among these men. The theory of organization, therefore, has to do with the structure of co-ordination imposed upon the work-division units of an enterprise. Hence it is not possible to determine how an activity is to be organized without, at the same time, considering how the work in question is to be divided. Work division is the foundation of organization; indeed, the reason for organization.

1. The Division of Work

It is appropriate at the outset of this discussion to consider the reasons for and the effect of the division of work. It is sufficient for our purpose to note the following factors.

Why Divide Work?

Because men differ in nature, capacity and skill, and gain greatly in dexterity by specialization;
Because the same man cannot be at two places at the same time;
Because one man cannot do two things at the same time;
Because the range of knowledge and skill is so great that a man cannot within his life-span know more than a small fraction of it. In other words, it is a question of human nature, time, and space.

The introduction of machinery accentuates the division of work. Even such a simple thing as a saw, a typewriter, or a transit requires increased specialization, and serves to divide workers into those who can and those who cannot use the particular instrument effectively. Division of work on the basis of the tools and machines used in work rests no doubt in part on aptitude, but primarily upon the development and maintenance of skill through continued manipulation.

Specialized skills are developed not alone in connection with machines and tools. They evolve naturally from the materials handled, like wood, or cattle, or paint, or cement. They arise similarly in activities which center in a complicated series of interrelated concepts, principles, and techniques. These are most clearly recognized in the professions, particularly those based on the

Papers on the Science of Administration (New York: Institute of Public Administration, 1937), pp. 3–45.

application of scientific knowledge, as in engineering, medicine, and chemistry. They are none the less equally present in law, ministry, teaching, accountancy, navigation, aviation, and other fields.

The nature of these subdivisions is essentially pragmatic, in spite of the fact that there is an element of logic underlying them. They are therefore subject to a gradual evolution with the advance of science, the invention of new machines, the progress of technology and the change of the social system. In the last analysis, however, they appear to be based upon differences in individual human beings. But it is not to be concluded that the apparent stability of "human nature," whatever that may be, limits the probable development of specialization. The situation is quite the reverse. As each field of knowledge and work is advanced, constituting a continually larger and more complicated nexus of related principles, practices and skills, any individual will be less and less able to encompass it and maintain intimate knowledge and facility over the entire area, and there will thus arise a more minute specialization because knowledge and skill advance while man stands still. Division of work and integrated organization are the bootstraps by which mankind lifts itself in the process of civilization.

The Limits of Division

There are three clear limitations beyond which the division of work cannot to advantage go. The first is practical and arises from the volume of work involved in man-hours. Nothing is gained by subdividing work if that further subdivision results in setting up a task which requires less than the full time of one man. This is too obvious to need demonstration. The only exception arises where space interferes, and in such cases the part-time expert must fill in his spare time at other tasks, so that as a matter of fact a new combination is introduced.

The second limitation arises from technology and custom at a given time and place. In some areas nothing would be gained by separating undertaking from the custody and cleaning of churches, because by custom the sexton is the undertaker; in building construction it is extraordinarily difficult to re-divide certain aspects of electrical and plumbing work and to combine them in a more effective way, because of the jurisdictional conflicts of craft unions; and it is clearly impracticable to establish a division of cost accounting in a field in which no technique of costing has yet been developed.

This second limitation is obviously elastic. It may be changed by invention and by education. If this were not the fact, we should face a static division of labor. It should be noted, however, that a marked change has two dangers. It greatly restricts the labor market from which workers may be drawn and greatly lessens the opportunities open to those who are trained for the particular specialization.

The third limitation is that the subdivisions of work must not pass beyond physical division into organic division. It might seem far more efficient to have the front half of the cow in the pasture grazing and the rear half of the barn being milked all of the time, but this organic division would fail. Similarly there is no gain from splitting a single movement or gesture like licking an envelope, or tearing apart a series of intimately and intricately related activities.

It may be said that there is in this an element of reasoning in a circle; that the test here applied as to whether an activity is organic or not is whether it is divisible or not—which is what we set out to define. This charge is true. It must be a pragmatic test. Does the division work out? Is something vital destroyed and lost? Does it bleed?

The Whole and the Parts

It is axiomatic that the whole is equal to the sum of its parts. But in dividing up any "whole," one must be certain that every part, including unseen elements and relationships, is accounted for. The marble sand to which the Venus de Milo may be reduced by a vandal does not equal the statue, though every last grain be preserved; nor is a thrush just so much feathers, bones, flesh, and blood; nor a typewriter merely so much steel, glass, paint, and rubber. Similarly a piece of work to be done cannot be subdivided into the obvious component parts without great danger that the central design, the operating relationships, the imprisoned idea, will be lost.

A simple illustration will make this clear. One man can build a house. He can lay the foundation, cut the beams and boards, make the window frames and doors, lay the floors, raise the roof, plaster the walls, fit in the heating and water systems, install the electric wiring, hang the paper, and paint the structure. But if he did, most of the work would be done by hands unskilled in the work; much material would be spoiled, and the work would require many months of his time. On the other hand, the whole job of building the house might be divided among a group of men. One man could do the foundation, build the chimney, and plaster the walls; another could erect the frame, cut the timbers and the boards, raise the roof, and do all the carpentry; another all the plumbing; another all the paper hanging and painting; another all the electric wiring. But this would not make a house unless someone—an architect—made a plan for the house, so that each skilled worker could know what to do and when to do it.

When one man builds a house alone he plans as he works; he decides what to do first and what next, that is, he "co-ordinates the work." When many men work together to build a house this part of the work, the co-ordinating, must not be lost sight of.

In the "division of the work" among the various skilled specialists, a specialist in planning and co-ordination must be sought as well. Otherwise, a great deal of time may be lost, workers may get in each other's way, material may not be on hand when needed, things may be done in the wrong order, and there may even be a difference of opinion as to where the various doors and windows are to go. It is self-evident that the more the work is subdivided, the greater is the danger of confusion, and the greater is the need of overall supervision and co-ordination. Co-ordination is not something that develops by accident. It must be won by intelligent, vigorous, persistent and organized effort.

2. The Co-ordination of Work

If subdivision of work is inescapable, co-ordination becomes mandatory. There is, however, no one way to co-ordination. Experience shows that it may be achieved in two primary ways. These are:

1. By organization, that is, by interrelating the subdivisions of work by allotting them to men who are placed in a structure of authority, so that the work may be co-ordinated by orders of superiors to subordinates, reaching from the top to the bottom of the entire enterprise.

2. By the dominance of an idea, that is, the development of intelligent singleness of purpose in the minds and wills of those who are working together as a group, so that each worker will of his own accord fit his task into the whole with skill and enthusiasm.

These two principles of co-ordination are not mutually exclusive, in fact, no enterprise is really effective without the extensive utilization of both.

Size and time are the great limiting factors in the development of co-ordination. In a small project, the problem is not difficult; the structure of authority is simple, and the central purpose is real to every worker. In a large complicated enterprise, the organization becomes involved, the lines of authority tangled, and there is danger that the workers will forget that there is any central purpose, and so devote their best energies only to their own individual advancement and advantage.

The interrelated elements of time and habit are extraordinarily important in co-ordination. Man is a creature of habit. When an enterprise is built up gradually from small beginnings the staff can be "broken in" step by step. And when difficulties develop, they can be ironed out, and the new method followed from that point on as a matter of habit, with the knowledge that that particular difficulty will not develop again. Routines may even be mastered by drill as they are in the army. When, however, a large new enterprise must be set up or altered overnight, then the real difficulties of co-ordination make their appearance. The factor of habit, which is thus an important foundation of co-ordination when time is available, becomes a serious handicap when time is not available, that is, when rules change. The question of co-ordination therefore must be approached with different emphasis in small and in large enterprises; in simple and in complex situations; in stable and in new or changing organizations.

Co-ordination Through Organization

Organization as a way of co-ordination requires the establishment of a system of authority whereby the central purpose or objective of an enterprise is translated into reality through the combined efforts of many specialists, each working in his own field at a particular time and place.

It is clear from long experience in human affairs that such a structure of authority requires not only many men at work in many places at selected times, but also a single directing executive authority. The problem of organization thus becomes the problem of building up between the executive at the center and the subdivisions of work on the periphery an effective network of communication and control.

The following outline may serve further to define the problem:

1. First step: Define the job to be done, such as the furnishing of pure water to all of the people and industries within a given area at the lowest possible cost;
2. Second step: Provide a director to see that the objective is realized;
3. Third step: Determine the nature and number of individualized and specialized work units into which the job will have to be divided. As has been seen above, this subdivision depends partly upon the size of the job (no ultimate subdivision can generally be so small as to require less than the full time of one worker) and upon the status of technological and social development at a given time;
4. Fourth step: Establish and perfect the structure of authority between the director and the ultimate work subdivisions. . . .

The Span of Control

In this undertaking, we are confronted at the start by the inexorable limits of human nature. Just as the hand of man can span only a limited number of notes on the piano, so the mind and will of man can span but a limited number of immediate managerial contacts. . . . The limit of control is partly a matter of the limits of knowledge, but even more is it a matter of the limits of time and of energy. As a result the executive of any enterprise can personally direct only a few persons. He must depend upon these to direct others, and upon them in turn to direct still others, until the last man in the organization is reached.

This condition placed upon all human organization by the limits of the span of control obviously differs in different kinds of work and in organizations of different sizes. Where the work is of a routine, repetitive, measurable, and homogeneous character, one man can perhaps direct several score workers. This is particularly true when the workers are all in a single room. Where the work is diversified, qualitative, and particularly when the workers are scattered, one man can supervise only a few. This diversification, dispersion, and non-measurability is of course most evident at the very top of any organization. It follows that the limitations imposed by the span of control are most evident at the top of an organization, directly under the executive himself.

But when we seek to determine how many immediate subordinates the director of an enterprise can effectively supervise, we enter a realm of experience which has not been brought under sufficient scientific study to furnish a final answer.

⚜ ⚜ ⚜

But without further research we may conclude that the chief executive of an organization can deal with only a few immediate subordinates; that this number is determined not only by the nature of the work, but also by the nature of the executive; and that the number of immediate subordinates in a large, diversified and dispersed organization must be even less than in a homogeneous and unified organization to achieve the same measure of co-ordination.

One Master

From the earliest times it has been recognized that nothing but confusion arises under multiple command. "A man cannot serve two masters" was adduced as a theological argument because it was already accepted as a principle of human relation in everyday life. In administration this is known as the principle of "unity of command." The principle may be stated as follows: A workman subject to orders from several superiors will be confused, inefficient, and irresponsible; a workman subject to orders from but one superior may be methodical, efficient, and responsible. Unity of command thus refers to those who are commanded, not to those who issue the commands.

The significance of this principle in the process of co-ordination and organization must not be lost sight of. In building a structure of co-ordination, it is often tempting to set up more than one boss for a man who is doing work which has more than one relationship. Even as great a philosopher of management as Taylor fell into this error in setting up separate foremen to deal with machinery, with materials, with speed, etc., each with the power of giving orders directly to the individual workman. The rigid adherence to the principle of unity of command may have its absurdities; these are, however, unimportant in comparison with the certainty of confusion, inefficiency, and irresponsibility which arise from the violation of the principle.

Technical Efficiency

⚜ ⚜ ⚜

It has been observed by authorities in many fields that the efficiency of a group working together is directly related to the homogeneity of the work they are performing, of the processes they are utilizing, and of the purposes which actuate them. From top to bottom, the group must be unified. It must work together.

It follows from this (1) that any organizational structure which brings together in a single unit work divisions which are non-homogeneous in work, in technology, or in purpose will encounter the danger of friction and inefficiency; and (2) that a unit based on a given specialization cannot be given technical direction by a layman.

In the realm of government it is not difficult to find many illustrations of the unsatisfactory results of non-homogeneous administrative combinations. It is generally agreed that agricultural development and education cannot be administered by the same men who enforce pest and disease control, because the success of the former rests upon friendly co-operation and trust of the farmers, while the latter engenders resentment and suspicion. Similarly, activities like drug control established in protection of the consumer do not find appropriate homes in departments dominated by the interests of the producer. In the larger cities and in states it has been found that hospitals cannot be so well administered by the health department directly as they can be when set up independently in a separate department, or at least in a bureau with extensive autonomy, and it is generally agreed that public welfare administration and police administration require separation, as do public health administration and welfare administration, though both of these combinations may be found in successful operation under special conditions. No one would think of combining water supply and public education, or tax administration and public recreation. In every one of these cases, it will be seen that there is some element either of work to be done, or of the technology used, or of the end sought which is non-homogeneous. . . .

Caveamus Expertum

At this point a word of caution is necessary. The application of the principle of homogeneity has its pitfalls. Every highly trained technician, particularly in the learned professions, has a profound sense of omniscience and a great desire for complete independence in the service of society. When employed by government he knows exactly what the people need better than they do themselves, and he knows how to render this service. He tends to be utterly oblivious of all other needs, because, after all, is not his particular technology the road to salvation? Any restraint applied to him is "limitation of freedom," and any criticism "springs from ignorance and jealousy." Every budget increase he secures is "in the public interest," while every increase secured elsewhere is "a sheer waste." His efforts and maneuvers to expand are "public education" and "civic organization," while similar efforts by others are "propaganda" and "politics."

Another trait of the expert is his tendency to assume knowledge and authority in fields in which he has no competence. In this particular, educators, lawyers, priests, admirals, doctors, scientists, engineers, accountants, merchants, and bankers are all the same—having achieved technical competence or "success" in one field, they come to think this competence is a general quality detachable from the field and inherent in themselves. They step without embarrassment into other areas. They do not remember that the robes of authority of one kingdom confer no sovereignty in another; but that there they are merely a masquerade.

The expert knows his "stuff." Society needs him, and must have him more and more as man's technical knowledge becomes more and more extensive. But history shows us that the common man is a better judge of his own needs in the long run than any cult of experts. Kings and ruling classes, priests and prophets, soldiers and lawyers, when permitted to rule rather than serve mankind, have in the end done more to check the advance of human welfare than they have to advance it. The true place of the expert is, as A.E. said so well, "on tap, not on top." The essential validity of democracy rests upon this philosophy, for democracy is a way of government in which the common man is the final judge of what is good for him.

Efficiency is one of the things that is good for him because it makes life richer and safer. That efficiency is to be secured more and more through the use of technical specialists. These specialists have no right to ask for, and must not be given freedom from supervisory control, but in establishing that control, a government which ignores the conditions of efficiency cannot expect to achieve efficiency.

3. Organizational Patterns

Organizing the Executive

We do not . . . expect the chief executive to write his own letters. We give him a private secretary, who is part of his office and assists him to do this part of his job. This secretary is not a part of any department, he is a subdivision of the executive himself. In just this way, though on a different plane, other phases of the job of the chief executive may be organized.

Before doing this, however, it is necessary to have a clear picture of the job itself. This brings us directly to the question, "What is the work of the chief executive? What does he do?"

The answer is POSDCORB.

POSDCORB is, of course, a made-up word designed to call attention to the various functional elements of the work of a chief executive because "administration" and "management" have lost all specific content. POSDCORB is made up of the initials and stands for the following activities:

> Planning, that is working out in broad outline the things that need to be done and the methods for doing them to accomplish the purpose set for the enterprise;
> Organizing, that is the establishment of the formal structure of authority through which work subdivisions are arranged, defined, and co-ordinated for the defined objective;

Staffing, that is the whole personnel function of bringing in and training the staff and maintaining favorable conditions of work;

Directing, that is the continuous task of making decisions and embodying them in specific and general orders and instructions and serving as the leader of the enterprise;

Co-ordinating, that is the all important duty of interrelating the various parts of the work;

Reporting, that is keeping those to whom the executive is responsible informed as to what is going on, which thus includes keeping himself and his subordinates informed through records, research and inspection;

Budgeting, with all that goes with budgeting in the form of fiscal planning, accounting, and control.

If these seven elements may be accepted as the major duties of the chief executive, it follows that they *may* be separately organized as subdivisions of the executive. The need for such subdivision depends entirely on the size and complexity of the enterprise. In the largest enterprises, particularly where the chief executive is as a matter of fact unable to do the work that is thrown upon him, it may be presumed that one or more parts of POSDCORB should be suborganized.

Aggregating the Work Units

In building the organization from the bottom up we are confronted by the task of analyzing everything that has to be done and determining in what grouping it can be placed without violating the principle of homogeneity. This is not a simple matter, either practically or theoretically. It will be found that each worker in each position must be characterized by:

1. The major *purpose* he is serving, such as furnishing water, controlling crime, or conducting education;
2. The *process* he is using, such as engineering, medicine, carpentry, stenography, statistics, accounting;
3. The *persons or things* dealt with or served, such as immigrants, veterans, Indians, forests, mines, parks, orphans, farmers, automobiles, or the poor;
4. The *place* where he renders his service, such as Hawaii, Boston, Washington, the Dust Bowl, Alabama, or Central High School.

Organization by Major Purpose

Organization by major purpose, such as water supply, crime control, or education, serves to bring together in a single large department all of those who are at work endeavoring to render a particular service. Under such a policy, the department of education will contain not only teachers and school administrators, but also architects, engineers, chauffeurs, auto mechanics, electricians, carpenters, janitors, gardeners, nurses, doctors, lawyers, and accountants. Everything that has to do with the schools would be included, extending perhaps even to the control of traffic about school properties. Similarly the department of water supply would include not only engineers and maintenance gangs, but also planners, statisticians, lawyers, architects, accountants, meter readers, bacteriologists, and public health experts.

The advantages of this type of organization are three: first, it makes more certain the accomplishment of any given broad purpose or project by bringing the whole job under a single director with immediate control of all the experts, agencies, and services which are required in the performance of the work. No one can interfere. The director does not have to wait for others, nor negotiate for their help and co-operation; nor appeal to the chief executive to untangle a conflict. He can devote all his energies to getting on with the job.

Second, from the standpoint of self-government, organization by purpose seems to conform best to the objectives of government as they are recognized and understood by the public. The public sees the end result, and cannot understand the methodology. It can therefore express its approval or disapproval with less confusion and more effectiveness regarding major purposes than it can regarding the processes.

Third, it apparently serves as the best basis for eliciting the energies and loyalties of the personnel and for giving a focus and central drive to the whole activity, because purpose is understandable by the entire personnel down to the last clerk and inspector.

The statement of these strong points of organization by major purpose points the way to its dangers. These are to be found, first, in the impossibility of cleanly dividing all of the work of any government into a few such major purposes which do not overlap extensively. For example, education overlaps immediately with health and with recreation, as does public works with law enforcement. The strong internal co-ordination and drive tends to precipitate extensive and serious external conflict and confusion, just as there is more danger of accident with a high-powered motor car. This is apparent particularly in the development of a reasonable city plan, or in arriving at a consistent policy throughout the departments for the maintenance of properties, or in handling legal matters, or arranging similar work and salary conditions. The lawyers, engineers, accountants, doctors of different departments will all have their own ideas as to how similar matters are to be dealt with.

Second, there is danger that an organization erected on the basis of purpose will fail to make use of the most up-to-date technical devices and specialists because the dominance of purpose generally tends to obscure the element of process, and because there may not be enough work of a given technical sort to permit efficient subdivision.

Third, there is also danger in such an organization that subordinate parts of the work will be unduly suppressed or lost sight of because of the singleness of purpose, enthusiasm, and drive of the head of the department. For example, medical work with children when established under the department of education as a division is likely to receive less encouragement than it would if independently established in the health department, because after all the department of education is primarily interested in schools and has its own great needs and problems.

Fourth, a department established on the basis of purpose falls easily into the habit of overcentralization, and thus fails to fit its service effectively to the people. Or if it does decentralize its services, as do the fire department, the police department, the health department, and the department of education of New York City, the representatives of these departments in the field do not always make the best use of each other's assistance and co-operation, and when any difficulty does arise, it is such a long way to the top where co-ordination can be worked out, that it is easier to get along without it.

Fifth, an organization fully equipped from top to bottom with all of the direct and collateral services required for the accomplishment of its central purpose, without the need of any assistance from other departments, drifts very easily into an attitude and position of complete independence from all other activities and even from democratic control itself.

Organization by Major Process

Organization by major process, such as engineering, teaching, the law, or medicine, tends to bring together in a single department all of those who are at work making use of a given special skill or technology, or are members of a given profession. Under such a policy the department of law would comprise all of the lawyers and law clerks, including those who are devoting their time to school matters, or water supply suits, or drafting ordinances. The department of engineering and public works would have all the engineers, including those concerned with planning, design, construction, maintenance and other phases of engineering work, wherever that work was found. This would include the work in the parks, on the streets, in the schools, and in connection with water, sewer, waste and other services. The department of health would include all of the doctors, nurses, and bacteriologists, and would not only carry on the general public health work, but would do the medical and nursing work for the schools, the water department, the department of social welfare, etc., as has been outlined above.

In every one of these cases it will be observed that the basis of organization is the bringing together in a single office or department of all the workers who are using some particular kind of skill, knowledge, machinery, or profession. This principle of organization has the following advantages:

First, it guarantees the maximum utilization of up-to-date technical skill and by bringing together in a single office a large amount of each kind of work (technologically measured), makes it possible in each case to make use of the most effective divisions of work and specialization.

Second, it makes possible also the economies of the maximum use of labor saving machinery and mass production. These economies arise not from the total mass of the work to be performed, not from the fact that the work performed serves the same general purpose but from the fact that the work is performed with the same machine, with the same technique, with the same motions. For example, economy in printing comes from skill in typesetting, printing, and binding and the use of modern equipment. It makes no difference to the printer whether he is printing a pamphlet for the schools, a report for the police department, or a form for the comptroller. Unit costs, efficiency in the doing of the job, rest upon the process, not the purpose.

Third, organization by process encourages co-ordination in all of the technical and skilled work of the enterprise, because all of those engaged in any field are brought together under the same supervision, instead of being scattered in several departments as is the case when organization is based upon some other principle.

Fourth, it furnishes an excellent approach to the development of central co-ordination and control when certain of the services such as budgeting, accounting, purchasing, and planning are set up on a process basis and used as instruments of integration even where other activities are set up on some other basis.

Fifth, organization by process is best adapted to the development of career service, and the stimulation of professional standards and pride. A career ladder can be erected very much more easily in a department which is from top to bottom engineers, or doctors, or statisticians, or clerks, than it can in a department which is partly engineers, partly doctors, partly statisticians, partly clerks. In the vertical departments, the rungs of a professional ladder are a flying trapeze requiring the employee in his upward course to swing from department to department. This cannot be accomplished "with the greatest of ease."

These are the major advantages of organization on the basis of process. There are, of course, offsetting difficulties. As in the case of any other principle of organization, it is impossible to aggregate all of the work of the government on such a basis alone. It is not difficult to do so for engineering and medicine and teaching, but it becomes impossible when we reach typing and clerical work. It cannot furnish a satisfactory basis for doing the whole job in any large or complicated enterprise.

In the second place, there is always the danger that organization by process will hinder the accomplishment of major purposes, because the process departments may be more interested in *how* things are done than in *what* is accomplished. For example, a housing department which must clear the slums, build new low cost tenements and manage them, and inspect existing housing and approve new building plans, may find it difficult to make rapid progress if it must draw its legal help from the corporation counsel, its architects from the department of engineering, its enforcement officers from the police department, and its plans from the planning commission, particularly if one or more of these departments regards public housing as a nuisance and passing fad. There are also accountants who think that the only reason for the running of a government is the keeping of the books!

Third, experience seems to indicate that a department built around a given profession or skill tends to show a greater degree or arrogance and unwillingness to accept democratic control. This is perhaps a natural outgrowth of the insolence of professionalism to which reference has already been made.

Fourth, organization by process is perhaps less favorable to the development of a separate administrative service, because it tends to bring rather narrow professional specialists to the top of each department, men who are thereby disqualified for transfer to administrative posts in other fields.

And finally, the necessity of effective co-ordination is greatly increased. Purpose departments must be co-ordinated so that they will not conflict but will work shoulder to shoulder. But whether they do, or do not, the individual major purposes will be accomplished to a considerable extent and a failure in any service is limited in its effect to that service. Process departments must be co-ordinated not only to prevent conflict, but also to guarantee positive co-operation. They work hand in hand. They must also time their work so that it will fit together, a factor of lesser significance in the purpose departments. A failure in one process affects the whole enterprise, and a failure to co-ordinate one process division, may destroy the effectiveness of all of the work that is being done.

While organization by process thus puts great efficiency within our reach, this efficiency cannot be realized unless the compensating structure of co-ordination is developed.

Organization by Clientele or Matériel

Organization on the basis of the persons served or dealt with, or on the basis of the things dealt with, tends to bring together in a single department, regardless of the purpose of the service, or the techniques used, all of those who are working with a given group or a given set of things. Examples are the veterans' administration which deals with all of the problems of the veteran, be they in health, in hospitals, in insurance, in welfare, or in education; and the immigration bureau which deals with immigrants at all points, including legal, financial, and medical services. Departmentalization on the basis of *matériel* is more common in private business than in public. Department stores, for example, have separate departments for furniture, hardware, drugs, jewelry, shoes, etc., and have separate buyers and sales forces for each. In many communities the school is in reality such a service, as it concentrates most of the community services touching children in school, including medical inspection, corrective treatment, free lunches, and recreation, and certain phases of juvenile crime. The Forest Service is another organization based on *matériel—in this case, trees.*

The great advantage of this type of organization is the simplification and co-ordination of the service of government in its contact with the consumer. He does not encounter first one and then another representative, each of whom does or demands something different or even something contradictory. At the international border one may be met by an immigration inspector who is interested in one's nationality and residence, by a customs inspector who is interested in goods brought in, by an agricultural inspector interested in certain pests, by a game warden interested in guns and rods, etc. In New York City, at one time, each tenement was subject to separate inspection at periodic intervals by men interested in slums, crime, fire escapes, plumbing, fire hazards, and electric wiring. Many cases have been reported of conflicting orders being issued to individual property owners under such a system.

A second advantage is found in the increasing skill which attends the handling over and over of the same material.

A third gain arises from the elimination of duplicate travel, particularly in dealing with widely separated or sparsely distributed work.

The disadvantages of an organization which brings together all of the contacts with a given individual or thing are:

First, it tends to sacrifice the efficiency of specialization, because it must after all perform several otherwise specialized functions through the same organization or even at times through the same agent. For example, if the effort is made to combine all building inspections in the field, the same man must examine plumbing, wiring, living conditions, and fire escapes. Or, at the international border, the same man must know and enforce the immigration law, the customs laws, the hunting laws, and the crop pest laws, and must possess the required special knowledge in the various technical fields involved. Or, in the veterans' administration the same director must supervise and direct specialists in medicine, institutional administration, insurance, and vocational education and rehabilitation.

It is to be noted that this difficulty has been overcome in certain notable instances by the creation of a new specialist profession to deal with the specific combination of functions brought together in a given service. The best illustration is the United States Forest Service. This can be done only where there is a large volume of work and an opportunity for a career within the service itself.

A second difficulty is found in the impossibility of applying the principle of division by persons served to all of the work of a government, without encountering extensive conflict and duplication. It is not difficult to pick out special groups like the aged, the youth, the criminal, the veteran, the real estate owner, etc., but when all is said and done there remains a great number of the ordinary citizens that does not fall into *any single* grouping. Each individual will appear in various groups at various times, and in the general group known as "the public" the rest of the time. And it is clearly impossible to organize a special department for the public, with all of the heterogeneous elements which this would entail from the standpoint of dissimilar technologies and conflicting objectives. It must be remembered also that even such departments as seem to be organized on the basis of persons served do not as a matter of fact cover all of the services rendered to or government contacts with a class of individuals. Taking even the most expanded school systems where the schools really are youth departments, it will be found that general quarantine is enforced by the health authorities, that children benefit also by police traffic and crime prevention work, that they drink water furnished by the water department, and milk protected by the division of foods, and live in homes supervised by the housing authority, and are protected by the fire department.

A third difficulty arises from the danger of dominance by favor-seeking pressure groups. Departments set up by clientele seldom escape political dominance by those groups, and are generally found to be special pleaders for those groups, at times in opposition to the general interest of society as a whole. This is in part due to the fact that the organization itself is often brought into being through the action of a pressure group and its demand for a special agency to serve it, but it is also continued through the efforts of the agency once established to marshal and maintain a group in its support. It follows that agencies so set up as to maintain or develop their own pressure backing are peculiarly difficult of democratic control and tend not to fit into a co-ordinated social policy.

Organization by Place

Organization on the basis of the place at which the service is performed brings together all of those who work in a limited area regardless of the service they are performing or of the techniques they represent. This is the general practice in territorial or colonial governments. Even where the home government has separate departments interested in health, education, law enforcement, natural resources, labor relations, and commercial development, it will be found that these departments have no direct representatives within a given territory or colony, but that there is a single representative of the home government there, under whom there are organized separate divisions to deal with health, education, law enforcement, natural resources, etc. In other words all or most of the representatives of the home government in the area are brought together in a single local agency, in place of serving as the far distant field representatives of the various central departments.

It is not only in colonial government that this plan is utilized. It is found also in greater or lesser degree in many of the regular departments of all large governmental units. In some of the largest city police systems the city is divided into precincts, and most of the police activities within a given area are under the complete direction of a precinct officer through whom all communication to and from headquarters must go. A similar situation is found in the postal system. Though the Washington office contains divisions in charge of mail delivery, stamp sale, postal savings, money orders, parcel post, and other services, these services do not each maintain independent local offices. A single local office is maintained with a postmaster in charge, under whom there are separate divisions for performing these particular services and for reporting the results of their work to the several supervisory and control divisions at headquarters. The Treasury Department, on the other hand, though it has customs officers, income tax examiners, bank examiners, narcotic officers, secret service, and others in the field representing various administrative divisions of the Treasury in Washington, does not establish a general local director of these field services, but supervises each in turn directly from Washington, or through some regional office which has no organic relationship with any one of the other services.

The most extreme cases of subdivision of the work of government are found in the American states where the state has not only subdivided itself into geographic areas for the performance of certain types of governmental service, but has actually turned over to these geographic areas a large measure of the right to determine how the local service shall be conducted. This is known as "home rule," and is found in all kinds of local government, particularly in the cities. It is common in the conduct of schools, the management of the police, the enforcement of justice, and the maintenance of the courts, all of which are legally "state functions." It is also the general basis of operation for poor relief, local highways, water supply, waste removal, property tax administration, and health administration. Where these functions are turned over to cities, villages, towns, or counties, they are in reality suborganized on a geographical basis. . . .

It should be noted that every department in every government of any size must be broken down geographically. In no other way can it reach the people who are to be served or who are to be controlled. In the government of the United States, only 20 percent of the employees are located in Washington, and thousands of this number are actually in the field. Eighty percent are regularly assigned to offices or work scattered throughout the country. They carry the government to the people and to the soil. The same is true of state governments and of city governments. Only a small part of the force actually works in the state capital or the city hall. The real work of government is done out among the people in the various sections of the state or city. In the supervision of these forces it is often necessary to establish some form of regional organization, if for no other reason than to save the time of the supervisory officers who cannot be in two places at once. It is thus generally a question as to how high up in the organization geographical subdivision shall be introduced. Obviously this may be done at the very top, as the first division of the work under the chief executive of an enterprise, or it may be introduced far down the line after the major divisions have been set up by purpose, by process, or by clientele. The former may be termed *primary* geographical subdivision and the latter *secondary, tertiary,* or *subordinate* geographical subdivision. A department or major activity, like the Tennessee Valley Authority, which is set up on the basis of geographical boundaries is in fact a primary geographical subdivision of the government.

The advantages of departmentalization on the basis of geographical areas, that is on the basis of superior geographical subdivision, are fairly obvious in practice. They consist first of the greater ease of co-ordination of services rendered and controls exercised within a given area; second, of the greater tendency to adapt the total program to the needs of the areas served, not alone because of the discretion resting within the divisions, but also because the needs and differences of the areas will be more vigorously represented at headquarters in the general consideration of broad policy; and third, of the greater ease with which co-operative relations may be established with subordinate governmental units, which are of necessity first of all geographically defined units. Decentralization of geographical divisions strengthens these tendencies, and serves, moreover, to reduce travel costs, short circuit adjustment problems, cut red tape, and speed up all joint activities and administrative decisions. It increases not only the awareness of the officials to local needs and to the interrelation of service and planning problems, but develops a new sensitivity to the process of democratic control through intimate association of the officials with the people served.

With decentralized subdivision a large amount of discretion must be delegated to the men in charge of field offices; in fact, they must be men of ability equal to if not superior to those who would be selected to head centralized departments of similar scope.

The difficulties of primary geographic subdivision are also not far to seek. They consist of the increased difficulty of maintaining a uniform nation-wide, state-wide, or city-wide policy; the danger of too narrow and short-sighted management; and the increased difficulty of making full use of technical services and the highest specialization because of the division of the work into limited blocks. Decentralization tends to enhance these difficulties by reason of physical isolation. It introduces other factors as well, such as higher costs for supervisory personnel, the general hesitancy of central administrative heads to delegate sufficient real power, the lesser prestige of localized officials, and the increased tendency of such a system to come under the control of localizing logrolling pressure groups. Political parties under our system of representation are based upon geographical areas. An administrative system also set up by areas is peculiarly subject to spoliation by politicians as long as we have the spoils system

Whenever the concept of geographic areas is introduced into the structure of organization, either as a primary or as a subordinate plan of division of work, there is always the further practical problem of delineating appropriate boundaries. This is particularly difficult when it is planned to deal with several activities widely differing in their nature and technology. There is always the danger that the tasks to be dealt with do not follow compact geographic boundaries and that the administrative separation introduced by the geographic division will complicate rather than simplify the work.

Line and Staff

The army has contributed much to the theory of organization. Not the least of these contributions has been the concept of line and staff. . . .

When the work of government is subjected to the dichotomy of "line" and "staff," there are included in staff all of those persons who devote their time exclusively to the knowing, thinking, and planning functions, and in the line all of the remainder who are, thus, chiefly concerned with the doing functions. The overhead directing authority of the staff group, usually a board or committee, is the "general staff."

Obviously those in the line are also thinking and planning, and making suggestions to superior officers. They cannot operate otherwise. But this does not make them staff officers. Those also in the staff are *doing* something; they do not merely sit and twiddle their thumbs. But they do not organize others, they do not direct or appoint personnel, they do not issue commands, they do not take responsibility for the job. Everything they suggest is referred up, not down, and is carried out, if at all, on the responsibility and under the direction of a line officer.

The important point of confusion in considering line and staff has arisen in speaking of the budget director, the purchasing agent, the controller, the public relations secretary as "staff" officers. On the basis of the definition it is clear that they are all line officers. They have important duties of direction and control. When administrative responsibility and power are added to any staff function, that function thereby becomes immediately and completely a line function. There is no middle ground.

The chief value of the line and staff classification is to point to the need (1) of developing an independent planning agency as an aid to the chief executive; and (2) of refusing to inject any element of administrative authority and control into such an agency.

The necessity for central purchase, for personnel administration, for budgeting and for fiscal control rests on other considerations and not on the philosophy of the general staff.

4. Interrelation of Systems of Departmentalization

Students of administration have long sought a single principle of effective departmentalization just as alchemists sought the philosophers' stone. But they have sought in vain. There is apparently no one most effective system of departmentalism.

Each of the four basic systems of organization is intimately related with the other three, because in any enterprise all four elements are present in the doing of the work and are embodied in every individual workman. Each member of the enterprise is working for some major purpose, uses some process, deals with some persons, and serves or works at some place.

If an organization is erected about any one of these four characteristics of work, it becomes immediately necessary to recognize the other characteristics in constructing the secondary and tertiary divisions of the work. For example, a government which is first divided on the basis of place will, in each geographical department, find it necessary to divide by purpose, by process, by clientele, or even again by place; and one divided in the first instance by purpose, may well be divided next by process and then by place. While the first or primary division of any enterprise is of very great significance, it must none the less be said that there is no one most effective pattern for determining the priority and order for the introduction of these interdependent principles. It will depend in any case upon the results which are desired at a given time and place.

An organization is a living and dynamic entity. Each activity is born, has its periods of experimental development, of vigorous and stable activity, and, in some cases, of decline. A principle of organization appropriate at one stage may not be appropriate at all during a succeeding stage, particularly in view of the different elements of strength and of weakness which we have seen to exist in the various systems of departmentalization. In any government various parts of its work will always stand at different stages of their life cycle. It will therefore be found that not all of the activities of any government may be appropriately departmentalized neatly on the basis of a single universal plan. Time is an essential element in the formula.

Another variable is technological development. The invention of machines, the advance of applied science, the rise of new specializations and professions, changes in society and in the way men work and move in their private life must be continually reflected in the work of government, and therefore in the structure of government. Medieval governments made use of warriors, priests, artists, builders, and tax gatherers; they had no place for sanitary engineers, chemists, entomologists, pneumatic drill operators, and typists. Before you organize a statistical division there must be statistical machinery and statistical science, but as soon as there are such machinery and science, any large organization which fails to recognize the fact in its organization may greatly lessen its utilization of the newly available tools and skills.

A further variable influencing the structure of any enterprise is its size, measured not so much by the amount of work done as by the number of men at work and their geographical dispersion. A drug store is an excellent illustration of the problem encountered. It must have a prescription department with a licensed pharmacist, no matter how small it is, because of the technological requirements involved. But it does not need to have a separate medicine and supply department, refreshment department, book department, toy department, sporting goods department, cigar department, and delivery department, each with a trained manager, buyer, and sales force, unless it is a big store. In the small store, the pharmacist may even be the manager, the soda jerker, and the book dispenser. If the business is big enough, it may be desirable to have more than one store in order to reach the customers, thus introducing geographical subdivision. Similarly, in government the nature of the organization must be adapted not only to the technological requirements but also to the size of the undertaking and the dispersion of its work.

Structure and Co-ordination

The major purpose of organization is co-ordination, as has been pointed out above. It should therefore be noted that each of the four principles of departmentalization plays a different role in co-ordination. In each case the highest degree of co-ordination takes place within the departments set up, and the greatest lack of co-ordination and danger of friction occurs between the departments, or at the points where they overlap.

If all of the departments are set up on the basis of purpose, then the task of the chief executive in the field of co-ordination will be to see that the major purposes are not in conflict and that the various processes which are used are consistent, and that the government as it touches classes of citizens or reaches areas of the community is appropriate, rational, and effective. He will not have to concern himself with co-ordination within the departments, as each department head will look after this.

If all of the departments are set up on the basis of process, the work methods will be well standardized on professional lines, and the chief executive will have to see that these are co-ordinated and timed to produce the results and render the services for which the government exists, and that the service rendered actually fits the needs of the persons or areas served.

If place be the basis of departmentalization, that is, if the services be decentralized, then the task of the chief executive is not to see that the activities are co-ordinated locally and fit the locality, but to see that each of these services makes use of the standard techniques and that the work in each area is part of a general program and policy.

If the work of the government be departmentalized in part on the basis of purpose, in part on the basis of process, in part on the basis of clientele, and in part on the basis of place, it will be seen that the problems of co-ordination and smooth operation are multiplied and that the task of the executive is increased. Moreover, the nature of his work is altered. In an organization in which all of the major divisions follow one philosophy, the executive himself must furnish the interdepartmental co-ordination and see that things do not fall between two stools. In an organization built on two or more bases of departmentalization, the executive may use, for example, the process departments as a routine means of co-ordinating the purpose departments. None the less the task of the executive is extraordinarily complicated. There is also great danger in such an organization that one department may fail to aid or actually proceed to obstruct another department. When departments cross each other at right angles, the danger of collision is far greater and far more serious than when their contacts are along parallel lines at their respective outer limits.

5. Co-ordination by Ideas

Any large and complicated enterprise would be incapable of effective operation if reliance for co-ordination were placed in organization alone. Organization is necessary; in a large enterprise it is essential, but it does not take the place of a dominant central idea as the foundation of action and self-co-ordination in the daily operation of all of the parts of the enterprise. Accordingly, the most difficult task of the chief executive is not command, it is leadership, that is, the development of the desire and will to work together for a purpose in the minds of those who are associated in any activity.

Human beings are compounded of cogitation and emotion and do not function well when treated as though they were merely cogs in motion. Their capacity for great and productive labor, creative co-operative work, and loyal self-sacrifice knows no limits provided the whole man, body-mind-and-spirit, is thrown into the program.

Implications

After all that has been written about morale in war and in work, the psychology of group effort, and the art of leadership, it is not necessary to elaborate this point here. It is appropriate, however, to note the following specific elements which bear directly upon the problem of co-ordination:

1. Personnel administration becomes of extraordinary significance, not merely from the standpoint of finding qualified appointees for the various positions, but even more from the standpoint of assisting in the selection of individuals and in the maintenance of conditions which will serve to create a foundation of loyalty and enthusiasm.

   The new drive for career government service and for in-service training derives its significance not so much from the fact that better persons will enter the service when the chance for promotion is held out to them, but from the fact that a career service is a growing and learning service, one that believes in the work and in the future of the enterprise.

2. Even where the structure of the organization is arranged to produce co-ordination by authority, and certainly in those realms in which the structure as such is wanting, the effort should be made to develop the driving ideas by co-operative effort and compromise so that there may be an understanding of the program, a sense of participation in its formulation, and enthusiasm in its realization.

3. Proper reporting on the results of the work of the departments and of the government as a whole to the public and to the controlling legislative body, and public appreciation of good service rendered by public employees is essential, not merely as a part of the process of democratic control, but also as a means to the development of service morale.

4. As a matter of public policy the government should encourage the development of professional associations among the employees of the government, in recognition of the fact that such associations can assist powerfully in the development of standards and ideals. In situations where it is natural, office and shop committees should be built up.

5. A developing organization must be continually engaged in research bearing upon the major technical and policy problems encountered, and upon the efficiency of the processes of work. In both types of research, but particularly in the latter, members of the staff at every level should be led to participate in the inquiries and in the development of solutions.

6. There is need for a national system of honor awards which may be conspicuously conferred upon men and women who render distinguished and faithful, though not necessarily highly advertised public service.

7. The structure of any organization must reflect not only the logic of the work to be done, but also the special aptitudes of the particular human beings who are brought together in the organization to carry through a particular project. It is the men and not the organization chart that do the work.

Dominant Ideals

The power of an idea to serve as the foundation of co-ordination is so great that one may observe many examples of co-ordination even in the absence of any single leader or of any framework of authority. The best illustration is perhaps a nation at war. Every element steps into line and swings into high gear "to help win the war." The co-ordination is enthusiastic and complete, within the limits of knowledge of course. In an old stable community, small enough for each person to know the other, even competing businesses generally work along together in harmony. The town board, the school board, the park commission, the overseer of the poor, though answerable to no single executive, manage to get along with each other and each to fit his part of the work into that of the others to arrive at a sensible result for the whole picture. Men of intelligence and good will find little difficulty in working together for a given purpose even without an organization. They do not need to be held in line or driven to do a specific task in a specific way at a specific time. They carry on because of their inner compulsion, and may in the end accomplish a far better result for that very reason.

Hire and Fire

Closely akin to these considerations is the place of discipline in the technique of co-ordination. In most American thinking on management it has been assumed that the power to hire and fire must of necessity follow the hierarchical lines of the organization. Even students of administration have assumed that a chart of any organization may be drawn in terms either of the lines of appointment or in terms of the duties performed, because it was thought that the two are coincident, or should be. American business men have shared the same view. In their labor relations they take the traditional position that no man can run a business unless he has the free and unlimited power to hire and fire. It is the cornerstone of their thinking.

From the standpoint of modern management, however, competent observers have come to see that this approach is neither justified by the facts nor conducive to effective results. In practical situations employers do not as a matter of fact have the power to fire, even when they have the legal right. There are public relations, and increasingly there are labor unions. Frequently employers do not have the unlimited power to appoint. Here again there are standards, public relations, and closed shops. An individual minor executive in a large corporation generally has his employees selected for him. He is not free either to hire or to fire. These limitations of the right to hire and fire are destined, it is clear, to become more and more restrictive.

It becomes increasingly clear, therefore, that the task of the administrator must be accomplished less and less by coercion and discipline and more and more by persuasion. In other words, management of the future must look more to leadership and less to authority as the primary means of co-ordination.

These undoubted facts of experience are re-emphasized here not for the purpose of arguing that the consideration of the philosophy of organization is after all a "fools' contest," but rather to insist that the more important and the more difficult part of co-ordination is to be sought not through systems of authority, but through ideas and persuasion, and to make clear the point that the absurdities of the hierarchical system of authority are made sweet and reasonable through unity of purpose. It may well be that the system of organization, the structure of authority, is primarily important in co-ordination because it makes it easy to deal with the routine affairs, and thereby lessens the strain placed upon leadership, so that it can thus devote itself more fully to the supreme task of developing consent, participation, loyalty, enthusiasm, and creative devotion.

6. Co-ordination and Change

The Limits of Co-ordination

Are there limits to co-ordination? Is mankind capable of undertaking activities which though interrelated are beyond man's power of systematic co-ordination?

In the field of big business, economists and lawyers have raised this question, and have asked whether some of the larger corporations were not already too large for effective operation. Certainly in government, we face what often seem superhuman tasks because of their size and complexity. And not too encouraging are such efforts as we have seen in Italy, Germany, and Russia, where government is co-ordinating not only the social controls but also production and distribution. In a lesser degree, and with greater reliance upon voluntary action within a broad framework of regulation, England, France, and the United States are also striving for the same ends, with greater and greater imposition of public controls. There are apparently no limits to the effort mankind is prepared to make to render life more secure and more abundant through socially enforced co-ordination. If there are limits to man's power of co-ordination, it would be well to recognize their nature now rather than at some future time.

Considerable light is thrown upon this question by the techniques which have been worked out in the authoritarian states. In every case we find: the abolition of representative government; the extinguishment of local government, including home rule; the transfer of all policy determination as well as execution to a single executive, the legislative assembly becoming a channel for manufacturing consent; the erection of an immense bureaucratic machine responsible also for the control of conduct and of economic life; the determination of production programs and quotas; the establishment of a factional party in supreme control and subject to no discipline but its own; the rise of a single powerful leader; the disappearance of compromise as a basis of action; the stringent control and use of press, radio, schools, universities, public assembly, and all private associations to condition the whole nation, particularly the rising generation; the intensification of separatist nationalism and race consciousness; the fabrication of national scapegoats; the stimulation of great mass diversions, particularly in sport and expeditions; the extinction of criticism and difference of opinion; and the termination of free inquiry.

It will be observed that there are two great efforts in this whole program, first to make the government all powerful in every important sphere of life so that it may have the facilities and authority for the co-ordination of all of life; and second, to create absolute and universal consent and enthusiastic adherence to the program of the state. The attention which is devoted to this latter objective by the authoritarian states is a powerful testimonial to the power of ideas in co-ordinating the activities of humanity.

It is clear also from the observation of these experiments, in which direction the limitations of co-ordination lie. The difficulties arise from:

1. The uncertainty of the future, not only as to natural phenomena like rain and crops, but even more as to the behavior of individuals and of peoples;
2. The lack of knowledge, experience, wisdom, and character among leaders and their confused and conflicting ideals and objectives;
3. The lack of administrative skill and technique;

4. The vast number of variables involved and the incompleteness of human knowledge, particularly with regard to man and life;
5. The lack of orderly methods of developing, considering, perfecting, and adopting new ideas and programs.

It may also be noted that the authoritarian states are in trouble internationally. Some regard this as intentional, as part of the diversion and scapegoat technique, while others think that it is more or less inevitable because of the very co-ordination of the economic activities of the individual nations in question. If this latter explanation is correct, then we may regard the increased friction at the periphery experienced by co-ordinated states as a further illustration of the general principle noted above.

It is a striking fact that the authoritarian states have thus far found little difficulty in regimenting the thinking and conduct of the masses of the population. This is the least of their troubles. The upper and middle classes and the educated are no exception to the rule. It is of course too early to accept the dominion of opinion that has been established as a long-time phenomenon, and there have been those who have before this predicted its early collapse. It must be recorded, however, that there is no indication of this breakdown as yet. It is difficult to see how such a collapse can come except through a failure of the administration or of the economic policies of the government. In other words, the weak link in the chain is not the securing of popular support; it is rather in the field of policy and execution. It is at this point that the lack of a systematic method for bringing in new ideas, the corrective of free criticism, and the common man's appraisal of the end results may prove disastrous. Certainly a state which attempts the extraordinarily difficult task of co-ordinating most of life will need these sources of regeneration and correction even more than a state which undertakes a more limited responsibility.

If this analysis is sound, the limits of co-ordination are to be found in lack of knowledge and lack of administrative skill. It would therefore be sound policy (1) to advance knowledge through research in public affairs, and administration both through research and through the adoption of improved techniques. It would seem also desirable (2) to advance the area of attempted co-ordination in sectors and experimentally so that the necessary skill may be gained through trial and error. This would mean a deliberate advance in a wave motion, with periods of pause and consolidation after each forward move.

If this course of action is adopted there is no need of accepting the view that there are fixed limits of co-ordination beyond which mankind can never go. It is also probable that the area of co-ordination will always be less extensive than all of life because the ability of mankind to co-ordinate, though continually advancing, can never overtake the creative capacity of individuals to invent new fields of activity and knowledge.

Chester I. Barnard (1886–1961)

For most of his working life, Chester Barnard's primary occupation was in private business, the telephone industry, which he joined as a statistician in 1909 in Boston. Following a series of increasingly important assignments he became the first president of the New Jersey Bell Telephone Company in 1927, a post which he held until 1948. But he also served in a great variety of nonbusiness capacities. Beginning in 1931, he organized and directed the New Jersey Emergency Relief Administration; later he was a director of the Regional Plan Association, the National Probation Association, and the United States Chamber of Commerce. During World War II, he was national president of the United Services Organization (USO) and from 1948 to 1952 was president of the Rockefeller Foundation. He was not an academic; in fact, he never received a bachelor's degree though he studied three years at Harvard. Yet he was one of the truly seminal thinkers in administration and organization in American history. He was widely read, but most of his insights and theories derived from his own experiences and observations in his private and public professional life. He was not in the mainstream of the public administration movement when his major and only full-scale book, *The Functions of the Executive,*[1] was published in 1938. It challenged many of the assumptions and premises of both business and public administration and at the same time charted new courses and perspectives for scholars in both fields, which would have tremendous impact particularly after World War II.

Barnard's concepts were so wide-ranging and at the same time so closely integrated that it is impossible to choose a single essay—or even two or three—to comprehend his thoughts. He was the first, or surely one of the first, to relate sociological and psychological theory to formal organizations; to focus on decision-making (including the decision not to decide); to analyze informal organization; to develop an economy of incentives as applied to organization; to describe authority in organization as derivative of responsibility; to explore the moral ingredients of responsibility; to penetrate the

---

1. The book, published by Harvard University Press, was actually a revision of and expansion upon a series of lectures Barnard delivered at Harvard in 1937. A second volume, *Organization and Management,* consisting of a collection of selected papers by Barnard, was published by the same press in 1948. The two books, in retrospect, seem to have been misnamed. *Functions* was really a theory of organization with emphasis in the latter part on the role and responsibilities of executives. The later volume was a series of unrelated essays, some expanding upon and explaining parts of the first, others on distinct new topics.

essence of leadership; and to explore in depth the nature, the functions, and the pathologies of status in organizations.[2] The essay that follows, on the executive functions, perhaps comes closest to providing a focus for his widely ranging formulations on a subject of dominant interest to him.

F.C.M.

The Functions of the Executive

The Executive Functions

The coordination of efforts essential to a system of cooperation requires, as we have seen, an organization system of communication. Such a system of communication implies centers or points of interconnection and can only operate as these centers are occupied by persons who are called executives. It might be said, then, that the function of executives is to serve as channels of communication so far as communications must pass through central positions. But since the object of the communication system is coordination of all aspects of organization, it follows that the functions of executives relate to all the work essential to the vitality and endurance of an organization, so far, at least, as it must be accomplished through formal coordination.

It is important to observe, however, that not all work done by persons who occupy executive positions is in connection with the executive functions, the coordination of activities of others. Some of the work of such persons, though *organization* work, is not executive. For example, if the president of a corporation goes out personally to sell products of his company or engages in some of the production work, these are not executive services. If the president of a university gives lectures to a class of students, this is not executive work. If the head of a government department spends time on complaints or disputes about services rendered by the department, this is not necessarily executive work. Executive work is not that *of* the organization, but the specialized work of *maintaining* the organization in operation.

Probably all executives do a considerable amount of non-executive work. Sometimes this work is more valuable than the executive work they do. This intermixture of functions is a matter of convenience and often of economy, because of the scarcity of abilities; or there may be other reasons for it. As a result of the combination of executive with non-executive functions, however, it is difficult in practice merely by comparison of titles or of nominal

2. Most of these subjects are treated in *The Functions of the Executive*. Barnard's essays on leadership and status are contained in *Organization and Management*.

Chapter 15, *The Functions of the Executive* (Cambridge: Harvard University Press, 1968; reprint of the 1938 edition), pp. 215–234. Reprinted by permission of the publishers. Copyright 1938 by the President and Fellows of Harvard College, © renewed 1966 by Grace F. N. Barnard.

functions to determine the comparative methods of executive work in different organizations. If we mean by executive functions the specialized work of maintaining systems of cooperative effort, we may best proceed for general purposes to find out what work has to be done, and then, when desirable, to trace out who are doing that work in a particular organization.

This is especially true because executive work is itself often complexly organized. In an organization of moderate size there may be a hundred persons who are engaged part of the time in executive work; and some of them, for example clerks or stenographers, are not executives in any ordinary sense. Nevertheless, the activities of these persons constitute the executive organization. It is to the functions of this organization as a special unit that our attention should be given primarily, the distribution of work between persons or positions being for general purposes quite of secondary importance. This chapter will be devoted to the functions of the executive organization as a whole which exists exclusively for the coordination of the efforts of the entire organization.

The executive functions serve to maintain a system of cooperative effort. They are impersonal. The functions are not, as so frequently stated, to manage a group of persons. I do not think a correct understanding of executive work can be had if this narrower, convenient, but strictly speaking erroneous, conception obtains. It is not even quite correct to say that the executive functions are to manage the system of cooperative efforts. As a whole it is managed by itself, not by the executive organization, which is a part of it. The functions with which we are concerned are like those of the nervous system, including the brain, in relation to the rest of the body. It exists to maintain the bodily system by directing those actions which are necessary more effectively to adjust to the environment, but it can hardly be said to manage the body, a large part of whose functions are independent of it and upon which it in turn depends.

The essential executive functions, as I shall present them . . . are, first, to provide the system of communication; second, to promote the securing of essential efforts; and third, to formulate and define purpose. Since the elements of organization are interrelated and interdependent, the executive functions are so likewise; nevertheless they are subject to considerable specialization and as functions are to a substantial degree separable in practice. We shall deal with them only as found in complex, though not necessarily large, organizations.

I. The Maintenance of Organization Communication

We have noticed . . . that, when a complex of more than one unit is in question, centers of communication and corresponding executives are necessary. The need of a definite system of communication creates the first task of the organizer and is the immediate origin of executive organization. If the purpose of an organization is conceived initially in the mind of one person, he is likely very early to find necessary the selection of lieutenants; and if the organization is spontaneous its very first task is likely to be the selection of a leader. Since communication will be accomplished only through the agency of persons, the selection of persons for executive functions is the concrete method of establishing the *means* of communication, though it must be immediately followed by the creation of positions, that is, a *system* of communication; and, especially in establishing organizations, the positions will exist to be filled in the event of vacancies.

In other words, communication position and the "locating" of the services of a person are complementary phases of the same thing. The center of communication is the organization service of a person at a place. Persons without positions cannot function as executives, they mean nothing but potentiality. Conversely, positions vacant are as defunct as dead nerve centers. This is why executives, when functioning strictly as executives, are unable to appraise men in the abstract, in an organization vacuum, as it were. Men are neither good nor bad, but only good or bad in this or that position. This is why they not infrequently "change the organization," the arrangement of positions, if men suitable to fill them are not available. In fact, "executive organization" in practice cannot be divorced from "executive personnel"; and "executive personnel" is without important meaning except in conjunction with a specific arrangement of positions.

Therefore, the problem of the establishment and maintenance of the system of communication, that is, the primary task of the executive organization, is perpetually that of obtaining the coalescence of the two phases, executive personnel and executive positions. Each phase in turn is the strategic factor of the executive problem—first one, then the other phase, must be adjusted. This is the central problem of the executive functions. Its solution is not in itself sufficient to accomplish the work of all these functions; but no others can be accomplished without it, and none well unless it is well done.

Although this communication function has two phases, it is usually necessary in practice to deal with one phase at a time, and the problems of each phase are of quite different kinds. The problems of positions are those of location and the geographical, temporal, social, and functional specializations of unit and group organizations. The personnel problems are a special case of general personnel problems—the recruiting of contributors who have appropriate qualifications, and the development of the inducements, incentives, persuasion, and objective authority that can make those qualifications effective executive services in the organization.

1. The Scheme of Organization.   Let us call the first phase of the function—the definition of organization positions—the "scheme of organization." This is the aspect of organization which receives relatively excessive formal attention because it can apparently be reduced to organization charts, specifications of duties, and descriptions of divisions of labor, etc. It rests upon or represents a coordination chiefly of the work to be done by the organization, that is, its purposes broken up into subsidiary purposes, specializations, tasks, etc., . . . the kind and quality of *services* of personnel that can be obtained; the kind and quantity of *persons* that must be included in the cooperative system for this purpose; the inducements that are required; and the places at which and the times when these factors can be combined, which will not be specifically discussed here.

It is evident that these are mutually dependent factors, and that they all involve other executive functions which we shall discuss later. So far as the *scheme* of organization is separately attacked, it is always on the assumption that it is then the strategic factor, the other factors of organization remaining fixed for the time being; but since the underlying purpose of any change in a scheme of organization is to affect these other factors as a whole favorably, any scheme of organization at any given time represents necessarily a result of previous successive approximations through a period of time. It has always necessarily to be attacked on the basis of the present situation.

2. Personnel.   The scheme of organization is dependent not only upon the general factors of the organization as a whole, but likewise, as we have indicated, on the availability of various kinds of services for the executive positions. This becomes in its turn the strategic factor. In general, the principles of the economy of incentives apply here as well as to other more general personnel problems. The balance of factors and the technical problems of this special class, however, are not only different from those generally to be found in other spheres of organization economy but are highly special in different types of organizations.

The most important single contribution required of the executive, certainly the most universal qualification, is loyalty, domination by the organization personality. This is the first necessity because the lines of communication cannot function at all unless the personal contributions of executives will be present at the required positions, at the times necessary, without default for ordinary personal reasons. This, as a personal qualification, is known in secular organizations as the quality of "responsibility"; in political organizations as "regularity"; in government organizations as fealty or loyalty; in religious organizations as "complete submission" to the faith and to the hierarchy of objective religious authority.

The contribution of personal loyalty and submission is least susceptible to tangible inducements. It cannot be bought either by material inducements or by other positive incentives, except all other things be equal. This is as true of industrial organizations, I believe, as of any others. It is rather generally understood that although money or other material inducements must usually be paid to responsible persons, responsibility itself does not arise from such inducements.

However, love of prestige is, in general, a much more important inducement in the case of executives than with the rest of the personnel. Interest in work and pride in organization are other incentives that usually must be present. These facts are much obscured as respects commercial organizations, where material inducements appear to be the effective factors partly because such inducements are more readily offered in such organizations and partly because, since the other incentives are often equal as between such organizations, material inducements are the only available differential factor. It also becomes an important secondary factor to individuals in many cases, because prestige and official responsibilities impose heavy material burdens on them. Hence neither churches nor socialistic states have been able to escape the necessity of direct or indirect material inducements for high dignitaries or officials. But this is probably incidental and superficial in all organizations. It appears to be true that in all of them adequate incentives to executive services are difficult to offer. Those most available in the present age are tangible, materialistic; but on the whole they are both insufficient and often abortive.

Following loyalty, responsibility, and capacity to be dominated by organization personality, come the more specific personal abilities. They are roughly divided into two classes: relatively general abilities, involving general alertness, comprehensiveness of interest, flexibility, faculty of adjustment, poise, courage, etc.; and specialized abilities based on particular aptitudes and acquired techniques. The first kind is relatively difficult to appraise because it depends upon innate characteristics developed through general experience. It is not greatly susceptible to immediate inculcation. The second kind may be less rare because the division of labor, that is, organization itself, fosters it automatically, and because it is susceptible to development (at a cost) by training and education. We deliberately and more and more turn out specialists; but we do not develop general executives well by specific efforts, and we know very little about how to do it.

The higher the positions in the line of authority, the more general the abilities required. The scarcity of such abilities, together with the necessity for keeping the lines of authority as short as feasible, controls the organization of executive work. It leads to the reduction of the number of formally executive positions to the minimum, a measure made possible by creating about the executives in many cases staffs of specialists who supplement them in time, energy, and technical capacities. This is made feasible by elaborate and often delicate arrangements to correct error resulting from the faults of over-specialization and the paucity of line executives.

The operation of such systems of complex executive organization requires the highest development of the executive arts. Its various forms and techniques are most definitely exemplified in the armies and navies of the major powers, the Postal Administrations of several European countries, the Bell Telephone System, some of the great railway systems, and the Catholic Church; and perhaps in the political organization of the British Empire. One of the first limitations of world-wide or even a much more restricted international organization is the necessity for the development of these forms and techniques far beyond their present status.

Thus, jointly with the development of the scheme of organization, the selection, promotion, demotion, and dismissal of men becomes the essence of maintaining the system of communication without which no organization can exist. The selection in part, but especially the promotion, demotion, and dismissal of men, depend upon the exercise of supervision or what is often called "control."

Control relates directly, and in conscious application chiefly, to the work of the organization as a whole rather than to the work of executives as such. But so heavily dependent is the success of cooperation upon the functioning of the executive organization that practically the control is over executives for the most part. If the work of an organization is not successful, if it is inefficient, if it cannot maintain the services of its personnel, the conclusion is that its "management" is wrong; that is, that the scheme of communication or the associated personnel or both, that is, the executive department directly related, are at fault. This is, sometimes at least, not true, but often it is. Moreover, for the correction of such faults the first reliance is upon executive organization. The methods by which control is exercised are, of course, numerous and largely technical to each organization, and need not be further discussed here.

3. Informal Executive Organizations.   So far we have considered the first executive function only as it relates to the formal communication system. It has been emphasized several times in this treatise that informal organization is essential to formal organizations, particularly with reference to communication. This is true not only of the organization as a whole, or of its ultimate subordinate units, but also of that special part which we call the executive organization. The communication function of executives includes the maintenance of informal executive organization as an essential means of communication.

Although I have never heard it stated that this is an executive function or that such a thing as an informal executive organization exists, in all the good organizations I have observed the most careful attention is paid to it. In all of them informal organizations operate. This is usually not apparent except to those directly concerned.

The general method of maintaining an informal executive organization is so to operate and to select and promote executives that a general condition of compatibility of personnel is maintained. Perhaps often and certainly occasionally men cannot be promoted or selected, or even must be relieved, because they cannot function, because they "do not fit," where there is no question of formal competence. This question of "fitness" involves such matters as education, experience, age, sex, personal distinctions, prestige, race, nationality, faith, politics, sectional antecedents; and such very specific personal traits as manners, speech, personal appearance, etc. It goes by few if any rules, except those based at least nominally on other, formal, considerations. It represents in its best sense the political aspects of personal relationship in formal organization. I suspect it to be most highly developed in political, labor, church, and university organizations, for the very reason that the intangible types of personal services are relatively more important in them than in most other, especially industrial, organizations. But it is certainly of major importance in all organizations.

This compatibility is promoted by educational requirements (armies, navies, churches, schools); by requirement of certain background (European armies, navies, labor unions, Soviet and Fascist governments, political parties); by conferences and conventions; by specifically social activities; by class distinctions connected with privileges and "authority" (in armies, navies, churches, universities). A certain conformity is required by unwritten understanding that can sometimes be formally enforced, expressed for its negative aspect by the phrase "conduct unbecoming a gentleman and an officer." There are, however, innumerable other processes, many of which are not consciously employed for this purpose.

It must not be understood that the desired degree of compatibility is always the same or is the maximum possible. On the contrary it seems to me to be often the case that excessive compatibility or harmony is deleterious, resulting in "single track minds" and excessively crystallized attitudes and in the destruction of personal responsibility; but I know from experience in operating with new emergency organizations, in which there was no time and little immediate basis for the growth of an informal organization properly coordinated with formal organization that it is almost impossible to secure effective and efficient cooperation without it.

The functions of informal executive organizations are the communication of intangible facts, opinions, suggestions, suspicions, that cannot pass through formal channels without raising issues calling for decisions, without dissipating dignity and objective authority, and without overloading executive positions; also to minimize excessive cliques of political types arising from too great divergence of interests and views; to promote self-discipline of the group; and to make possible the development of important personal influences in the organization. There are probably other functions.

I shall comment on only two functions of informal executive organization. The necessity for avoiding formal issues, that is, for avoiding the issuance of numerous formal orders except on routine matters and except in emergencies, is important. I know of major executives who issue an order or judgment settling an important issue rather seldom, although they are functioning all the time. The obvious desire of politicians to avoid important issues (and to impose them on their opponents) is based upon a thorough sense of organization. Neither authority nor cooperative disposition (largely the same things) will stand much overt division on formal issues in the present stage of human development. Hence most laws, executive orders, decisions, etc., are in effect formal notice that all is well—there is agreement, authority is not questioned.

The question of personal influence is very subtle. Probably most good organizations have somewhere a Colonel House; and many men not only exercise beneficent influence far beyond that implied by their formal status, but most of them, at the time, would lose their influence if they had corresponding formal status. The reason may be that many men have personal qualifications of high order that will not operate under the stress of commensurate official responsibility. By analogy I may mention the golfers of first class skill who cannot "stand up" in public tournaments.

To summarize: the first executive function is to develop and maintain a system of communication. This involves jointly a scheme of organization and an executive personnel. The processes by which the latter is accomplished include chiefly the selection of men and the offering of incentives; techniques of control permitting effectiveness in promoting, demoting, and dismissing men; and finally the securing of an informal organization in which the essential property is compatibility of personnel. The chief functions of this informal organization are expansion of the means of communication with reduction in the necessity for formal decisions, the minimizing of undesirable influences, and the promotion of desirable influences concordant with the scheme of formal responsibilities.

II. The Securing of Essential Services from Individuals

The second function of the executive organization is to promote the securing of the personal services that constitute the material of organizations.

The work divides into two main divisions: (1) the bringing of persons into cooperative relationship with the organization; (2) the eliciting of the services after such persons have been brought into that relationship.

1.   The characteristic fact of the first division is that the organization is acting upon persons who are in every sense outside it. Such action is necessary not merely to secure the personnel of new organizations, or to supply the material for the growth of existing organizations, but also to replace the losses that continually take place by reason of death, resignation, "backsliding," emigration, discharge, excommunication, ostracism. These factors of growth or replacement of contributors require bringing persons by organization effort within range of the consideration of the incentives available in order to induce some of these persons to attach themselves to the organization. Accordingly the task involves two parts: (a) bringing persons within reach of specific effort to secure services; and (b) the application of that effort when they have been brought near enough. Often both parts of the task occupy the efforts of the same persons or parts of an organization; but they are clearly distinct elements and considerable specialization is found with respect to them.

(a) Bringing persons within reach of recruiting or proselyting influence is a task which differs in practical emphasis among organizations in respect both to scope and to method. Some religious organizations—especially the Catholic Church, several Protestant Churches, the Mormon Church, for example—have as ideal goals the attachment of all persons to their organizations, and the wide world is the field of proselyting propaganda. During many decades the United States of America invited all who could reach its shores to become American citizens. Other organizations, having limits on the volume of their activities, restrict the field of propaganda. Thus many nations in effect now restrict substantial growth to those who acquire a national status by birth; the American Legion restricts its membership to those who have acquired a status by a certain type of previous service, etc. Others restrict their fields practically on the basis of proportions. Thus universities "in principle" are open to all or to all with educational and character qualifications but may restrict their appeals to geographical, racial, and class proportions, so as to preserve the cosmopolitan character of their bodies, or to preserve predominance of nationals, etc. Industrial and commercial organizations are theoretically limited usually by considerations of social compatibility and additionally by the costs of propaganda. They usually attempt no appeal when the geographic remoteness makes it ineffective.

Although the scope of the field of propaganda is for most organizations not clearly conceived or stated and as a problem only requires active consideration at intervals usually long, the question is nevertheless fundamental. This is best indicated by the methods practically employed in connection with it. In churches the organization of mission work and its territorial scope are the best indications of its importance. In most governments, at present, the accretion of members takes the form of stimulating reproduction by active promotional efforts, as in France and Italy, for example, or by the ease of acquiring citizenship and free land, as until recently in the United States. In many industrial organizations foreign recruiting was once an important aspect of their work, and directly or indirectly the appeal for contributors of capital or credit has been fundamentally international in scope until recent exchange restrictions. In fact, the most universal aspect of industrial organization appeal has been in respect to this type of contributor—for many practical purposes he is not usually regarded as the material of organization, though in the present study he is.

(b) The effort to induce specific persons who by the general appeal are brought into contact with an organization actually to become identified with it constitutes the more regular and routine work of securing contributors. This involves in its general aspects the method of persuasion which has already been described, the establishment of inducements and incentives, and direct negotiation. The methods required are indefinitely large in number and of very wide variety. . . .

2. Although the work of recruiting is important in most organizations, and especially so in those which are new or rapidly expanding or which have high "turnover," nevertheless in established and enduring organizations the eliciting of the quantity and quality of efforts from their adherents is usually

more important and occupies the greater part of personnel effort. Because of the more tangible character of "membership," being an "employee," etc., recruiting is apt to receive more attention as a field of personnel work than the business of promoting the actual output of efforts and influences, which are the real material of organization. Membership, nominal adherence, is merely the starting point; and the minimum contributions which can be conceived as enabling retention of such connection would generally be insufficient for the survival of active or productive organization. Hence every church, every government, every other important organization, has to intensify or multiply the contributions which its members will make above the level or volume which would occur if no such effort were made. Thus churches must strengthen the faith, secure compliance by public and private acknowledgments of faith or devotion, and secure material contributions from their members. Governments are concerned with increasing the quality of the citizenry—promoting national solidarity, loyalty, patriotism, discipline, and competence. Other organizations are similarly occupied in securing loyalty, reliability, responsibility, enthusiasm, quality of efforts, output. In short, every organization to survive must deliberately attend to the maintenance and growth of its authority to do the things necessary for coordination, effectiveness, and efficiency. This, as we have seen, depends upon its appeal to persons who are already related to the organization.

The methods, the inducements and incentives, by which this is done have already been in general indicated in our discussion of incentives and authority. As executive functions they may be distinguished as the maintenance of morale, the maintenance of the scheme of inducements, the maintenance of schemes of deterrents, supervision and control, inspection, education and training.

III. The Formulation of Purpose and Objectives

The third executive function is to formulate and define the purposes, objectives, ends, of the organization. It has already been made clear that, strictly speaking, purpose is defined more nearly by the aggregate of action taken than by any formulation in words; but that that aggregate of action is a residuum of the decisions relative to purpose and the environment, resulting in closer and closer approximations to the concrete acts. It has also been emphasized that purpose is something that must be accepted by all the contributors to the system of efforts. Again, it has been stated that purpose must be broken into fragments, specific objectives, not only ordered in time so that detailed purpose and detailed action follow in the series of progressive cooperation, but also ordered contemporaneously into the specializations—geographical, social, and functional—that each unit organization implies. It is more apparent here than with other executive functions that it is an entire executive organization that formulates, redefines, breaks into details, and decides on the innumerable simultaneous and progressive actions that are the stream of syntheses constituting purpose or action. No single executive can under any conditions accomplish this function alone, but only that part of it which relates to his position in the executive organization.

Hence the critical aspect of this function is the assignment of responsibility—the delegation of objective authority. Thus in one sense this function is that of the scheme of positions, the system of communication, already discussed. That is its potential aspect. Its other aspect is the actual decisions and conduct which make the scheme a working system. Accordingly, the general executive states that "this is the purpose, this the objective, this the direction, in general terms, in which we wish to move, before next year." His department heads, or the heads of his main territorial divisions, say to their departments or suborganizations: "This means for us these things now, then others next month, then others later, to be better defined after experience." Their subdepartment or division heads say: "This means for us such and such operations now at these places, such others at those places, something today here, others tomorrow there." Then district or bureau chiefs in turn become more and more specific, their sub-chiefs still more so as to place, group, time, until finally purpose is merely jobs, specific groups, definite men, definite times, accomplished results. But meanwhile, back and forth, up and down, the communications pass, reporting obstacles, difficulties, impossibilities, accomplishments; redefining, modifying purposes level after level.

Thus the organization for the definition of purpose is the organization for the specification of work to do; and the specifications are made in their final stage when and where the work is being done. I suspect that at least nine-tenths of all organization activity is on the responsibility, the authority, and the specifications of those who make the last contributions, who apply personal energies to the final concrete objectives. There is no meaning to personal specialization, personal experience, personal training, personal location, personal ability, eyes and ears, arms and legs, brains and emotions, if this is not so. What must be added to the indispensable authority, responsibility, and capability of each contributor is the indispensable coordination. This requires a pyramiding of the formulation of purpose that becomes more and more general as the number of units of basic organization becomes larger, and more and more remote in future time. Responsibility for abstract, generalizing, prospective, long-run decision is delegated *up* the line, responsibility for definition, action, remains always at the base where the authority for effort resides.

The formulation and definition of purpose is then a widely distributed function, only the more general part of which is executive. In this fact lies the most important inherent difficulty in the operation of cooperative systems— the necessity for indoctrinating those at the lower levels with general purposes, the major decisions, so that they remain cohesive and able to make the ultimate detailed decisions coherent; and the necessity, for those at the higher levels, of constantly understanding the concrete conditions and the specific decisions of the "ultimate" contributors from which and from whom executives are often insulated. Without that up-and-down-the-line coordination of purposeful decisions, general decisions and general purposes are mere intellectual processes in an organization vacuum, insulated from realities by layers of misunderstanding. The function of formulating grand purposes and providing for their redefinition is one which needs sensitive systems of communication, experience in interpretation, imagination, and delegation of responsibility.

❀   ❀   ❀

Charles A. Beard (1874–1948)

Although best known and remembered as a scholar and writer of American and European history, Charles A. Beard was also a major contributor to the development of public administration in this country. His voluminous works included several dealing primarily with politics and administration. Between 1917 and 1922, he directed the Training School for Public Service, associated with the New York Bureau of Municipal Research, and for many subsequent years pushed for the development of the field of public administration. He participated in the formation of the American Society for Public Administration in 1939, and in December of that year delivered a ringing address on the importance of public administration before the American Political Science Association. Most of that address is reprinted below.

F.C.M.

Administration, A Foundation of Government

The authors of the Constitution of the United States regarded it as a triumph for the human spirit in America that a new form of government could be established by the process of discussion, deliberation, and popular action, as distinguished from the age-long processes of violence. Looking backward from their time and forward into our own, we may say that they were justified in their celebration.

With reference to a far less momentous occurrence, this modest occasion, we may properly regard as a triumph for the same spirit a voluntary action of public officials and interested citizens looking to the resolute and continuous improvement of the public services. It is this action, the establishment of a Society for Public Administration, that we are ratifying and approving today. These officials and these citizens are no hirelings of a despotic power, taking orders from above. They are not seeking the aggrandizement of a class, bent on exploiting and holding down a subject people. They are not concerned

"Administration, A Foundation of Government," *American Political Science Review,* Vol. XXXIV (April, 1940), pp. 232–235.

primarily with emoluments, promotions, and honors as such. On the contrary, they are proposing to search their own hearts and minds, to study ways and means of making more efficient and economical the services rendered by government to the people. They do not wish to diminish either civil liberties or individual responsibilities in society. On the contrary, they cherish these eternal values and intend to discover and develop schemes and methods of administration deliberately adapted to the perpetuation of these precious elements in the American heritage.

The step taken today, though it may seem novel to some, is only the culmination of a long chain of events, extending over a period of forty years and more. The establishment of systematic instruction in comparative administration under the auspices of the late Frank J. Goodnow at Columbia University long ago was among the great beginnings. The organization of the New York Bureau of Municipal Research was another advance. The foundation of the Governmental Research Association was still another. The spread of instruction in administration among our universities, the creation of numerous societies of public officials, the growth of civil service legislation, the self-dedicated and distinguished careers of innumerable men and women in various branches of public administration, the deepening recognition of the vital relation between efficient and honorable administration and the very existence of our society and form of government—all these and more have signaled through the years the coming of this day and the action which is here taken. . . .

Paraphrasing the language of my distinguished friend, Dr. Alfred Cohn, specialist in cardiac diseases at the Rockefeller Institute, I may remark, by way of preface, that it is the business of science, in dealing with any subject, to make true statements about it, of the utmost generality, and in the fewest possible words. Remembering this admonition, I present, for what it is worth, and may prove to be worth, the following bill of axioms or aphorisms on public administration, as fitting this important occasion:

1. The continuous and fairly efficient discharge of certain functions by government, central and local, is a necessary condition for the existence of any great society.

2. As a society becomes more complicated, as its division of labor ramifies more widely, as its commerce extends, as technology takes the place of handicrafts and local self-sufficiency, the functions of government increase in number and in their vital relationships to the fortunes of society and of individuals.

3. Any government in such a complicated society, consequently any such society itself, is strong in proportion to its capacity to administer the functions that are brought into being.

4. Legislation respecting these functions, difficult as it is, is relatively easy as compared with the enforcement of legislation, that is, the effective discharge of these functions in their most minute ramifications and for the public welfare.

5. When a form of government, such as ours, provides for legal changes, by the process of discussion and open decision, to fit social changes, then effective and wise administration becomes the central prerequisite for the perdurance of government and society—to use a metaphor, becomes a foundation of government as a going concern.

6. Unless the members of an administrative system are drawn from various classes and regions, unless careers are open in it to talents, unless the way is prepared by an appropriate scheme of general education, unless public officials are subjected to internal and external criticism of a constructive nature, then the public personnel will become a bureaucracy dangerous to society and to popular government.

7. Unless, as David Lilienthal has recently pointed out in an address on the Tennessee Valley Authority, an administrative system is so constructed and operated as to keep alive local and individual responsibilities, it is likely to destroy the basic well-springs of activity, hope, and enthusiasm necessary to popular government and to the flowering of a democratic civilization.

The validity of these axioms may be illustrated, though not proved, by reference to the fate of that great society, the Roman Empire of antiquity, which perished from the earth. Historians of the decline and fall are fairly well agreed that in the latter years of the Empire, its administrative system, which had grown ever more complicated and centralized in the days of prosperity, at last destroyed local autonomy, proved to be incompetent for its tasks, and sank into ruins with the society which it had once powerfully helped to sustain.

If these things be true and of good report, it follows that this occasion, which may seem trivial amid the rush and roar of affairs, may receive a strange elevation at the hands of those historians who, in distant years, seek to trace the trajectory of our civilization. At all events, we may be well assured that good work, honestly done, with an unfailing interest in the public welfare, is worthy of great talents and high aspirations, brings its own rewards and satisfactions, and somehow anchors itself in the economy of universal history. With this assurance and under this sign, the new society, launched today, may look forward to a service which will not end until the language of the Gettysburg address is heard no more on this continent.

V. O. Key (1908-1963)

V. O. Key is probably best and properly remembered as one of the most eminent students of American politics, parties, voting behavior, and pressure groups, the principal subjects of his teaching and writing during the last two decades of his life. It is less well known that during the early years of his professional career, a primary field of interest for him was public administration. His first book was a seminal work on federal grants in aid. During the 1930s, he was a member of the staff of the Committee on Public Administration (of the Social Science Research Council) and of the National Resources Planning Board. During World War II, he was a staff member of the Bureau of the Budget.

The article on budgeting that follows was written two years before he went to work at the bureau. In it he put his finger on the basic problem of public budgeting, a problem which has plagued budgeteers, politicians, and scholars before and since: determining the criteria for allocating public expenditures among competing purposes and programs. Almost a decade after the article was written, the first Hoover Commission made a stab at the problem with its proposal for performance budgeting. In the mid-1960s, with the enthusiastic support of President Lyndon B. Johnson, federal economists made a more penetrating effort with their Planning-Programming-Budgeting System (PPBS), based in large part upon cost-benefit analysis. But in 1971 Alice Rivlin, one of the leaders in that push, wrote: "Little progress has been made in comparing the benefits of different social programs."[1] More recently, President Carter inaugurated a new effort in the same direction, dubbed "zero-base budgeting." One need not denigrate the positive byproducts of these various initiatives, but it seems safe to judge that none has solved Key's problem. Indeed, much that has gone on in the field of budgeting seems analogous to Wallace Sayre's observation in the field of personnel—the triumph of technique over purpose.[2]

No one before or since has more clearly enunciated this basic problem of public budgeting than did V. O. Key in 1940. In his closing remarks, he called upon political philosophers to help in resolving the problem. Yet I am not aware of many political philosophers who have contributed toward an answer—or even have addressed the question.

F.C.M.

1.   In her book, *Systematic Thinking for Social Action* (Brookings Institution, 1971), p. 7.
2.   See the Sayre article in Part IV.

The Lack of a Budgetary Theory

... On the most significant aspect of public budgeting, i.e., the allocation of expenditures among different purposes so as to achieve the greatest return, American budgetary literature is singularly arid. Toilers in the budgetary field have busied themselves primarily with the organization and procedure for budget preparation, the forms for the submission of requests for funds, the form of the budget document itself, and like questions. That these things have deserved the consideration given them cannot be denied when the unbelievable resistance to the adoption of the most rudimentary essentials of budgeting is recalled and their unsatisfactory condition in many jurisdictions even now is observed. Nevertheless, the absorption of energies in the establishment of the mechanical foundations for budgeting has diverted attention from the basic budgeting problem (on the expenditure side), namely: On what basis shall it be decided to allocate x dollars to activity A instead of activity B?

Writers on budgeting say little or nothing about the purely economic aspects of public expenditure. "Economics," says Professor Robbins, "is the science which studies human behavior as a relationship between ends and scarce means which have alternative uses." Whether budgetary behavior is economic or political is open to fruitless debate; nevertheless, the point of view and the mode of thought of the economic theorist are relevant, both in the study of and action concerning public expenditure. The budget-maker never has enough revenue to meet the requests of all spending agencies, and he must decide (subject, of course, to subsequent legislative action) how scarce means shall be allocated to alternative uses. The completed budgetary document (although the budget-maker may be quite unaware of it) represents a judgment upon how scarce means should be allocated to bring the maximum return in social utility.

In their discussions of the review of estimates, budget authorities rarely go beyond the question of how to judge the estimates for particular functions, i.e., ends; and the approach to the review of the estimate of the individual agency is generally directed toward the efficiency with which the particular end is to be achieved. Even in this sort of review, budget-makers have developed few standards of evaluation, acting, rather, on the basis of their impressionistic judgment, of a rudimentary cost accounting, or, perhaps, of the findings of administrative surveys. For decisions on the requests of individual agencies, the techniques have by no means reached perfection. It is sometimes possible to compute with fair accuracy whether the increased efficiency from new public works, such as a particular highway project, will

American Political Science Review, Vol. XXXIV (December, 1940): 1137–1144. Reprinted with permission.

warrant the capital outlay. Or, given the desirability of a particular objective, it may be feasible to evaluate fairly precisely alternative means for achieving that end. Whether a particular agency is utilizing, and plans to utilize, its resources with the maximum efficiency is of great importance, but this approach leaves untouched a more fundamental problem. If it is assumed that an agency is operating at maximum efficiency, the question remains whether the function is worth carrying out at all, or whether it should be carried out on a reduced or enlarged scale, with resulting transfers of funds to or from other activities of greater or lesser social utility.

Nor is there found in the works of the public finance experts much enlightenment on the question herein considered. They generally dispose of the subject of expenditures with a few perfunctory chapters and hurry on to the core of their interest—taxation and other sources of revenue. On the expenditure side, they differentiate, not very plausibly, between productive and unproductive expenditure; they consider the classification of public expenditures; they demonstrate that public expenditures have been increasing; and they discuss the determination of the optimum aggregate of public expenditure; but they do not generally come to grips with the question of the allocation of public revenues among different objects of expenditure. The issue is recognized, as when Pigou says: "As regards the distribution, as distinct from the aggregate cost, of optional government expenditure, it is clear that, just as an individual will get more satisfaction out of his income by maintaining a certain balance between different sorts of expenditure, so also will a community through its government. The principle of balance in both cases is provided by the postulate that resources should be so distributed among different uses that the marginal return of satisfaction is the same for all of them. . . . Expenditure should be distributed between battleships and poor relief in such wise that the last shilling devoted to each of them yields the same real return. We have here, so far as theory goes, a test by means of which the distribution of expenditure along different lines can be settled." But Pigou dismisses the subject with a paragraph, and the discussion by others is not voluminous.

The only American writer on public finance who has given extended attention to the problem of the distribution of expenditures is Mabel Walker. In her *Municipal Expenditures,* she reviews the theories of public expenditure and devises a method for ascertaining the tendencies in distribution of expenditures on the assumption that the way would be pointed to "a norm of expenditures consistent with the state of progress at present achieved by society." While her method would be inapplicable to the federal budget, and would probably be of less relevance in the analysis of state than of municipal expenditures, her study deserves reflective perusal by municipal budget officers and by students of the problem.

Literature skirting the edges of the problem is found in the writings of those economists who have concerned themselves with the economic problems of the socialist state. In recent years, a new critique of socialism has appeared. This attack, in the words of one who attempts to refute it, is ". . . more subtle and technical than the previous ones, based on the supposed inability of a socialist community to solve purely economic problems. . . . What is asserted is that, even with highly developed technique, adequate incentives to activity, and rational control of population, the economic directors of a socialist commonwealth would be unable to balance against each other the worthwhileness of different lines of production or the relative advantages of different ways of producing the same good." Those who believe this problem not insoluble in a socialist economy set out to answer the question: "What is the proper method of determining just what commodities shall be produced from the economic resources at the disposal of a given community?" One would anticipate from those seeking to answer this question some light on the problems of the budget-maker in a capitalist state. But they are concerned only with the pricing of state-produced goods for sale to individuals in a socialist economy. Professor Dickinson, for example, excludes from his discussion goods and services provided in a socialist economy "free of charge to all members of society, as the result of a decision, based on other grounds than market demands, made by some authoritative economic organ of the community." That exclusion removes from consideration the point at issue. Nevertheless, the critics of socialist theory do at least raise essentially the same problem as that posed in the present discussion; and their comment is suggestive.

Various studies of the economics of public works touch the periphery of the problem concerning the allocation of public expenditures. The principal inquiries have been prosecuted under the auspices of the National Resources Planning Board and its predecessor organizations. These reports, however, are concerned in the main with the question of how much in the aggregate should be spent, and when, in order to function as the most effective absorber of the shocks incidental to cyclical fluctuations. Two studies, by Arthur D. Gayer and John M. Clark, deal with public works outlays as stabilizers of the economic order and with related matters. These works suggest factors relevant in the determination of the total amount of the capital budget; but in them the problem of selection among alternative public works projects is not tackled. In another study, the latter issue is approached by Russell V. Black from a rich background of city planning experience, and he formulates a suggestive but tentative set of criteria for the selection and programming of public works projects.

Planning agencies and professional planners have been more interested in the abstract problem of ascertaining the relative utility of public outlays than has any other group. The issue is stated theoretically in a recent report: "The problem is essentially one of the development of criteria for selecting the objects of public expenditure. As a larger and larger proportion of the national income is spent for public purposes, the sphere of the price system with its freedom of choice of objects of expenditure is more and more restricted. Concurrently, the necessity for developing methods by which public officials may select objects of expenditure which will bring the greatest utility or return and most accurately achieve social aspirations becomes more pressing. In a sense, this constitutes the central problem of the productive state. If planning is to be 'over-all' planning, it must devise techniques for the balancing of values within a framework that gives due regard both to the diverse interests of the present and to the interests of the future." Planning agencies have not succeeded in formulating any convincing principles, either descriptive or normative, concerning the allocation of public funds, but they have, within limited spheres, created governmental machinery facilitating the consideration of related alternative expenditures. The most impressive example is the Water Resources Committee (of the National Resources Planning Board) and its subsidiary drainage-basin committees. Through this machinery, it is possible to consider alternatives in objectives and sequences of expenditure—questions that would not arise concretely without such machinery. Perhaps the approach toward the practical working out of the issue lies in the canalizing of decisions through the governmental machinery so as to place alternatives in juxtaposition and compel consideration of relative values. This is the effect of many existing institutional arrangements; but the issue is rarely so stated, and the structure of government, particularly the federal-state division, frequently prevents the weighing of alternatives.

It may be argued that for the best performance of individual public functions a high degree of stability in the amount of funds available year after year is desirable, and that the notion that there is, or needs to be, mobility of resources as among functions is erroneous. Considerable weight is undoubtedly to be attached to this view. Yet over periods of a few years important shifts occur in relative financial emphasis on different functions of government. Even in minor adjustments, the small change up or down at the margin may be of considerable significance. Like an individual consumer, the state may have certain minimum expenditures generally agreed upon, but care in weighing the relative utility of alternative expenditures becomes more essential as the point of marginal utility is approached. Moreover, within the public economy, frictions (principally institutional in character) exist to obstruct and delay adjustments in the allocation of resources in keeping with changing wants probably to a greater extent than in the private economy.

Efforts to ascertain more precisely the relative "values" of public services may be thought fruitless because of the influence of pressure groups in the determination of the allocation of funds. Each spending agency has its clientele, which it marshals for battle before budgetary and appropriating agencies. And there are those who might contend that the pattern of expenditures resultant from the interplay of these forces constitutes a maximization of return from public expenditure, since it presumably reflects the social consensus on the relative values of different services. If this be true, the more efficient utilization of resources would be promoted by the devising of means more accurately to measure the political strength of interests competing for appropriations. That the appropriation bill expresses a social consensus sounds akin to the mystic doctrine of the "general will." Constantly, choices have to be made between the demands of different groups; and it is probably true that factors other than estimates of the relative political strength of contending groups frequently enter into the decisions. The pressure theory suggests the potential development in budget bureaus and related agencies of a strong bureaucracy strategically situated, and with a vested interest in the general welfare, in contrast with the particularistic drives of the spending agencies.

It is not to be concluded that by excogitation a set of principles may be formulated on the basis of which the harassed budget official may devise an automatic technique for the allocation of financial resources. Yet the problem needs study in several directions. Further examination from the viewpoints of economic theory and political philosophy could produce valuable results. The doctrine of marginal utility, developed most finely in the analysis of the market economy, has a ring of unreality when applied to public expenditures. The most advantageous utilization of public funds resolves itself into a matter of value preferences between ends lacking a common denominator. As such, the question is a problem in political philosophy; keen analyses in these terms would be of the utmost importance in creating an awareness of the problems of the budgetary implementation of programs of political action of whatever shade. The discussion also suggests the desirability of careful and comprehensive analyses of the budgetary process. In detail, what forces go into the making of state budgets? What factors govern decisions of budgetary officials? Precisely what is the role of the legislature? On the federal level, the field for inquiry is broader, including not only the central budgetary agency, but departmental budget offices as well. Studies of congressional appropriating processes are especially needed. For the working budget official, the implications of the discussion rest primarily in a point of view in the consideration of estimates in terms of alternatives—decisions which are always made, but not always consciously. For the personnel policy of budget agencies, the question occurs whether almost sole reliance on persons trained primarily in accounting and fiscal procedure is wise. The thousands of little decisions made in budgetary agencies grow by accretion into formidable budgetary documents which from their sheer mass are apt often to overwhelm those with the power of final decision. We need to look carefully at the training and working assumptions of these officials, to the end that the budget may most truly reflect the public interest.

Carl Joachim Friedrich (1901–) and Herman Finer (1898–1969)

During the years just preceding the United States' entry into World War II, two distinguished professors of political science engaged in a warm intellectual debate on a subject that is still of dominant importance in public administration: administrative responsibility. Interestingly, both of these individuals were of European origin, although their argument related primarily to American government. Professor Friedrich of Harvard was born, brought up, and educated in Germany prior to moving to the United States in 1922 and later becoming a naturalized American citizen. He is one of our most brilliant and prolific scholars and an ardent supporter of democratic institutions. Professor Finer, an Englishman, had conducted research and taught in this country. He too was an eminent scholar and an ardent supporter of democratic institutions.

The debate was apparently provoked by a monograph written by Friedrich in 1935 on *Responsible Government Service Under the American Constitution,* the third chapter of which was directed to responsibility.[1] The following year, Finer criticized Friedrich's propositions on responsibility in an article in a political science journal.[2] Friedrich came back in 1940 with a more extended statement of his views, entitled "Public Policy and the Nature of Administrative Responsibility";[3] and Finer responded, with vigor and some vitriol, in an article on "Administrative Responsibility in Democratic Government," published in the summer of 1941.[4]

Extracts of the last two articles, Friedrich's in 1940 and Finer's, in 1941, are reprinted below. Following the Vietnam War and Watergate, and with the current concern about professionalism and administrative ethics, the issues that they pose seem even more cogent for the 1980s than at the time when they were written.

F.C.M.

1. This was one of the monographs prepared for the Commission of Inquiry on Public Service Personnel, discussed and quoted from above. It was published as part of a book entitled *Problems of the American Public Service* (McGraw-Hill, 1935).

2. *The Political Science Quarterly* 51, 4 Dec. 1936, pp. 569–599.

3. In the book, *Public Policy,* then published annually by the Harvard University Press.

4. *Public Administration Review,* vol. I, pp. 335–350.

Carl Joachim Friedrich

Public Policy and the Nature of Administrative Responsibility

❊ ❊ ❊

Responsibility and Policy Formation

The starting point of any study of responsibility must be that even under the best arrangements a considerable margin of irresponsible conduct of administrative activities is inevitable. For if a responsible person is one who is answerable for his acts to some other person or body, who has to give an account of his doings (Oxford English Dictionary), it should be clear without further argument that there must be some agreement between such a responsible agent and his principal concerning the action in hand or at least the end to be achieved. When one considers the complexity of modern governmental activities, it is at once evident that such agreement can only be partial and incomplete, no matter who is involved. Once the electorate and legislative assemblies are seen, not through the smoke screen of traditional prejudice, but as they are, it is evident that such principals cannot effectively bring about the responsible conduct of public affairs, unless elaborate techniques make explicit what purposes and activities are involved in all the many different phases of public policy. It is at this point that the decisive importance of policy determination becomes apparent. Too often it is taken for granted that as long as we can keep the government from doing wrong we have made it responsible. What is more important is to insure effective action of any sort. To stimulate initiative, even at the risk of mistakes, must nowadays never be lost sight of as a task in making the government's services responsible. An official should be as responsible for inaction as for wrong action; certainly the average voter will criticize the government as severely for one as for the other.

Without a well-defined and well-worked-out policy, responsibility becomes very difficult to bring about. Yet such policies are the exception rather than the rule. Many of the most severe breakdowns in contemporary administration, accompanied by violent public reactions against irresponsible bureaucracy, will be found to trace back to contradictory and ill-defined policy, as embodied in faulty legislation. There are numerous familiar illustrations.

Public Policy (Cambridge: Harvard University Press, 1940), pp. 3–24. Copyright 1940, © renewed 1967 by the President and Fellows of Harvard College. Reprinted by permission of John Wiley & Sons, Inc.

Nor should it be imagined that legislation in this sense is merely embodied in the formal statutes passed by Congress or Parliament. An even more common source of contradictory policy is administrative rules and regulations adopted by the several departments in the process of executing the statutory provisions.

Hence, administrative responsibility can no longer be looked upon as merely a responsibility for executing policies already formulated. We have to face the fact that this responsibility is much more comprehensive in scope.

Policy-Making and Policy Execution

It has long been customary to distinguish between policy-making and policy execution. Frank J. Goodnow, in his well-known work, *Politics and Administration,* undertook to build an almost absolute distinction upon this functional difference. . . . But while the distinction has a great deal of value as a relative matter of emphasis, it cannot any longer be accepted in this absolute form. Admittedly, this misleading distinction has become a fetish, a stereotype in the minds of theorists and practitioners alike. The result has been a great deal of confusion and argument. The reason for making this distinction an absolute antithesis is probably to be found in building it upon the metaphysical, if not abstruse, idea of a will of the state. This neo-Hegelian (and Fascist) notion is purely speculative. Even if the concept "state" is retained—and I personally see no good ground for it—the idea that this state has a will immediately entangles one in all the difficulties of assuming a group personality or something akin to it. In other words, a problem which is already complicated enough by itself—that is, how a public policy is adopted and carried out—is bogged down by a vast ideological superstructure which contributes little or nothing to its solution. . . . The concrete patterns of public policy formation and execution reveal that politics and administration are not two mutually exclusive boxes, or absolute distinctions, but that they are two closely linked aspects of the same process. Public policy, to put it flatly, is a continuous process, the formation of which is inseparable from its execution. Public policy is being formed as it is being executed, and it is likewise being executed as it is being formed. Politics and administration play a continuous role in both formation and execution, though there is probably more politics in the formation of policy, more administration in the execution of it. Insofar as particular individuals or groups are gaining or losing power or control in a given area, there is politics; insofar as officials act or propose action in the name of public interest, there is administration.

The same problem may be considered from another angle. Policies in the common meaning of the term are decisions about what to do or not to do in given situations. It is characteristic of our age that most legislation is looked upon as policy-deciding. Hence policy-making in the broad sense is not supposed to be part of administration. While these propositions are true in a general way, they tend to obscure two important facts, namely, (1) that many policies are not ordained with a stroke of the legislative or dictatorial pen but evolve slowly over long periods of time; and (2) that administrative officials participate continuously and significantly in this process of evolving policy. To commence with the latter fact, it is evident that in the process of doing something the administrator may discover another and better way of accomplishing the same result, or he discovers that the thing cannot be done at all, or that something else has to be done first, before the desired step can be taken. In our recent agricultural policy, examples of all these "administrative" policy determinations can be cited, as likewise in our social security policy. The discussions now taking place in both fields amply illustrate these points. What is more, such administrative participation alone renders policy-making a continuous process, so much in a state of flux that it is difficult, if not impossible, to state with precision what the policy in any given field is at any particular time. But, if this is true, it follows as a corollary that public policy will often be contradictory and conflicting in its effects upon society. Our myth-makers, of course, remain adamant in proclaiming that this should not be so and let it go at that. It is hard to disagree with them, but we still have to face the question of responsibility, seeing that policies are in fact contradictory and conflicting. Who is responsible for what and to whom? To what extent does such responsibility affect the actual conduct of affairs? A complex pattern appears when we attempt to answer such questions.

Some time ago I pointed out that administrative responsibility had not kept pace with our administrative tasks. In relying upon the political responsibility of policy-making persons and bodies, we had lost sight of the deeper issues involved. At that time I wrote:

> . . . autocratic and arbitrary abuse of power has characterized the officialdom of a government service bound only by the dictates of conscience. Nor has the political responsibility based upon the election of legislatures and chief executives succeeded in permeating a highly technical, differentiated government service any more than the religious responsibility of well-intentioned kings. Even a good and pious king would be discredited by arbitrary "bureaucrats"; even a high-minded legislature or an aspiring chief executive pursuing the public interest would be thwarted by a restive officialdom.

An offended commentator from the British Isles exclaimed loudly that if I imagined that to be true of England I was "simply wrong." But I think it would be easy to show that the officials of a seventeenth-century prince were more responsible, i.e., answerable, to him, their sovereign, than the officials of any modern democracy are as yet to the people, their supposed sovereign. In the comparison there was no judgment as to the positive amount of responsibility found in either. Admittedly, many commentators have dwelt at length upon the frequently irresponsible conduct of public affairs in Great Britain and elsewhere.

The New Imperative: Functional Responsibility

It is interesting that the administrators themselves attach so little weight to the influence of parliamentary or legislative bodies. Leading Swiss officials—and Switzerland has as responsible a government service as any country in the world—told the author that "responsibility of the public service in Switzerland results from a sense of duty, a desire to be approved by his fellow officials, and a tendency to subordinate one's own judgment as a matter of course. Still, in the case like the arrival of Social Democrats into the Federal Council, it might happen that official conduct would be slow to respond to the new situation." They also felt that officials are not unwilling to allow a measure to lapse, although actually provided for in legislation, if considerable opposition is felt which the public might be expected to share. Thus a wine tax was quietly allowed to drop out of sight, just as the potato control act remained a dead letter in the United States. There are, of course, ways by which the legislature secures a measure of control that enables it to enforce responsibility, usually of the negative kind which prevents abuses. Legislative committees act as watchdogs over all expenditure.

What is true of Switzerland and the United States without "parliamentary responsibility" seems to be equally true of England and France. In both countries complaints against the increasing independence of officials are constantly being voiced. In a very important discourse, Sir Josiah Stamp called attention to the creative role the civil servant is called upon to play in Great Britain. "I am quite clear that the official must be the mainspring of the new society, suggesting, promoting, advising at every stage." Sir Josiah insisted that this trend was inevitable, irresistible, and therefore called for a new type of administrator. An editorial writer of *The Times,* though critical of this development, agreed "that the practice, as opposed to the theory, of administration has long been moving in this direction." He added, "In practice, they [the officials] possess that influence which cannot be denied to exhaustive knowledge; and this influence, owing to the congestion of parliamentary business and other causes, manifests itself more and more effectively as an initiative in public affairs." Testimony of this sort could be indefinitely multiplied; and as we are interested in practice, not in ideology, we must consider the question of responsibility in terms of the actualities. Such cases throw a disquieting light upon the idea that the mere dependence of a cabinet upon the "confidence" of an elected assembly insures responsible conduct on the part of the officials in charge of the initiation and execution of public policy, when those officials hold permanent positions. It is no accident that the Goodnow school should fully share such illusions. After pointing out that the British Cabinet unites in its hands power of legislation and administration, and thus both formulates and executes policies, Goodnow remarks:

> So long as their action meets with the approval of Parliament . . . there is none to gainsay them. If, however, they fail to gain such approval . . . they must resign their powers to others whose policy is approved by Parliament. . . . In this way the entire English government is made responsible to Parliament, which in turn is responsible to the people.

This is no longer very true. It is objectionable to consider administrative responsibility secure by this simple device, not merely because of interstitial violations but because there is a fundamental flaw in the view of politics and policy here assumed. The range of public policy is nowadays so far-flung that the largely inoperative "right" of the parliamentary majority to oust a Cabinet from power belongs in that rather numerous group of rights for which there is no remedy. The majority supporting the Cabinet may violently disagree with this, that, and the other policy advocated and adopted by the Cabinet, but considerations of party politics, in the broadest sense, will throttle their objections because the particular issue is "not worth a general election" and the chance of the M.P.'s losing his seat. As contrasted with the detailed and continuous criticism and control of administrative activity afforded by Congressional committees, this parliamentary responsibility is largely inoperative and certainly ineffectual. When one considers the extent of public disapproval directed against Franklin D. Roosevelt's Congressional supporters who were commonly dubbed "rubber stamps," it is astonishing that anyone extolling the virtues of British parliamentarism should get a hearing at all. For what has the parliamentary majority in Britain been in the last few years but a rubber stamp of an automatic docility undreamt of in the United States?

A Dual Standard of Administrative Responsibility

But are there any possible arrangements under which the exercise of such discretionary power can be made more responsible? The difficulties are evidently very great. Before we go any further in suggesting institutional safeguards, it becomes necessary to elucidate a bit more the actual psychic conditions which might predispose any agent toward responsible conduct. Palpably, a modern administrator is in many cases dealing with problems so novel and complex that they call for the highest creative ability. This need for creative solutions effectively focuses attention upon the need for action. The pious formulas about the will of the people are all very well, but when it comes to these issues of social maladjustment the popular will has little content, except the desire to see such maladjustments removed. A solution which fails in this regard, or which causes new and perhaps greater maladjustments, is bad; we have a right to call such a policy irresponsible if it can be shown that it was adopted without proper regard to the existing sum of human knowledge concerning the technical issues involved; we also have a right to call it irresponsible if it can be shown that it was adopted without proper regard for existing preferences in the community, and more particularly its prevailing majority. Consequently, the responsible administrator is one who is responsive to these two dominant factors: technical knowledge and popular sentiment. Any policy which violates either standard, or which fails to crystallize in spite of their urgent imperatives, renders the official responsible for it liable to the charge of irresponsible conduct.

In writing of the first of these factors, technical knowledge, I said some years ago:

> Administrative officials seeking to apply scientific "standards" have to account for their action in terms of a somewhat rationalized and previously established set of hypotheses. Any deviation from these hypotheses will be subjected to thorough scrutiny by their colleagues in what is known as the "fellowship of science." . . . If a specific designation were desirable, it might be well to call this type of responsibility "functional" and "objective," as contrasted with the general and "subjective" types, such as religious, moral, and political responsibility. For in the former case, action is tested in terms of relatively objective problems which, if their presence is not evident, can be demonstrated to exist, since they refer to specific functions. Subjective elements appear wherever the possibility of relatively voluntary choice enters in, and here political responsibility is the only method which will insure action in accordance with popular preference. . . .

Yet this view has been objected to as inconceivable by one who claimed that he could not see how the term "responsibility" could be applied except where the governed have the power to dismiss or at least seriously damage the officeholder. Thus, with one stroke of the pen, all the permanent officials of the British government, as well as our own and other supposedly popular governments are once and for all rendered irresponsible. According to this commentator, political responsibility alone is "objective," because it involves a control by a body external to the one who is responsible. He also claims that its standards may be stated with finality and exactitude and its rewards and punishments made peremptory. For all of which British foreign policy leading up to Munich no doubt provides a particularly illuminating illustration.

It seems like an argument over words. The words, as a matter of fact, do not matter particularly. If you happen to feel that the word "objective" spells praise, and the word "subjective" blame, it may be better to speak of "technical" as contrasted with "political" responsibility, or perhaps "functional" and "political" will appeal. Whether we call it "objective" or "functional" or "technical," the fact remains that throughout the length and breadth of our technical civilization there is arising a type of responsibility on the part of the permanent administrator, the man who is called upon to seek and find the creative solutions for our crying technical needs, which cannot be effectively enforced except by fellow-technicians who are capable of judging his policy in terms of the scientific knowledge bearing upon it.

"Nature's laws are always enforced," and a public policy which neglects them is bound to come to grief, no matter how eloquently it may be advocated by popular orators, eager partisans, or smart careerists.

Shall We Enforce or Elicit Responsible Conduct?

Those old-timers who are enamored of strict subserviency undoubtedly will be inclined to argue that the foregoing is all very well, but that it depends entirely for its effectiveness upon the good will of the administrator, and that as soon as he is indifferent or hostile to such public reactions he can and will discard them. There is unquestionably some truth in this objection. Responsible conduct of administrative functions is not so much enforced as it is elicited. But it has been the contention all along that responsible conduct is never strictly enforceable, that even under the most tyrannical despot administrative officials will escape effective control—in short, that the problem of how to bring about responsible conduct of the administrative staff of a large organization is, particularly in a democratic society, very largely a question of sound work rules and effective morale.

The whole range of activities involving constant direct contact of the administrator with the public and its problems shows that our conception of administrative responsibility is undergoing profound change. The emphasis is shifting; instead of subserviency to arbitrary will we require responsiveness to commonly felt needs and wants. The trend of the creative evolution of American democracy from a negative conception to a positive ideal of social service posits such a transformation. As the range of government services expands, we are all becoming each other's servants in the common endeavor of operating our complex industrial society.

It seems desirable to consider one further problem of especial significance in this area, and that is the role and the importance of satisfactory relations of the government to its employees of all ranks and classes. Private employers are becoming increasingly aware of the decisive role which all their employees must play in the public relations of business concerns. Competition through service is becoming an ever more important factor, and the contact of the general public with particular businesses is through their employees. It is evident that the government through its expanding services is placed in a similar position. The Postal Service has long recognized this and has evolved careful regulations concerning the dealings of its employees with the public. As a result, the letter carrier has become a symbol of cheerful service. By contrast, the arbitrary official of authoritarian regimes abroad has always been acknowledged as the antithesis of democracy. Although such conduct was often condoned as part of administrative efficiency, we know today that this view is mistaken. Just as morale within the service is of decisive importance in bringing about responsible administration, so likewise morale should extend beyond the confines of the service itself.

The most serious issue revolves around the problem of the employees' right to organize, to bargain collectively, and to strike if their demands are rejected. It is difficult to see how popular government can recognize a right to strike, though it seems equally questionable to deny it. Whatever the abstract arguments, the right to strike is not recognized by most democratic governments. At any rate, most public employees recognize that such strikes are not in their true interest. But it is obvious that in lieu of the possibility of bringing their complaints and grievances forcibly to the attention of their employer, the government, government employees must be provided with exceptionally well-ordered institutional safeguards for mediation and arbitration.

Conclusion

The ways, then, by which a measure of genuine responsibility can be secured under modern conditions appear to be manifold, and they must all be utilized for achieving the best effect. No mere reliance upon some one traditional device, like the dependence of the Cabinet upon majority support in Parliament, or popular election of the chief executive (neither of which exists in Switzerland), can be accepted as satisfactory evidence. At best, responsibility in a democracy will remain fragmentary because of the indistinct voice of the principal whose agents the officials are supposed to be—the vast heterogeneous masses composing the people. Even the greatest faith in the common man (and I am prepared to carry this very far) cannot any longer justify a simple acceptance of the mythology of "the will of the people." Still, if all the different devices are kept operative and new ones developed as opportunity offers, democratic government by pooling many different interests and points of view continues to provide the nearest approximation to a policy-making process which will give the "right" results. Right policies are policies which seem right to the community at large and at the same time do not violate "objective" scientific standards. Only thus can public policy contribute to what the people consider their happiness.

Herman Finer

Administrative Responsibility in Democratic Government

My chief difference with Professor Friedrich was and is my insistence upon distinguishing responsibility as an arrangement of correction and punishment even up to dismissal both of politicians and officials while he believed and believes in reliance upon responsibility as a sense of responsibility, largely unsanctioned, except by deference or loyalty to professional standards. I still maintain my belief while in a more recent article, Professor Friedrich maintains his, so far as I am able to follow his argument. I propose therefore to treat the subject in two divisions, first, a more extended version of my own beliefs and, second, a critical examination of his article.

Are the servants of the public to decide their own course, or is their course of action to be decided by a body outside themselves? My answer is that the servants of the public are not to decide their own course; they are to be responsible to the elected representatives of the public, and these are to determine the course of action of the public servants to the most minute degree that is technically feasible. Both of these propositions are important: the main proposition of responsibility, as well as the limitation and auxiliary institutions implied in the phrase, "that is technically feasible." This kind of responsibility is what democracy means; and though there may be other devices which provide "good" government, I cannot yield on the cardinal issue of democratic government. In the ensuing discussion I have in mind that there is the dual problem of securing the responsibility of officials, (a) through the courts and disciplinary controls within the hierarchy of the administrative departments; and, also (b) through the authority exercised over officials by responsible ministers based on sanctions exercised by the representative assembly. In one way or another this dual control obtains in

Reprinted from *Public Administration Review,* Vol. 1 (Summer, 1941), pp. 335–350. © 1941 by The American Society for Public Administration. All rights reserved.

all the democratic countries, though naturally its purposes and procedures vary from country to country.

What are we to mean by responsibility? There are two definitions. First, responsibility may mean that X is accountable for Y to Z. Second, responsibility may mean an inward personal sense of moral obligation. In the first definition the essence is the externality of the agency or persons to whom an account is to be rendered, and it can mean very little without that agency having authority over X, determining the lines of X's obligation and the terms of its continuance or revocation. The second definition puts the emphasis on the conscience of the agent, and it follows from the definition that if he commits an error it is an error only when recognized by his own conscience, and that the punishment of the agent will be merely the twinges thereof. The one implies public execution: the other hara-kiri. While reliance on an official's conscience may be reliance on an official's accomplice, in democratic administration all parties, official, public, and Parliament, will breathe more freely if a censor is in the offing. . . .

Democratic systems are chiefly embodiments of the first mentioned notion of responsibility, and dictatorial systems chiefly of the second.

In the democratic system, however, there is either a direct declaration in the constitution of the primacy of the people over officeholders, whether politicians or employees, or else in authoritative documents or popular proverbs the constitutional omission is made good. Thus, in the Weimar Constitution, Article I declared the issuance of sovereignty from the people. Thus, the Committee on Indian Reforms of 1934 said, "so there arise two familiar British conceptions; that good government is not an acceptable substitute for self government, and that the only form of self government worthy of the name is government through ministers responsible to an elective legislature." And thus, we are all familiar with the essential meaning of the American dictum, "where annual election ends tyranny begins."

Democratic governments, in attempting to secure the responsibility of politicians and officeholders to the people, have founded themselves broadly upon the recognition of three doctrines. First, the mastership of the public, in the sense that politicians and employees are working not for the good of the public in the sense of what the public needs, but of the wants of the public as expressed by the public. Second, recognition that this mastership needs institutions, and particularly the centrality of an elected organ, for its expression and the exertion of its authority. More important than these two is the third notion, namely, that the function of the public and of its elected institutions is not merely the exhibition of its mastership by informing governments and officials of what it wants, but the authority and power to exercise an effect upon the course which the latter are to pursue, the power to exact obedience to orders.

Democratic government proceeded upon the lines mentioned because the political and administrative history of all ages, the benevolent as well as the tyrannical, the theological as well as the secular, has demonstrated without the shadow of a doubt that sooner or later there is an abuse of power when external punitive controls are lacking. This abuse of power has shown itself roughly in three ways. Governments and officials have been guilty of non-feasance, that is to say, they have not done what law or custom required them to do owing to laziness, ignorance, or want of care for their charges, or corrupt influence. Again there may be malfeasance, where a duty is carried out, but is carried out with waste and damage because of ignorance, negligence, and technical incompetence. Third, there is what may be called over-feasance, where a duty is undertaken beyond what law and custom oblige or empower; overfeasance may result from dictatorial temper, the vanity and ambition of the jack in office, or genuine, sincere, public-spirited zeal. As a matter of fact, the doctrine of the separation of powers as developed by Montesquieu was as much concerned with the aberrations of public-spirited zeal on the part of the executive as with the other classes of the abuse of power. Indeed, his phrase deserves to be put into the center of every modern discussion of administrative responsibility, *virtue itself hath need of limits.* We in public administration must beware of the too good man as well as the too bad; each in his own way may give the public what it doesn't want. If we wish the public to want things that are better in our estimation, there is a stronger case for teaching the public than for the imposition of our zealotry. A system which gives the "good" man freedom of action, in the expectation of benefiting from all the "good" he has in him, must sooner or later (since no man is without faults) cause his faults to be loaded on to the public also.

As a consequence of bitter experience and sad reflection, democratic governments have gradually devised the responsible executive and an elected assembly which enacts the responsibility. Within the system, there has been a particular concentration on the subservience of the officials to the legislature, ultimately through ministers and cabinet in a cabinet system, and through the chief executive where the separation of powers is the essential form of the organization of authority. Where officials have been or are spoilsmen, the need for holding them to subservience is particularly acute, since the spoilsmen have not even a professional preparation to act as a support and guide and guarantee of capacity. With career men, the capacity may be present. What is needed, however, is not technical capacity per se, but technical capacity in the service of the public welfare as defined by the public and its authorized representatives.

Legislatures and public have realized that officials are monopolist no less than the grand men of business who have arrogated to themselves the exclusive control of the manufacture or sale of a commodity and therewith the domination, without appeal by the victim, of an entire sector of national life.

The philosophy and experience of the Sherman Anti-Trust Act have significant applications to administrative procedures in public administration. The official participates in the monopoly of a service to society so outstanding that it has been taken over from a potential private monopolist by the government. This monopoly is exercisable through a sovereign agency armed with all the force of society and subject to no appeal outside the institutions which the government itself creates. This is to be subject to a potentially grievous servitude.

To overcome the potential evils flowing from public monopoly, democratic governments have set up various controls. It is these controls, and especially their modern deficiencies, which seem to have worried Professor Friedrich into a position where he practically throws the baby out with the bath. He feels that there is need of some elasticity in the power of the official, some discretion, some space for the "inner check," and he sees also that existent controls (either intentionally or by the accident of their own institutional deficiencies) do actually leave some latitude to the official. He argues therefore that heavy and, indeed, primary reliance in the making of public policy and its execution should be placed on moral responsibility, and he pooh-poohs the efficacy of and need for political responsibility. He gives the impression of stepping over the dead body of political responsibility to grasp the promissory incandescence of the moral variety.

Let us review the chief controls exercised over politicians and officials in democratic government, and their deficiencies and the remedy of these deficiencies. In traversing their inadequacies I am dealing with those loopholes for administrative discretion or the policy-making power of officials which have given Professor Friedrich so much concern. First, the legislative definition of the duties and powers of officials may not be precise because the legislators were not very clear about what they wanted. It is doubtful, for example, whether the planning clauses in the T.V.A. statute represented any clarity of purpose in the legislative mind. Legislative draftsmanship may be slipshod. Or the statute may be simply misunderstood, thus offering latitude to officials. If all the items of administrative determination arising out of the elbowroom allowed by these causes were gathered together they would no doubt be considerable. Since this latitude exists, it calls for one or both of the available remedies: the continuing control of the representative and judicial agencies over the official and an omnipresent sense of duty *to the public* on the part of the official. But the remedy is not as Professor Friedrich suggests, the institution of specific legislative policies which may please the heart of the technical expert or the technocrat. I again insist upon subservience, for I still am of the belief with Rousseau that the people can be unwise but cannot be wrong. The devices for securing the continuing responsiveness of the official are, of course, the law courts, the procedure of criticism, question, debate, and fact-finding, and parliamentary control of the purse within the assembly, and, in the U.S.A., the election of executive or administrative officials and their recall.

Next, the enormous congestion of modern legislative assemblies and the heritage of antiquated procedure mean that a sufficiently frequent review of legislation and its administrative outcrops cannot be secured to remedy, or to punish,or to act by power of anticipation on the official mind. But these are not insuperable problems and there is no need for us, seeing contemporary deficiencies, to jettison political responsibility prematurely.

Third, there may be a want of understanding by members of Parliament and congressmen of technical issues involved in the law and the administration, and this shortcoming has meant a leaning upon the supply of these things available in public employees. But the growth of advisory bodies, formal and informal, in the major governments of our own time has tremendously limited the need to rely wholly upon official initiative. Attention to the further development of advisory bodies is the line of progress here, not surely the handing over of our fate to officials who, by the way, are themselves only too grateful for instruction by such bodies.

It is true, further, that the exercise of the power of control by the legislature, such for example as Congress' detailed attention to and itemization of financial appropriations, may destroy movement, flexibility, and the like, on the part of the administration. This point is stressed by Professor Friedrich; queerly enough, he does not deduce from this criticism that a more rational parliamentary procedure is required, but that there is need of more administrative discretion. He even goes to the inexplicable extreme of proposing that some action is better than none, whatever the action is!

In short, these various drawbacks of political control can be remedied. They can be highly improved, and it is therefore unnecessary to proceed along the line definitely approved by Professor Friedrich of more administrative policy making. As a democrat, I should incline to the belief that the remedying of these drawbacks is precisely our task for the future. The legitimate conclusion from the analysis of the relationship between Parliament and administration is not that the administration should be given its head, but on the contrary that legislative bodies should be improved. Conceding the growing power of officials we may discover the remedy in the improvement of the quality of political parties and elections, if our minds are ready to explore.

Let us commence the critical discussion with a passage of Professor Friedrich's on Goodnow's *Politics and Administration.* In 1900 Professor F. J. Goodnow's work, one of the pioneer incursions into a fairly untilled field, made the following distinction between politics and administration. . . . Professor Friedrich imputes to Goodnow "an almost absolute distinction" in this functional difference. As a matter of fact, Goodnow uses the term "mainly busied with the discharge of one of these functions," and deserves credit for the broad distinction.

The distinction in the present writer's mind is this. By the "political" phase of government we mean all that part which is concerned with eliciting the will and winning the authority of the people. The process is carried on differently in democratic and dictatorial states. The elements of coercion and persuasion differ in magnitude and kind, and the place of the electorate, parties, parliaments, and ministers differs. This process ends with a law; with the approval (by positive ratification or by lapse of time for rejection) of administrative rules based on the original statute; and with control of the application of the law. The distinctive mark of this political part of the governmental process is that its agencies are practically unfettered in their authority over the making of policy and its execution. Where a written constitution and judicial review are absent, these political agencies are bounded only by the hopes and fears arising out of the electoral process. What of the administrative side? Administration begins where the legislature says it shall begin. It begins where the administrator begins, and the legislature decides that. Administration may include the making of rules and policy, which looks like legislation or politics, but its essence is that the administrator, elected or appointed (and most usually in modern states the latter), cannot himself determine the range or object of that policy. He has authority, but it is a conditioned, derived authority.

Thus, in the governmental process in general, there are agencies which are concerned with making and executing policy, and there is a descending narrowing latitude of discretion in the making of policy. The latitude is greatest where electorate meets legislature; it then tapers down through a descending line of the administrative hierarchy until the discretion left to the messenger and the charwoman and the minor manipulative grades is almost nil. . . .

Professor Friedrich calls this distinction of Goodnow's (shared by all other authorities I can recall), "misleading," a "fetish," a "stereotype," in the minds of theorists and practitioners alike. . . .

Later on, Professor Friedrich is constrained to admit: "Politics and administration play a continuous role in both formation and execution [of policy], though there is probably more politics in the formation of policy, more administration in the execution of it." "More" is a delicious understatement. But the understatement is not intended; it is part of a thesis that the amount of policy made by modern officials is of very great magnitude, in terms of proposing and later executing with latitude of interpretation. But this is only a play on the words "making" and "policy." What important "policy" does any federal official "make"? Has any federal official more authority than to propose? Certainly we expect those who are paid by the public to think and propound solutions to do their job well. But this is nothing new. By misusing the word "make" to suggest instituting and carrying into the law of the land, and only by this torsion of meaning, can Professor Friedrich's thesis at all come into court—that administrative responsibility to the legislature, the real policy-forming body of the nation, is in modern conditions impossible or unnecessary.

In the effort not to let reconsideration correct his first misconception of "responsibility," Professor Friedrich finds himself compelled to adopt quite an undemocratic view of government, and to throw scorn upon the popular will. I do not think for a moment that he really is antidemocratic, but his line of argument presses him to enunciate views which might lead to this suspicion. The error in his conception leads to an error in the consequence; and the error in the consequence is precisely what officials (not constrained by principle and institutions to the dictates of political responsibility) would begin to use as an argument to justify their irresponsibility: conceit of themselves and scorn of the popular will. . . .

The answer to this argument is this. It is demonstrable that the will of the people has content, not only about what it desires, but how maladjustments can be remedied, and some of its ideas are quite wise. The popular will may not be learned, but nevertheless the public's own experience teaches it something, the press of all kind teaches it more, and political parties and the more instructed members of the community play quite a part. "The people" consist of many kinds of minds and degrees of talent, not of undifferentiated ignorance and empty-mindedness. Legislative assemblies created by election, in which political parties play a vital part, also exist; and they are not so dumb. Their sagacity is not to be ignored or derided. Second, a policy which is based upon an incomplete or faulty grasp of technical knowledge is not an irresponsible policy, for to use the word "irresponsible" here is to pervert it by substituting it for the words "incomplete" or "faulty" or "unwise." It is surely wisest to say that the full grasp of knowledge is to be used by the official within the terms of the obligation and policy established for him by the legislature or his departmental superior; otherwise it looks as though an independent position were being claimed for the official. Nor is it wise to make responsibility to "the community" an addendum to a "proper regard to the existing sum of human knowledge, etc. etc." And, by the way, the state seems to have cropped up again in the word community!

"Consequently," continues Professor Friedrich, "the responsible administrator is one who is responsible to these two dominant factors: technical knowledge and popular sentiment. Any policy which violates either standard, or which fails to crystallize in spite of their urgent imperatives, renders the official responsible for it liable to the charge of irresponsible conduct." But just as surely there is no responsibility unless there is an obligation to someone else; no one is interested in a question of responsibility as a relationship between a man and a science, but as it involves a problem of duty—and the problem of duty is an interpersonal, not a personal, matter. Responsibility in the sense of an interpersonal, externally sanctioned duty is, then, the dominant consideration for public administration; and it includes and does not merely stand by the side of responsibility to the standards of one's craft in the dubious position of a Cinderella. If the community does not command, there is no call for the technical knowledge whatever; and however magnificent the grasp of technical knowledge and the desire to use it, it must be declared irresponsible whenever it becomes operative except under a direct or implied obligation. Many a burglar has been positively hated for his technical skill.

Professor Friedrich seems to be so obsessed by modern technology, and the important part which the knowledge of it must play in the establishment of policy, that he seems to forget how old this problem is, and what the answer of the ages has been to the very problem he poses. Does he think there was no question of "technical needs" three hundred years or three thousand years ago, or of the relationship of those who provided the knowledge and service to those members of the public who were its consumers? Governments owned warships, weapons, sewers, baths, roads, and irrigation works, and even had mines and forests to administer, and domestic and foreign trade to regulate. The relationship of the public to the mysteries of religion and ecclesiastical procedures—a very important technique in the context of good living—was for centuries one of the most critical problems in the history of political responsibility. "The creative solutions for our crying technical needs," as Professor Friedrich calls them, have for centuries been offered by the experts of various kinds, and the verdict of mankind has been that they need the expert on tap and not on top. All important questions are begged by throwing in the word "creative." It is no news to tell us, as we are told here, that nature will have her revenge if her laws are not understood and followed in any particular piece of administration. Of course that is so. But there is a wider concept of nature than that which relates to interest in the "technical"; there is also the nature of man as a political animal. We are entitled to believe, from the reading of his millennial administrative history, that *his* nature, as well as physical nature, is thwarted where the primacy of public responsibility is challenged by blurred interpretations, theoretical and practical, of the term responsibility.

The foregoing critical analysis of Professor Friedrich's view on administrative responsibility as stated in *Public Policy* shows, I think, its untenability both in its main drift and in most of its particular secondary though related aspects. The analysis reveals the following propositions as cogent and justifiable, in contradiction to Professor Friedrich's contentions.

Never was the political responsibility of officials so momentous a necessity as in our own era. Moral responsibility is likely to operate in direct proportion to the strictness and efficiency of political responsibility, and to fall away into all sorts of perversions when the latter is weakly enforced. While professional standards, duty to the public, and pursuit of technological efficiency are factors in sound administrative operation, they are but ingredients, and not continuously motivating factors, of sound policy, and they require public and political control and direction.

The public and the political assemblies are adequately sagacious to direct policy—they know not only where the shoe pinches, but have a shrewd idea as to the last and leather of their footwear: and where they lack technical knowledge their officials are appointed to offer it to them for their guidance, and not to secure official domination; and, within these limits the practice of giving administrative latitude to officials is sound.

Contemporary devices to secure closer cooperation of officials with public and legislatures are properly auxiliaries to and not substitutes for political control of public officials through exertion of the sovereign authority of the public. Thus, political responsibility is the major concern of those who work for healthy relationships between the officials and the public, and moral responsibility, although a valuable conception and institutional form, is minor and subsidiary.

PART IV

EXPANDING
HORIZONS

During the New Deal and to a far greater extent during the war that followed it, most of those who had taught or studied public administration, as well as those who would later become associated with its study, gained immediate experience in government operations, either in civil or in military agencies. What they saw and experienced did not correspond very well with the concepts and descriptions of the earlier books and articles about the federal government and about the work of large-scale administrative organizations in general. Those with a scholarly turn of mind questioned many of the old approaches and doctrines; they developed new perspectives and new frames of reference. For example, during an era when most public policies and military strategies were so obviously developed as well as carried out in administrative agencies, it was difficult to discern the traditional dichotomy between policy and administration. In the new agencies and the military services, established rules, procedures, and structures were deliberately abandoned, overlooked, or suspended. Organizations were forced to become more fluid and dynamic than those pictured in the books. The work of administration itself came to be perceived more in terms of negotiation, less in terms of Fayol's categories or Gulick's POSDCORB.[1]

The growing dissatisfaction with the traditional models of public administration had a number of consequences in the years following World War II. One was the development of more realistic descriptions and analyses of what actually happens in the administration of public programs. This was reflected in a great variety of semi-autobiographical accounts and recollections of individual experiences. It was reflected, too, in the development of a rising number and variety of case studies, usually focused on significant administrative decisions, and the effort to build from them generalizations about behavior in public organizations.[2] Both the autobiographical reviews and the cases stressed the interrelationship of administration with policymaking and therefore also with politics and power. The emphasis on these topics greatly increased while that on efficiency and economy in their narrower, traditional sense declined.

Others, of whom Herbert A. Simon was the conspicuous early leader, were dissatisfied with, if not downright scornful of, previous efforts to build a science of administration and sought new theoretical frameworks. This

1. As described in Fayol's and Gulick's articles in Parts II and III.

2. The origin of this kind of public administration case study was a seminar at Harvard, begun in 1945. Later, in 1948, a group of universities established a Committee on Public Administration Cases, which, greatly enlarged, became the Inter-University Case Program in 1951.

search led them inevitably into the approaches and methodologies of other social sciences, notably sociology, psychology and social psychology, cultural anthropology, and, somewhat later, economics.[3] It also contributed to a reawakened interest in quantitative methods and to rationales for reducing or eliminating the unscientific play of politics in the analysis of administrative decisions and processes.

The extension of public administration into other social disciplines was accompanied and, in fact, preceded and sparked by a burst of interest and knowledge within those disciplines themselves in associational and organizational behavior. That burst was spurred in part by the studies of workers and their supervisors conducted in the late 1920s and early 1930s at the Hawthorne plant of the Western Electric Company (see the Roethlisberger excerpt below). Another kind of impulse was that of Kurt Lewin in his studies, during the 1930s and later, of behavior and change in small groups, which gave rise to the field of group dynamics. Still another was the discovery and, after World War II, the translation into English by American sociologists of the writings about bureaucracy of Max Weber, which had actually been written more than twenty-five years earlier.

In the interest of continuity of fields of thought, if not of strict chronology, the selections that follow are arranged in two sections. The first concerns studies and writings by authors outside of the field of public administration, most of these published before or during World War II. The second consists of articles or excerpts of books published at the close of that war or later by scholars or participants in public administration.

---

3.   This outreach of public administration into other disciplines was reflected particularly in two significant books published at or shortly after the close of the period covered herein. The first was a distinctly different kind of text, *Public Administration* by Herbert A. Simon, Donald W. Smithburg, and Victor K. Thompson, (1950); the second, *The Policy Sciences,* edited by Harold Lasswell and Daniel Lerner (1951).

Max Weber (1864–1920)

The name of Max Weber must now be familiar to every self-respecting student of public administration. Such was not always the case. I have found almost no references to Weber in the literature on American public administration until after World War II. Most of his voluminous output was produced before or during World War I. A substantial portion of it was not published in German until some years after his death in 1920, at the age of fifty-six. And that part of his work dealing with bureaucracy, mostly from *Wirtschaft und Gesellschaft*, was not translated into English until 1946. It does not appear that many early scholars or practitioners in American public administration, even those who studied in Germany, were influenced by Weber, if they knew of his existence at all.

Weber's theory and generalizations on bureaucracy in modern society were partly based upon his own experiences in and observations of the Prussian military, the German civil service, and giant German corporations. They reached the United States via leaders in the field of sociology, who first translated his works and later criticized the consequences of bureaucracy, often with vehemence. Weber wrote that bureaucracy was the most efficient form of large-scale organization. His "ideal type" of bureaucracy became a model against which to measure public organizations, both in theory and in practice. It provided a socio-scientific base for studying large-scale organization. It also suggested that the word *bureaucracy,* and its relatives *bureaucrat* and *bureaucratization,* might be neutralized: made into scientific constructs, not pejoratives. It now appears that this possibility has not been generally realized. Nonetheless, the study of bureaucracy has become a central theme in social science, including public administration, and many modern students of organization theory begin with Max Weber's definitions and descriptions of bureaucracy.

F.C.M.

The Theory of Social and Economic Organization

Legal Authority with a Bureaucratic Administrative Staff

Legal Authority: The Pure Type with Employment of a Bureaucratic Administrative Staff

The effectiveness of legal authority rests on the acceptance of the validity of the following mutually inter-dependent ideas.

1. That any given legal norm may be established by agreement or by imposition, on grounds of expediency or rational values or both, with a claim to obedience at least on the part of the members of the corporate group. This is, however, usually extended to include all persons within the sphere of authority or of power in question—which in the case of territorial bodies is the territorial area—who stand in certain social relationships or carry out forms of social action which in the order governing the corporate group have been declared to be relevant.

2. That every body of law consists essentially in a consistent system of abstract rules which have normally been intentionally established. Furthermore, administration of law is held to consist in the application of these rules to particular cases; the administrative process in the rational pursuit of the interests which are specified in the order governing the corporate group within the limits laid down by legal precepts and following principles which are capable of generalized formulation and are approved in the order governing the group, or at least not disapproved in it.

3. That thus the typical person in authority occupies an "office." In the action associated with his status, including the commands he issues to others, he is subject to an impersonal order to which his actions are oriented. This is true not only for persons exercising legal authority who are in the usual sense "officials," but, for instance, for the elected president of a state.

4. That the person who obeys authority does so, as it is usually stated, only in his capacity as a "member" of the corporate group and what he obeys is only "the law." He may in this connexion be the member of an association, of a territorial commune, of a church, or a citizen of a state.

5. In conformity with point 3, it is held that the members of the corporate group, in so far as they obey a person in authority, do not owe this obedience to him as an individual, but to the impersonal order. Hence, it follows that there is an obligation to obedience only within the sphere of the rationally

The Theory of Social and Economic Organization. Translated by A. M. Henderson and T. Parsons (New York: Oxford University Press, 1947), pp. 329–341. Reprinted with permission of Macmillan Publishing Co., Inc. Copyright 1947, renewed 1975 by Talcott Parsons.

delimited authority which, in terms of the order, has been conferred upon him.

The following may thus be said to be the fundamental categories of rational legal authority:

(1) A continuous organization of official functions bound by rules.

(2) A specified sphere of competence. This involves (a) a sphere of obligations to perform functions which has been marked off as part of a systematic division of labor. (b) The provision of the incumbent with the necessary authority to carry out these functions. (c) That the necessary means of compulsion are clearly defined and their use is subject to definite conditions. A unit exercising authority which is organized in this way will be called an "administrative organ."

There are administrative organs in this sense in large-scale private organizations, in parties and armies, as well as in the state and the church. An elected president, a cabinet of ministers, or a body of elected representatives also in this sense constitute administrative organs. This is not, however, the place to discuss these concepts. Not every administrative organ is provided with compulsory powers. But this distinction is not important for present purposes.

(3) The organization of offices follows the principle of hierarchy; that is, each lower office is under the control and supervision of a higher one. There is a right of appeal and of statement of grievances from the lower to the higher. Hierarchies differ in respect to whether and in what cases complaints can lead to a ruling from an authority at various points higher in the scale, and as to whether changes are imposed from higher up or the responsibility for such changes is left to the lower office, the conduct of which was the subject of complaint.

(4) The rules which regulate the conduct of an office may be technical rules or norms. In both cases, if their application is to be fully rational, specialized training is necessary. It is thus normally true that only a person who has demonstrated an adequate technical training is qualified to be a member of the administrative staff of such an organized group, and hence only such persons are eligible for appointment to official positions. The administrative staff of a rational corporate group thus typically consists of "officials," whether the organization be devoted to political, religious, economic—in particular, capitalistic—or other ends.

(5) In the rational type it is a matter of principle that the members of the administrative staff should be completely separated from ownership of the means of production or administration. Officials, employees, and workers attached to the administrative staff do not themselves own the non-human means of production and administration. These are rather provided for their use in kind or in money, and the official is obligated to render an accounting of their use. There exists, furthermore, in principle complete separation of the property belonging to the organization, which is controlled within the sphere of office, and the personal property of the official, which is available for his own

private uses. There is a corresponding separation of the place in which official functions are carried out, the "office" in the sense of premises, from living quarters.

(6) In the rational type case, there is also a complete absence of appropriation of his official position by the incumbent. Where "rights" to an office exist, as in the case of judges, and recently of an increasing proportion of officials and even of workers, they do not normally serve the purpose of appropriation by the official, but of securing the purely objective and independent character of the conduct of the office so that it is oriented only to the relevant norms.

(7) Administrative acts, decisions, and rules are formulated and recorded in writing, even in cases where oral discussion is the rule or is even mandatory. This applies at least to preliminary discussions and proposals, to final decisions, and to all sorts of orders and rules. The combination of written documents and a continuous organization of official functions constitutes the "office"—which is the central focus of all types of modern corporate action.

The purest type of exercise of legal authority is that which employs a bureaucratic administrative staff. Only the supreme chief of the organization occupies his position of authority by virtue of appropriation, of election, or of having been designated for the succession. But even *his* authority consists in a sphere of legal "competence." The whole administrative staff under the supreme authority then consists, in the purest type, of individual officials who are appointed and function according to the following criteria:

(1) They are personally free and subject to authority only with respect to their impersonal official obligations.

(2) They are organized in a clearly defined hierarchy of offices.

(3) Each office has a clearly defined sphere of competence in the legal sense.

(4) The office is filled by a free contractual relationship. Thus, in principle, there is free selection.

(5) Candidates are selected on the basis of technical qualifications. In the most rational case, this is tested by examination or guaranteed by diplomas certifying technical training, or both. They are *appointed,* not elected.

(6) They are remunerated by fixed salaries in money, for the most part with a right to pensions. Only under certain circumstances does the employing authority, especially in private organizations, have a right to terminate the appointment, but the official is always free to resign. The salary scale is primarily graded according to rank in the hierarchy; but in addition to this criterion, the responsibility of the position and the requirements of the incumbent's social status may be taken into account.

(7) The office is treated as the sole, or at least the primary, occupation of the incumbent.

(8) It constitutes a career. There is a system of "promotion" according to seniority or to achievement, or both. Promotion is dependent on the judgment of superiors.

(9) The official works entirely separated from ownership of the means of administration and without appropriation of his position.

(10) He is subject to strict and systematic discipline and control in the conduct of the office.

This type of organization is in principle applicable with equal facility to a wide variety of different fields. It may be applied in profit-making business or in charitable organizations, or in any number of other types of private enterprises serving ideal or material ends. It is equally applicable to political and to religious organizations. With varying degrees of approximation to a pure type, its historical existence can be demonstrated in all these fields.

1. For example, this type of bureaucracy is found in private clinics, as in endowed hospitals or the hospitals maintained by religious orders. Bureaucratic organization has played a major role in the Catholic Church. It is well illustrated by the administrative role of the priesthood in the modern church, which has expropriated almost all of the old church benefices, which were in former days to a large extent subject to private appropriation. It is also illustrated by the conception of the universal Episcopate, which is thought of as formally constituting a universal legal competence in religious matters. Similarly, the doctrine of Papal infallibility is thought of as in fact involving a universal competence but only one which functions "ex cathedra" in the sphere of the office, thus implying the typical distinction between the sphere of office and that of the private affairs of the incumbent. The same phenomena are found in the large-scale capitalistic enterprise; and the larger it is, the greater their role. And this is not less true of political parties, which will be discussed separately. Finally, the modern army is essentially a bureaucratic organization administered by that peculiar type of military functionary, the "officer."

2. Bureaucratic authority is carried out in its purest form where it is most clearly dominated by the principle of appointment. There is no such thing as a hierarchy of elected officials in the same sense as there is a hierarchical organization of appointed officials. In the first place, election makes it impossible to attain a stringency of discipline even approaching that in the appointed type. For it is open to a subordinate official to compete for elective honors on the same terms as his superiors, and his prospects are not dependent on the superior's judgment.

3. Appointment by free contract, which makes free selection possible, is essential to modern bureaucracy. Where there is a hierarchical organization with impersonal spheres of competence, but occupied by unfree officials— like slaves or dependents, who, however, function in a formally bureaucratic manner—the term "patrimonial bureaucracy" will be used.

4. The role of technical qualifications in bureaucratic organizations is continually increasing. Even an official in a party or a trade-union organization

is in need of specialized knowledge, though it is usually of an empirical character, developed by experience, rather than by formal training. In the modern state, the only "offices" for which no technical qualifications are required are those of ministers and presidents. This only goes to prove that they are "officials" only in a formal sense, and not substantively, as is true of the managing director or president of a large business corporation. There is no question but that the "position" of the capitalistic entrepreneur is as definitely appropriated as is that of a monarch. Thus at the top of a bureaucratic organization, there is necessarily an element which is at least not purely bureaucratic. The category of bureaucracy is one applying only to the exercise of control by means of a particular kind of administrative staff.

5. The bureaucratic official normally receives a fixed salary. By contrast, sources of income which are privately appropriated will be called "benefices." Bureaucratic salaries are also normally paid in money. Though this is not essential to the concept of bureaucracy, it is the arrangement which best fits the pure type. Payments in kind are apt to have the character of benefices, and the receipt of a benefice normally implies the appropriation of opportunities for earnings and of positions. There are, however, gradual transitions in this field with many intermediate types. Appropriation by virtue of leasing or sale of offices or the pledge of income from office are phenomena foreign to the pure type of bureaucracy.

6. . . . The typical "bureaucratic" official occupies the office as his principal occupation.

7. With respect to the separation of the official from ownership of the means of administration, the situation is essentially the same in the field of public administration and in private bureaucratic organizations, such as the large-scale capitalistic enterprise.

8. Collegial bodies . . . are rapidly decreasing in importance in favor of types of organization which are in fact, and for the most part formally as well, subject to the authority of a single head. For instance, the collegial "governments" in Prussia have long since given way to the monocratic "district president." The decisive factor in this development has been the need for rapid, clear decisions, free of the necessity of compromise between different opinions and also free of shifting majorities.

9. The modern army officer is a type of appointed official who is clearly marked off by certain class distinctions. This will be discussed elsewhere. In this respect such officers differ radically from elected military leaders, from charismatic condottieri, from the type of officers who recruit and lead mercenary armies as a capitalistic enterprise, and, finally, from the incumbents of commissions which have been purchased. There may be gradual transitions between these types. The patrimonial "retainer," who is separated from the means of carrying out his function, and the proprietor of a mercenary army for capitalistic purposes have, along with the private capitalistic entrepreneur, been pioneers in the organization of the modern type of bureaucracy. . . .

The Monocratic Type of Bureaucratic Administration

Experience tends universally to show that the purely bureaucratic type of administrative organization—that is, the monocratic variety of bureaucracy— is, from a purely technical point of view, capable of attaining the highest degree of efficiency and is in this sense formally the most rational known means of carrying out imperative control over human beings. It is superior to any other form in precision, in stability, in the stringency of its discipline, and in its reliability. It thus makes possible a particularly high degree of calcula- bility of results for the heads of the organization and for those acting in relation to it. It is finally superior both in intensive efficiency and in the scope of its operations, and is formally capable of application to all kinds of administrative tasks.

The development of the modern form of the organization of corporate groups in all fields is nothing less than identical with the development and continual spread of bureaucratic administration. This is true of church and state, of armies, political parties, economic enterprises, organizations to promote all kinds of causes, private associations, clubs, and many others. Its development is, to take the most striking case, the most crucial phenomenon of the modern Western state. However many forms there may be which do not appear to fit this pattern, such as collegial representative bodies, parlia- mentary committees, soviets, honorary officers, lay judges, and what not, and however much people may complain about the "evils of bureaucracy," it would be sheer illusion to think for a moment that continuous administrative work can be carried out in any field except by means of officials working in offices. The whole pattern of everyday life is cut to fit this framework. For bureaucratic administration is, other things being equal, always, from a formal, technical point of view, the most rational type. For the needs of mass administration today, it is completely indispensable. The choice is only that between bureaucracy and dilettantism in the field of administration.

The primary source of the superiority of bureaucratic administration lies in the role of technical knowledge which, through the development of modern technology and business methods in the production of goods, has become completely indispensable. In this respect, it makes no difference whether the economic system is organized on a capitalistic or a socialistic basis. Indeed, if in the latter case a comparable level of technical efficiency were to be achieved, it would mean a tremendous increase in the importance of special- ized bureaucracy.

When those subject to bureaucratic control seek to escape the influence of the existing bureaucratic apparatus, this is normally possible only by creating an organization of their own which is equally subject to the process of bureaucratization. Similarly the existing bureaucratic apparatus is driven to continue functioning by the most powerful interests which are material and objective, but also ideal in character. Without it, a society like our own—with a separation of officials, employees, and workers from ownership of the means of administration, dependent on discipline and on technical training—could no longer function. The only exception would be those groups, such as the peasantry, who are still in possession of their own means of subsistence. Even in case of revolution by force or of occupation by an enemy, the bureaucratic machinery will normally continue to function just as it has for the previous legal government.

The question is always who controls the existing bureaucratic machinery. And such control is possible only in a very limited degree to persons who are not technical specialists. Generally speaking, the trained permanent official is more likely to get his way in the long run than his nominal superior, the Cabinet minister, who is not a specialist.

Bureaucratic administration means fundamentally the exercise of control on the basis of knowledge. This is the feature of it which makes it specifically rational. This consists on the one hand in technical knowledge which, by itself, is sufficient to ensure it a position of extraordinary power. But in addition to this, bureaucratic organizations, or the holders of power who make use of them, have the tendency to increase their power still further by the knowledge growing out of experience in the service. For they acquire through the conduct of office a special knowledge of facts and have available a store of documentary material peculiar to themselves. While not peculiar to bureaucratic organizations, the concept of "official secrets" is certainly typical of them. It stands in relation to technical knowledge in somewhat the same position as commercial secrets do to technological training. It is a product of striving for power.

Bureaucracy is superior in knowledge, including both technical knowledge and knowledge of the concrete fact within its own sphere of interest, which is usually confined to the interests of a private business—a capitalistic enterprise. The capitalistic entrepreneur is, in our society, the only type who has been able to maintain at least relative immunity from subjection to the control of rational bureaucratic knowledge. All the rest of the population have tended to be organized in large-scale corporate groups which are inevitably subject to bureaucratic control. This is as inevitable as the dominance of precision machinery in the mass production of goods.

The following are the principal, more general social consequences of bureaucratic control:

(1) The tendency to "levelling" in the interest of the broadest possible basis of recruitment in terms of technical competence.

(2) The tendency to plutocracy growing out of the interest in the greatest possible length of technical training. Today this often lasts up to the age of thirty.

(3) The dominance of a spirit of formalistic impersonality, *"Sine ira et studio,"* without hatred or passion, and hence without affection or enthusiasm.

The dominant norms are concepts of straightforward duty without regard to personal considerations. Everyone is subject to formal equality of treatment; that is, everyone in the same empirical situation. This is the spirit in which the ideal official conducts his office.

The development of bureaucracy greatly favours the levelling of social classes and this can be shown historically to be the normal tendency. Conversely, every process of social levelling creates a favorable situation for the development of bureaucracy; for it tends to eliminate class privileges, which include the appropriation of means of administration and the appropriation of authority as well as the occupation of offices on an honorary basis or as an avocation by virtue of wealth. This combination everywhere inevitably foreshadows the development of mass democracy. . . .

The "spirit" of rational bureaucracy has normally the following general characteristics:

(1) Formalism, which is promoted by all the interests which are concerned with the security of their own personal situation, whatever this may consist in. Otherwise the door would be open to arbitrariness and hence formalism is the line of least resistance.

(2) There is another tendency, which is apparently in contradiction to the above, a contradiction which is in part genuine. It is the tendency of officials to treat their official function from what is substantively a utilitarian point of view in the interest of the welfare of those under their authority. But this utilitarian tendency is generally expressed in the enactment of corresponding regulatory measures which themselves have a formal character and tend to be treated in a formalistic spirit. This tendency to substantive rationality is supported by all those subject to authority who are not included in the class mentioned above as interested in the security of advantages already controlled. The problems which open up at this point belong in the theory of "democracy."

Mary Parker Follett (1868–1933)

Following her graduation from Radcliffe College in 1898, Mary Parker Follett pursued a variety of careers. Her early activities were dedicated largely to social and educational work with children of poor families in her native Boston, and to vocational guidance. Her interest and avid scholarship in problems of government led to publication of two works in political science, *The Speaker of the House of Representatives* (1909) and *The New State* (1920). These were followed in 1924 by *Creative Experience,* a philosophical treatise grounded in psychology, emphasizing the reciprocal character of human relationships. In the 1920s and until her death in 1933, she developed a growing concern with business organization and management. She consulted with many business leaders, drafted papers, and delivered lectures in this field. Several of her papers were later collected and published in the volume, *Dynamic Administration* (1940), edited by Henry C. Metcalf and L. Urwick.

Despite the broad range of her interests and writing, there was quite a remarkable consistency in Follett's thought. It focused on principles she had developed at an early age concerning the individual and human relationships in any kind of association. Her key words and expressions, sprinkled through her papers and books, included coordination, cooperation, circular response, the law of the situation, integration, and others. Her foundations were psychological; her principles, normative and optimistic.

Follett was influential with many progressive business leaders and some in public administration; yet, in some respects, she was about a generation ahead of her time. Her ideas expressed during the 1920s and early 1930s were clear forerunners to movements that began after World War II: human relations, group dynamics, and later, organization development. The paper reproduced below was originally presented by her at a conference in 1925.

F.C.M.

Dynamic Administration

Constructive Conflict

I wish to consider in this paper the most fruitful way of dealing with conflict. At the outset I should like to ask you to agree for the moment to think of conflict as neither good nor bad; to consider it without ethical pre-judgment; to think of it not as warfare, but as appearance of difference, difference of opinions, of interests. For that is what conflict means—difference. We shall not consider merely the differences between employer and employee, but those between managers, between the directors at Board meetings or wherever difference appears.

As conflict—difference—is here in the world, as we cannot avoid it, we should, I think, use it. Instead of condemning it, we should set it to work for us. Why not? What does the mechanical engineer do with friction? Of course his chief job is to eliminate friction, but it is true that he also capitalizes friction. The transmission of power by belts depends on friction between the

Dynamic Administration (New York: Harper & Brothers, 1940), pp. 30–49. Reprinted with permission.

belt and the pulley. The friction between the driving wheel of the locomotive and the track is necessary to haul the train. All polishing is done by friction. The music of the violin we get by friction. We left the savage state when we discovered fire by friction. We talk of the friction of mind on mind as a good thing. So in business, too, we have to know when to try to eliminate friction and when to try to capitalize it, when to see what work we can make it do. That is what I wish to consider here, whether we can set conflict to work and make it *do* something for us.

Methods of Dealing With Conflict

There are three main ways of dealing with conflict: domination, compromise, and integration. Domination, obviously, is a victory of one side over the other. This is the easiest way of dealing with conflict, the easiest for the moment but not usually successful in the long run, as we can see from what has happened since the War.

The second way of dealing with conflict, that of compromise, we understand well, for it is the way we settle most of our controversies; each side gives up a little in order to have peace, or, to speak more accurately, in order that the activity which has been interrupted by the conflict may go on. Compromise is the basis of trade union tactics. In collective bargaining, the trade unionist asks for more than he expects to get, allows for what is going to be lopped off in the conference. Thus we often do not know what he really thinks he should have, and this ignorance is a great barrier to dealing with conflict fruitfully. At the time of a certain wage controversy in Massachusetts, the lowest paid girls in the industry were getting about $8.00 or $9.00 a week. The demand made by two of the representatives of the girls was for $22.40 (for a minimum wage, note), obviously too great an increase for anyone seriously to think of getting at one time. Thus the employers were as far as ever from knowing what the girls really thought they ought to have.

But I certainly ought not to imply that compromise is peculiarly a trade union method. It is the accepted, the approved, way of ending controversy. Yet no one really wants to compromise, because that means a giving up of something. Is there then any other method of ending conflict? There is a way beginning now to be recognized at least, and even occasionally followed: when two desires are *integrated,* that means a solution has been found in which both desires have found a place, that neither side has had to sacrifice anything. Let us take some very simple illustration. In the Harvard Library one day, in one of the smaller rooms, someone wanted the window open, I wanted it shut. We opened the window in the next room, where no one was sitting. This was not a compromise because there was no curtailing of desire; we both got what we really wanted. For I did not want a closed room, I simply did not want the north wind to blow directly on me; likewise the other occupant did not want that particular window open, he merely wanted more air in the room. . . .

Let us take another illustration. A Dairymen's Co-operative League almost went to pieces last year on the question of precedence in unloading cans at a creamery platform. The men who came down the hill (the creamery was on a down grade) thought they should have precedence; the men who came up the hill thought they should unload first. The thinking of both sides in the controversy was thus confined within the walls of these two possibilities, and this prevented their even trying to find a way of settling the dispute which would avoid these alternatives. The solution was obviously to change the position of the platform so that both up-hillers and down-hillers could unload at the same time. But this solution was not found until they had asked the advice of a more or less professional integrator. When, however, it was pointed out to them, they were quite ready to accept it. Integration involves invention, and the clever thing is to recognize this, and not to let one's thinking stay within the boundaries of two alternatives which are mutually exclusive.

Take another case. There is sometimes a question whether the meetings of works committees should be held in the plant or outside: the argument for meeting inside is the obvious advantage of being near one's work; the argument against, the fear of company influence. I know one factory that made what I consider an integration by having the meetings of the works committee held in the separate club building of the employees situated within the factory grounds. Here the men felt much freer than in any other part of the plant.

Some people tell me that they like what I have written on integration, but say that I am talking of what ought to be instead of what is. But indeed I am not; I am talking neither of what is, to any great extent, nor of what ought to be merely, but of what perhaps may be. This we can discover only by experiment. That is all I am urging, that we try experiments in methods of resolving differences; differences on the Board of Directors, with fellow managers or heads of departments, with employees, or in other relations. If we do this, we may take a different attitude toward conflict.

The key-word of psychology today is desire. If we wish to speak of conflict in the language of contemporary psychology, we might call it a moment in the interacting of desires. Thus we take from it any connotation of good or bad. Thus we shall not be afraid of conflict, but shall recognize that there is a destructive way of dealing with such moments and a constructive way. Conflict as the moment of the appearing and focusing of difference may be a sign of health, a prophecy of progress. If the Dairymen's League had not fought over the question of precedence, the improved method of unloading would not have been thought of. The conflict in this case was constructive. And this was because, instead of compromising, they sought a way of integrating. Compromise does not create, it deals with what already exists;

integration creates something new, in this case a different way of unloading. And because this not only settled the controversy but was actually better technique, saved time for both the farmers and the creamery, I call this: setting friction to work, making it *do* something.

Thus we see that while conflict as continued unintegrated difference is pathological, difference itself is not pathological. . . . What I think we should do in business organization is to try to find the machinery best suited for the normal appearing and uniting of diversity so that the difference does not stay too long crystallized, so that the pathological stage shall not be reached.

One advantage of integration over compromise I have not yet mentioned. If we get only compromise, the conflict will come up again and again in some other form, for in compromise we give up part of our desire, and because we shall not be content to rest there, sometime we shall try to get the whole of our desire. Watch industrial controversy, watch international controversy, and see how often this occurs. Only integration really stabilizes. But by stabilization I do not mean anything stationary. Nothing ever stays put. I mean only that that particular conflict is settled and the next occurs on a higher level.

Psychology has given us the phrase "progressive integratings"; we need also the phrase progressive differings. We can often measure our progress by watching the nature of our conflicts. Social progress is in this respect like individual progress; we become spiritually more and more developed as our conflicts rise to higher levels. If a man should tell you that his chief daily conflict within himself is—Shall I steal or not steal?—you would know what to think of his stage of development. As someone has said, "A man is known by the dilemmas he keeps." In the same way, one test of your business organization is not how many conflicts you have, for conflicts are the essence of life, but *what* are your conflicts? And how do you deal with them? It is to be hoped that we shall not always have strikes, but it is equally to be hoped that we shall always have conflict, the kind which leads to invention, to the emergence of new values.

Having suggested integration as perhaps the way by which we can deal most fruitfully with conflict, with difference, we should now consider the method by which integration can be obtained. But before we do that I want to say definitely that I do not think integration is possible in all cases. When two men want to marry the same woman, there can be no integration; when two sons both want the old family home, there can usually be no integration. And there are many such cases, some of little, some of great seriousness. I do not say that there is no tragedy in life. All that I say is that if we were alive to its advantages, we could often integrate instead of compromising. . . .

Bases of Integration

If, then, we do not think that differing necessarily means fighting, even when two desires both claim right of way, if we think that integration is more profitable than conquering or compromising, the first step toward this con-summation is *to bring the differences into the open.* We cannot hope to integrate our differences unless we know what they are. I will give some illustrations of the opposite method—evading or suppressing the issue.

I know a factory where, after the War, the employees asked for a 5 percent increase in wages, but it was not clear to either side whether this meant a 5 percent raise over present wages or over pre-War wages. Moreover, it was seen that neither side wished to know! The employees naturally preferred to think the former, the managers the latter. It was some time before both sides were willing to face the exact issue; each, unconsciously, hoped to win by keeping the whole problem hazy.

One of the longest discussions I ever heard on a minimum wage board was in regard to the question of fares to and from work: first, whether this item should be included at all with board, lodging, etc., in a cost-of-living budget, that is, whether transportation to and from the plant should be a cost on production. When finally it was decided to leave the item in and allow 60 cents a week for it, instead of the $1.20 which the 10-cent Boston car fare would necessitate if this item were to be allowed for in full, it seemed to me a clear case of evasion or suppression. That is, the employers were not willing to face at that moment the question whether wages should include transpor-tation. I sat on that board as a representative of the public, and I suggested more than once during the discussion that we should find out whether most of the girls in that particular industry did live near the plant or at a distance too great for walking. Also I suggested that we should find out whether, if they lived near the plant, the cost of board and lodging in that neighborhood was so high that it would more than offset car fares. But the employers in this instance were not ready to face the issue, and therefore the clearly evasive decision of 60 cents was made.

Another interesting case of suppression occurred in a committee of which I was a member. The question was a disagreement concerning the pay of two stenographers who were working for us. Those who urged the higher amount persisted in speaking of the stenographers' day as an eight-hour day because the hours are from nine to five, although with the hour out for lunch that obviously makes a seven-hour day.

Wherever you have the fight-set, you are in danger of obscurities, con-scious or unconscious. As long as trade unionism is a defensive movement, as long as employers' associations are defensive movements, we shall have obscurities. As long as internationalism is what it is, evasion will go on. Of course not to *appear* to evade is part of good diplomacy, for you don't want the other side to think you are trying to "get by" on anything. But we shall continue to evade or suppress as long as our real aim is not agreement, but domination. . . .

The psychiatrist tells his patient that he cannot help him unless he is honest in wanting his conflict to end. The "uncovering" which every book on psychology has rubbed into us for many years now as a process of the utmost importance for solving the conflicts which the individual has within himself is equally important for the relations between individuals, or between groups, classes, races, nations. In business, the employer, in dealing either with his associates or his employees, has to get underneath all the camouflage, has to find the real demand as against the demand put forward, distinguish declared motive from real motive, alleged cause from real cause, and to remember that sometimes the underlying motive is deliberately concealed and that sometimes it exists unconsciously.

The first rule, then, for obtaining integration is to put your cards on the table, face the real issue, uncover the conflict, bring the whole thing into the open.

One of the most important reasons for bringing the desires of each side to a place where they can be clearly examined and valued is that evaluation often leads to *revaluation.* We progress by a revaluation of desire, but usually we do not stop to examine a desire until another is disputing right of way with it. Watch the evolution of your desires from childhood, through youth, etc. The baby has many infantile desires which are not compatible with his wish for approbation; therefore he revalues his desires. We see this all through our life. We want to do so-and-so, but we do not estimate how much this really means to us until it comes into conflict with another desire. Revaluation is the flower of comparison.

This conception of the revaluation of desire it is necessary to keep in the foreground of our thinking in dealing with conflict, for neither side ever "gives in" really, it is hopeless to expect it, but there often comes a moment when there is a simultaneous revaluation of interests on both sides and unity precipitates itself. . . . Integration is often more a spontaneous flowing together of desire than one might think from what I have said; the revaluing of interests on both sides may lead the interests to fit into each other, so that all find some place in the final solution.

The bearing of all this on business administration is, I hope, obvious. A business should be so organized (this is one of the tests for us to apply to our organization) that full opportunity is given in any conflict, in any coming together of different desires, for the whole field of desire to be viewed. Our employees should be able to see, as we should be able ourselves to see, the whole field of desire. The *field of desire* is an important psychological and sociological conception; many conflicts could, I believe, be prevented from ending disastrously by getting the desires of each side into one field of vision where they could be viewed together and compared. We all believe to a certain extent in Freud's "sublimation," but I believe still more that various desires get orientated toward one another and take on different values in the process of orientation.

It will be understood, of course, that all this applies to ourselves as well as to the other side; we have to uncover our sub-articulate egoisms, and then, when we see them in relation to other facts and desires, we may estimate them differently. We often think it is a question of eliminating motives when it is only a question of subordinating them. We often, for instance, treat personal motives as more ignoble than we need. There is nothing necessarily discreditable in the politician "standing by" his friends. The only ethical question is how much that motive is weighing against others. The unethical thing is to persuade yourself that it is not weighing at all.

I have time barely to mention a very important point: the connection between the *realignment of groups* and a revaluation of interests. I have found this important in watching the realignments of political parties. We must in any conflict between groups watch every realignment to see how far it changes the confronting desires, for this means how far it changes the conflict.

I began this section by saying that the first step in integration is to bring the differences into the open. If the first step is to put clearly before ourselves what there is to integrate, there is something very important for us to note— namely, that the highest lights in a situation are not always those which are most indicative of the real issues involved. Many situations are decidedly complex, involve numerous and varied activities, overlapping activities. There is too great a tendency (perhaps encouraged by popular journalism) to deal with the dramatic moments, forgetting that these are not always the most significant moments. We should not follow literary analogies here. You may have a good curtain with, to quote Kipling, the lovers loving and the parents signing cheques. Yet, after all, this may not be the controlling moment in the lives of these people. To *find the significant rather than the dramatic features* of industrial controversy, of a disagreement in regard to policy on board of directors or between managers, is essential to integrative business policies.

Such search is part of what seems to me the second step in integration. If the first step is to uncover the real conflict, the next is to take the demands of both sides and break them up into their constituent parts. Contemporary psychology shows how fatal it is to try to deal with conglomerates. I know a boy who wanted a college education. His father died and he had to go to work at once to support his mother. Had he then to give up his desire? No, for on analysis he found that what he wanted was not a college education, but an education, and there were still ways of his getting that. You remember the southern girl who said, "Why, I always thought damned Yankee was one word until I came north."

You will notice that to break up a problem into its various parts involves the *examination of symbols,* involves, that is, the careful scrutiny of the language used to see what it really means. A friend of mine wanted to go to Europe, but also she did not want to spend the money it would cost. Was there any integration? Yes, she found one. In order to understand it, let us use the method I am advocating; let us ask, what did "going to Europe" symbolize to her? In order to do that, we have to break up this whole, "going to

Europe." What does "going to Europe" stand for to different people? A sea voyage, seeing beautiful places, meeting new people, a rest or change from daily duties, and a dozen other things. Now, this woman had taught for a few years after leaving college and then had gone away and led a somewhat secluded life for a good many years. "Going to Europe" was to her a symbol, not of snow mountains, or cathedrals, or pictures, but of meeting people— that was what she wanted. When she was asked to teach in a summer school of young men and women where she would meet a rather interesting staff of teachers and a rather interesting group of students, she immediately accepted. This was her integration. This was not a substitution for her wish, it was her *real* wish fulfilled.

It is, of course, unavoidable to use symbols; all language is symbolic; but we should be always on our guard as to what is symbolized. . . . Every day we use many more not-understood symbols, many more whole-words, unanalysed words, than we ought to. Much of what is written of the "consumer" is inaccurate because consumer is used as a whole-word, whereas it is quite obvious that the consumer of large wealth has different desires and motives from the consumer of small means.

We have been considering the breaking up of the whole-demand. On the other hand, one often has to do just the opposite; find the whole-demand, the real demand, which is being obscured by miscellaneous minor claims or by ineffective presentation. The man with a genius for leadership is the one who can make articulate the whole-demand, unless it is a matter of tactics deliberately to conceal it. . . .

Mr. Earl Howard, labor manager for Hart, Schaffner and Marx, said to me once, "It isn't enough merely to study the actual reaction of your employees; you must anticipate their reactions, beat them to it." That—to beat them to it—is exactly what each firm does try to do with its competing firms, but I do not think many managers study and anticipate the reactions of their employees as carefully as they do those of competing firms. It would be just as useful.

You could probably give me many illustrations of the *anticipation of response*. We could find innumerable examples in our households. A man liked motoring, his wife walking; he anticipated what her response might be to a suggestion that they motor on Sunday afternoon by tiring her out playing tennis in the morning.

The anticipation of conflict, it should be noted, does not mean necessarily the avoidance of conflict, but playing the game differently. That is, you integrate the different interests without making all the moves. A friend of mine says that my theory of integration is like a game of chess. I think it is something like that. The tyro has to find his solution by making his actual moves, by the crude method of changing the places of his chessmen. A good chessplayer does not need to do this, he sees the possibilities without playing them out. The business man in dealing with competitive firms is like the good chess player. As the real conflict between two good chess players is a conflict of possibilities that would be realized if they played them out, so in business you do not have to make all the moves to make your integrations; you deal with antecedents, premonitory symptoms, etc. You do not avoid doing certain things, you have done them without doing them.

But assuming that in our business we do watch response and anticipate response, that still is not going far enough. It is not enough to ask to what our employee or our business confrère or business competitor is responding, nor even to what he is likely to respond. We have to prepare the way for response, we have to try to build up in him a certain attitude. . . .

Yet even *preparation for response* is only a small part of the matter; we shall have to go deeper than that. There is *circular* as well as *linear* response, and the exposition of that is I think the most interesting contribution of contemporary psychology to the social sciences. A good example of circular response is a game of tennis. A serves. The way B returns the ball depends partly on the way it was served to him. A's next play will depend on his own original serve plus the return of B, and so on and so on. We see this in discussion. We see this in most activity between one and another. Mischievous or idle boys say, "Let's start something"; we must remember that whenever we act we have always "started something," behavior precipitates behavior in others. Every employer should remember this. One of the managers in a factory expressed it to me thus: "I am in command of a situation until I behave; when I act I have lost control of the situation." This does not mean that we should not act! It is, however, something to which it is very important that we give full consideration.

Circular response seems a simple matter, quite obvious, something we must all accept. Yet every day we try to evade it, every day we act and hope to avoid the inescapable response. . . .

The conception of circular behavior throws much light on conflict, for I now realize that I can never fight you, I am always fighting you plus me. I have put it this way: that response is always to a relation. I respond, not only to you, but to the relation between you and me. Employees do not respond only to their employers, but to the relation between themselves and their employer. Trade unionism is responding, not only to capitalism, but to the relation between itself and capitalism. . . .

Obstacles to Integration

Finally, let us consider the chief *obstacles to integration*. It requires a high order of intelligence, keen perception and discrimination, more than all, a brilliant inventiveness; it is easier for the trade union to fight than to suggest a better way of running the factory. . . .

Another obstacle to integration is that our way of life has habituated many of us to enjoy domination. Integration seems to many a tamer affair; it leaves no "thrills" of conquest. I knew a dispute within a trade union where, by the skilful action of the chairman, a true integration was discovered and accepted, but instead of the satisfaction one might have expected from such a happy result, the evening seemed to end rather dully, flatly; there was no climax, there was no side left swelling its chest, no one had conquered, no one had "won out." It is even true that to some people defeat, as well as conquest, is more interesting than integration. That is, the person with decided fight habits feels more at home, happier, in the fight movement. Moreover, it leaves the door open for further fighting, with the possibility of conquest the next time.

Another obstacle to integration is that the matter in dispute is often theorized over instead of being taken up as a proposed activity. I think this important in business administration. Intellectual agreement does not alone bring full integration. . . .

I have been interested to watch how often disagreement disappears when theorizing ends and the question is of some definite activity to be undertaken. At a trade union conference, someone brought up the question of waste: how could the workmen help to eliminate waste? But it was found that most of the union men did not think it the job of the workmen to eliminate waste; that belonged to the management. Moreover, they did not think it in their interest to eliminate waste; wages were fixed by the union, by collective bargaining; everything saved went to swell profits; no more went into their pockets. It was seen, however, that there was another side, and the argument went on, but without coming to any agreement. Finally, however, by some maneuvering on the part of the chairman, it was acknowledged that there were certain forms of waste which the unions could be got to take cognizance of. A machinist, a plumber, and a carpenter undertook to take up with their unions the question of how far they could agree to take some responsibility for these particular types of waste. I hope the fact then emerged, when it was considered as a practical issue, that for some forms of waste the management is responsible, for some forms the employees, and for some forms the union.

A serious obstacle to integration which every business man should consider is the language used. We have noted the necessity of making preparation in the other man, and in ourselves too, for the attitude most favorable to conciliation. A trade unionist said to me, "Our representatives didn't manage it right. If instead of a 15 percent increase they had asked for an adjustment of wages, the management would have been more willing to listen to us; it would have put them in a different frame of mind." I don't quite see why we are not more careful about our language in business, for in most delicate situations we quite consciously choose that which will not arouse antagonism. You say to your wife at breakfast, "Let's reconsider that decision we came to last night." You do not say, "I wish to give you my criticism of the decision you made last night."

I cannot refrain from mentioning a personal experience. I went into the Edison Electric Light Company and said to a young woman at a counter, "Where shall I go to speak about my bill?" "Room D for complaints" she replied. "But I don't wish to make a complaint," I said. "I thought there was a mistake in your bill." "I think there is," I said, "but I don't wish to complain about it; it was a very natural mistake." The girl looked nonplussed, and as she was obviously speechless a man came out from behind a desk and said: "You would prefer to ask for an adjustment, wouldn't you?" and we had a chat about it.

I have left untouched one of the chief obstacles to integration—namely, the undue influence of leaders—the manipulation of the unscrupulous on the one hand and the suggestibility of the crowd on the other. Moreover, even when the power of suggestion is not used deliberately, it exists in all meetings between people; the whole emotional field of human intercourse has to be taken fully into account in dealing with methods of reconciliation. . . .

Finally, perhaps the greatest of all obstacles to integration is our lack of training for it. In our college debates we try always to beat the other side. In the circular announcing the courses to be given at the Bryn Mawr Summer School for Workers, I find: "English Composition and Public Speaking; to develop the art of oral and written expression." I think that in addition to this there should be classes in discussion which should aim to teach the "art" of co-operative thinking, and I was disappointed that there was no such course in the program of a school for workers. Managers need it just as much. I have found, in the case of the wage boards which I have been on, that many employers (I ought in fairness to say not the majority) came to these joint conferences of employers and employees with little notion of conferring, but to push through, to force through, plans *previously* arrived at, based on *preconceived* ideas of what employees are like. It seems as if the methods of genuine conference have yet to be learned. Even if there were not the barriers of an unenlightened self-interest, of prejudice, rigidity, dogmatism, routine, there would still be required training and practice for us to master the technique of integration. A friend of mine said to me, "Open-mindedness is the whole thing, isn't it?" No, it isn't; it needs just as great a respect for your own view as for that of others, and a firm upholding of it until you are convinced. Mushy people are no more good at this than stubborn people.

As an indirect summing up of this discussion, I should like to emphasize our responsibility for integration. We saw in our consideration of circular response that my behavior helps create the situation to which I am responding. That implies (what we have daily to take into account) that my behavior is helping to *develop* the situation to which I am responding. The standard of living goes up not only while, but partly because, it is being studied. This conception of the developing situation is of the utmost importance for business administration. It makes it impossible to construct a map of the future, yet all our maxims of foresight hold good; every business should reconcile these two statements. We should work always with the evolving situation, and note what part our own activities have in that evolving situation.

This is the most important word, not only for business relations, but for all human relations: not to adapt ourselves to a situation—we are all more necessary to the world than that; neither to mold a situation to *our* liking—we are all, or rather each, of too little importance to the world for that; but to take account of that reciprocal adjustment, that interactive behaviour between the situation and ourselves which means a change in both the situation and ourselves. One test of business administration should be: is the organization such that both employers and employees, or co-managers, co-directors, are stimulated to a reciprocal activity which will give more than mere adjustment, more than an equilibrium? Our outlook is narrowed, our activity is restricted, our chances of business success largely diminished when our thinking is constrained within the limits of what has been called an either-or situation. We should never allow ourselves to be bullied by an "either-or." There is often the possibility of something better than either of two given alternatives. Every one of us interested in any form of constructive work is looking for the plus values of our activity. . . .

F. J. Roethlisberger (1898–1974)

During the late 1920s and early 1930s one of the most ambitious series of social experiments in American history was conducted, certainly up to that time. The site was the Hawthorne plant of the Western Electric Company near Chicago; the subject, the workers in that plant, their effectiveness, and their relationships with each other and with management. Led by Elton Mayo, the study team included a number of scholars, many from the Harvard School of Business, specialized in industrial psychology, sociology, and cultural anthropology. Their experiments and findings were reported and analyzed in an imposing number of books over the following years, which collectively formed the principal launching pad for the field of human relations. That field burgeoned after World War II and its influence extended far beyond the management of factories into other areas of organized endeavor, including, of course, public administration.

Professor F. J. (Fritz) Roethlisberger of the Harvard School participated in the studies and later wrote extensively about them. The second chapter of his book *Management and Morale*, which is reprinted below, is perhaps the most succinct account of the studies themselves and of the conclusions the researchers drew from them.

The initial focus and the assumptions of those involved in the Hawthorne studies seem largely to have been based upon those of scientific management as propounded by Frederick W. Taylor several decades earlier. Both were concerned centrally with the workers, their motivations, their efficiency, and the impact upon them of the reward system and conditions of work. The Hawthorne studies indicated that Taylor's science was inadequate because it took too little account of human factors. Yet both scientific management and human relations came under fire from organized labor, which charged them with encouraging the manipulation of workers primarily for the benefit of management.

F.C.M.

Management and Morale

The Road Back to Sanity

At a recent meeting the researches in personnel at the Hawthorne plant of the Western Electric Company were mentioned by both a management man and a union man. There seemed to be no difference of opinion between the two regarding the importance or relevance of these research findings for effective management-employee relations. This seemed to me interesting because it suggested that the labor situation can be discussed at a level where both sides can roughly agree. The question of what this level is can be answered only after closer examination of these studies.

In the February, 1941, issue of the *Reader's Digest* there appeared a summary statement of these researches by Stuart Chase, under the title, "What Makes the Worker Like to Work?" At the conclusion of his article, Stuart Chase said, "There is an idea here so big that it leaves one gasping." Just what Mr. Chase meant by this statement is not explained, but to find out one can go back to the actual studies and see what was learned from them. In my opinion, the results were very simple and obvious—as Sherlock Holmes used to say to Dr. Watson, "Elementary, my dear Watson." Now this is what may have left Stuart Chase "gasping"—the systematic exploitation of the simple and the obvious which these studies represent.

There seems to be an assumption today that we need a complex set of ideas to handle the complex problems of this complex world in which we live.

Chapter 2, *Management and Morale* (Cambridge: Harvard University Press, 1941), pp. 7–26. Reprinted by permission of the publishers. Copyright 1941 by the President and Fellows of Harvard College; © 1969 by F. J. Roethlisberger.

We assume that a big problem needs a big idea; a complex problem needs a complex idea for its solution. As a result, our thinking tends to become more and more tortuous and muddled. Nowhere is this more true than in matters of human behavior. It seems to me that the road back to sanity—and here is where my title comes in—lies:

(1) In having a few simple and clear ideas about the world in which we live.

(2) In complicating our ideas, not in a vacuum, but only in reference to things we can observe, see, feel, hear, and touch. Let us not generalize from verbal definitions; let us know in fact what we are talking about.

(3) In having a very simple method by means of which we can explore our complex world. We need a tool which will allow us to get the data from which our generalizations are to be drawn. We need a simple skill to keep us in touch with what is sometimes referred to as "reality."

(4) In being "tough-minded," i.e. in not letting ourselves be too disappointed because the complex world never quite fulfills our most cherished expectations of it. Let us remember that the concrete phenomena will always elude any set of abstractions that we can make of them.

(5) In knowing very clearly the class of phenomena to which our ideas and methods relate. Now, this is merely a way of saying, "Do not use a saw as a hammer." A saw is a useful tool precisely because it is limited and designed for a certain purpose. Do not criticize the usefulness of a saw because it does not make a good hammer.

Although this last statement is obvious with regard to such things as "saws" and "hammers," it is less well understood in the area of human relations. Too often we try to solve human problems with nonhuman tools and, what is still more extraordinary, in terms of nonhuman data. We take data from which all human meaning has been deleted and then are surprised to find that we reach conclusions which have no human significance.

It is my simple thesis that a human problem requires a human solution. First, we have to learn to recognize a human problem when we see one; and second, upon recognizing it, we have to learn to deal with it as such and not as if it were something else. Too often at the verbal level we talk glibly about the importance of the human factor; and too seldom at the concrete level of behavior do we recognize a human problem for what it is and deal with it as such. *A human problem to be brought to a human solution requires human data and human tools.* It is my purpose to use the Western Electric researches as an illustration of what I mean by this statement, because, if they deserve the publicity and acclaim which they have received, it is because, in my opinion, they have so conclusively demonstrated this point. In this sense they are the road back to sanity in management-employee relations.

Experiments in Illumination

The Western Electric researches started about sixteen years ago, in the Hawthorne plant, with a series of experiments on illumination. The purpose was to find out the relation of the quality and quantity of illumination to the efficiency of industrial workers. These studies lasted several years, and I shall not describe them in detail. It will suffice to point out that the results were quite different from what had been expected.

In one experiment the workers were divided into two groups. One group, called the "test group," was to work under different illumination intensities. The other group, called the "control group," was to work under an intensity of illumination, as nearly constant as possible. During the first experiment, the test group was submitted to three different intensities of illumination of increasing magnitude, 24, 46, and 70 foot candles. What were the results of this early experiment? Production increased in both rooms—in both the test group and the control group—and the rise in output was roughly of the same magnitude in both cases.

In another experiment, the light under which the test group worked was decreased from 10 to 3 foot candles, while the control group worked, as before, under a constant level of illumination intensity. In this case the output rate in the test group went up instead of down. It also went up in the control group.

In still another experiment, the workers were allowed to believe that the illumination was being increased, although, in fact, no change in intensity was made. The workers commented favorably on the improved lighting condition, but there was no appreciable change in output. At another time, the workers were allowed to believe that the intensity of illumination was being decreased, although again, in fact, no actual change was made. The workers complained somewhat about the poorer lighting, but again there was no appreciable effect on output.

And finally, in another experiment, the intensity of illumination was decreased to .06 of a foot candle, which is the intensity of illumination approximately equivalent to that of ordinary moonlight. Not until this point was reached was there any appreciable decline in the output rate.

What did the experimenters learn? Obviously, as Stuart Chase said, there was something "screwy," but the experimenters were not quite sure who or what was screwy—they themselves, the subjects, or the results. One thing was clear: the results were negative. Nothing of a positive nature had been learned about the relation of illumination to industrial efficiency. If the results were to be taken at their face value, it would appear that there was no relation between illumination and industrial efficiency. However, the investigators were not yet quite willing to draw this conclusion. They realized the difficulty of testing for the effect of a single variable in a situation where there were many uncontrolled variables. It was thought therefore that another experiment should be devised in which other variables affecting the output of workers could be better controlled.

A few of the tough-minded experimenters already were beginning to suspect their basic ideas and assumptions with regard to human motivation. It occurred to them that the trouble was not so much with the results or with the subjects as it was with their notion regarding the way their subjects were supposed to behave—the notion of a simple cause-and-effect, direct relationship between certain physical changes in the workers' environment and the responses of the workers to these changes. Such a notion completely ignored the human meaning of these changes to the people who were subjected to them.

In the illumination experiments, therefore, we have a classic example of trying to deal with a human situation in nonhuman terms. The experimenters had obtained no human data; they had been handling electric-light bulbs and plotting average output curves. Hence their results had no human significance. That is why they seemed screwy. Let me suggest here, however, that the results were not screwy, but the experimenters were—a "screwy" person being by definition one who is not acting in accordance with the customary human values of the situation in which he finds himself.

The Relay Assembly Test Room

Another experiment was framed, in which it was planned to submit a segregated group of workers to different kinds of working conditions. The idea was very simple: A group of five girls were placed in a separate room where their conditions of work could be carefully controlled, where their output could be measured, and where they could be closely observed. It was decided to introduce at specified intervals different changes in working conditions and to see what effect these innovations had on output. Also, records were kept, such as the temperature and humidity of the room, the number of hours each girl slept at night, the kind and amount of food she ate for breakfast, lunch, and dinner. Output was carefully measured, the time it took each girl to assemble a telephone relay of approximately forty parts (roughly a minute) being automatically recorded each time; quality records were kept; each girl had a physical examination at regular intervals. Under these conditions of close observation the girls were studied for a period of five years. Literally tons of material were collected. Probably nowhere in the world has so much material been collected about a small group of workers for such a long period of time.

But what about the results? They can be stated very briefly. When all is said and done, they amount roughly to this: A skillful statistician spent several years trying to relate variations in output with variations in the physical circumstances of these five operators. For example, he correlated the hours that each girl spent in bed the night before with variations in output the following day. Inasmuch as some people said that the effect of being out late one night was not felt the following day but the day after that, he correlated variations in output with the amount of rest the operators had had two nights before. I mention this just to point out the fact that he missed no obvious tricks and that he did a careful job and a thorough one, and it took him many years to do it. The attempt to relate changes in physical circumstances to variations in output resulted in not a single correlation of enough statistical significance to be recognized by any competent statistician as having any meaning.

Now, of course, it would be misleading to say that this negative result was the only conclusion reached. There were positive conclusions, and it did not take the experimenters more than two years to find out that they had missed the boat. After two years of work, certain things happened which made them sit up and take notice. Different experimental conditions of work, in the nature of changes in the number and duration of rest pauses and differences in the length of the working day and week, had been introduced in this Relay Assembly Test Room. For example, the investigators first introduced two five-minute rests, one in the morning and one in the afternoon. Then they increased the length of these rests, and after that they introduced the rests at different times of the day. During one experimental period they served the operators a specially prepared lunch during the rest. In the later periods, they decreased the length of the working day by one-half hour and then by one hour. They gave the operators Saturday morning off for a while. Altogether, thirteen such periods of different working conditions were introduced in the first two years.

During the first year and a half of the experiment, everybody was happy, both the investigators and the operators. The investigators were happy because as conditions of work improved the output rate rose steadily. Here, it appeared, was strong evidence in favor of their preconceived hypothesis that fatigue was the major factor limiting output. The operators were happy because their conditions of work were being improved, they were earning more money, and they were objects of considerable attention from top management. But then one investigator—one of those tough-minded fellows—suggested that they restore the original conditions of work, that is, go back to a full forty-eight-hour week without rests, lunches, and what not. This was Period XII. Then the happy state of affairs, when everything was going along as it theoretically should, went sour. Output, instead of taking the expected nose dive, maintained its high level.

Again the investigators were forcibly reminded that human situations are likely to be complex. In any human situation, whenever a simple change is introduced—a rest pause, for example—other changes, unwanted and unanticipated, may also be brought about. What I am saying here is very simple. If one experiments on a stone, the stone does not know it is being experimented upon—all of which makes it simple for people experimenting on stones. But if a human being is being experimented upon, he is likely to know it. Therefore, his attitudes toward the experiment and toward the experimenters become very important factors in determining his responses to the situation.

Now that is what happened in the Relay Assembly Test Room. To the investigators, it was essential that the workers give their full and whole-hearted cooperation to the experiment. They did not want the operators to work harder or easier depending upon their attitude toward the conditions that were imposed. They wanted them to work as they felt, so that they could be sure that the different physical conditions of work were solely responsible for the variations in output. For each of the experimental changes, they wanted subjects whose responses would be uninfluenced by so-called "psychological factors."

In order to bring this about, the investigators did everything in their power to secure the complete cooperation of their subjects, with the result that almost all the practices common to the shop were altered. The operators were consulted about the changes to be made, and, indeed, several plans were abandoned because they met with the disapproval of the girls. They were questioned sympathetically about their reactions to the conditions imposed, and many of these conferences took place in the office of the superintendent. The girls were allowed to talk at work; their "bogey" was eliminated. Their physical health and well-being became matters of great concern. Their opinions, hopes, and fears were eagerly sought. What happened was that in the very process of setting the conditions for the test—a so-called "controlled" experiment—the experimenters had completely altered the social situation of the room. Inadvertently a change had been introduced which was far more important than the planned experimental innovations: the customary supervision in the room had been revolutionized. This accounted for the better attitudes of the girls and their improved rate of work.

The Development of a New and More Fruitful Point of View

After Period XII in the Relay Assembly Test Room, the investigators decided to change their ideas radically. What all their experiments had dramatically and conclusively demonstrated was the importance of employee attitudes and sentiments. It was clear that the responses of workers to what was happening about them were dependent upon the significance these events had for them. In most work situations the meaning of a change is likely to be as important, if not more so, than the change itself. This was the great *éclaircissement*, the new illumination, that came from the research. It was an illumination quite different from what they had expected from the illumination studies. Curiously enough, this discovery is nothing very new or startling. It is something which anyone who has had some concrete experience in handling other people intuitively recognizes and practices. Whether or not a person is going to give his services whole-heartedly to a group depends, in good part, on the way he feels about his job, his fellow workers, and supervisors—the meaning for him of what is happening about him.

However, when the experimenters began to tackle the problem of employee attitudes and the factors determining such attitudes—when they began to tackle the problem of "meaning"—they entered a sort of twilight zone where things are never quite what they seem. Moreover, overnight, as it were, they were robbed of all the tools they had so carefully forged; for all their previous tools were nonhuman tools concerned with the measurement of output, temperature, humidity, etc., and these were no longer useful for the human data that they now wanted to obtain. What the experimenters now wanted to know was how a person felt, what his intimate thinking, reflections, and preoccupations were, and what he liked and disliked about his work environment. In short, what did the whole blooming business—his job, his supervision, his working conditions—mean to him? Now this was human stuff, and there were no tools, or at least the experimenters knew of none, for obtaining and evaluating this kind of material.

Fortunately, there were a few courageous souls among the experimenters. These men were not metaphysicians, psychologists, academicians, professors, intellectuals, or what have you. They were men of common sense and of practical affairs. They were not driven by any great heroic desire to change the world. They were true experimenters, that is, men compelled to follow the implications of their own monkey business. All the evidence of their studies was pointing in one direction. Would they take the jump? They did.

Experiments in Interviewing Workers

A few tough-minded experimenters decided to go into the shops and—completely disarmed and denuded of their elaborate logical equipment and in all humility—to see if they could learn how to get the workers to talk about things that were important to them and could learn to understand what the workers were trying to tell them. This was a revolutionary idea in the year 1928, when this interviewing program started—the idea of getting a worker to talk to you and to listen sympathetically, but intelligently, to what he had to say. In that year a new era of personnel relations began. It was the first real attempt to get human data and to forge human tools to get them. In that year a novel idea was born; dimly the experimenters perceived a new method of human control. In that year the Rubicon was crossed from which there could be no return to the "good old days." Not that the experimenters ever wanted to return, because they now entered a world so exciting, so intriguing, and so full of promise that it made the "good old days" seem like the prattle and play of children.

When these experimenters decided to enter the world of "meaning," with very few tools, but with a strong sense of curiosity and a willingness to learn, they had many interesting adventures. It would be too long a story to tell all of them, or even a small part of them. They made plenty of mistakes, but they were not afraid to learn.

At first, they found it difficult to learn to give full and complete attention to what a person had to say without interrupting him before he was through. They found it difficult to learn not to give advice, not to make or imply moral judgments about the speaker, not to argue, not to be too clever, not to dominate the conversation. not to ask leading questions. They found it difficult to get the person to talk about matters which were important to him and not to the interviewer. But, most important of all, they found it difficult to learn that perhaps the thing most significant to a person was not something in his immediate work situation.

Gradually, however, they learned these things. They discovered that sooner or later a person tends to talk about what is uppermost in his mind to a sympathetic and skillful listener, and they became more proficient in interpreting what a person is saying or trying to say. Of course they protected the confidences given to them and made absolutely sure that nothing an employee said could ever be used against him. Slowly they began to forge a simple human tool—imperfect, to be sure—to get the kind of data they wanted. They called this method "interviewing." I would hesitate to say the number of man-hours of labor which went into the forging of this tool. There followed from studies made through its use a gradually changing conception of the worker and his behavior.

A New Way of Viewing Employee Satisfaction and Dissatisfaction

When the experimenters started to study employee likes and dislikes, they assumed, at first, that they would find a simple and logical relation between a person's likes or dislikes and certain items and events in his immediate work situation. They expected to find a simple connection, for example, between a person's complaint and the object about which he was complaining. Hence, the solution would be easy: correct the object of the complaint, if possible, and presto! the complaint would disappear. Unfortunately, however, the world of human behavior is not so simple as this conception of it; and it took the investigators several arduous and painful years to find this out. I will mention only a few interesting experiences they had.

Several times they changed the objects of the complaint only to find that the attitudes of the complainants remained unchanged. In these cases, correcting the object of the complaint did not remedy the complaint or the attitude of the person expressing it. A certain complaint might disappear, to be sure, only to have another one arise. Here the investigators were running into so-called "chronic kickers," people whose dissatisfactions were more deeply rooted in factors related to their personal histories. For such people the simple remedy of changing the object of the complaint was not enough.

Several times they did absolutely nothing about the object of the complaint, but after the interview, curiously enough, the complaint disappeared. A typical example of this was that of a woman who complained at great length and with considerable feeling about the poor food being served in the company restaurant. When, a few days later, she chanced to meet the interviewer, she commented with great enthusiasm upon the improved food and thanked the interviewer for communicating her grievance to management and for securing such prompt action. Here no change had been made in the thing criticized; yet the employee felt that something had been done.

Many times they found that people did not really want anything done about the things of which they were complaining. What they did want was an opportunity to talk about their troubles to a sympathetic listener. It was astonishing to find the number of instances in which workers complained about things which had happened many, many years ago, but which they described as vividly as if they had happened just a day before.

Here again, something was "screwy," but this time the experimenters realized that it was their assumptions which were screwy. They were assuming that the meanings which people assign to their experience are essentially logical. They were carrying in their heads the notion of the "economic man," a man primarily motivated by economic interests, whose logical capacities were being used in the service of this self-interest.

Gradually and painfully in the light of the evidence, which was overwhelming, the experimenters had been forced to abandon this conception of the worker and his behavior. Only with a new working hypothesis could they make sense of the data they had collected. The conception of the worker which they developed is actually nothing very new or startling; it is one which any effective administrator intuitively recognizes and practices in handling human beings.

First, they found that the behavior of workers could not be understood apart from their feelings or sentiments. I shall use the word "sentiment" hereafter to refer not only to such things as feelings and emotions, but also to a much wider range of phenomena which may not be expressed in violent feelings or emotions—phenomena that are referred to by such words as "loyalty," "integrity," "solidarity."

Secondly, they found that sentiments are easily disguised, and hence are difficult to recognize and to study. Manifestations of sentiment take a number of different forms. Feelings of personal integrity, for example, can be expressed by a handshake; they can also be expressed, when violated, by a sitdown strike. Moreover, people like to rationalize their sentiments and to objectify them. We are not so likely to say "I feel bad," as to say "The world is bad." In other words, we like to endow the world with those attributes and qualities which will justify and account for the feelings and sentiments we have toward it; we tend to project our sentiments on the outside world.

Thirdly, they found that manifestations of sentiment could not be understood as things in and by themselves, but only in terms of the total situation of the person. To comprehend why a person felt the way he did, a wider range of phenomena had to be explored. The following three diagrams illustrate roughly the development of this point of view.

It will be remembered that at first the investigators assumed a simple and direct relation between certain physical changes in the worker's environment and his responses to them. This simple state of mind is illustrated in diagram I. But all the evidence of the early experiments showed that the responses of employees to changes in their immediate working environment can be understood only in terms of their attitudes—the "meaning" these changes have for them. This point of view is represented in diagram II. However, the "meaning" which these changes have for the worker is not

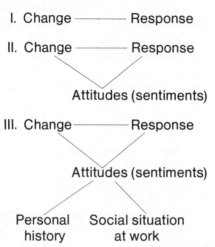

I. Change ———— Response

II. Change ———— Response

Attitudes (sentiments)

III. Change ———— Response

Attitudes (sentiments)

Personal   Social situation
history   at work

strictly and primarily logical, for they are fraught with human feelings and values. The "meaning," therefore, which any individual worker assigns to a particular change depends upon (1) his social "conditioning," or what sentiments (values, hopes, fears, expectations, etc.) he is bringing to the work situation because of his previous family and group associations, and hence the relation of the change to these sentiments; and (2) the kind of human satisfaction he is deriving from his social participation with other workers and supervisors in the immediate work group of which he is a member, and hence the effect of the change of his customary interpersonal relations. This way of regarding the responses of workers (both verbal and overt) is represented in diagram III. It says briefly: Sentiments do not appear in a vacuum; they do not come out of the blue; they appear in a social context. They have to be considered in terms of that context, and apart from it they are likely to be misunderstood.

One further point should be made about that aspect of the worker's environment designated "Social situation at work" in diagram III. What is meant is that the worker is not an isolated, atomic individual; he is a member of a group, or of groups. Within each of these groups the individuals have feelings and sentiments toward each other, which bind them together in collaborative effort. Moreover, these collective sentiments can, and do, become attached to every item and object in the industrial environment— even to output. Material goods, output, wages, hours of work, and so on, cannot be treated as things in themselves. Instead, they must be interpreted as carriers of social value.

Output as a Form of Social Behavior

That output is a form of social behavior was well illustrated in a study made by the Hawthorne experimenters, called the Bank Wiring Observation Room. This room contained fourteen workmen representing three occupational groups—wiremen, soldermen, and inspectors. These men were on group piecework, where the more they turned out the more they earned. In such a situation one might have expected that they would have been interested in maintaining total output and that the faster workers would have put pressure on the slower workers to improve their efficiency. But this was not the case. Operating within this group were four basic sentiments, which can be expressed briefly as follows: (1) You should not turn out too much work; if you do, you are a "rate buster." (2) You should not turn out too little work; if you do, you are a "chiseler." (3) You should not say anything to a supervisor which would react to the detriment of one of your associates; if you do, you are a "squealer." (4) You should not be too officious; that is, if you are an inspector you should not act like one.

To be an accepted member of the group a man had to act in accordance with these social standards. One man in this group exceeded the group standard of what constituted a fair day's work. Social pressure was put on him to conform, but without avail, since he enjoyed doing things the others disliked. The best-liked person in the group was the one who kept his output exactly where the group agreed it should be.

Inasmuch as the operators were agreed as to what constituted a day's work, one might have expected rate of output to be about the same for each member of the group. This was by no means the case; there were marked differences. At first the experimenters thought that the differences in individual performance were related to differences in ability, so they compared each worker's relative rank in output with his relative rank in intelligence and dexterity as measured by certain tests. The results were interesting: the lowest producer in the room ranked first in intelligence and third in dexterity; the highest producer in the room was seventh in dexterity and lowest in intelligence. Here surely was a situation in which the native capacities of the men were not finding expression. From the viewpoint of logical, economic behavior, this room did not make sense. Only in terms of powerful sentiments could these individual differences in output level be explained. Each worker's level of output reflected his position in the informal organization of the group.

What Makes the Worker Not Want to Cooperate

As a result of the Bank Wiring Observation Room, the Hawthorne researchers became more and more interested in the informal employee groups which tend to form within the formal organization of the company, and which are not likely to be represented in the organization chart. They became interested in the beliefs and creeds which have the effect of making each individual feel an integral part of the group and which make the group appear as a single unit, in the social codes and norms of behavior by means of which employees automatically work together in a group without any conscious choice as to whether they will or will not cooperate. They studied the important social functions these groups perform for their members, the histories of these informal work groups, how they spontaneously appear, how they tend to perpetuate themselves, multiply, and disappear, how they are in constant jeopardy from technical change, and hence how they tend to resist innovation. In particular, they became interested in those groups whose norms and codes of behavior are at variance with the technical and economic objectives of the company as a whole. They examined the social conditions under which it is more likely for the employee group to separate itself out in opposition to the remainder of the groups which make up the total organization. In such phenomena they felt that they had at last arrived at the heart of the problem of effective collaboration. They obtained a new enlightenment of the present industrial scene; from this point of view, many perplexing problems became more intelligible.

Some people claim, for example, that the size of the pay envelope is the major demand which the employee is making on his job. All the worker wants is to be told what to do and to get paid for doing it. If we look at him and his job in terms of sentiments, this is far from being as generally true as we would like to believe. Most of us want the satisfaction that comes from being accepted and recognized as people of worth by our friends and work associates. Money is only a small part of this social recognition. The way we are greeted by our boss, being asked to help a newcomer, being asked to keep an eye on a difficult operation, being given a job requiring special skill—all of these are acts of social recognition. They tell us how we stand in our work group. We all want tangible evidence of our social importance. We want to have a skill that is socially recognized as useful. We want the feeling of security that comes not so much from the amount of money we have in the bank as from being an accepted member of a group. A man whose job is without social function is like a man without a country; the activity to which he has to give the major portion of his life is robbed of all human meaning and significance.

If this is true—and all the evidence of the Western Electric researches points in this direction—have we not a clue as to the possible basis for labor unrest and disputes? Granted that these disputes are often stated in terms of wages, hours of work, and physical conditions of work, is it not possible that these demands are disguising, or in part are the symptomatic expression of, much more deeply rooted human situations which we have not as yet learned to recognize, to understand, or to control? It has been said there is an irresistible urge on the part of workers to tell the boss off, to tell the boss to go to hell. For some workers this generalization may hold, and I have no reason to believe it does not. But, in those situations where it does, it is telling us something very important about these particular workers and their work situations. Workers who want to tell their boss to go to hell sound to me like people whose feelings of personal integrity have been seriously injured. What in their work situations has shattered their feelings of personal integrity? Until we understand better the answer to this question, we cannot handle effectively people who manifest such sentiments. Without such understanding we are dealing only with words and not with human situations—as I fear only overlogicized machinery for handling employee grievances sometimes does.

The matters of importance to workers which the Hawthorne researches disclosed are not settled primarily by negotiating contracts. If industry today is filled with people living in a social void and without social function, a labor contract can do little to make cooperation possible. If, on the other hand, the workers are an integral part of the social situations in which they work, a legal contract is not of the first importance. Too many of us are more interested in getting our words legally straight than in getting our situations humanly straight.

In summary, therefore, the Western Electric researches seem to me like a beginning on the road back to sanity in employee relations because (1) they offer a fruitful working hypothesis, a few simple and relatively clear ideas for the study and understanding of human situations in business; (2) they offer a simple method by means of which we can explore and deal with the complex human problems in a business organization—this method is a human method: it deals with things which are important to people; and (3) they throw a new light on the precondition for effective collaboration. Too often we think of collaboration as something which can be logically or legally contrived. The Western Electric studies indicate that it is far more a matter of sentiment than a matter of logic. Workers are not isolated, unrelated individuals; they are social animals and should be treated as such.

This statement—the worker is a social animal and should be treated as such—is simple, but the systematic and consistent practice of this point of view is not. If it were systematically practiced, it would revolutionize present-day personnel work. Our technological development in the past hundred years has been tremendous. Our methods of handling people are still archaic. If this civilization is to survive, we must obtain a new understanding of human motivation and behavior in business organizations—an understanding which can be simply but effectively practiced. The Western Electric researches contribute a first step in this direction.

Robert K. Merton (1910–   )

One of America's prominent sociologists, Professor Robert K. Merton, began his academic career at Harvard as a student of Talcott Parsons and others. Like Parsons he was a student of bureaucracy as defined and described by Max Weber. This was but one of a myriad of his interests in sociological theory, but for the purposes of this collection it was probably most relevant. He was concerned with the unintended and unanticipated human consequences of bureaucracy, a subject that Weber did not explore extensively. A number of Merton's own students pursued the secondary and the dysfunctional effects of bureaucratic organization.

The selection which follows was written by Merton just before World War II and before Weber was widely known in the United States. I have deleted the first part, which is largely a summary of Weber with emphases upon the positive attributes of bureaucracy. The remainder, reprinted here, emphasizes the negative influence of bureaucratic forms on the human personality and on organizational effectiveness.

F.C.M.

Bureaucratic Structure and Personality

❊   ❊   ❊

In these bold outlines,* the positive attainments and functions of bureaucratic organization are emphasized and the internal stresses and strains of such structures are almost wholly neglected. The community at large, however, evidently emphasizes the imperfections of bureaucracy, as is suggested by the fact that the "horrid hybrid," bureaucrat, has become a *Schimpfwort*. The transition to a study of the negative aspects of bureaucracy is afforded by the application of Veblen's concept of "trained incapacity," Dewey's notion of "occupational psychosis," or Warnotte's view of "professional deformation." Trained incapacity refers to that state of affairs in which one's abilities function as inadequacies or blind spots. Actions based upon training

---

*The author here refers to the earlier paragraphs, which are essentially a summary of Weber's description of bureaucracy. *Ed.*

Social Forces, Vol. 18 (May, 1940), pp. 560–568.

and skills which have been successfully applied in the past may result in inappropriate responses *under changed conditions*. An inadequate flexibility in the application of skills will, in a changing milieu, result in more or less serious maladjustments. Thus, to adopt a barnyard illustration used in this connection by Burke, chickens may be readily conditioned to interpret the sound of a bell as a signal for food. The same bell may now be used to summon the "trained chickens" to their doom as they are assembled to suffer decapitation. In general, one adopts measures in keeping with his past training and, under new conditions which are not recognized as *significantly* different, the very soundness of this training may lead to the adoption of the wrong procedures. Again, in Burke's almost echolalic phrase, "people may be unfitted by being fit in an unfit fitness"; their training may become an incapacity.

Dewey's concept of occupational psychosis rests upon much the same observations. As a result of their day to day routines, people develop special preferences, antipathies, discriminations, and emphases. (The term psychosis is used by Dewey to denote a "pronounced character of the mind.") These psychoses develop through demands put upon the individual by the particular organization of his occupational role.

The concepts of both Veblen and Dewey refer to a fundamental ambivalence. Any action can be considered in terms of what it attains or what it fails to attain. "A way of seeing is also a way of not seeing—a focus upon object A involves a neglect of object B." In his discussion, Weber is almost exclusively concerned with what the bureaucratic structure attains: precision, reliability, efficiency. This same structure may be examined from another perspective provided by the ambivalence. What are the limitations of the organization designed to attain these goals?

For reasons which we have already noted, the bureaucratic structure exerts a constant pressure upon the official to be "methodical, prudent, disciplined." If the bureaucracy is to operate successfully, it must attain a high degree of reliability of behavior, an unusual degree of conformity with prescribed patterns of action. Hence, the fundamental importance of discipline which may be as highly developed in a religious or economic bureaucracy as in the army. Discipline can be effective only if the ideal patterns are buttressed by strong sentiments which entail devotion to one's duties, a keen sense of the limitation of one's authority and competence, and methodical performance of routine activities. The efficacy of social structure depends ultimately upon infusing group participants with appropriate attitudes and sentiments. As we shall see, there are definite arrangements in the bureaucracy for inculcating and reinforcing these sentiments.

At the moment, it suffices to observe that in order to ensure discipline (the necessary reliability of response), these sentiments are often more intense than is technically necessary. There is a margin of safety, so to speak, in the pressure exerted by these sentiments upon the bureaucrat to conform to his patterned obligations, in much the same sense that added allowances (precautionary over-estimations) are made by the engineer in designing the supports for a bridge. But this very emphasis leads to a transference of the sentiments from the *aims* of the organization onto the particular details of behavior required by the rules. Adherence to the rules, originally conceived as a means, becomes transformed into an end-in-itself; there occurs the familiar process of *displacement of goals* whereby "an instrumental value becomes a terminal value." Discipline, readily interpreted as conformance with regulations, whatever the situation, is seen not as a measure designed for specific purposes but becomes an immediate value in the life-organization of the bureaucrat. This emphasis, resulting from the displacement of the original goals, develops into rigidities and an inability to adjust readily. Formalism, even ritualism, ensues with an unchallenged insistence upon punctilious adherence to formalized procedures. This may be exaggerated to the point where primary concern with conformity to the rules interferes with the achievement of the purposes of the organization, in which case we have the familiar phenomenon of the technicism or red tape of the official. An extreme product of this process of displacement of goals is the bureaucratic virtuoso, who never forgets a single rule binding his action and hence is unable to assist many of his clients. A case in point, where strict recognition of the limits of authority and literal adherence to rules produced this result, is the pathetic plight of Bernt Balchen, Admiral Byrd's pilot in the flight over the South Pole.

> According to a ruling of the department of labor Bernt Balchen . . . cannot receive his citizenship papers. Balchen, a native of Norway, declared his intention in 1927. It is held that he has failed to meet the condition of five years' continuous residence in the United States. The Byrd antarctic voyage took him out of the country, although he was on a ship flying the American flag, was an invaluable member of an American expedition, and in a region to which there is an American claim because of the exploration and occupation of it by Americans, this region being Little America.
>
> The bureau of naturalization explains that it cannot proceed on the assumption that Little America is American soil. That would be *trespass on international questions* where it has no sanction. So far as the bureau is concerned, Balchen was out of the country and *technically* has not complied with the law of naturalization.

Such inadequacies in orientation which involve trained incapacity clearly derive from structural sources. The process may be briefly recapitulated. (1) An effective bureaucracy demands reliability of response and strict devotion to regulations. (2) Such devotion to the rules leads to their transformation into absolutes; they are no longer conceived as relative to a given set of purposes. (3) This interferes with ready adaptation under special conditions not clearly envisaged by those who drew up the general rules. (4) Thus, the very elements which conduce toward efficiency in general produce inefficiency in specific instances. Full realization of the inadequacy is seldom attained by members of the group who have not divorced themselves from the "meanings" which the rules have for them. These rules in time become symbolic in cast, rather than strictly utilitarian.

Thus far, we have treated the ingrained sentiments making for rigorous discipline simply as data, as given. However, definite features of the bureaucratic structure may be seen to conduce to these sentiments. The bureaucrat's official life is planned for him in terms of a graded career, through the organizational devices of promotion by seniority, pensions, incremental salaries, *etc.*, all of which are designed to provide incentives for disciplined action and conformity to the official regulations. The official is tacitly expected to and largely does adapt his thoughts, feelings, and actions to the prospect of this career. But *these very devices* which increase the probability of conformance also lead to an over-concern with strict adherence to regulations which induces timidity, conservatism, and technicism. Displacement of sentiments from goals onto means is fostered by the tremendous symbolic significance of the means (rules).

Another feature of the bureaucratic structure tends to produce much the same result. Functionaries have the sense of a common destiny for all those who work together. They share the same interests, especially since there is relatively little competition insofar as promotion is in terms of seniority. In-group aggression is thus minimized and this arrangement is therefore conceived to be positively functional for the bureaucracy. However, the esprit de corps and informal social organization which typically develops in such situations often leads the personnel to defend their entrenched interests rather than to assist their clientele and elected higher officials. As President Lowell reports, if the bureaucrats believe that their status is not adequately recognized by an incoming elected official, detailed information will be withheld from him, leading him to errors for which he is held responsible. Or, if he seeks to dominate fully, and thus violates the sentiment of self-integrity of the bureaucrats, he may have documents brought to him in such numbers that he cannot manage to sign them all, let alone read them. This illustrates the defensive informal organization which tends to arise whenever there is an apparent threat to the integrity of the group.

It would be much too facile and partly erroneous to attribute such resistance by bureaucrats simply to vested interests. Vested interests oppose any new order which either eliminates or at least makes uncertain their differential advantage deriving from the current arrangements. This is undoubtedly involved in part in bureaucratic resistance to change but another process is perhaps more significant. As we have seen, bureaucratic officials affectively identify themselves with their way of life. They have a pride of craft which leads them to resist change in established routines; at least, those changes which are felt to be imposed by persons outside the inner circle of coworkers. This nonlogical pride of craft is a familiar pattern found even, to judge from Sutherland's *Professional Thief,* among pickpockets who, despite the risk, delight in mastering the prestige-bearing feat of "beating a left breech" (picking the left front trousers pocket).

In a stimulating paper, Hughes has applied the concepts of "secular" and "sacred" to various types of division of labor; "the sacredness" of caste and *Stände* prerogatives contrasts sharply with the increasing secularism of occupational differentiation in our mobile society. However, as our discussion suggests, there may ensue, in particular vocations and in particular types of organization, the *process of sanctification* (viewed as the counterpart of the process of secularization). This is to say that through sentiment-formation, emotional dependence upon bureaucratic symbols and status, and affective involvement in spheres of competence and authority, there develop prerogatives involving attitudes of moral legitimacy which are established as values in their own right, and are no longer viewed as merely technical means for expediting administration. One may note a tendency for certain bureaucratic norms, originally introduced for technical reasons, to become rigidified and sacred, although, as Durkheim would say, they are *laique en apparence.* Durkheim has touched on this general process in his description of the attitudes and values which persist in the organic solidarity of a highly differentiated society.

Another feature of the bureaucratic structure, the stress on depersonalization of relationships, also plays its part in the bureaucrat's trained incapacity. The personality pattern of the bureaucrat is nucleated about this norm of impersonality. Both this and the categorizing tendency, which develops from the dominant role of general, abstract rules, tend to produce conflict in the bureaucrat's contacts with the public or clientele. Since functionaries minimize personal relations and resort to categorization, the peculiarities of individual cases are often ignored. But the client who, quite understandably, is convinced of the "special features" of *his* own problem often objects to such categorical treatment. Stereotyped behavior is not adapted to the exigencies of individual problems. The impersonal treatment of affairs which are at times of great personal significance to the client give rise to the charge of "arrogance" and "haughtiness" of the bureaucrat. . . .

Still another source of conflict with the public derives from the bureaucratic structure. The bureaucrat, in part irrespective of his position within the hierarchy, acts as a representative of the power and prestige of the entire structure. In his official role he is vested with definite authority. This often leads to an actual or apparent domineering attitude, which may only be exaggerated by a discrepancy between his position within the hierarchy and his position with reference to the public. Protest and recourse to other officials on the part of the client are often ineffective or largely precluded by the previously mentioned esprit de corps which joins the officials into a more or less solidary in-group. This source of conflict *may* be minimized in private enterprise since the client can register an effective protest by transferring his trade to another organization within the competitive system. But with the monopolistic nature of the public organization, no such alternative is possible. Moreover, in this case, tension is increased because of a discrepancy between ideology and fact: the governmental personnel are held to be "servants of the people," but in fact they are usually superordinate, and release of tension can seldom be afforded by turning to other agencies for the necessary service. This tension is in part attributable to the confusion of status of bureaucrat and client; the client may consider himself socially superior to the official who is at the moment dominant.

Thus, with respect to the relations between officials and clientele, one structural source of conflict is the pressure for formal and impersonal treatment when individual, personalized consideration is desired by the client. The conflict may be viewed, then, as deriving from the introduction of inappropriate attitudes and relationships. Conflict within the bureaucratic structure arises from the converse situation, namely, when personalized relationships are substituted for the structurally required impersonal relationships. This type of conflict may be characterized as follows.

The bureaucracy, as we have seen, is organized as a secondary, formal group. The normal responses involved in this organized network of social expectations are supported by affective attitudes of members of the group. Since the group is oriented toward secondary norms of impersonality, any failure to conform to these norms will arouse antagonism from those who have identified themselves with the legitimacy of these rules. Hence, the substitution of personal for impersonal treatment within the structure is met with widespread disapproval and is characterized by such epithets as graft, favoritism, nepotism, apple-polishing, etc. These epithets are clearly manifestations of injured sentiments. The function of such "automatic resentment" can be clearly seen in terms of the requirements of bureaucratic structure.

Bureaucracy is a secondary group mechanism designed to carry on certain activities which cannot be satisfactorily performed on the basis of primary group criteria. Hence behavior which runs counter to these formalized norms becomes the object of emotionalized disapproval. This constitutes a functionally significant defense set up against tendencies which jeopardize the performance of socially necessary activities. To be sure, these reactions are not rationally determined practices explicitly designed for the fulfilment of this function. Rather, viewed in terms of the individual's interpretation of the situation, such resentment is simply an immediate response opposing the "dishonesty" of those who violate the rules of the game. However, this subjective frame of reference notwithstanding, these reactions serve the function of maintaining the essential structural elements of bureaucracy by reaffirming the necessity for formalized, secondary relations and by helping to prevent the disintegration of the bureaucratic structure which would occur should these be supplanted by personalized relations. This type of conflict may be generically described as the intrusion of primary group attitudes when secondary group attitudes are institutionally demanded, just as the bureaucrat-client conflict often derives from interaction on impersonal terms when personal treatment is individually demanded.

The trend toward increasing bureaucratization in Western society, which Weber had long since foreseen, is not the sole reason for sociologists to turn their attention to this field. Empirical studies of the interaction of bureaucracy and personality should especially increase our understanding of social structure. A large number of specific questions invite our attention. To what extent are particular personality types selected and modified by the various bureaucracies (private enterprise, public service, the quasi-legal political machine, religious orders)? Inasmuch as ascendancy and submission are held to be traits of personality, despite their variability in different stimulus-situations, do bureaucracies select personalities of particularly submissive or ascendant tendencies? And since various studies have shown that these traits can be modified, does participation in bureaucratic office tend to increase ascendant tendencies? Do various systems of recruitment (e.g. patronage, open competition involving specialized knowledge or "general mental capacity," practical experience) select different personality types? Does promotion through seniority lessen competitive anxieties and enhance administrative efficiency? A detailed examination of mechanisms for imbuing the bureaucratic codes with affect would be instructive both sociologically and psychologically. Does the general anonymity of civil service decisions tend to restrict the area of prestige-symbols to a narrowly defined inner circle? Is there a tendency for differential association to be especially marked among bureaucrats?

The range of theoretically significant and practically important questions would seem to be limited only by the accessibility of the concrete data. Studies of religious, educational, military, economic, and political bureaucracies dealing with the interdependence of social organization and personality formation should constitute an avenue for fruitful research. On that avenue, the functional analysis of concrete structures may yet build a Solomon's House for sociologists.

Abraham H. Maslow (1908–1970)

Many years ago, Abraham H. Maslow, a psychologist, developed a theory of motivation grounded in an analysis and classification of human needs in five basic categories. With the growing concern after World War II for employee morale and organizational health, in business, public, and other administration, his thesis was picked up by a school of psychologists interested in organization and its development. During the 1960s and 1970s, his five categories—particularly the fifth, self-actualization—were widely referred to in public administration literature. The selection that follows is his very brief summary of his theory of motivation, which closed his 1943 article on the subject.

F.C.M.

A Theory of Human Motivation

Summary

(1) There are at least five sets of goals, which we may call basic needs. These are briefly physiological, safety, love, esteem, and self-actualization. In addition, we are motivated by the desire to achieve or maintain the various conditions upon which these basic satisfactions rest and by certain more intellectual desires.

(2) These basic goals are related to each other, being arranged in a hierarchy of prepotency. This means that the most prepotent goal will monopolize consciousness and will tend to itself to organize the recruitment of the various capacities of the organism. The less prepotent needs are minimized, even forgotten or denied. But when a need is fairly well satisfied, the next prepotent ("higher") need emerges, in turn to dominate the conscious life and to serve as the center of organization of behavior, since gratified needs are not active motivators.

Thus man is a perpetually wanting animal. Ordinarily the satisfaction of these wants is not altogether mutually exclusive, but only tends to be. The average member of our society is most often partially satisfied and partially unsatisfied in all of his wants. The hierarchy principle is usually empirically observed in terms of increasing percentages of non-satisfaction as we go up the hierarchy. Reversals of the average order of the hierarchy are sometimes observed. Also it has been observed that an individual may permanently lose the higher wants in the hierarchy under special conditions. There are not only ordinarily multiple motivations for usual behavior, but in addition many determinants other than motives.

(3) Any thwarting or possibility of thwarting of these basic human goals, or danger to the defenses which protect them, or to the conditions upon which they rest, is considered to be a psychological threat. With a few exceptions, all psychopathology may be partially traced to such threats. A basically thwarted man may actually be defined as a "sick" man, if we wish.

(4) It is such basic threats which bring about the general emergency reactions.

Summary, "A Theory of Human Motivation," *Psychological Review,* Vol. 50 (July, 1943), pp. 370–396.

Herbert A. Simon (1916–   )

Herbert A. Simon's interest in the theory of organizations began before World War II when he was working toward his Ph.D. in political science at the University of Chicago and was a staff member of the International City Managers' Association. Although his early work was directed primarily to governmental organizations, it even then revealed interests going well beyond the orthodox public administration in psychology, sociology, and philosophy. It reflected a considerable dissatisfaction with the "principles" of public administration, which he criticized as mutually contradictory "proverbs,"[1] and undertook to develop a firmer grounding for a theory of organizations. His subsequent works, many of which dealt with private as well as public organizations, have been extensive, original, and incisive. They have included a number of books and many articles and speeches, dealing with such subjects and themes as: rationality and its limits in decision-making; values versus facts; "satisficing" as against optimizing; the uses of computers in organizational decisions; organizational goals; the criteria of efficiency. Indicative of the catholicity of his interests and the creativity of his work was the award to him in 1978 of the Nobel Prize in economics.

For students of public administration, Simon's first major book, *Administrative Behavior* (1947), has long been and continues to be a basic text in organizational theory. Simon's ideas at that time undoubtedly grew in part from the writings of Chester I. Barnard, who wrote the foreword for Simon's book. In it Barnard said: "This book conveys what I have experienced as common to all and what is in this sense essential in all organization and administration. It has the right 'feel.' This means that I find Professor Simon's apprehension of the structure of organized action consonant with my experience. It therefore appeals to me as sound" (p. ix).

The following selection reprints Chapter 1 of *Administrative Behavior.* It focuses on Simon's underlying theme, administrative decision-making, and undergirds much of the argument of later chapters of the book and, indeed, of Simon's later career.

F.C.M.

---

1. As demonstrated in an article in a journal which was later largely reproduced as Chapter 2 of his book *Administrative Behavior,* Chapter 1 of which is reprinted here.

Administrative Behavior

Decision Making and Administrative Operation

Administration is ordinarily discussed as the art of "getting things done." Emphasis is placed upon processes and methods for insuring incisive action. Principles are set forth for securing concerted action from groups of men. In all this discussion, however, not very much attention is paid to the choice which prefaces all action—to the determining of what is to be done rather than to the actual doing. It is with this problem—the process of choice which leads to action—that the present study is concerned. . . .

Although any practical activity involves both "deciding" and "doing," it has not commonly been recognized that a theory of administration should be concerned with the processes of decision as well as with the processes of action. This neglect perhaps stems from the notion that decision-making is confined to the formulation of over-all policy. On the contrary, the process of decision does not come to an end when the general purpose of an organization has been determined. The task of "deciding" pervades the entire administrative organization quite as much as does the task of "doing"— indeed, it is integrally tied up with the latter. A general theory of administration must include principles of organization that will insure correct decision-making, just as it must include principles that will insure effective action.

Decision-Making and the Execution of Decisions

It is clear that the actual physical task of carrying out an organization's objectives falls to the persons at the lowest level of the administrative hierarchy. The automobile, as a physical object, is built not by the engineer or the executive, but by the mechanic on the assembly line. The fire is extinguished, not by the fire chief or the captain, but by the team of firemen who play a hose on the blaze.

It is equally clear that the persons above this lowest or operative level in the administrative hierarchy are not mere surplus baggage, and that they too must have an essential role to play in the accomplishment of the agency's objectives. Even though, as far as physical cause and effect are concerned, it is the machine gunner and not the major who fights battles, the major is likely to have a greater influence upon the outcome of a battle than any single machine gunner.

Chapter 1, *Administrative Behavior*, first edition (New York: Macmillan 1947), pp.1–19. Reprinted with permission of Macmillan Publishing Co., Inc. Copyright © 1947, renewed 1975 by Herbert A. Simon.

How, then, do the administrative and supervisory staff of an organization affect that organization's work? The nonoperative staff of an administrative organization participate in the accomplishment of the objectives of that organization to the extent that they influence the decisions of the operatives—the persons at the lowest level of the administrative hierarchy. The major can influence the battle to the extent that his head is able to direct the machine gunner's hand. By deploying his forces in the battle area and assigning specific tasks to subordinate units he determines for the machine gunner where he will take his stand and what his objective will be. In very small organizations the influence of all supervisory employees upon the operative employees may be direct, but in units of any size there are interposed between the top supervisors and the operative employees several levels of intermediate supervisors who are themselves subject to influences from above, and who transmit, elaborate, and modify these influences before they reach the operatives.

If this is a correct description of the administrative process, then the construction of an efficient administrative organization is a problem in social psychology. It is a task of setting up an operative staff and superimposing on that staff a supervisory staff capable of influencing the operative group toward a pattern of coordinated and effective behavior. The term "influencing" rather than "directing" is used here, for direction—that is, the use of administrative authority—is only one of several ways in which the administrative staff may affect the decisions of the operative staff; and, consequently, the construction of an administrative organization involves more than a mere assignment of functions and allocation of authority.

In the study of organization, the operative employee must be at the focus of attention, for the success of the structure will be judged by his performance within it. Insight into the structure and function of an organization can best be gained by analyzing the manner in which the decisions and behavior of such employees are influenced within and by the organization.

Choice and Behavior

All behavior involves conscious or unconscious selection of particular actions out of all those which are physically possible to the actor and to those persons over whom he exercises influence and authority. The term "selection" is used here without any implication of a conscious or deliberate process. It refers simply to the fact that, if the individual follows one particular course of action, there are other courses of action that he thereby forgoes. In many cases the selection process consists simply in an established reflex action—a typist hits a particular key with a finger because a reflex has been established between a letter on the printed page and this particular key. Here the action is, in some sense at least, rational (i.e. goal-oriented), yet no element of consciousness or deliberation is involved.

In other cases the selection is itself the product of a complex chain of activities called "planning" or "design" activities. An engineer, for example, may decide upon the basis of extensive analysis that a particular bridge should be of cantilever design. His design, further implemented by detailed plans for the structure, will lead to a whole chain of behaviors by the individuals constructing the bridge.

In this volume many examples will be given of all varieties of selection process. All these examples have in common the following characteristics: At any moment there are a multitude of alternative (physically) possible actions, any one of which a given individual may undertake; by some process these numerous alternatives are narrowed down to that one which is in fact acted out. The words "choice" and "decision" will be used interchangeably in this study to refer to this process. Since these terms as ordinarily used carry connotations of self-conscious, deliberate, rational selection, it should be emphasized that as used here they include any process of selection, regardless of whether the above elements are present to any degree.

Value and Fact in Decision

A great deal of behavior, and particularly the behavior of individuals within administrative organizations, is purposive—oriented toward goals or objectives. This purposiveness brings about an integration in the pattern of behavior, in the absence of which administration would be meaningless; for, if administration consists in "getting things done" by groups of people, purpose provides a principal criterion in determining what things are to be done.

The minute decisions that govern specific actions are inevitably instances of the application of broader decisions relative to purpose and to method. The walker contracts his leg muscles in order to take a step; he takes a step in order to proceed toward his destination; he is going to the destination, a mail box, in order to mail a letter; he is sending a letter in order to transmit certain information to another person, and so forth. Each decision involves the selection of a goal, and a behavior relevant to it; this goal may in turn be mediate to a somewhat more distant goal; and so on, until a relatively final aim is reached. In so far as decisions lead toward the selection of final goals, they will be called "value judgments"; so far as they involve the implementation of such goals they will be called "factual judgments."

Unfortunately, problems do not come to the administrator carefully wrapped in bundles with the value elements and the factual elements neatly sorted. For one thing, goals or final objectives of governmental organization and activity are usually formulated in very general and ambiguous terms— "justice," "the general welfare," or "liberty." Then, too, the objectives as defined may be merely intermediate to the attainment of more final aims. For example, in certain spheres of action, the behavior of men is generally oriented around the "economic motive." Yet, for most men, economic gain is not usually an end in itself, but a means of attaining more final ends: security, comfort, and prestige.

Finally, the value and factual elements may be combined, in some cases, in a single objective. The apprehension of criminals is commonly set up as an objective of a municipal police department. To a certain extent this objective is conceived as an end in itself, that is, as aimed toward the apprehension and punishment of offenders against the law but from another point of view apprehension is considered a means for protecting citizens, for rehabilitating offenders, and for discouraging potential offenders.

The Hierarchy of Decisions.   The concept of *purposiveness* involves a notion of a hierarchy of decisions—each step downward in the hierarchy consisting in an implementation of the goals set forth in the step immediately above. Behavior is purposive in so far as it is guided by general goals or objectives; it is rational in so far as it selects alternatives which are conducive to the achievement of the previously selected goals.

It should not be inferred that this hierarchy or pyramid of goals is perfectly organized or integrated in any actual behavior. A governmental agency, for instance, may be directed simultaneously toward several distinct objectives: a recreation department may seek to improve the health of children, to provide them with good uses for their leisure time, and to prevent juvenile delinquency, as well as to achieve similar goals for the adults in the community.

Even when no conscious or deliberate integration of these goals takes place in decision, it should be noted that an integration generally takes place in fact. Although in making decisions for his agency, the recreation administrator may fail to weigh the diverse and sometimes conflicting objectives against one another in terms of their relative importance, yet his actual decisions, and the direction which he gives to the policy of his agency will amount in practice to a particular set of weights for these objectives. If the program emphasizes athletics for adolescent boys, then this objective is given an actual weight in practice which it may, or may not, have had in the consciousness of the administrator planning the program. Hence, although the administrator may refuse the task, or be unable to perform it, of consciously and deliberately integrating his system of objectives, he cannot avoid the implications of his actual decisions, which achieve such a synthesis in fact.

The Relative Element in Decision.   In an important sense, all decision is a matter of compromise. The alternative that is finally selected never permits a complete or perfect achievement of objectives, but is merely the best solution that is available under the circumstances. The environmental situation inevitably limits the alternatives that are available, and hence sets a maximum to the level of attainment of purpose that is possible.

This relative element in achievement—this element of compromise—makes even more inescapable the necessity of finding a common denominator when behavior is aimed simultaneously at several objectives. For instance, if experience showed that an organization like the Work Projects Administration could at one and the same time dispense relief and construct public works without handicapping either objective, then the agency might attempt to attain at the same time both of these objectives. If, on the other hand, experience showed that the accomplishment of either of these objectives through the organization seriously impeded the accomplishment of the other, one would have to be selected as the objective of the agency, and the other sacrificed. In balancing the one aim against the other, and in attempting to find a common denominator, it would be necessary to cease thinking of the two aims as ends in themselves, and instead to conceive them as means to some more general end.

An Illustration of the Process of Decision.   In order to understand more clearly the intimate relationships that exist in any practical administrative problem between judgments of value and fact, it will be helpful to study an example from the field of municipal government.

What questions of value and fact arise in the opening and improvement of a new street? It is necessary to determine: (1) the design of the street; (2) the proper relationship of the street to the master plan; (3) means of financing the project; (4) whether the project should be let on contract or done by force account; (5) the relation of this project to construction that may be required subsequent to the improvement (e.g., utility cuts in this particular street); and (6) numerous other questions of like nature. These are questions for which answers must be found—each one combining value and factual elements. A partial separation of the two elements can be achieved by distinguishing the purposes of the project from its procedures.

On the one hand, decisions regarding these questions must be based upon the purposes for which the street is intended, and the social values affected by its construction—among them, (1) speed and convenience in transportation; (2) traffic safety; (3) effect of street layout on property values; (4) construction costs; and (5) distribution of cost among taxpayers.

On the other hand, the decisions must be made in the light of scientific and practical knowledge as to the effect particular measures will have in realizing their values. Included here are (1) the relative smoothness, permanence, and cost of each type of pavement; (2) relative advantages of alternate routes from the standpoint of cost and convenience to traffic; and (3) the total cost and distribution of cost for alternative methods of financing.

The final decision, then, will depend both on the relative weight that is given to the different objectives and on judgment as to the extent to which any given plan will attain each objective.

This brief account will serve to indicate some of the basic features of the process of decision—features that will be further elaborated in this study.

Decision-Making in the Administrative Process

Administrative activity is group activity. Simple situations are familiar where a man plans and executes his own work; but as soon as a task grows to the point where the efforts of several persons are required to accomplish it this is no longer possible, and it becomes necessary to develop processes for the application of organized effort to the group task. The techniques which facilitate this application are the administrative processes.

It should be noted that the administrative processes are decisional processes: they consist in segregating certain elements in the decisions of members of the organization, and establishing regular organizational procedures to select and determine these elements and to communicate them to the members concerned. If the task of the group is to build a ship, a design for the ship is drawn and adopted by the organization, and this design limits and guides the activities of the persons who actually construct the ship.

The organization, then, takes from the individual some of his decisional autonomy, and substitutes for it an organizational decision-making process. The decisions which the organization makes for the individual ordinarily (1) specify his function, that is, the general scope and nature of his duties; (2) allocate authority, that is, determine who in the organization is to have power to make further decisions for the individual; and (3) set such other limits to his choice as are needed to coordinate the activities of several individuals in the organization.

The administrative organization is characterized by specialization—particular tasks are delegated to particular parts of the organization. It has already been noted above that this specialization may take the form of "vertical" division of labor. A pyramid or hierarchy of authority may be established, with greater or less formality, and decision-making functions may be specialized among the members of this hierarchy.

Most analyses of organization have emphasized "horizontal" specialization—the division of work—as the basic characteristic of organized activity. Luther Gulick, for example, in his "Notes on the Theory of Organization," says: "Work division is the foundation of organization; indeed, the reason for organization." In this study we shall be primarily concerned with "vertical" specialization—the division of decision-making duties between operative and supervisory personnel. One inquiry will be into the reasons why the operative employees are deprived of a portion of their autonomy in the making of decisions and subjected to the authority and influence of supervisors.

There would seem to be at least three reasons for vertical specialization in organization. First, if there is any horizontal specialization, vertical specialization is absolutely essential to achieve coordination among the operative employees. Second, just as horizontal specialization permits greater skill and expertise to be developed by the operative group in the performance of their tasks, so vertical specialization permits greater expertise in the making of decisions. Third, vertical specialization permits the operative personnel to be held accountable for their decisions: to the board of directors in the case of a business organization; to the legislative body in the case of a public agency.

Coordination. Group behavior requires not only the adoption of correct decisions, but also the adoption by all members of the group of the same decisions. Suppose ten persons decide to cooperate in building a boat. If each has his own plan, and they do not communicate their plans, the chances are that the resulting craft will not be very seaworthy; they would probably meet with better success if they adopted even a very mediocre design, and if then all followed this same design.

By the exercise of authority or other forms of influence, it is possible to centralize the function of deciding so that a general plan of operations will govern the activities of all members of the organization. This coordination may be either procedural or substantive in nature: by procedural coordination is meant the specification of the organization itself—that is, the generalized description of the behaviors and relationships of the members of the organization. Procedural coordination establishes the lines of authority and outlines the sphere of activity of each organization member, while substantive coordination specifies the content of his work. In an automobile factory, an organization chart is an aspect of procedural coordination; blueprints for the engine block of the car being manufactured are an aspect of substantive coordination.

Expertise. To gain the advantages of specialized skill at the operative level, the work of an organization must be so subdivided that all processes requiring a particular skill can be performed by persons possessing that skill. Likewise, to gain the advantages of expertise in decision-making, the responsibility for decisions must be so allocated that all decisions requiring a particular skill can be made by persons possessing that skill.

To subdivide decisions is rather more complicated than to subdivide performance; for, while it is not usually possible to combine the sharp eye of one workman with the steady hand of another to secure greater precision in a particular operation, it is often possible to add the knowledge of a lawyer to that of an engineer in order to improve the quality of a particular decision.

Responsibility. Writers on the political and legal aspects of authority have emphasized that a primary function of organization is to enforce the conformity of the individual to norms laid down by the group, or by its authority-wielding members. The discretion of subordinate personnel is limited by policies determined near the top of the administrative hierarchy. When the maintenance of responsibility is a central concern, the purpose of vertical specialization is to assure legislative control over the administrator, leaving to the administrative staff adequate discretion to deal with technical matters which a legislative body composed of laymen would not be competent to decide.

Modes of Organizational Influence

Decisions reached in the higher ranks of the organization hierarchy will have no effect upon the activities of operative employees unless they are communicated downward. Consideration of the process requires an examination of the ways in which the behavior of the operative employee can be influenced. These influences fall roughly into two categories: (1) establishing in the operative employee *himself* attitudes, habits, and a state of mind which lead him to reach that decision which is advantageous to the organization; and (2) imposing on the operative employee decisions reached elsewhere in the organization. The first type of influence operates by inculcating in the employee organizational loyalties and a concern with efficiency, and more generally by training him. The second type of influence depends primarily upon authority and upon advisory and informational services. It is not insisted that these categories are either exhaustive or mutually exclusive, but they will serve the purposes of this introductory discussion.

As a matter of fact, the present discussion is somewhat more general than the preceding paragraph suggests, for it is concerned with organizational influences not only upon operative employees but upon all individuals making decisions within the organization.

Authority. The concept of authority has been analyzed at length by students of administration. We shall employ here a definition substantially equivalent to that put forth by C. I. Barnard. A subordinate is said to accept authority whenever he permits his behavior to be guided by the decision of a superior, without independently examining the merits of that decision. When exercising authority, the superior does not seek to convince the subordinate, but only to obtain his acquiescence. In actual practice, of course, authority is usually liberally admixed with suggestion and persuasion.

Although it is an important function of authority to permit a decision to be made and carried out even when agreement cannot be reached, perhaps this arbitrary aspect of authority has been overemphasized. In any event, if it is attempted to carry authority beyond a certain point, which may be described as the subordinate's "zone of acceptance," disobedience will follow. The magnitude of the zone of acceptance depends upon the sanctions which authority has available to enforce its commands. The term "sanctions" must be interpreted broadly in this connection, for positive and neutral stimuli—such as community of purpose, habit, and leadership—are at least as important in securing acceptance of authority as the threat of physical or economic punishment.

It follows that authority, in the sense here defined, can operate "upward" and "sidewise" as well as "downward" in the organization. If an executive delegates to his secretary a decision about file cabinets and accepts her recommendation without reexamination of its merits, he is accepting her authority. The "lines of authority" represented on organization charts do have a special significance, however, for they are commonly resorted to in order to terminate debate when it proves impossible to reach a consensus on a particular decision. Since this appellate use of authority generally requires sanctions to be effective, the structure of formal authority in an organization usually is related to the appointment, disciplining, and dismissal of personnel. These formal lines of authority are commonly supplemented by informal authority relations in the day-to-day work of the organization, while the formal hierarchy is largely reserved for the settlement of disputes.

Organizational Loyalties. It is a prevalent characteristic of human behavior that members of an organized group tend to identify with that group. In making decisions their organizational loyalty leads them to evaluate alternative courses of action in terms of the consequences of their action for the group. When a person prefers a particular course of action because it is "good for America," he identifies himself with Americans, when he prefers it because it will "boost business in Berkeley," he identifies himself with Berkeleyans. National and class loyalties are examples of identifications which are of fundamental importance in the structure of modern society.

The loyalties that are of particular interest in the study of administration are those which attach to administrative organizations or segments of such organizations. The regimental battle flag is the traditional symbol of this identification in military administration; in civil administration, a frequently encountered evidence of loyalty is the cry, "Our Bureau needs more funds!"

This phenomenon of identification, or organizational loyalty, performs one very important function in administration. If an administrator, each time he is faced with a decision, must perforce evaluate that decision in terms of the whole range of human values, rationality in administration is impossible. If he need consider the decision only in the light of limited organizational aims, his task is more nearly within the range of human powers. The fireman can concentrate on the problems of fires, the health officer on problems of disease, without irrelevant considerations entering in.

Furthermore, this concentration on a limited range of values is almost essential if the administrator is to be held accountable for his decisions. When the organization's objectives are specified by some higher authority, the major value-premise of the administrator's decisions is thereby given him, leaving to him only the implementation of these objectives. If the fire chief were permitted to roam over the whole field of human values—to decide that parks were more important than fire trucks, and consequently to remake his fire department into a recreation department—chaos would displace organization, and responsibility would disappear.

Organizational loyalties lead also, however, to certain difficulties which should not be underestimated. The principal undesirable effect of identification is that it prevents the institutionalized individual from making correct decisions in cases where the restricted area of values with which he identifies himself must be weighed against other values outside that area. This is a principal cause of the interbureau competition and wrangling which characterize any large administrative organization. The organization members, identifying themselves with the bureau instead of with the over-all organization, believe the bureau's welfare more important than the general welfare when the two conflict. This problem is frequently evident in the case of "housekeeping" agencies, where the facilitative and auxiliary nature of the agency is lost sight of in the effort to force the line agencies to follow standard procedures.

Organizational loyalties also result in incapacitating almost any department head for the task of balancing the financial needs of his department against the financial needs of other departments—whence the need for a centrally located budget agency that is free from these psychological biases. The higher we go in the administrative hierarchy, and the broader becomes the range of social values that must come within the administrator's purview, the more harmful is the effect of valuation bias, and the more important is it that the administrator be freed from his narrower identifications.

The Criterion of Efficiency. We have seen that the exercise of authority and the development of organizational loyalties are two principal means whereby the individual's value-premises are influenced by the organization. What about the issues of fact that underlie his decisions? These are largely determined by a principle that is implied in all rational behavior: the criterion of efficiency. In its broadest sense, to be efficient simply means to take the shortest path, the cheapest means, toward the attainment of the desired goals. The efficiency criterion is completely neutral as to what goals are to be attained. The commandment, "Be efficient!" is a major organizational influence over the decisions of the members of any administrative agency; and a determination whether this commandment has been obeyed is a major function of the review process.

Advice and Information. Many of the influences the organization exercises over its members are of a less formal nature than those we have been discussing. These influences are perhaps most realistically viewed as a form of internal public relations, for there is nothing to guarantee that advice produced at one point in an organization will have any effect at another point in the organization unless the lines of communication are adequate to its transmission, and unless it is transmitted in such form as to be persuasive. It is a prevalent misconception in headquarters offices that the internal advisory function consists in preparing precisely worded explanatory bulletins and making certain that the proper number of these are prepared, and that they are placed in the proper compartment of the "router." No plague has produced a rate of mortality higher than the rate that customarily afflicts central-office communications between the time they leave the issuing office and the moment when they are assumed to be effected in the revised practice of the operative employees.

Information and advice flow in all directions through the organization—

not merely from the top downward. Many of the facts that are relevant to decision are of a rapidly changing nature, ascertainable only at the moment of decision, and often ascertainable only by operative employees. For instance, in military operations knowledge of the disposition of the enemy's forces is of crucial importance, and military organization has developed elaborate procedures for transmitting to a person who is to make a decision all relevant facts that he is not in a position to ascertain personally.

Training.   Like organizational loyalties and the efficiency criterion, and unlike the other modes of influence we have been discussing, training influences decisions "from the inside out." That is, training prepares the organization member to reach satisfactory decisions himself, without the need for the constant exercise of authority or advice. In this sense, training procedures are alternatives to the exercise of authority or advice as means of control over the subordinate's decisions.

Training may be of an in-service or a pre-service nature. When persons with particular educational qualifications are recruited for certain jobs, the organization is depending upon this pre-training as a principal means of assuring correct decisions in their work. The mutual relation between training and the range of discretion that may be permitted an employee is an important factor to be taken into consideration in designing the administrative organization. That is, it may often be possible to minimize, or even dispense with, certain review processes by giving the subordinates training that enables them to perform their work with less supervision. Similarly, in drafting the qualifications required of applicants for particular positions, the possibility should be considered of lowering personnel costs by drafting semi-skilled employees and training them for particular jobs.

Training is applicable to the process of decision whenever the same elements are involved in a large number of decisions. Training may supply the trainee with the facts necessary in dealing with these decisions; it may provide him a frame of reference for his thinking; it may teach him "approved" solutions; or it may indoctrinate him with the values in terms of which his decisions are to be made.

The Equilibrium of the Organization

The question may next be raised why the individual *accepts* these organizational influences—why he accommodates his behavior to the demands the organization makes upon him. To understand how the behavior of the individual becomes a part of the system of behavior of the organization, it is necessary to study the relation between the personal motivation of the individual and the objectives toward which the activity of the organization is oriented.

If a business organization be taken, for the moment, as the type, three kinds of participants can be distinguished: entrepreneurs, employees, and customers. Entrepreneurs are distinguished by the fact that their decisions ultimately control the activities of employees; employees, by the fact that they contribute their (undifferentiated) time and efforts to the organization in return for wages; customers, by the fact that they contribute money to the organization in return for its products. (Any actual human being can, of course, stand in more than one of these relations to an organization, e.g. a Red Cross volunteer, who is really a composite customer and employee.)

Each of these participants has his own personal motives for engaging in these organizational activites. Simplifying the motives and adopting the standpoint of economic theory, we may say that the entrepreneur seeks profit (i.e. an excess of revenues over expenditures), the employees seek wages, and the customers find (at certain prices) the exchange of money for products attractive. The entrepreneur gains the right to dispose of the employees' time by entering into employment contracts with them; he obtains funds to pay wages by entering into sales contracts with the customers. If these two sets of contracts are sufficiently advantageous, the entrepreneur makes a profit and, what is perhaps more important for our purposes, the organization remains in existence. If the contracts are not sufficiently advantageous, the entrepreneur becomes unable to maintain inducements to keep others in organized activity with him, and may even lose his own inducement to continue his organizational efforts. In either event, the organization disappears unless an equilibrium can be reached at some level of activity. In any actual organization, of course, the entrepreneur will depend upon many inducements other than the purely economic ones mentioned above: prestige, "good will," loyalty, and others.

In an organization such as that just described, there appears, in addition to the personal aims of the participants, an *organization* objective, or objectives. If the organization is a shoe factory, for example, it assumes the objective of making shoes. Whose objective is this—the entrepreneur's, the customers', or the employees'? To deny that it belongs to any of these would seem to posit some "group mind," some organismic entity which is over and above its human components. The true explanation is simpler: the organization objective is, indirectly, a personal objective of *all* the participants. It is the means whereby their organizational activity is bound together to achieve a satisfaction of their own diverse personal motives. It is by employing workers to make shoes and by selling them that the entrepreneur makes his profit; it is by accepting the direction of the entrepreneur in the making of shoes that the employee earns his wage; and it is by buying the finished shoes that the customer obtains his satisfaction from the organization. Since the entrepreneur wishes a profit, and since he controls the behavior of the employees (within their respective areas of acceptance), it behooves him to guide the behavior of the employees by the criterion of "making shoes as efficiently as possible." In so far, then, as he can control behavior in the organization, he establishes this as the objective of the behavior.

It is to be noted that the objectives of the customer are very closely, and rather directly, related to the *objectives* of the organization; the objectives of the entrepreneur are closely related to the *survival* of the organization; while the objectives of the employee are directly related to neither of these, but are brought into the organization scheme by the existence of his area of acceptance. Granted that pure "entrepreneurs," "customers," and "employees" do not exist; granted further that this scheme needs to be modified somewhat to fit voluntary, religious, and governmental organizations, still it is the existence of these three type roles which gives behavior in administrative organizations the particular character that we recognize.

Robert A. Dahl (1915–   )

Before World War II, Robert A. Dahl served as a management analyst in the U.S. Department of Agriculture. During that war, he was on the professional staff of two civilian war agencies before entering the military service in 1943. Following his discharge, he joined the political science faculty at Yale University, where he has taught ever since. His early interest in public administration represented only a fraction of his scope of concerns, which came to encompass almost the entire spectrum of political science: political theory, political behavior, economics and politics, elites, and other areas. The article that follows, written soon after he went to Yale, is one of the few of his many writings specifically directed to public administration. Like Simon, though for somewhat different reasons, he questioned the underpinnings of the orthodox public administration and its legitimacy as a science.

F.C.M.

The Science of Public Administration: Three Problems

The effort to create a science of public administration has often led to the formulation of universal laws or, more commonly, to the assertion that such universal laws *could* be formulated for public administration. In an attempt to make the science of public administration analogous to the natural sciences,

Reprinted from *Public Administration Review,* Vol. VII (Winter, 1947), pp. 1–11. © 1947 by The American Society for Public Administration. All rights reserved.

the laws or putative laws are stripped of normative values, of the distortions caused by the incorrigible individual psyche, and of the presumably irrelevant effects of the cultural environment. It is often implied that "principles of public administration" have a universal validity independent not only of moral and political ends, but of the frequently nonconformist personality of the individual, and the social and cultural setting as well.

Perhaps the best known expression of this kind is that of W. F. Willoughby. Although he refused to commit himself as to the propriety of designating administration as a science, Willoughby nevertheless asserted that "in administration, there are certain fundamental principles of general application analogous to those characterizing any science. . . ." A more recent statement, and evidently an equally influential one, is L. Urwick's contention that "there are certain principles which govern the association of human beings *for any purpose,* just as there are certain engineering principles which govern the building of a bridge."

Others argue merely that it is possible to discover general principles of wide, although not necessarily of universal validity. Surely this more modest assessment of the role of public administration as a study is not, as an abstract statement, open to controversy. Yet even the discovery of these more limited principles is handicapped by the three basic problems of values, the individual personality, and the social framework.

Public Administration and Normative Values

The first difficulty of constructing a science of public administration stems from the frequent impossibility of excluding normative considerations from the problems of public administration. Science as such is not concerned with the discovery or elucidation of normative values; indeed, the doctrine is generally, if not quite universally, accepted that science *cannot* demonstrate moral values, that science cannot construct a bridge across the great gap from "is" to "ought." So long as the naturalistic fallacy is a stumbling block to philosophers, it must likewise impede the progress of social scientists.

Much could be gained if the clandestine smuggling of moral values into the social sciences could be converted into open and honest commerce. Writers on public administration often assume that they are snugly insulated from the storms of clashing values; usually, however, they are most concerned with ends at the very moment that they profess to be least concerned with them. The doctrine of efficiency is a case in point; it runs like a half-visible thread through the fabric of public administration literature as a dominant goal of administration. Harvey Walker has stated that "the objective of administration is to secure the maximum beneficial result contemplated by the law with the minimum expenditure of the social resources." The term "social resources" is sufficiently ambiguous to allow for almost any interpretation, but it suggests that the general concept involved is one of maximizing "output" minimizing "cost." Likewise, many of the promised benefits of administrative reorganization in state governments are presumed to follow from proposed improvements in "efficiency in operation." And yet, as Charles Hyneman has so trenchantly observed, there are in a democratic society other criteria than simple efficiency in operation.

Luther Gulick concedes that the goal of efficiency is limited by other values.

> In the science of administration, whether public or private, the basic "good" is efficiency. The fundamental objective of the science of administration is the accomplishment of the work in hand with the least expenditure of man-power and materials. Efficiency is thus axiom number one in the value scale of administration. This brings administration into apparent conflict with certain elements of the value scale of politics, whether we use that term in its scientific or in its popular sense. But both public administration and politics are branches of political science, so that we are in the end compelled to mitigate the pure concept of efficiency in the light of the value scale of politics and the social order.

He concludes, nevertheless, "that these interferences with efficiency [do not] in any way eliminate efficiency as the fundamental value upon which the science of administration may be erected. They serve to condition and to complicate, but not to change the single ultimate test of value in administration."

It is far from clear what Gulick means to imply in saying that "interferences with efficiency" caused by ultimate political values may "condition" and "complicate" but do not "change" the "single ultimate test" of efficiency as the goal of administration. Is efficiency the supreme goal not only of private administration, but also of public administration, as Gulick contends? If so, how can one say, as Gulick does, that "there are . . . highly inefficient arrangements like citizen boards and small local governments which *may* be necessary in a democracy as educational devices"? Why speak of efficiency as the "single ultimate test of value in administration" if it is not ultimate at all—if, that is to say, in a conflict between efficiency and "the democratic dogma" (to use Gulick's expression) the latter must prevail? Must this dogma prevail only because it has greater political and social force behind it than the dogma of efficiency; or ought it to prevail because it has, in some sense, greater value? How can administrators and students of public administration discriminate between those parts of the democratic dogma that are so strategic they ought to prevail in any conflict with efficiency and those that are essentially subordinate, irrelevant, or even false intrusions into the democratic hypothesis? What *is* efficiency? Belsen and Dachau were "efficient" by one scale of values. And in any case, why is efficiency the ultimate test? According to what and whose scale of values is efficiency placed on the highest pedestal? Is not the worship of efficiency itself a particular expression of a special value judgment? Does it not stem from a mode of thinking and a special moral hypothesis resting on a sharp distinction between means and ends?

The basic problems of *public* administration as a discipline and as a potential science are much wider than the problems of mere *administration*. The necessarily wider preoccupation of a study of *public* administration, as contrasted with *private* administration, inevitably enmeshes the programs of public administration in the toils of ethical considerations. Thus the tangled question of the right of public employees to strike can scarcely be answered without a tacit normative assumption of some kind. A pragmatic answer is satisfactory only so long as no one raises the question of the "rights" involved. And to resolve the question of rights merely by reciting *legal* norms is to beg the whole issue; it is to confess that an answer to this vital problem of public personnel must be sought elsewhere than with students of public administration. Moreover, if one were content to rest one's case on legal rights, it would be impossible to reconcile in a single "science of public administration" the diverse legal and institutional aspects of the right to strike in France, Great Britain, and the United States.

The great question of responsibility, certainly a central one to the study of public administration once it is raised above the level of academic disquisitions on office management, hinges ultimately on some definition of ends, purposes, and values in society. The sharp conflict of views on responsibility expressed several years ago by Carl Friedrich and Herman Finer resulted from basically different interpretations of the nature and purposes of democratic government. Friedrich tacitly assumed certain values in his discussion of the importance of the bureaucrat's "inner check" as an instrument of control. Finer brought Friedrich's unexpressed values into sharp focus and in a warm criticism challenged their compatibility with the democratic faith.

It is difficult, moreover, to escape the conclusion that much of the debate over delegated legislation and administrative adjudication, both in this country and in England, actually arises from a concealed conflict in objectives. Those to whom economic regulation and control are anathema have with considerable consistency opposed the growth of delegated legislation and the expansion of the powers of administrative tribunals—no doubt from a conviction that previously existing economic rights and privileges are safer in the courts than in administrative tribunals; whereas those who support this expansion of administrative power and techniques generally also favor a larger measure of economic regulation and control. Much of the debate that has been phrased in terms of means ought more properly to be evaluated as a conflict over general social goals.

One might justifiably contend that it is the function of a science of public administration, not to determine ends, but to devise the best means to the ends established by those agencies entrusted with the setting of social policy. The science of public administration, it might be argued, would be totally nonnormative, and its doctrines would apply with equal validity to any regime, democratic or totalitarian, once the ends were made clear. "Tell me what you wish to achieve," the public administration scientist might say, "and I will tell you what administrative means are best designed for your purposes." Yet even this view has difficulties, for in most societies, and particularly in democratic ones, ends are often in dispute; rarely are they clearly and unequivocally determined. Nor can ends and means ever be sharply distinguished, since ends determine means and often means ultimately determine ends.

The student of public administration cannot avoid a concern with ends. What he *ought* to avoid is the failure to make explicit the ends or values that form the groundwork of his doctrine. If purposes and normative considerations were consistently made plain, a net gain to the science of public administration would result. But to refuse to recognize that the study of public administration must be founded on some clarification of ends is to perpetuate the gobbledygook of science in the area of moral purposes.

A science of public administration might proceed, then, along these lines:

1. *Establishing a basic hypothesis.* A nonnormative science of public administration might rest on a basic hypothesis that removed ethical problems from the area covered by the science. The *science* of public administration would begin where the *basic hypothesis* leaves off. One could quarrel with the moral or metaphysical assumptions in the basic hypothesis; but all normative argument would have to be carried on at that level, and not at the level of the science. The science, as such, would have no ethical content.

   Can such a basic hypothesis be created? To this writer the problem appears loaded with enormous and perhaps insuperable difficulties; yet it is unlikely that a science of public administration will ever be possible until this initial step is taken.

2. *Stating ends honestly.* Some problems of the public services, like that of responsibility, evidently cannot be divorced from certain ends implied in the society served by the public services. If this is true, there can never be a universal science of public administration so long as societies and states vary in their objectives. In all cases where problems of public administration are inherently related to specific social ends and purposes, the most that can be done is to force all normative assumptions into the open, and not let them lie half concealed in the jungle of fact and inference to slaughter the unwary.

Public Administration and Human Behavior

A second major problem stems from the inescapable fact that a science of public administration must be a study of certain aspects of human behavior. To be sure, there are parts of public administration in which man's behavior can safely be ignored; perhaps it is possible to discuss the question of governmental accounting and auditing without much consideration of the behavior patterns of governmental accountants and auditors. But most problems of public administration revolve around human beings; and the study of public administration is therefore essentially a study of human beings as they have behaved, and as they may be expected or predicted to behave, under certain special circumstances. What marks off the field of public administration from psychology or sociology or political institutions is its concern with *human* behavior in the area of services performed by governmental agencies. This concern with human behavior greatly limits the immediate potentialities of a science of public administration. First, it diminishes the possibility of using experimental procedures; and experiment, though perhaps not indispensable to the scientific method, is of enormous aid. Second, concern with human behavior seriously limits the uniformity of data, since the datum is the discrete and highly variable man or woman. Third, because the data concerning human behavior constitute an incredibly vast and complex mass, the part played by the preferences of the observer is exaggerated, and possibilities of independent verification are diminished. Fourth, concern with human action weakens the reliability of all "laws of public administration," since too little is known of the mainsprings of human action to insure certitude, or even high probability, in predictions about man's conduct.

All these weaknesses have been pointed out so often in discussing the problems of the social sciences that it should be unnecessary to repeat them here. And yet many of the supposed laws of public administration and much of the claim to a science of public administration derive from assumptions about the nature of man that are scarcely tenable at this late date.

The field of organizational theory serves as an extreme example, for it is there particularly that the nature of man is often lost sight of in the interminable discussions over idealized and abstract organizational forms. In this development, writers on public administration have been heavily influenced by the rational character that capitalism has imposed on the organization of production, and have ignored the irrational qualities of man himself.

Capitalism, especially in its industrial form, was essentially an attempt to organize production along rational lines. In the organization of the productive process, the capitalistic entrepreneur sought to destroy the old restrictive practices and standards of feudalism and mercantilism; to rid the productive process of the inherited cluster of methods and technics that characterized the guilds and medieval craftsmen; in short, to organize production according to rational rather than traditional concepts. Combined with a new acquisitive ideal, this rational approach to production transformed not only the whole economic process but society itself. The rapid growth of mechanization, routine, and specialization of labor further increased the technically rational quality of capitalist production. It was perhaps inevitable that concepts should arise which subordinated individual vagaries and differences to the ordered requirements of the productive process: for it was this very subordination that the replacement of feudal and mercantilist institutions by capitalism had accomplished. The organization (though not the control) of production became the concern of the engineer; and because the restrictive practices authorized by tradition, the protective standards of the guilds, the benevolent regulations of a mercantilist monarchy, and even the nonacquisitive ideals of the individual had all been swept away, it was actually feasible to organize production without much regard for the varying individual personalities of those in the productive process. The productive process, which to the medieval craftsman was both a means and an end in itself, became wholly a means.

Ultimately, of course, men like Taylor provided an imposing theoretical basis for regarding function, based on a logical distribution and specialization of labor, as the true basis of organization. Men like Urwick modified and carried forward Taylor's work, and in the process have tremendously influenced writers on public administration. Urwick, so it must have appeared, provided a basis for a genuine science of administration. "There are principles," he wrote, "*which should govern arrangements for human association of any kind. These principles can be studied as a technical question, irrespective of the purpose of the enterprise, the personnel composing it, or any constitutional, political, or social theory underlying its creation.*" And again, "Whatever the motive underlying persistence in bad structure it is always more hurtful to the greatest number than good structure."

Sweeping generalizations such as these gave promise of a set of "universal principles": i.e., a science. American students of public administration could not fail to be impressed.

Aside from the fact that Urwick ignored the whole question of ends, it is clear that he also presupposed (though he nowhere stated what sort of human personality he *did* presuppose) an essentially rational, amenable individual; he presupposed, that is to say, individuals who would accept logical organization and would not (for irrelevant and irrational reasons) rebel against it or silently supersede it with an informal organization better suited to their personality needs. Urwick must have supposed this. For if there is a large measure of irrationality in human behavior, then an organizational structure formed on "logical" lines may in practice frustrate, anger, and embitter its personnel. By contrast, an organization not based on the logic of organizational principles may better utilize the peculiar and varying personalities of its members. Is there any evidence to suggest that in such a case the "logical" organization will achieve its purposes in some sense "better" or more efficiently than the organization that adapts personality needs to the purposes of the organization? On what kind of evidence are we compelled to assume that the rationality of organizational structure will prevail over the irrationality of man?

Patently the contention that one system of organization is more rational than another, *and therefore better,* is valid only (a) if individuals are dominated by reason or (b) if they are so thoroughly dominated by the technical process (as on the assembly line, perhaps) that their individual preferences may safely be ignored. However much the latter assumption might apply to industry (a matter of considerable doubt), clearly it has little application to public administration, where technical processes are, on the whole, of quite subordinate importance. As for the first assumption, it has been discredited by all the findings of modern psychology. The science of organization had learned too much from industry and not enough from Freud.

The more that writers on public administration have moved from the classroom to the administrator's office, the more Urwick's universal principles have receded. As early as 1930, in a pioneering work, Harold Lasswell described the irrational and unconscious elements in the successful and unsuccessful administrator. Meanwhile, experiments in the Hawthorne plant of Western Electric Company were indicating beyond doubt that individual personalities and social relationships had great effects even on routinized work in industry. Increased output was the result of "the organization of human relations, rather than the organization of techniques." Urwick had said (with little or no supporting evidence): "The idea that organizations should be built up round and adjusted to individual idiosyncracies, rather than that individuals should be adapted to the requirements of sound principles of organization, is . . . foolish. . . ." The Hawthorne experiment demonstrated, on the contrary, that ". . . no study of human situations which fails to take account of the nonlogical social routines can hope for practical success."

In 1939, Leonard White seriously qualified the principle of subordinating individuals to structure by adding the saving phrase of the neo-classical economists: "in the long run." . . . In the most recent text on public administration, the importance of personality is frankly admitted. ". . . administrative research," say the authors, "does not seek its goal in the formulation of mechanical rules or equations, into which human behavior must be molded. Rather, it looks toward the systematic ordering of functions *and human relationships* so that organizational decisions can and will be based upon the certainty that each step taken will actually serve the purpose of the organization as a whole." And one whole chapter of this text is devoted to informal organizations—the shadow relationships that frequently dominate the formal structure of the organization.

Thus by a lengthy and circumspect route, man has been led through the back door and readmitted to respectability. It is convenient to exile man from the science of public administration; it is simpler to forget man and write with "scientific" precision than to remember him and be cursed with his maddening unpredictability. Yet his exclusion is certain to make the study of public administration sterile, unrewarding, and essentially unreal.

If there is ever to be a science of public administration it must derive from an understanding of man's behavior in the area marked off by the boundaries of public administration. This area, to be sure, can never be clearly separated from man's behavior in other fields; all the social sciences are interdependent and all are limited by the basic lack of understanding of man's motivations and responses. Yet the ground of peculiar concern for a prospective science of public administration is that broad region of services administered by the government; until the manifold motivations and actions in this broad region have been explored and rendered predictable, there can be no science of public administration.

It is easier to define this area in space than in depth. One can arbitrarily restrict the prospective science of public administration to a certain region of human activity; but one cannot say with certainty how deeply one must mine

this region in order to uncover its secrets. Does concern with human behavior mean that the researcher in public administration must be a psychiatrist and a sociologist? Or does it mean rather that in plumbing human
behavior the researcher must be capable of using the investigations of the
psychiatrist and sociologist? The need for specialization—a need, inciden-
tally, which science itself seems to impose on human inquiry—suggests that
the latter alternative must be the pragmatic answer.

Development of a science of public administration implies the development of a science of man in the area of services administered by the public.
No such development can be brought about merely by the constantly reiterated assertion that public administration is already a science. We cannot
achieve a science by creating in a mechanized "administrative man" a
modern descendant of the eighteenth century's rational man, whose only
existence is in books on public administration and whose only activity is
strict obedience to "universal laws of the science of administration."

Public Administration and the Social Setting

If we know precious little about "administrative man" as an individual,
perhaps we know even less about him as a social animal. Yet we cannot
afford to ignore the relationship between public administration and its social
setting.

No anthropologist would suggest that a social principle drawn from one
distinct culture is likely to be transmitted unchanged to another culture; Ruth
Benedict's descriptions of the Pueblo Indians of Zuñi, the Melanesians of
Dobu, and the Kwakiutl Indians of Vancouver Island leave little doubt that
cultures can be integrated on such distinctly different lines as to be almost
noncomparable. If the nation-states of western civilization by no means
possess such wholly contrasting cultures as the natives of Zuñi, Dobu, and
Vancouver Island, nevertheless few political scientists would contend that
a principle of political organization drawn from one nation could be adopted
with equal success by another; one would scarcely argue that federalism has
everywhere the same utility or that the unitary state would be equally viable
in Britain and the United States or that the American presidential system
would operate unchanged in France or Germany.

There should be no reason for supposing, then, that a principle of public
administration has equal validity in every nation-state, or that successful
public administration practices in one country will necessarily prove successful in a different social, economic, and political environment. A particular nation-state embodies the results of many historical episodes, traumas,
failures, and successes which have in turn created peculiar habits, mores,
institutionalized patterns of behavior, *Weltanschauungen,* and even "national psychologies." One cannot assume that public administration can
escape the effects of this conditioning; or that it is somehow independent of
and isolated from the culture of social setting in which it develops. At the

same time, as value can be gained by a comparative study of government based upon a due respect for differences in the political, social, and economic environment of nation-states, so too the comparative study of public administration ought to be rewarding. Yet the comparative aspects of public administration have largely been ignored; and as long as the study of public administration is not comparative, claims for "a science of public administration" sound rather hollow. Conceivably there might be a science of American public administration and a science of British public administration and a science of French public administration; but can there be "a science of public administration" in the sense of a body of generalized principles independent of their peculiar national setting?

Today we stand in almost total ignorance of the relationship between "principles of public administration" and their general setting. Can it be safely affirmed, on the basis of existing knowledge of comparative public administration, that there are *any* principles independent of their special environment?

The discussion over an administrative class in the civil service furnishes a useful example of the difficulties of any approach that does not rest on a thorough examination of developmental and environmental differences. The manifest benefits and merits of the British administrative class have sometimes led American students of public administration to suggest the development of an administrative class in the American civil service; but proposals of this kind have rarely depended on a thorough comparison of the historical factors that made the administrative class a successful achievement in Britain, and may or may not be duplicated here.

If these remarks . . . are well founded, then these conclusions suggest themselves:

1. Generalizations derived from the operation of public administration in the environment of one nation-state cannot be universalized and applied to public administration in a different environment. A principle *may* be applicable in a different framework. But its applicability can be determined only after a study of that particular framework.

2. There can be no truly universal generalizations about public administration without a profound study of varying national and social characteristics impinging on public administration, to determine what aspects of public administration, if any, are truly independent of the national and social setting. Are there discoverable principles of *universal* validity, or are all principles valid only in terms of a special environment?

3. It follows that the study of public administration inevitably must become a much more broadly based discipline, resting not on a narrowly defined knowledge of techniques and processes, but rather extending to the varying historical, sociological, economic, and other conditioning factors that give public administration its peculiar stamp in each country.

The relation of public administration to its peculiar environment has not been altogether ignored. Unhappily, however, comparative studies are all too infrequent; and at best they provide only the groundwork. We need many more studies of comparative administration before it will be possible to argue that there are any universal principles of public administration.

In Conclusion

We are a long way from a science of public administration. No science of public administration is possible unless: (1) the place of normative values is made clear; (2) the nature of man in the area of public administration is better understood and his conduct is more predictable; and (3) there is a body of comparative studies from which it may be possible to discover principles and generalities that transcend national boundaries and peculiar historical experiences.

John M. Gaus (1894–1969)

Beginning shortly after World War I, John M. Gaus was a scholar and professor of political science, concentrating particularly on public adminis- tration for most of his working life. But interspersed with his teaching were a wide variety of administrative and research assignments in state and national governments, experiences which contributed to his classes and writing. His interests were extraordinarily deep, in terms of history, and broad, in terms of the interrelationships between public administration and the society which it was intended to serve. He was more concerned with the people and their mores, the social institutions, and the land and other physical resources that provide the environment of public administration than with its legitimacy as a science. This point of view is epitomized in the following selection, which was originally the first of a series of lectures he delivered at the University of Alabama, later published as a book. To my knowledge, this was the first time the biological term *ecology*, meaning the interdependence of an organism with its environment, was used in connection with government.

F.C.M.

Reflections on Public Administration

The Ecology of Government

It is useful for us to start with the fact of criticism of the public service at a time when it has been so widely extended. The attack is not new. It was well diagnosed by Felix Frankfurter in a lecture which he delivered in 1930 at Yale University. He noted that then, too, the attack accompanied an expanding reliance upon the thing attacked. "The paradox of both distrusting and burdening government reveals the lack of a conscious philosophy of politics. It betrays some unresolved inner conflict about the interaction of government and society. I suspect that it implies an uncritical continuance of past assumptions about government and society. We have not adjusted our thinking about government to the overwhelming facts of modern life, and so carry over old mental habits, traditional schoolbook platitudes and campaign slogans as to the role, the purposes and the methods of government."

Unresolved inner conflicts . . . too often spill over into ugly social conflicts, too often supply materials for use by the greedy, the irresponsible, the perverted, the rabble-rousers, who pile up future trouble for us all when the opiates of hatred and fanaticism wear off. The abuse accompanying the use of government is therefore worth our examination beyond the benefits we may gain from a knowledge of the errors of government; such an examination may give us light on the wider and deeper problem of man in society, of human relations generally. But for our present purposes, it warns us that the study of public administration must begin with some explanation of why people burden themselves with something which many of them, at least, resent.

The effort to relate government functions to the environment is necessary, and the recognition of its validity by various observers and scholars confirms one's own effort. In the same lecture from which I have already quoted, Professor Frankfurter (as he then was) asserts, "Before we can consider the aptness of political ideas or the adequacy of political machinery, the relevance of past experience or the promise of new proposals, we must be fully alive to what might be called the raw material of politics—the nature and extent of the demands made upon the machinery of government, and the environment

Chapter 1, *Reflections on Public Administration* (University, Ala.: University of Alabama Press, 1947), pp. 1–19.

in which it moves." A. V. Dicey, in search for the causes of the current which he discerned in English policy in the nineteenth century as a movement from laissez-faire to collectivism, suggested that one explanation is "the existence of patent facts which impress upon ordinary Englishmen the Interdependence of Private and Public Interest." Elihu Root, in his address of acceptance of his election to the United States Senate by the New York State Legislature remarked that "The intimate connection between the people of every locality and of every other state, largely brought about by the increase of communication . . . has forced upon the National Government the performance of a great variety of duties which formerly were performed by the states within the limits of their comparatively isolated communities. . . . This is not a matter of what we wish or what we do not wish; it is not a matter of political program or platform, it is a plain fact to be seen by any one and a fact to be considered."

You will have noted the use by these analysts of government, differing in background and outlook, of such terms as "the nature and extent of the demands made upon the machinery of government," "the existence of patent facts," "has forced upon the national Government the performance of a great variety of duties" and "it is a plain fact." In their several ways, these observers are reminding us that there is an explanation of the functions of government in the changes which take place in its environment, changes which coerce us into the use of government as an instrument of public housekeeping and adjustment. It is not enough to look upon government as an instrument of spoils, whether of an economic class or party or factional machine, although it may at any time and place serve such purposes. But there may also be environmental changes so extensive as to require and obtain a response that is public rather than private. It is at this point of analysis that the Frankfurter lecture and the series of lectures by John Dewey published under the title *The Public and Its Problems* become so valuable to the student of public administration. He needs these efforts to explain and make intelligible the confusing shifts in the use of government; he can benefit from these searches for an explanation of the meaning of "public"; and he needs to assimilate and develop his own working ideas of this basic question of functions in order to clarify for busy citizens what is happening. Unless the causes of public administration are clearer to them, they will lack standards to measure and control the resulting costs in taxation and the regulation of conduct. Indifference, cynicism, and at one extreme a kind of nihilism (which characterized one phase of the Nazi technique in German politics) will prevail; and at another extreme, sheer pressure, plunder and racketeering, a spoils system limited only by bankruptcy.

Hence the study of public administration must include its ecology. "Ecology," states the Webster Dictionary, "is the mutual relations, collectively, between organisms and their environment." J. W. Bews points out that "the word itself is derived from the Greek *oikos*, a house or home, the same root word as occurs in economy and economics. Economics is a subject with which ecology has much in common, but ecology is much wider. It deals with all the inter-relationships of living organisms and their environment." Some social scientists have been returning to the use of the term, chiefly employed by the biologist and botanist, especially under the stimulus of studies of anthropologists, sociologists, and pioneers who defy easy classification, such as the late Sir Patrick Geddes in Britain. In the lecture of Frankfurter's already quoted, the linkage between physical area, population, transport, and government is concretely indicated.

An ecological approach to public administration builds, then, quite literally from the ground up; from the elements of a place—soils, climate, location, for example—to the people who live there—their numbers and ages and knowledge, and the ways of physical and social technology by which from the place and in relationships with one another, they get their living. It is within this setting that their instruments and practices of public housekeeping should be studied so that they may better understand what they are doing, and appraise reasonably how they are doing it. Such an approach is of particular interest to us as students seeking to co-operate in our studies; for it invites—indeed is dependent upon—careful observation by many people in different environments of the roots of government functions, civic attitudes, and operating problems.

With no claim to originality, therefore, and indeed with every emphasis on the collaborative nature of the task, I put before you a list of the factors which I have found useful as explaining the ebb and flow of the functions of government. They are: people, place, physical technology, social technology, wishes and ideas, catastrophe, and personality. . . .

By illustrating concretely the relation of these environmental factors, a co-operative testing of the theory will be facilitated. The changes in the distribution of the people of a governmental unit by time, age, and place throw light on the origins of public policy and administration. At our first census we were a people 80 percent of whom lived on farms; at our last census, one hundred and fifty years later, 80 percent of us did not live on farms. Over a third are now living in a relatively few metropolitan areas; but the growth of these areas is not in the core or mother city; it is in the surrounding suburbs, separate political entities, frequently also separate economic-status and cultural entities, yet sharing with the mother city, which is often absolutely declining in population, the public housekeeping problems of a metropolitan organism for which no—or no adequate—political organization exists. Our population is increasingly one with a larger proportion distributed among the older age classes. These raw facts—too little known and appreciated by citizens, which should be at once placed before them in discussing many of our public questions—in themselves explain much about our functions of government. Coupled with factors of place and technology, they clarify many an issue that is usually expressed in sterile conflicts. For example, the old people in the more frequent large family on a farm of a century ago, where more goods and services were provided on the farm, had a function still to perform and a more meaningful place in the lives of younger generations of the family. In a more pecuniary economy, separated from the family-subsistence economy, ignored in the allocation of the work and rewards of an industrial society, the demand for pensions became irresistible.

The movement of people (by characteristic age and income groups) from the mother city to suburbs (as guided by factors of time-space and cost in the journey to work, the dispersal of shopping centers, the search of industry for land space for straight-line production facilitated by paved roads, trucks, and distribution of power by wires, and other technological changes, and changes in what we wish for in residential environment) produces its repercussion in the values of land and buildings, in the tax basis for public services already existent in older areas and demanded in the new, in the differential requirements and capacities-to-pay of people for housing (including the site and neighborhood equipment) and in the adjustment of transport and utility requirements for the ever-changing metropolitan organism.

Thus the factors of people and place are inextricably interwoven. And not merely in crowded urban centers. I have watched the same process of change in sparsely settled areas of farm and forest, and its potent effect on government.

My own generation has had a great lesson in the importance of change in physical technology in witnessing the adoption of the automobile and the role it has come to play. It may be noted that its widespread use was made possible by the development of paved highways provided necessarily as a public service. Highway expansion and design have been affected by the coercion of political forces created by the physical invention. Groups of automobile users, manufacturers, hotel proprietors, road builders, road machinery and materials suppliers, persons seeking jobs in highway construction and administration, and many others, have contended with those using horses, carriage and harness makers, and persons opposed to the increased taxation that paved roads would require. The original causes—a combination of physical inventions such as the internal combustion engine and the vulcanization of rubber—get obscured in the ultimate disputes over taxation, jurisdiction, requirement of liability insurance and examination for drivers' licenses, or over the merits or defects of systems of traffic control or the financing of overhead crossings or express highways. The citizen blames "bureaucrats" and "politicians" because the basic ecological causes have not been clarified for him. This process of public function adoption may also be reversed by other changes—as we see, for example, in the abandonment of many publicly financed and constructed canals, when new technologies of transport rendered them obsolete.

Changes in physical technology, however slowly their institutional influences may spread, are more obvious even to the point of being dramatic, to the citizen. But he sometimes forgets the importance of the invention of social institutions or devices, and their continuing influences which coerce us. Thus the pooling and application of the savings of many through the invention of the corporation has set new forces to ripple through the social order, disarranging human relationships and creating new possibilities of large scale enterprise financially capable of utilizing extensive equipment and personnel and creating new relationships between buyer and seller, employer and employee—from which coercions for a new balance of forces, through consumer, labor, and investor standards, have resulted.

You will have noted how interrelated all of these factors are in their operation. Perhaps the subtlest one is that for which I have difficulty in finding a satisfactory term. I have used the words "wishes and ideas." What you don't know, it is said, won't hurt you. I wonder whether this is true. If you do know that some new drug, or method of treatment of disease, will prevent the illness or perhaps death of those dear to you, you will have a new imperative for action, even if that action requires a public program. If you know or think you know that a combination of legislative and administrative measures will safeguard your bank deposit or insurance from destruction, that idea will have a coercive effect upon your political action. If you think that public officials are corrupt, that a tariff act or a regulation of a trade is a "racket," that too will influence the political decisions of your time. If you value material well-being, and if that desire takes so definite a form as a house and yard and garden, there are inevitable consequences in standards of public services that will facilitate the realization of your desire. Down that long road one will find the public insurance of mortgages to achieve lower interest rates and longer-term financing and zoning ordinances.

Catastrophe, especially when leadership and knowledge are prepared with long-time programs into which the immediate hurried relief action can be fitted, has its place in the ecology of administration. It not only is destructive, so that relief and repair are required on a scale so large that collective action is necessary, but it also disrupts, jostles, or challenges views and attitudes, and affords to the inner self as well as to others a respectable and face-saving reason for changing one's views as to policy. The atomic bomb gave to many, perhaps, a determining reason for a change of attitude toward international organization. But I incline to the view that the effects of catastrophe on our thinking are relatively short-lived, and confined to relatively smaller institutional changes, and that older forces flood back with great strength to cancel most of the first reaction. A frightened and frustrated society is not one in which really significant changes will take root, unless careful preparation and wise administration of the relief period are available. The night club fire in

Boston in recent years in which so many service men from various parts of the country were killed is a tragic example of one role of catastrophe. In the lurid glare of that fire, weaknesses in building codes and the administration of them were revealed. So many vested interests of materials, construction, and crafts center in building codes that they are difficult to keep in tune with invention and changing social needs. The fact that many in the fire were from remote places, and were men in the armed services, gave unusually wide reporting of the tragedy for some days, especially as many victims lingered on in hospitals. One result of the shock of the catastrophe was therefore action in cities throughout the world to inspect their places of public amusement and survey their fire-prevention legislation and administration. On a vaster scale, the catastrophe of economic world depression led to a varied array of responses through collective action in which there was much similarity despite regional and ideological differences among the various states of the world, since there were also like ecological factors, common to modern power industry and the price system. World wars illustrate the extent to which a large area of collective action is necessarily adopted under modern conditions of total war—and equally illustrate the tremendous pull of older customary views at the close, when the pressure to remove the controls rises, and individuals in office are held responsible for the frustrations once borne as a patriotic offering. Wise and fortunate indeed is that community that has so analyzed its problems and needs, and has so prepared to make use of catastrophe should it come by plans for carrying out programs of improvements, that the aftermath of tragedy finds its victims as well cared for as humanly possible and in addition some tangible new advance in the equipment and life of the community. I have seen some communities which, because they had equipped themselves with personnel capable of fresh thinking, had obtained from depression work-relief programs recreation facilities that were their first amenities.

Such an approach as this to our study of public administration is difficult, in that it makes demands upon our powers to observe, upon a sensitive awareness of changes and maladjustment and upon our willingness to face the political—that is, the public-housekeeping—basis of administration. These factors . . . in various combinations lie behind a public agency. In their combination will be found the reasons for its existence, and the reasons for attack upon it as well. Only in so far as we can find some essentially public core in the combination can we hope to have an agency free from spoils or abuse of power. The process of growth and formulation of a public policy out of these environmental materials links environment and administration. We may be too responsive to change, or we may fail to achieve our best selves by ignoring what we might do to advantage ourselves by collective action, if we perform this task of politics badly.

"When I pay taxes," wrote Justice Holmes to his friend Sir Frederick Pollock, "I buy civilization." It is no easy task of the citizen in this complicated world to get fair value in what he buys. That task is one of discovery of the causes of problems, of the communication of possible remedies, of the organizing of citizens, of the formulation of law. It is the task, in short, of politics. The task will be more fruitfully performed if the citizen, and his agents in public offices, understand the ecology of government.

Wallace S. Sayre (1905-1972)

During the years preceding, during, and following World War II, Wallace Sayre was one of the most knowledgeable, astute, and prescient scholars in all of public administration. He taught at a number of universities, finally at Columbia, and wrote a variety of articles, monographs, and books of which probably the most notable was *Governing New York City* (with Herbert S. Kaufman). In addition to his scholarly work, Sayre served in a variety of governmental capacities. He was a member of New York City's civil service commission in the 1930s. During World War II, he was director of personnel for the Office of Price Administration, and later he was adviser and consultant to a variety of federal and local agencies. In fact, he died of a heart attack in the mayor's office when he was advising the mayor of New York, John Lindsay.

Among Sayre's greatest contributions was his challenging of conventional wisdom about public administration. The excerpt that follows was directed primarily to personnel administration as practiced by the national government, but its basic theme, the usurpation of ends by means, could apply to almost any aspect of administration. The selection is drawn from a review of a text on industrial personnel management with particular emphasis upon human relations: Paul Pigors and Charles A. Meyers' *Personnel Administration: A Point of View and a Method* (McGraw-Hill, 1947). But Sayre's main points are addressed to public, not industrial, personnel management, and I have deleted most of the specific references to the Pigors-Meyers book.

F.C.M.

The Triumph of Techniques
over Purpose

The concepts and the methodology of contemporary public personnel administration are, of course, the product of the dominant objectives set by, and for, the students and the practitioners of the craft. It is possible to identify these goals in separate terms, even though they overlap and have always exerted powerful reciprocal influences upon each other. . . .

The earliest of these, and still the source of the most distinctive public personnel practices, is the goal of eliminating party patronage from the management of the civil service. This definition of purpose has been the most enduring, the most widely understood and embraced, and consequently the most influential article of faith in the growth of the profession. From this premise the basic structure of civil service administration has been derived: central personnel control agencies, bipartisan commissions, quantitative techniques, the "rule of three," and the whole familiar arsenal of devices to neutralize and divert patronage pressures. On the whole, the means were once appropriate to the problem. But, as Gordon Clapp observed in this *Review* as early as 1941, the merit system advocates having clearly won the day in most jurisdictions, the question now is what to do with the victory— which of these methods are today appropriate to the new priority objectives? And what are the new objectives?

A second, closely associated purpose was gradually made explicit in the development of the public personnel program. This goal is the guarantee of equal treatment to all applicants for public employment and among all public employees. This is clearly a positive ethic of great appeal in a democratic society, and it has won an increasing emphasis from public personnel specialists. The contribution of this goal to personnel methodology has been substantial. Its main effect has been to move personnel administration, in the words of Gordon Clapp, "into the cold objective atmosphere of tests, scores, weighted indices, and split-digit ranking" so completely that "these technical trappings have become the symbols of the merit system."

Still another stream of influence has contributed to the fulfillment of this tendency. The logic of scientific management, the paramount ideology of articulate business management between the two wars, has also exerted a powerful attraction for the personnel administrators. The impersonal goals of management logic made the precise, quantitative techniques of the efficiency engineer plausible and attractive methods for the "scientific" personnel

Reprinted from *Public Administration Review,* Vol. VIII (Spring, 1948), pp. 134–137.

manager. Job classification, factor analysis, numerical efficiency ratings, formal promotion charts, and all their procedural relatives acquired a new and impressive endorsement—the personnel system could now lay claim to the combined virtues of merit, equality in competition, and scientific management.

Finally, public personnel policies and methods have been measurably affected by the goal of a public career service. Stated in its most positive terms, this objective represents an effort to provide the conditions of work which will attract and hold a public service of optimum talents. In its negative aspects, the goal has been translated into an elaborate system of protectionism. In the area of methodology the negative connotations have slowly but surely won the dominant position. The concept of status and the concept of rights earned by seniority, to use but two examples from a large network, have been molded from precedent to precedent into a personnel jurisprudence in which all but the most expert technicians lose their way.

In sum, the personnel administration produced by the confluence of these four streams of influence represents a triumph of techniques over purpose. This is not an unusual outcome in the field of administration. Nor does the conclusion mean that great historical accomplishments should not be recorded. What it does suggest is that both ends and means now urgently need fundamental reexamination.

Private personnel administration has not escaped similar pressures. In particular, it has responded in its development to "scientific" management and to a modified version of careerism. The resulting complex of concepts and methods makes up a formidable system of quantitative techniques and formal rules in private personnel administration. Here, too, one may conclude that the ends have been made captive by the means.

Personnel administration, then, has tended to become characterized more by procedure, rule, and technique than by purpose or results. In the public field especially, quantitative devices have overshadowed qualitative. Standardization and uniformity have been enshrined as major virtues. Universal (and therefore arbitrary) methods have been preferred to experiment and variety. From the perspective of the clientele (the public, the managers, and the employees), these traits increasingly connote rigidity, bureaucracy, institutionalism;—and they are now beginning to evoke a reciprocal system of formal and informal techniques of evasion. Among personnel people there is an accompanying growth of frustration and a loss of satisfying participation in the real work of the organization.

Personnel administration, seen in this context, mirrors the dilemma of all orthodox administration. The traditional conceptual and methodical apparatus of administration has rested heavily upon the fallacy of an "administrative man" comparable to the synthetic, rational "economic man" of the classical economists. During the past fifteen years this fiction of the "administrative man" (which Elton Mayo so aptly called the "rabble hypothesis") has been steadily undermined not only by the painstaking inquiries of many students of human behavior but even more by the movement of great social forces. In the growth of personnel administration this rise of mature dissent may be traced, in large part at least, from its clearest beginnings in the reflections of John Dewey and Mary Follett upon the nature and structure of authority, in the efforts of Ordway Tead and Henry Metcalf to introduce more democratic precepts into the practice of personnel administration, and in the pioneering Hawthorne studies at Western Electric by Elton Mayo, F. J. Roethlisberger, and others. The efficiency engineer and the logician of management have slowly given way, at least at the level of administrative theory, to the psychologist, the sociologist, and other social scientists.

❊   ❊   ❊

The authors[1] are not altogether successful in their attempt to transmute formal personnel procedures into useful human relations instruments. This relative failure highlights one of the most difficult judgments which the human relations group must now make: to what extent can they accept and work within the present structure and methods of personnel administration? What are the hazards that any such acceptance will adulterate their concepts and inhibit further exploration and growth?

The answer, especially in public personnel administration, would seem to lie in a different perspective on the values and uses of quantitative techniques. It is not the techniques per se which have constructed the straightjacket that now imprisons so much of personnel administration. The basic techniques are, when properly used, of considerable value and of even greater potential promise. The real difficulty lies in the fact that (1) the techniques are usually inadequate for the full purpose they are relied upon to accomplish, yet accomplishment is gradually taken for granted; (2) the techniques are prematurely frozen into regulations and procedures for universal application in greatly varying administrative environments, thus stifling at birth the process of genuine research and technical development; and (3) the techniques gradually obscure the ends they were designed to serve. The contrast between this tendency of personnel specialists toward eager installation and canonization of rudimentary techniques and the stubborn experimentalism of the physical sciences is instructive. Even many of those who might be assumed to be the least susceptible to this tendency—the psychologists, with their strong experimental tradition—reveal their imprisonment within the system by devoting their energies to the refinement of the installed methods of testing skills and personality "traits" rather than to the working out of new techniques and applications in the fields of attitudes, motivation, and group dynamics.

The immediate trends as well as some of the most deeply imbedded concepts of public personnel administration are opposed to the human

---

1.   Sayre is here referring to the authors of the book he is reviewing. Ed.

relations point of view. Although this is not the whole problem, it is a revealing index of the crisis in civil service administration. At a time when the urgency, difficulty, and complexity of governmental performance are daily increasing, at a time when industrial personnel administration is moving toward a recognition of the values of experimental and thorough inquiry into human behavior, tempered in application by informality and flexibility in the human relations of organized effort, the public service becomes steadily more dependent upon a cold, impersonal, rigid quantification of human ability and worth in public employment. Nor is even this the full measure of the inadequacy. The methods relied upon lack the objectivity which is their sole claim to usefulness; they provide merely the appearance, not the substance, of the relevant measurement of ability and merit. The variables of personnel administration are too many and too subtle to be contained within a purely statistical frame of reference. In contrast, a prime virtue of the human relations group is its relative lack of conceit about the immutability of its concepts and techniques.

Some readers may wonder whether this review overlooks the "new trends" in federal personnel administration. These trends need to be more carefully examined than opportunity here affords. However, some tentative observations are in order. During the war years, many useful explorations were made in the direction of personnel policies and methods which would be appropriate and adequate for the great tasks of federal administration. Some of these experiments still endure, but the surrounding climate is not encouraging. With perhaps the sole exception of TVA among the federal agencies, there has been uniformly a net loss of opportunity for the development of agency personnel programs responsive to the special needs of agency assignment and climate. The prewar pattern of uniform rules, designed to impose an artificial appearance of order and objectivity upon the federal establishments, has been restored and strengthened, not relaxed. "Decentralization" has been the main theme of "progress" in the postwar federal personnel program. It is relevant to inquire: what is the substance of the program being decentralized? The ultimate values of decentralization depend upon the quality of the program. The decentralization of work load under strict procedural instructions binding those who do the work is a dubious administrative economy; it certainly does not represent an important new trend in the development of an adequate philosophy and method of personnel administration.

Norton E. Long (1910–   )

Since 1936, when he began teaching, Norton E. Long has been a scholar and professor of political science at a number of universities. His academic career was interrupted for several years during and following World War II when he served in administrative posts in the national government and subsequently by research assignments and consultations for state, local, and foreign governments. Following his experience in the 1940s, Long wrote a number of provocative articles about the national government and its administration, most of which were later incorporated in a book of essays, *The Polity* (Rand McNally, 1962). His interests and writings since the mid-1950s have focused primarily on government in cities and metropolitan areas. The selection that follows deals with one of Long's favorite themes, one that he thought had been long neglected in the study of public administration: political power in administration and its relation to the executive and the legislature.

F.C.M.

Power and Administration

There is no more forlorn spectacle in the administrative world than an agency and a program possessed of statutory life, armed with executive orders, sustained in the courts, yet stricken with paralysis and deprived of power. An object of contempt to its enemies and of despair to its friends.

The lifeblood of administration is power. Its attainment, maintenance, increase, dissipation, and loss are subjects the practitioner and student can ill afford to neglect. Loss of realism and failure are almost certain consequences. This is not to deny that important parts of public administration are so deeply entrenched in the habits of the community, so firmly supported by the public, or so clearly necessary as to be able to take their power base for granted and concentrate on the purely professional side of their problems. But even these islands of the blessed are not immune from the plague of politics. . . . Power is only one of the considerations that must be weighed in administration, but of all it is the most overlooked in theory and the most dangerous to overlook in practice.

The power resources of an administrator or an agency are not disclosed by a

Reprinted from *Public Administration Review,* Vol. IX (Autumn, 1949), pp. 257–264.

legal search of titles and court decisions or by examining appropriations or budgetary allotments. Legal authority and a treasury balance are necessary but politically insufficient bases of administration. Administrative rationality requires a critical evaluation of the whole range of complex and shifting forces on whose support, acquiescence, or temporary impotence the power to act depends.

Analysis of the sources from which power is derived and the limitations they impose is as much a dictate of prudent administration as sound budgetary procedure. The bankruptcy that comes from an unbalanced power budget has consequences far more disastrous than the necessity of seeking a deficiency appropriation. The budgeting of power is a basic subject matter of a realistic science of administration.

It may be urged that for all but the top hierarchy of the administrative structure the question of power is irrelevant. Legislative authority and administrative orders suffice. Power adequate to the function to be performed flows down the chain of command. Neither statute nor executive order, however, confers more than legal authority to act. Whether Congress or President can impart the substance of power as well as the form depends upon the line-up of forces in the particular case. A price control law wrung from a reluctant Congress by an amorphous and unstable combination of consumer and labor groups is formally the same as a law enacting a support price program for agriculture backed by the disciplined organizations of farmers and their congressmen. The differences for the scope and effectiveness of administration are obvious. The Presidency, like Congress, responds to and translates the pressures that play upon it. The real mandate contained in an Executive order varies with the political strength of the group demand embodied in it, and in the context of other group demands.

Both Congress and President do focus the general political energies of the community and so are considerably more than mere means for transmitting organized pressures. Yet power is not concentrated by the structure of government or politics into the hands of a leadership with a capacity to budget it among a diverse set of administrative activities. A picture of the Presidency as a reservoir of authority from which the lower echelons of administration draw life and vigor is an idealized distortion of reality.

A similar criticism applies to any like claim for an agency head in his agency. Only in varying degrees can the powers of subordinate officials be explained as resulting from the chain of command. Rarely is such an explanation a satisfactory account of the sources of power.

To deny that power is derived exclusively from superiors in the hierarchy is to assert that subordinates stand in a feudal relation in which to a degree they fend for themselves and acquire support peculiarly their own. A structure of interests friendly or hostile, vague and general or compact and well-defined, encloses each significant center of administrative discretion. This structure is an important determinant of the scope of possible action. As a source of power and authority it is a competitor of the formal hierarchy.

Not only does political power flow in from the sides of an organization, as it were; it also flows up the organization to the center from the constituent parts. . . .

It is clear that the American system of politics does not generate enough power at any focal point of leadership to provide the conditions for an even partially successful divorce of politics from administration. Subordinates cannot depend on the formal chain of command to deliver enough political power to permit them to do their jobs. Accordingly they must supplement the resources available through the hierarchy with those they can muster on their own, or accept the consequences in frustration—a course itself not without danger. Administrative rationality demands that objectives be determined and sights set in conformity with a realistic appraisal of power position and potential.

The theory of administration has neglected the problem of the sources and adequacy of power, in all probability because of a distaste for the disorderliness of American political life and a belief that this disorderliness is transitory. An idealized picture of the British parliamentary system as a Platonic form to be realized or approximated has exerted a baneful fascination in the field. The majority party with a mandate at the polls and a firmly seated leadership in the Cabinet seems to solve adequately the problem of the supply of power necessary to permit administration to concentrate on the fulfillment of accepted objectives. It is a commonplace that the American party system provides neither a mandate for a platform nor a mandate for a leadership.

Accordingly, the election over, its political meaning must be explored by the diverse leaders in the executive and legislative branches. Since the parties have failed to discuss issues, mobilize majorities in their terms, and create a working political consensus on measures to be carried out, the task is left for others—most prominently the agencies concerned. Legislation passed and powers granted are frequently politically premature. . . . The agencies to which tasks are assigned must devote themselves to the creation of an adequate concensus to permit administration. The mandate that the parties do not supply must be attained through public relations and the mobilization of group support. . . .

The theory that agencies should confine themselves to communicating policy suggestions to executive and legislature, and refrain from appealing to their clientele and the public, neglects the failure of the parties to provide either a clear-cut decision as to what they should do or an adequately mobilized political support for a course of action. The bureaucracy under the American political system has a large share of responsibility for the public promotion of policy and even more in organizing the political basis for its survival and growth. It is generally recognized that the agencies have a special competence in the technical aspects of their fields which of necessity gives them a rightful policy initiative. In addition, they have or develop a shrewd understanding of the politically feasible in the group structure within which they work. Above all, in the eyes of their supporters and their enemies they represent the institutionalized embodiment of policy, an enduring organization actually or potentially capable of mobilizing power behind policy. The survival interests and creative drives of administrative organizations combine with clientele pressures to compel such mobilization. The party system provides no enduring institutional representation for group interest at all comparable to that of the bureaus of the Department of Agriculture. Even the subject matter committees of Congress function in the shadow of agency permanency.

The bureaucracy is recognized by all interested groups as a major channel of representation to such an extent that Congress rightly feels the competition of a rival. The weakness in party structure both permits and makes necessary the present dimensions of the political activities of the administrative branch— permits because it fails to protect administration from pressures and fails to provide adequate direction and support, makes necessary because it fails to develop a consensus on a leadership and a program that makes possible administration on the basis of accepted decisional premises.

Agencies and bureaus more or less perforce are in the business of building, maintaining, and increasing their political support. They lead and in large part are led by the diverse groups whose influence sustains them. Frequently they lead and are themselves led in conflicting directions. This is not due to a dull-witted incapacity to see the contradictions in their behavior but is an almost inevitable result of the contradictory nature of their support.

To varying degrees, dependent on the breadth of acceptance of their programs, officials at every level of significant discretion must make their estimates of the situation, take stock of their resources, and plan accordingly. A keen appreciation of the real components of their organization is the beginning of wisdom. These components will be found to stretch far beyond the government payroll. Within the government they will encompass Congress, congressmen, committees, courts, other agencies, presidential advisers, and the President. . . .

The broad alliance of conflicting groups that makes up presidential majorities scarcely coheres about any definite pattern of objectives, nor has it by the alchemy of the party system had its collective power concentrated in an accepted leadership with a personal mandate. The conciliation and maintenance of this support is a necessary condition of the attainment and retention of office involving, as Madison so well saw, "the spirit of party and faction in the necessary and ordinary operations of government." The President must in large part be, if not all things to all men, at least many things to many men. As a consequence, the contradictions in his power base invade administration. The often criticized apparent cross-purposes of the Roosevelt regime cannot be put down to inept administration until the political facts are weighed. Were these apparently self-defeating measures reasonably related to the general maintenance of the composite majority of the Administration? The first objective—ultimate patriotism apart—of the administrator is the attainment and retention of the power on which his tenure of office depends. This is the necessary pre-condition for the accomplishment of all other objectives.

The same ambiguities that arouse the scorn of the naive in the electoral campaigns of the parties are equally inevitable in administration and for the same reasons. Victory at the polls does not yield either a clear-cut grant of power or a unified majority support for a coherent program. The task of the Presidency lies in feeling out the alternatives of policy which are consistent with the retention and increase of the group support on which the Administration rests. The lack of a budgetary theory (so frequently deplored) is not due to any incapacity to apply rational analysis to the comparative contribution of the various activities of government to a determinate hierarchy of purposes. It more probably stems from a fastidious distaste for the frank recognition of the budget as a politically expedient allocation of resources. Appraisal in terms of their political contribution to the Administration provides almost a sole common denominator between the Forest Service and the Bureau of Engraving.

❊   ❊   ❊

In ordinary times the manifold pressures of our pluralistic society work themselves out in accordance with the balance of forces prevailing in Congress and the agencies. Only to a limited degree is the process subject to responsible direction or review by President or party leadership.

❊   ❊   ❊

The difficulty of coordinating government agencies lies not only in the fact that bureaucratic organizations are institutions having survival interests which may conflict with their rational adaptation to over-all purpose, but even more in their having roots in society. Coordination of the varied activities of a modern government almost of necessity involves a substantial degree of coordination of the economy. Coordination of government agencies involves far more than changing the behavior and offices of officials in Washington and the field. It involves the publics that are implicated in their normal functioning. To coordinate fiscal policy, agricultural policy, labor policy, foreign policy, and military policy, to name a few major areas, moves beyond the range of government charts and the habitat of the bureaucrats to the market place and to where the people live and work. This suggests that the reason why government reorganization is so difficult is that far more than government in the formal sense is involved in reorganization. . . .

Basic to the problem of administrative rationality is that of organizational identification and point of view. To whom is one loyal—unit, section, branch, division, bureau, department, administration, government, country, people, world history, or what? Administrative analysis frequently assumes that organizational identification should occur in such a way as to merge primary organization loyalty in a larger synthesis. The good of the part is to give way to the reasoned good of the whole. This is most frequently illustrated in the rationalizations used to counter self-centered demands of primary groups for funds and personnel. Actually the competition between governmental power centers, rather than the rationalizations, is the effective instrument of coordination.

Most students of administration are planners of some sort. Most congressmen would fly the label like the plague. Most bureaucrats, whatever their private faith, live under two jealous gods, their particular clientele and the loyalty check. Such a condition might, if it exists as described, cast doubt on whether even the intellectual conditions for rational administrative coordination exist. Be that as it may, the transition from a government organized in clientele departments and bureaus, each responding to the massive feudal power of organized business, organized agriculture, and organized labor, to a government integrated about a paramount national purpose will require a political power at least as great as that which tamed the earlier feudalism. It takes a sharp eye or a tinted glass to see such an organized power on the American scene.

A Presidency backed by a disciplined party controlling a majority in Congress would probably assimilate itself to a premiership by association of legislative leadership in the formulation of policy and administration. In either line of development the crucial matter is party organization. For the spirit of the party system determines the character of the government.

Attempts to solve administrative problems in isolation from the structure of power and purpose in the polity are bound to prove illusory. The reorganization of Congress to create responsibility in advance of the development of party responsibility was an act of piety to principle, of educational value; but as a practical matter it raised a structure without foundation. In the same way, reorganization of the executive branch to centralize administrative power in the Presidency while political power remains dispersed and divided may effect improvement, but in a large sense it must fail. The basic prerequisite to the administration of the textbooks is a responsible two party system.

The means to its attainment are a number one problem for students of administration. What Schattschneider calls the struggle for party government may sometime yield us the responsible parliamentary two party system needed to underpin our present administrative theory. Until that happy time, exploration of the needs and necessities of our present system is a high priority task of responsible scholarship.

Paul H. Appleby (1891–1963)

Initially a journalist and a newspaper publisher, Paul H. Appleby began his government service at the start of the New Deal when Henry Wallace, the Secretary of Agriculture, appointed him as his executive assistant. He later became Undersecretary of Agriculture, served on a variety of overseas missions during World War II, and, in 1944, was appointed Assistant Director of the Budget. He did not enter academia on a full-time basis until 1947 when, at age fifty-six, he was appointed dean of the Maxwell School at Syracuse University. Later, beginning in 1955, he served as Director of the Budget of New York State under Governor Averell Harriman.

Appleby was an astute observer as well as participant; he had a rare ability to generalize from his observations and a creative, original mind which built new thoughts from perspectives that differed from traditional viewpoints of political science and public administration. All of his governmental appointments were political, and though not a politician himself, he usually served as a bridge between top political executives and the career bureaucracy. More than most of the earlier theorists, he viewed public administration as essentially political (in the larger, not necessarily partisan, sense of the term). Indeed in the second chapter of the book quoted below, he described the administrative process as one of the essential political processes.

In his four books, the first of which was *Big Democracy* in 1945 (Knopf), and a wide variety of articles, Appleby treated a range of subjects almost as broad as public administration itself. But his pervasive theme was the interpenetration of administration with policy and politics. Perhaps the most incisive treatment of this theme was contained in the opening chapter of his second book, *Policy and Administration*, most of which is reprinted below.

F.C.M.

Policy and Administration

Fallacies and Definitions

The makers of the American Constitution built it in some respects on the basis of erroneous descriptions—such as Montesquieu's—of the British system. This in particular is the origin of the formal separation of powers which, however qualified in the Constitution or in practice, is a central feature of American governmental structure.

Most scholarly efforts in the field of government (curiously similar to pressure-group efforts) were long, and quite naturally, attempts to look at government from single, separate vantage points on the basis of certain simplifying assumptions. For a half-century or so, while political science was developing as a distinct discipline, much of its literature tended to accept as substantially real a separation of powers which excluded from administration any—or at least any important—policy-making functions. Under such a theory of separation, a civil service system was justified, accepted, and probably to a small extent over-sold.

The President was recognized as an outstanding exception, but the President's office was conceived of in personal rather than institutional terms. He was a policy-maker as an individual and as President, not as Chief Executive. He occupied a level not merely a long step higher than his Cabinet but almost in another world.

Other exceptions were noted and struggled with, both by political scientists and by politicians. Some positions, altogether not making any very clear pattern, were recognized as policy-making and therefore subject to Senatorial confirmation. In professional circles, efforts were made to distinguish between "administrative" and "executive," some elevating the first term, others the second. But generally it was long believed that administrative personnel were not policy-making. This was at a time when the executive government did not differ markedly in nature from its successor segments of the government of today.

In the meantime, however, the government has gone on, developing in some parts under restraint of prevailing theory, in some parts in disregard of theory, in all parts reflecting governmental efforts to survive under changing conditions.

Chapter 1, *Policy and Administration* (University, Ala.: University of Alabama Press, 1949), pp. 1–25.

It is widely believed that Congress has an exclusive responsibility for policy-making. Yet it is also widely believed that policy is freely made by every government official. Many citizens also have accepted Justice Field's distinction between judicial and legislative acts ("The one determines what the law is, and what the rights of parties are with reference to transactions already had; the other prescribes what the law shall be in future cases arising under it.") and have observed all three branches of the government performing both of the functions he described. Without extensively exploring the ramifications of all three branches, these papers will consider ways in which policy is made in the course of administration.

In normal fashion the discussion would begin with some definitions. But definition in social science is generally difficult, and often the source of the misunderstanding one seeks to reduce. Definition is particularly difficult when it has to do with living, complex processes; when achieved, it is often so broad as to have little meaning. The attempt here is to describe.

Both courts and administrators find in law things Congress or legislatures had never consciously put there. In other cases, both resolve difficulties Congress or legislature had consciously left for them to resolve.

Congress and legislatures make policy for the future, but have no monopoly on that function, as the courts have no monopoly on the determination of what the law is. Administrators are continually laying down rules for the future, and administrators are continually determining what the law is, what it means in terms of action, what the rights of parties are with respect both to transactions in process and transactions in prospect. Administrators make thousands of such decisions to one made by the courts. They act with regard for what the courts have decided and would be likely to decide, of course, but in considerable degree the power of the courts over administration is a reserve power. The power of legislative bodies is in a considerable degree, also, a reserve power over administration.

Administrators also participate in another way in the making of policy for the future; they formulate recommendations for legislation, and this is a part of the function of policy-making, even that policy-making which can be done fully only at the legislative level. Both administrative change and legislative change grow out of the popular scene, grow out of reactions to conditions as they have developed, reactions to what has been legislated, to what is being administered and the way it is being administered. Citizen reactions flow to the legislative body directly, and through the executive branch, and both currents are essential to the final product. As the current of citizen reaction moves through the executive branch, it is given a certain organization. It gains also contributions growing out of administrative and expert considerations. The two currents from the people equip the legislature more fully than would the direct people-to-legislature current alone. In channeling one of the currents, the executive branch participates in policy-making.

It might be said, then, that legislative bodies make very general policy, and that administrators make policy by applying that general policy at successively less abstract levels. While there is truth in this, it is by no means uniformly valid. Claims bills regularly enacted in considerable number provide one familiar example of quite specific policy-making by Congress. Small claims of the same sort are settled administratively; the power of Congress with respect to claims is reserved not for the generally significant but for the large. Eliminations of specific appropriations for single jobs provide another kind of example. One may recall, too, the Congressional spanking given to a recent Secretary of the Treasury for changing the pay of charwomen in the Treasury building without specific Congressional approval.

On the other hand, many very broad policy decisions have been made within the executive branch. This is particularly true with respect to foreign policy, conduct of war, and public welfare. In New York State the Governor has great responsibility for very broad policy-making and legislative leadership.

The injection of Congress, or Congressional instrumentalities, into the "administrative" field further confuses the matter in the national government. Individual members of Congress, chairmen of committees, sub-committees and committees—none of which is "the Congress"—exercise a great deal of influence over, and sometimes actually exercise a direct control over, many matters that are commonly thought of as strictly administrative.

If one wishes, then, to define policy as that which Congress decides, and administration as that which the executive branch does, policy and administration may be regarded as separated, and the definitions, like so many others having to do with social processes, become rather meaningless. Similarly, within the executive branch, if policy is defined as decision-making at top levels and administration is decision-making and decision-application at lower levels, a kind of separation is achieved, but the definitions are not useful.

The position taken in this discussion is that description is more appropriate than definition; that many types of decisions involving policy-making are and must be delegated as a usual thing; that, on the other hand, almost any type of decision may become, on occasion, a matter for top-level consideration and determination, even for popular determination; that the movement of work materials and decisions perpendicularly and laterally in the levels and divisions of government is of the essence of both policy-making and administration; and that the whole governmental context is important to legislation, to administration, to policy-making, and to court decisions. By "context" it is intended to suggest that courts can be judged and their decision-making understood only in the light of what is done by Congress and by administrators; that administration can be judged and its policy-making understood only in the light of what is done by courts and Congress and the administrative hierarchy itself; that Congressional policy-making similarly can be understood only in the light of what is done by courts and by administrators; that the three branches can be understood only in the light of popular political activities.

The position here taken is also that exercise of discretion in decision-making is everywhere in the government of the same nature, but of many orders, and that the order of a particular decision is always subject to final determination in a great political complex of pressure and agitation present or prospective in which felt need, history, and precedent work through various interlocking governmental institutions, each distinguished by preponderant but not exclusive responsibilities. Constitutional structure and principle and law provide much of the history, precedent, and institutional pattern. Public sense of need and the institutions of government are in this aspect alike, and together are dynamic factors working through political means to effect ever new adjustment to an ever changing social whole. The institutions are flexible and dynamic in considerable part because of their political nature, their political environment and their political responsibility; politics brings felt need and governmental institutions into whatever harmony is achieved.

The great distinction between government and other organized undertakings is to be found in the wholly political character of government. The great distinction between public administration and other administration is likewise to be found in the political character of public administration. Policy-making in private business may take place with reasonable public safety at many levels because it is influenced by supply and demand, by competition and by an intra-organizational play of diverse interests. Policy-making may take place with reasonable public safety at many levels in the executive government because the order of any decision is always *subject* to political determination, and arrived at in a political environment. This is to say that by political agitation any decision normally or administratively treated as of a low order of importance and delegated to a low hierarchal level of responsibility may be called up for higher-level consideration.

Subject to such calling up, normal administrative or legislative fixing of the order of a particular decision—the level at which it may be made—is done by a subtle process of political evaluation. That evaluation is reached generally through anticipation of popular reaction; as a response to experience, convention, and precedent; under pressure from interests directly concerned; under pressures from other parts of the government; and in specific cases through popular debate, campaigns, and elections. The order of a particular decision is preliminarily and tentatively determined within the executive branch by political, administrative, procedural, technical, or factual and social evaluations. These evaluations constitute a more or less rough consensus of the horizontally and perpendicularly associated individuals and groups participating in the institutional and environmental context. The level at which a decision is to be made, therefore, may be shifted downward or upward as evaluations point to more or less controversy, or to more or less "importance." Importance within the administrative organization turns in some part on expert valuations; in some degree on novelty; in some parts on prerogatives and other institutional valuations; in some part on dimensions and scope of the action—the weight of impact it will have or has had on citizens, and the number of citizens affected; in some part on ideal values, such as are involved, for example, in questions of the *kind* of impact on even a single citizen. In very considerable part all this is reaction to diverse political forces.

It is a process, then, in which many unlike things are weighed on the same scales, and simultaneously. It is like, but much more complicated than, the process of economic evaluation in which investment and consumption goods through popular processes of supply and demand, and through competition and administration are weighed on dollar scales to determine relative values of a bottle of Lydia Pinkham's Vegetable Compound, a quart of milk, a shirt, and the Empire State Building. . . .

Judgments of values in the course of administration are all theoretically— and any one judgment in fact—subject to appeal to higher levels. The process of appeal usually is treated in restricted and legalistic terms, but it has a great and pervasive importance in the whole formal and informal operation of administrative business. Not merely the *nature* of citizen attitudes is weighed, but also the *intensity* of citizen feeling in the context of the whole social scene of the moment. Persistence of complaint, persistence of expressions of need, weighs heavily in political scales; but it weighs always in relation to other needs, hopes, complaints also on the scale, and their persistence. The reading of the scale changes constantly, and marked changes in reading send upward or downward in governmental levels the business to be decided.

An intricate process is subject to definition, but the definition must be made in such general terms as to reveal very little. Here administration is viewed as the government in direct action on behalf of and in restraint of citizens; policy-making in administration is the exercise of discretion with respect to such action. There are different orders of action, and different orders of policy, but these orders together are a continuum, with the funda-mental common character which use of that term requires. Confusion enters when the continuum is denied. Wisdom comes when the process of decision-making is considered as a whole.

Actually, the earlier professional belief in the separation of policy and administration was never so clear, consistent, or hard-and-fast as often has been assumed. The Constitution itself made no such complete separation. On the contrary, its provisions for a Presidential veto, for Presidential recom-mendations for legislation, and Presidential dominance in foreign and mili-tary policy injected the executive branch far into the policy-making field. Presidential responsibility of necessity was shared from the very beginning with the executive branch at large. White's administrative history, *The Federalists,* shows well begun in the first two administrations most of the kinds of policy-making now recognizable. If Hamilton, rather than Washington, exercised much of the policy leadership where Congress was concerned, it made the beginning more, not less, a foreshadowing of the general development.

Recognizing these Constitutional and historical facts and something of the actualities of practice, Goodnow's early discussion drew a line less abrupt between policy and administration than some who later quoted him seemed to know. Subsequently, many political scientists have noted the intermingling of policy-making and administration. Gulick as far back as 1933 positively denied their separation.

Louis Brownlow, a pioneer in the field of city managership, admitted years later that when he was a city manager he was an "important political figure." In a similar way, Professor Merriam in a series of lectures at Syracuse University in 1947 declared that "the executive has become fully as political as the legislature" and referred to policy-making and administration as a "circular process."

Thus, the long attempts to make sharp and real the separation of powers, the separations of policy-making and administration and politics and administration, have been undergoing abandonment. Perhaps the most stubborn withdrawal from their former ground is being made by lawyers. In their shift they are principal protagonists of an effort to secure a separation of powers within the executive branch as an extension of earlier thinking.

Executives do not sit at two different desks, treating policy at one and administration at the other. Even intellectually, they more often deal with whole problems than they deal with them as exclusively problems of policy or problems of administration.

A detailed analysis of jobs at each hierarchal level would show, it is believed, the same close relationships between policy-making and policy execution at each level of the administrative hierarchy. It is believed that the relationship exists even at the Congressional level. . . . A cabinet member similarly considers what to do and how to do it as one problem; his instructions about program goals have to be tied closely to, and are limited by, administrative directions designed to insure attainment of the goals. The reports he listens to or reads are both administrative reports and program reports of achievements, shortcomings, and difficulties. He receives administrative and policy recommendations alike. Some may be more strictly administrative, some more strictly pertaining to policy, but without program considerations there is no sense at all in administration, and without administration nothing would happen with respect to policy. The functions of policy-making can not actually be vested exclusively at any one point or level in the government. Wherever there is action affecting the public, there is policy-making. Policy is made by means of all the political processes by which government is carried on. The various processes interact. Because the processes are varied, and because they do interact, the parts of the government are not isolated, autonomous, or uncontrollable. Wherever the conduct of public affairs is not "taken out of politics," public control is possible; issues of administration as well as many others can be brought up for whatever consideration may be desired. Much administration may normally be left to administrators if all administration is a part of and subject to the various political processes. To this extent a rough, popular separation between policy and administration is valid.

It is where administrative questions become policy questions of a sort needing public debate that the two merge at the public level. They merge at every governmental level in precisely the same way. This is to say that certain aspects of administration and certain aspects of policy require treatment together at the level of Congress; certain aspects of administration and policy must be treated together at the level of the President; certain aspects of both must be treated at the level of a Department head—and so on down the administrative hierarchy. At every level, the answer to the question "What is my judgment about this which I have to decide, or about this one which I need to have a judgment?" is a policy question. In the perspective of each successive level everything decided at that level and above is "policy," and everything that may be left to a lower level is "administration." In the perspective of an outside observer, policy and administration are treated together at every level.

Top executives in their policy-making roles are as dependent upon lower executives as the lower executives are dependent on higher ones. It is a reciprocal process from a strictly policy-making standpoint, and the processes of administration and policy-making are reciprocal. The movement of administrative materials up and down a hierarchy and across on various levels of associated hierarchies is the reality by which administration and policy-making take place concurrently.

If there is ground for public fear because of a recognition of a policy-making function resting with administrative personnel, that fear needs to be considered. But one word of comfort on this point may not be out of place even in an introductory survey of the problem. The most extreme exercises of policy-making by executives have been admittedly unconstitutional, illegal, or highly questionable actions by certain Chief Executives. The Louisiana Purchase by Jefferson and the Emancipation Proclamation by Lincoln are outstanding examples. Reassurance would seem to lie in the fact that no one of the actions most seriously questioned from constitutional or legal standpoints has been itself disapproved by the people at the time or in subsequent history. This would suggest that the political institutions as a whole and the political environment within which the government operates have been in fact fully protective of the spirit even when the letter has been ignored. If this is true of the most dramatic and extensive exercises of power, may not the ordinary, organized, reciprocal operations of government, hedged in by pressures of many kinds, checked by competing and complementary prerogatives, exposed to publicity and opposition attack, with responsibility fixed in political officers who can be got at—may not this government be viewed with more than a little confidence and pride, as well as with constant concern?

Finally, it is submitted that the intermingling of policy and administration in our government is not new. It is more visible because both policy and administration are more visible; both have to do with many more things. But the *way* in which the government operates is largely the way in which it has been operated from the beginning.

"Administration" here is treated, therefore, as a broad term involving policy-making as well as execution. It is so treated because it is felt that a great deal of policy-making is implicit in what the executive branch does, and that it is important to recognize this policy-making function. "Management" involves the same intermingling of policy-making and execution, but it is here assigned arbitrarily to a lower level and used to signify executive action with least policy-making significance. Hence, public administration here becomes "that intermingling of policy-making and management which occurs below the levels of legislative, judicial, and popular-electoral policy determinations." Most presidential policy-making is on this level; a small part of it is on a level fully as elevated as the legislative and judicial levels. Some small part of the presidential policy-making power may be on a still higher level. But all of these levels are subordinate to the popular-electoral level.

Contents by Topic

Note: *Chapters excerpted from books are indicated by author and book title, not chapter title. Page numbers are, in most cases, the pages on which the books or articles begin in this collection. In a few cases, the page numbers refer to the pages in which the most relevant section of the article or book begins.*

Budget and Finance

Business Administration

The Discipline of Public Administration

Economy and Efficiency

Motivation and Human Relations

Organization Theory

Personnel and Civil Service

Politics, Policy and Administration

Professionalism

State and Local Government